Artificial Intelligence and Cognitive Science

Conceptual Issues

Series Editors

Andy Clark and Josefa Toribio
Washington University

A Garland Series

Series Contents

Machine Intelligence

Perspectives on the Computational Model

Edited with an introduction by

Andy Clark and Josefa Toribio
Washington University

GARLAND PUBLISHING, INC.
A MEMBER OF THE TAYLOR & FRANCIS GROUP
New York & London
1998

Library of Congress Cataloging-in-Publication Data

Machine intelligence : perspectives on the computational model / edited with introductions by Andy Clark and Josefa Toribio.
p. cm. — (Artificial intelligence and cognitive science ; 1)
Includes bibliographical references.
ISBN 0-8153-2768-4 (alk. paper)
1. Artificial intelligence. 2. Philosophy of mind. 3. Information theory. I. Clark, Andy, 1957– . II. Toribio, Josefa. III. Series.
Q335.M173 1998
006.3—dc21 98-27514
CIP

Printed on acid-free, 250-year-life paper
Manufactured in the United States of America

Contents

Information, Computation, and Representation

Introduction

Taking Care of Syntax

The papers gathered in this volume concern some of the most fundamental aspects of the computational approach to understanding the mind. In particular, they concern the original idea of the mind as, literally, a kind of computer program running on (implemented in) biological wetware. The idea here (see especially the papers by Turing, Haugeland, and Chalmers in section one) is that thought and reason are properties not so much of the physical stuff of which we are made (the organic tissues, etc.) but depend instead on organizational properties, and on the way that organization supports a certain kind of computational or information-processing profile. Just what this means (and the special problems it raises) will become clearer as our tale progresses.

Such a view, although it distinguishes the physical stuff from these organizational features, nonetheless stands opposed to spiritual or dualistic notions of the relation between mind and body, between the mental and the physical realms. The dualist, following in the giant footsteps of seventeenth-century philosopher René Descartes, holds that the mind is something ontologically and explanatorily separate from — indeed, in principle independent of — the physical body, brain, and central nervous system. Such a view is not crazy: Indeed, it is, in some ways, exactly what simple introspection suggests. Thoughts, ideas, and feelings certainly don't *seem* like other aspects of physical reality — they do not seem, for example, to be spatially localizable items extended in three or four dimensions! Yet out and out dualism, for all its introspective appeal, is a pretty much universally discredited position in both science and philosophy. The idea of something like a special, nonphysical substance seems puzzling and contradictory. And it seems superfluous given the close and intricate links between the mental and the physical plotted by neuroscience and psychopharmacology. Prozac, to take a mundane example, seems to operate not by affecting some special mental substance but by directly affecting the chemical balances of the biological brain. To assume that these effects then need to be (puzzlingly) propagated to some other ontological realm is to add needless complexity to our account. Insofar as the mental is in any sense special, according to the dominant computational model discussed in this volume, it is special because it depends on some specific and unusual ways in which ordinary physical stuff can be arranged and organized.

That special mode of organization, according to the proponents of what has been called the program of strong artificial intelligence, is *computational*. For computational organizations, unlike other modes of organizing physical stuff, show us how to link *syntax* (physical feature based systems of organization and structure) to *semantics* (the realm of meaning, thought, and reason), and to do so in the powerful context of an automatic device (see e.g., the papers by Haugeland, and by Dennett). The claim is thus not that the brain is somehow like a computing device (everything is like everything else in some respect or other, after all). It is that all that biological wetware just is, literally, nature's way of building a computing machine. By extension, the mind is realized in the brain in the same intimate-yet-relaxed way that a particular kind of information-processing is realized in a physical computer. There is nothing there over and above the physical stuff. Yet a different bedrock organization of such stuff could realize the very same information-processing profile (as when you run the same program on a PC and a Mac). And different physical substances could be used to build the actual devices. The mental is thus tied to the physical — but not so tightly as to require sameness of physical state whenever there is sameness of mental state.

This is a most alluring vision. It reveals the mental as special without making it ghostly. To really appreciate the idea, the reader should follow Haugeland's account (this volume) of how developments in formal logic, in the abstract theory of computation, and in real-world digital computing technology, conspired to put practical and conceptual flesh on the idea of an automatic device in which the unfolding of physical events is constrained (under an interpretation) to follow the rules of logic or of more general forms of "good reasoning." In such devices, to use John Haugeland's famous phrase, "if you take care of the syntax, the semantics will take of itself." Here syntax names the properties of the system that can be fixed as (ultimately) physical features: stuff that can be identified and responded to regardless of its meaning, just in virtue of shape, size, weight, or whatever. The pocket calculator, to take a very simple example, is just such a device: The organized flow of physical state changes guarantees that (under the usual interpretation) those state changes will respect the meanings of '2,' ' +,' '3' and so on.

Thus was born one of the deepest answers so far proposed to the eternal question "what is the nature of the mind?" Substance dualists had suggested that mind was a kind of special, albeit elusive, stuff. Reacting against this idea, so-called "philosophical behaviorists" (Ryle 1949) had instead identified mind with the actual and potential behavior patterns of the beings concerned — an answer that seemed, however, a little too shallow for scientific purposes. "Mind-brain identity theorists" (Smart 1959 and others) reacted, in turn, by proposing that mental states are simply identical with brain processes. This bold claim, however, seemed to yield rather too strong a connection. Thus Putnam (1960 and 1967) observed that such identity claims seemed to imply that creatures lacking brains *just like* ours could not share our beliefs or ideas. Such species-chauvinism seemed scientifically unprincipled and morally suspect. How, then, to do justice to both the bedrock physicality and the intuitive need for a kind of liberality and "multiple realizability"? The confluence of work in logic and formal systems, the theory of computation, and the creation of automatic digital devices suggested an apparently workable compromise: Look instead to the abstract, computational organization of the physical stuff — the web of formal state transitions that could be realized in flesh, silicon, or (for that matter) cream cheese (Putnam 1975, p. 291).

Such, in very broad brush strokes, is the research program most strongly represented in this volume. It is a program that, despite its enormous influence, confronts a number of quite serious difficulties. In the remainder of this brief introduction I will focus on three such difficulties, relating them to various treatments collected in this volume.

The first difficulty concerns the idea of neat, crisp, level-distinctions in nature. It might be phrased like this: Is there really a software level of organization in natural systems? Such a question arises, in very different forms, in the essays by Searle, Reeke and Edelman, and Dreyfus and Dreyfus. All these authors agree (despite other very large differences in view) that there may be something misleading in the standard computationalist emphasis on algorithms, symbols, and programs. And they all worry (again in very different ways) that the theoretical independence of algorithms and hardware may mislead us in our attempts to understand real brains and real biological intelligence.

For one thing, the apparent independence of algorithms from hardware is in large part an artifact of the persistent neglect of issues concerning actual timing of (and constraints arising from the need to support) rapid real-world action. An algorithm, considered independently of any implementation is just a sequence of steps with no inbuilt relation to real-world timing. Nature, however, can hardly afford to remain thus neutral. The project of discovering which algorithms (if any) the brain actually uses will be deeply informed by our knowledge of the processing speed (slow) and organization (parallel, with rich reciprocal and recurrent connectivity) of basic neural components. The shape and structure of biological information processing will, at the very least, be deeply dependent on such implementational details. The idea of trying to understand the computational structure of mind without deep and continuing reference to 'implementation' matters is thus sure to lead to fatal error. We must expect to confront an inner economy in which the software/hardware distinction is itself fuzzy, and in which the computational organization has been deeply sculpted by the nature and speed of neural components, the mechanics of the physical body, and the opportunities provided by the local physical environment (for an extended treatment of all this, see Clark 1997).

The broad notion of mind as 'syntactic engine,' it should be noted, is compatible with a very wide variety of types of computational story. Standard work in artificial intelligence invoked a kind of symbolic database and a set of rules for manipulating the symbols. Work in connectionism and artificial neural networks (see the papers by Churchland and Churchland, and by Dreyfus and Dreyfus) posits a much less linguaform style of inner encoding and a radically different set of basic processing operations. The bare idea of a computational organization thus tells us very little about either the form or structure of the inner realm.

Some theorists (notably Searle and perhaps to some extent Reeke and Edelman) think, however, that the problems go much deeper than I have so far suggested. What is at fault, these writers claim, is the very idea of mind as a computational phenomena, or as essentially information-processing. It is to such deeper challenges that I now turn.

A second difficulty, then, might be phrased like this: Why believe that a computational model provides anything more than a shallow, superficial simulacrum of intelligence and understanding? This issue is addressed, again in widely varying ways, in the essays by Harnad, Searle, Churchland and Churchland, Marr, Newell, and Dreyfus and Dreyfus. The worry is certainly a good one. There are clearly lots of ways in which a given program may count as just shallow mimicry, and fail dismally to illuminate (and even more dismally to replicate) a given aspect of our mental life. A chess computer such as Deep Blue may, at times, be capable of defeating even a grand master. But it relies heavily on the brute-force technique of using its fast processing speed to examine all potential outcomes for about seven moves ahead. This strategy looks quite unlike that of human experts (see especially the paper by Dreyfus and Dreyfus) who seem to rely much more heavily on shallow search with powerful pattern-recognition. At which point it seems hard to avoid thinking of Deep Blue as a kind of clever mimic that is somehow lacking in 'real' intelligence.

That said, we must clearly distinguish two questions. The first is whether a given program constitutes a good model of *human* intelligence. The second is whether the program, when up and running in a real physical device, constitutes some kind of real, but perhaps, nonhuman and alien form of intelligence. The latter question can easily seem impossible to decide. To insist on the use of similar computational strategies to our own threatens to repeat the "species chauvinism" error of early mind-brain identity theory, albeit in new computational clothes. But the only alternative seems to be (once again) a kind of sophisticated behaviorism — we might insist, for example, that any *real* intelligence must exhibit a broad and flexible range of responses to a multiplicity of environmental situations. Deep Blue might thus fail to make the grade not because it is not reasoning as we do (a dangerous kind of intellectual racism) but because its repertoire is too limited — it can recognize a checkmate, but it can't pursue a mate, or cook a decent meal. Something like this demand for flexibility underlies the proposal, in Turing's paper, of a kind of test for real intelligence involving the capacity to hold a proper conversation not restricted to any prespecified subject matter. A stronger demand, suggested in the paper by Stevan Harnad, might be that the system "ground" its representations in capacities to pick out and discriminate objects and features in the real world. Harnad (1991) suggests, in this spirit, an amended version of the Turing Test that would include 'robotic capacities.' The need to model whole systems rather than restricted fragments is pursued in the contribution by Allen Newell.

Might *all* computational models (as Searle wants to suggest) be somehow doomed to shallowness and 'mere mimicry'? My own view is that this only seems compelling when we unduly restrict our vision of possible computational organizations, for example, by identifying computational models with the chunky symbol systems of classical artificial intelligence. Thus imagine a program that, when up and running in an embodied, mobile robot, supports a wide variety of behaviors (from learning the piano, to studying philosophy, to offering advice to the lovelorn). And imagine, in addition, that its fine-grained reasoning profile is similar to our own. It uses shallow search, powerful pattern-recognition, etc. Surely such a program (up and running in its proper context, in the body, in the world) is a promising candidate for our moral respect — i.e., for the status of an actual exemplar of (nonbiological) intelligence? Isn't there, in short, some point at which the grain and fidelity of a computational model must be sufficient to usher into being a new intelligence?

Well maybe. And maybe not. For all this brings us to our final (third) Pandora's box of troubles: Why suppose mind is an *informational* phenomena at all?

Consider the following argument: Plants turn sunlight into energy (better, they turn one type of energy into another type, one that better suits their needs). No matter how detailed your computational model of this process, it won't ever carry out the actual transformation: A simulation is a simulation is a simulation. Now why, the argument continues, couldn't mindfulness be like that? Even if you get the overall set of neural state transitions perfectly described, a computer simulation will remain a mere simulation, and won't constitute a real mental life.

This kind of worry is most plausible, I suspect, when applied directly to the realm of *conscious* mental experiences. It is nicely expressed in Searle's (1992) example of the person suffering from a degenerative brain disease. In the hope of curing the disease she allows parts of her brain to be replaced by silicon chips. The chips preserve the state-transition functions of the neural matter, so the subject's behavior remains the same. She will even say things like "isn't this treatment wonderful." Yet all the while it is logically possible — Searle insists — that her conscious awareness is shrinking until one day it is all gone. She has become a kind of zombie — although her friends can never tell.

Such an example is conceptually problematic. It is not at all clear that we can really imagine what Searle suggests (see Dennett 1991 and Chalmers 1996). But it directs our attention to a good question: Why assume that the nature of our mental life is fixed by the abstract information-processing profile of the brain? Might not at least some aspects of our mental life depend much more directly upon the specifics of local physico-chemical processes, such that substituting a different but *informationally identical* process would nonetheless affect our mental state?

The computationalist can insist that such physico-chemical processes matter *only* for their information processing role. Hormones and chemicals matter, but only insofar as they affect the internal flow of information. The fundamental issue is thus: Which (none? all? some?) of the phenomena we intuitively describe as mental are ultimately *informational* and which (all? some? none?) are not? A lunch order (to take a nonmental example) is informational through and through. You can phone it, fax it, email it — and any 'simulation' of the order can itself count as a lunch order. But the actual *lunch* seems not to be! There is, of course, the famous internet pizza server. You specify size, consistency, and toppings and await on-screen arrival. But as James Gleick has commented (1995, p. 44) "By the time a heavily engineered software engine delivers the final product you begin to suspect that they've actually forgotten the difference between a pizza and *picture* of a pizza." Searle's claim is that conscious thought is more like a pizza than a lunch order — that it is simply *not* an informational phenomenon. Such a claim may seem initially plausible (though far from compelling — see various essays in volume three of this series) in the case of qualitative 'feels' and conscious experiences. The case of simple reason-guided choice and action lends itself rather naturally, by contrast, to an information-processing treatment. If I generate a plan to guide my actions, it is prima facie quite plausible to suppose that that very same mental state could be instantiated in any comparable complex system whose knowledge base and informational state-transitions were the same as mine.

Even in these "information-processing friendly " cases, however, there remain several unresolved issues. How, in detail, are we to unpack the notion of information itself? What do we mean when we talk of some information being explicitly represented in a system? How can a specific informational content (or indeed, any kind of content) play a causal-explanatory role in accounting for a specific action? These are amongst the deep and troubling questions addressed in the closing sequence of papers by Israel and Perry, Kirsh, Dretske, and Dennett. I shall forbear further comment here, save to say that the overall conceptual terrain is still pretty bumpy in places. Some especially nasty contours are developing, of late, around the problematic image of simple physical 'vehicles' of specific contents. Such vehicles, for anything that remotely resembles a high-level content (such as a concept, or belief), now look to be depressingly elusive. The 'vehicles,' if vehicle talk gets a grip at all, seem to involve widespread activity patterns in multiple neuronal populations, conspiring with real bodies, in real-world contexts. As a result, the whole idea of an inner neural code is, in all likelihood, in need of full reevaluation. Any such code will be very closely geared to the biomechanics, action-selecting needs, and local environmental context of a given agent. There is thus a trend, reflected in some of the essays in volume two of this collection — see also (Clark 1997 in press), (Reeke and Edelman this volume), (Kelso 1995), and (Thelen and Smith 1994) — toward a much more austere and less familiar vision of the kinds of information and knowledge encoded in biological brains. This is a vision of the inner syntactic engine stripped of much excess baggage and placed at a large interpretative remove from the basic contentful constructs of daily thought and reason. Yet for all that, I believe that the fundamental insight celebrated in the present volume remains largely compelling. This is the idea that it is, broadly speaking, the abstract causal organization of biological stuff (not the stuff itself) that yields minds and mentality. Computational descriptions can then, in essence, be seen as concise accounts of such abstract causal organization. (For a defense of this kind of 'minimal computationalism' see the paper by Chalmers in this volume.) And implementations — up, running, embodied versions of the minimally computational story — will exhibit that same causal-informational structure and hence count as instances, not mere simulacrums, of mentality. In short, we believe, despite all the problems, that a stripped down, subtly morphed version of the basic idea of mind as a syntactic engine should remain at the heart of the cognitive scientific endeavor. It is this fundamental vision that is developed, celebrated, challenged, and refined in the seminal treatments that follow.

Andy Clark and Josefa Toribio

References

Chalmers, D. (1996). *The Conscious Mind.* New York: Oxford University Press.

Clark, A. (1997). *Being There: Putting Brain, Body and World Together Again.* Cambridge: MIT Press.

Clark, A. (in press). "Where Brain, Body and World Collide." *Daedalus.*

Dennett, D. (1991). *Consciousness Explained.* New York: Little Brown and Co.

Gleick, J. (1995, Dec. 3). "Really Remote Control." *New York Times Magazine,* pp. 42–44.

Harnad, S. (1991). "Other Bodies, Other Minds." *Minds & Machines* 1: 43–54.

Kelso, S. (1995). *Dynamic Patterns.* Cambridge: MIT Press.

Putnam, H. (1960). "Minds and Machines." In S. Hook (ed.), *Dimensions of the Mind.* New York: New York University Press.

Putnam, H. (1967). "Psychological Predicates." In W. Capitan and D. Merill (eds.), *Art, Mind and Religion.* Pittsburgh: University of Pittsburgh Press.

Putnam, H. (1975). "The Meaning of 'Meaning.'" In H. Putnam (ed.), *Mind, Language and Reality,* pp. 215–75. Cambridge: Cambridge University Press.

Ryle, G. (1949). *The Concept of Mind.* London: Hutchinson.

Searle, J. (1992). *The Rediscovery of the Mind.* Cambridge: MIT Press.

Smart, J. (1959). "Sensations and Brain Processes." *Philosophical Review* 68: 141–56.

Thelen, E., and Smith, L. (1994). *A Dynamic Systems Approach to the Development of Cognition and Action.* Cambridge: MIT Press.

VOL. LIX. NO. 236.] [October, 1950

MIND

A QUARTERLY REVIEW

OF

PSYCHOLOGY AND PHILOSOPHY

I.—COMPUTING MACHINERY AND INTELLIGENCE

BY A. M. TURING

1. *The Imitation Game.*

I PROPOSE to consider the question, 'Can machines think ?' This should begin with definitions of the meaning of the terms 'machine' and 'think'. The definitions might be framed so as to reflect so far as possible the normal use of the words, but this attitude is dangerous. If the meaning of the words 'machine' and 'think' are to be found by examining how they are commonly used it is difficult to escape the conclusion that the meaning and the answer to the question, 'Can machines think ?' is to be sought in a statistical survey such as a Gallup poll. But this is absurd. Instead of attempting such a definition I shall replace the question by another, which is closely related to it and is expressed in relatively unambiguous words.

The new form of the problem can be described in terms of a game which we call the 'imitation game'. It is played with three people, a man (A), a woman (B), and an interrogator (C) who may be of either sex. The interrogator stays in a room apart from the other two. The object of the game for the interrogator is to determine which of the other two is the man and which is the woman. He knows them by labels X and Y, and at the end of the game he says either 'X is A and Y is B' or 'X is B and Y is A'. The interrogator is allowed to put questions to A and B thus :

C : Will X please tell me the length of his or her hair ?

Now suppose X is actually A, then A must answer. It is A's

object in the game to try and cause C to make the wrong identification. His answer might therefore be

'My hair is shingled, and the longest strands are about nine inches long.'

In order that tones of voice may not help the interrogator the answers should be written, or better still, typewritten. The ideal arrangement is to have a teleprinter communicating between the two rooms. Alternatively the question and answers can be repeated by an intermediary. The object of the game for the third player (B) is to help the interrogator. The best strategy for her is probably to give truthful answers. She can add such things as 'I am the woman, don't listen to him!' to her answers, but it will avail nothing as the man can make similar remarks.

We now ask the question, 'What will happen when a machine takes the part of A in this game?' Will the interrogator decide wrongly as often when the game is played like this as he does when the game is played between a man and a woman? These questions replace our original, 'Can machines think?'

2. *Critique of the New Problem.*

As well as asking, 'What is the answer to this new form of the question', one may ask, 'Is this new question a worthy one to investigate?' This latter question we investigate without further ado, thereby cutting short an infinite regress.

The new problem has the advantage of drawing a fairly sharp line between the physical and the intellectual capacities of a man. No engineer or chemist claims to be able to produce a material which is indistinguishable from the human skin. It is possible that at some time this might be done, but even supposing this invention available we should feel there was little point in trying to make a 'thinking machine' more human by dressing it up in such artificial flesh. The form in which we have set the problem reflects this fact in the condition which prevents the interrogator from seeing or touching the other competitors, or hearing their voices. Some other advantages of the proposed criterion may be shown up by specimen questions and answers. Thus:

Q: Please write me a sonnet on the subject of the Forth Bridge.
A: Count me out on this one. I never could write poetry.
Q: Add 34957 to 70764
A: (Pause about 30 seconds and then give as answer) 105621.
Q: Do you play chess?
A: Yes.

Q: I have K at my K1, and no other pieces. You have only K at K6 and R at R1. It is your move. What do you play ?

A: (After a pause of 15 seconds) R-R8 mate.

The question and answer method seems to be suitable for introducing almost any one of the fields of human endeavour that we wish to include. We do not wish to penalise the machine for its inability to shine in beauty competitions, nor to penalise a man for losing in a race against an aeroplane. The conditions of our game make these disabilities irrelevant. The 'witnesses' can brag, if they consider it advisable, as much as they please about their charms, strength or heroism, but the interrogator cannot demand practical demonstrations.

The game may perhaps be criticised on the ground that the odds are weighted too heavily against the machine. If the man were to try and pretend to be the machine he would clearly make a very poor showing. He would be given away at once by slowness and inaccuracy in arithmetic. May not machines carry out something which ought to be described as thinking but which is very different from what a man does ? This objection is a very strong one, but at least we can say that if, nevertheless, a machine can be constructed to play the imitation game satisfactorily, we need not be troubled by this objection.

It might be urged that when playing the 'imitation game' the best strategy for the machine may possibly be something other than imitation of the behaviour of a man. This may be, but I think it is unlikely that there is any great effect of this kind. In any case there is no intention to investigate here the theory of the game, and it will be assumed that the best strategy is to try to provide answers that would naturally be given by a man.

3. *The Machines concerned in the Game.*

The question which we put in § 1 will not be quite definite until we have specified what we mean by the word 'machine'. It is natural that we should wish to permit every kind of engineering technique to be used in our machines. We also wish to allow the possibility than an engineer or team of engineers may construct a machine which works, but whose manner of operation cannot be satisfactorily described by its constructors because they have applied a method which is largely experimental. Finally, we wish to exclude from the machines men born in the usual manner. It is difficult to frame the definitions so as to satisfy these three conditions. One might for instance insist that the team of engineers should be all of one sex, but this would not really be satisfactory, for it is probably possible to rear a complete individual from a single cell of the skin (say) of a man. To do so would be a feat of biological technique deserving of the very highest praise, but we would not be inclined to regard it as a case of 'constructing a thinking machine'. This prompts us to abandon the requirement that every kind of technique should be permitted. We are the more ready to do so in view of the fact that the present interest in 'thinking machines' has been aroused by a particular kind of machine, usually called an 'electronic computer' or 'digital computer'. Following this suggestion we only permit digital computers to take part in our game.

This restriction appears at first sight to be a very drastic one. I shall attempt to show that it is not so in reality. To do this necessitates a short account of the nature and properties of these computers.

It may also be said that this identification of machines with digital computers, like our criterion for 'thinking', will only be unsatisfactory if (contrary to my belief), it turns out that digital computers are unable to give a good showing in the game.

There are already a number of digital computers in working order, and it may be asked, 'Why not try the experiment straight away? It would be easy to satisfy the conditions of the game. A number of interrogators could be used, and statistics compiled to show how often the right identification was given.' The short answer is that we are not asking whether all digital computers would do well in the game nor whether the computers at present available would do well, but whether there are imaginable computers which would do well. But this is only the short answer. We shall see this question in a different light later.

4. *Digital Computers.*

The idea behind digital computers may be explained by saying that these machines are intended to carry out any operations which could be done by a human computer. The human computer is supposed to be following fixed rules; he has no authority to deviate from them in any detail. We may suppose that these rules are supplied in a book, which is altered whenever he is put on to a new job. He has also an unlimited supply of paper on which he does his calculations. He may also do his multiplications and additions on a 'desk machine', but this is not important.

If we use the above explanation as a definition we shall be in danger of circularity of argument. We avoid this by giving an outline of the means by which the desired effect is achieved. A digital computer can usually be regarded as consisting of three parts :

(i) Store.
(ii) Executive unit.
(iii) Control.

The store is a store of information, and corresponds to the human computer's paper, whether this is the paper on which he does his calculations or that on which his book of rules is printed. In so far as the human computer does calculations in his head a part of the store will correspond to his memory.

The executive unit is the part which carries out the various individual operations involved in a calculation. What these individual operations are will vary from machine to machine. Usually fairly lengthy operations can be done such as ' Multiply 3540675445 by 7076345687 ' but in some machines only very simple ones such as ' Write down 0 ' are possible.

We have mentioned that the ' book of rules ' supplied to the computer is replaced in the machine by a part of the store. It is then called the ' table of instructions '. It is the duty of the control to see that these instructions are obeyed correctly and in the right order. The control is so constructed that this necessarily happens.

The information in the store is usually broken up into packets of moderately small size. In one machine, for instance, a packet might consist of ten decimal digits. Numbers are assigned to the parts of the store in which the various packets of information are stored, in some systematic manner. A typical instruction might say—

' Add the number stored in position 6809 to that in 4302 and put the result back into the latter storage position '.

Needless to say it would not occur in the machine expressed in English. It would more likely be coded in a form such as 6809430217. Here 17 says which of various possible operations is to be performed on the two numbers. In this case the operation is that described above, *viz.* ' Add the number. . . .' It will be noticed that the instruction takes up 10 digits and so forms one packet of information, very conveniently. The control will normally take the instructions to be obeyed in the order of the positions in which they are stored, but occasionally an instruction such as

'Now obey the instruction stored in position 5606, and continue from there'

may be encountered, or again

'If position 4505 contains 0 obey next the instruction stored in 6707, otherwise continue straight on.'

Instructions of these latter types are very important because they make it possible for a sequence of operations to be repeated over and over again until some condition is fulfilled, but in doing so to obey, not fresh instructions on each repetition, but the same ones over and over again. To take a domestic analogy. Suppose Mother wants Tommy to call at the cobbler's every morning on his way to school to see if her shoes are done, she can ask him afresh every morning. Alternatively she can stick up a notice once and for all in the hall which he will see when he leaves for school and which tells him to call for the shoes, and also to destroy the notice when he comes back if he has the shoes with him.

The reader must accept it as a fact that digital computers can be constructed, and indeed have been constructed, according to the principles we have described, and that they can in fact mimic the actions of a human computer very closely.

The book of rules which we have described our human computer as using is of course a convenient fiction. Actual human computers really remember what they have got to do. If one wants to make a machine mimic the behaviour of the human computer in some complex operation one has to ask him how it is done, and then translate the answer into the form of an instruction table. Constructing instruction tables is usually described as 'programming'. To 'programme a machine to carry out the operation A' means to put the appropriate instruction table into the machine so that it will do A.

An interesting variant on the idea of a digital computer is a 'digital computer with a random element'. These have instructions involving the throwing of a die or some equivalent electronic process; one such instruction might for instance be, 'Throw the die and put the resulting number into store 1000'. Sometimes such a machine is described as having free will (though I would not use this phrase myself). It is not normally possible to determine from observing a machine whether it has a random element, for a similar effect can be produced by such devices as making the choices depend on the digits of the decimal for π.

Most actual digital computers have only a finite store. There is no theoretical difficulty in the idea of a computer with an unlimited store. Of course only a finite part can have been used at any one time. Likewise only a finite amount can have been constructed, but we can imagine more and more being added as required. Such computers have special theoretical interest and will be called infinitive capacity computers.

The idea of a digital computer is an old one. Charles Babbage, Lucasian Professor of Mathematics at Cambridge from 1828 to 1839, planned such a machine, called the Analytical Engine, but it was never completed. Although Babbage had all the essential ideas, his machine was not at that time such a very attractive prospect. The speed which would have been available would be definitely faster than a human computer but something like 100 times slower than the Manchester machine, itself one of the slower of the modern machines. The storage was to be purely mechanical, using wheels and cards.

The fact that Babbage's Analytical Engine was to be entirely mechanical will help us to rid ourselves of a superstition. Importance is often attached to the fact that modern digital computers are electrical, and that the nervous system also is electrical. Since Babbage's machine was not electrical, and since all digital computers are in a sense equivalent, we see that this use of electricity cannot be of theoretical importance. Of course electricity usually comes in where fast signalling is concerned, so that it is not surprising that we find it in both these connections. In the nervous system chemical phenomena are at least as important as electrical. In certain computers the storage system is mainly acoustic. The feature of using electricity is thus seen to be only a very superficial similarity. If we wish to find such similarities we should look rather for mathematical analogies of function.

5. *Universality of Digital Computers.*

The digital computers considered in the last section may be classified amongst the 'discrete state machines'. These are the machines which move by sudden jumps or clicks from one quite definite state to another. These states are sufficiently different for the possibility of confusion between them to be ignored. Strictly speaking there are no such machines. Everything really moves continuously. But there are many kinds of machine which can profitably be *thought of* as being discrete state machines. For instance in considering the switches for a lighting system it is a convenient fiction that each switch must be definitely on or definitely off. There must be intermediate positions, but for most purposes we can forget about them. As an example of a discrete state machine we might consider a wheel which clicks round through 120° once a second, but may be stopped by a lever which can be operated from outside ; in addition a lamp is to light in one of the positions of the wheel. This machine could be described abstractly as follows. The internal state of the machine (which is described by the position of the wheel) may be q_1, q_2 or q_3. There is an input signal i_0 or i_1 (position of lever). The internal state at any moment is determined by the last state and input signal according to the table

		Last State		
		q_1	q_2	q_3
Input	i_0	q_2	q_3	q_1
	i_1	q_1	q_2	q_3

The output signals, the only externally visible indication of the internal state (the light) are described by the table

State	q_1	q_2	q_3
Output	o_0	o_0	o_1

This example is typical of discrete state machines. They can be described by such tables provided they have only a finite number of possible states.

It will seem that given the initial state of the machine and the input signals it is always possible to predict all future states. This is reminiscent of Laplace's view that from the complete state of the universe at one moment of time, as described by the positions and velocities of all particles, it should be possible to predict all future states. The prediction which we are considering is, however, rather nearer to practicability than that considered by Laplace. The system of the 'universe as a whole' is such that quite small errors in the initial conditions can have an overwhelming effect at a later time. The displacement of a single electron by a billionth of a centimetre at one moment might make the difference between a man being killed by an avalanche a year later, or escaping. It is an essential property of the mechanical systems which we have called 'discrete state machines' that this phenomenon does not occur. Even when we consider the actual physical machines instead of the idealised machines, reasonably accurate knowledge of the state at one moment yields reasonably accurate knowledge any number of steps later.

As we have mentioned, digital computers fall within the class of discrete state machines. But the number of states of which such a machine is capable is usually enormously large. For instance, the number for the machine now working at Manchester it about $2^{165,000}$, *i.e.* about $10^{50,000}$. Compare this with our example of the clicking wheel described above, which had three states. It is not difficult to see why the number of states should be so immense. The computer includes a store corresponding to the paper used by a human computer. It must be possible to write into the store any one of the combinations of symbols which might have been written on the paper. For simplicity suppose that only digits from 0 to 9 are used as symbols. Variations in handwriting are ignored. Suppose the computer is allowed 100 sheets of paper each containing 50 lines each with room for 30 digits. Then the number of states is $10^{100\times50\times30}$, *i.e.* $10^{150,000}$. This is about the number of states of three Manchester machines put together. The logarithm to the base two of the number of states is usually called the ' storage capacity ' of the machine. Thus the Manchester machine has a storage capacity of about 165,000 and the wheel machine of our example about 1·6. If two machines are put together their capacities must be added to obtain the capacity of the resultant machine. This leads to the possibility of statements such as ' The Manchester machine contains 64 magnetic tracks each with a capacity of 2560, eight electronic tubes with a capacity of 1280. Miscellaneous storage amounts to about 300 making a total of 174,380.'

Given the table corresponding to a discrete state machine it is possible to predict what it will do. There is no reason why this calculation should not be carried out by means of a digital computer. Provided it could be carried out sufficiently quickly the digital computer could mimic the behaviour of any discrete state machine. The imitation game could then be played with the machine in question (as B) and the mimicking digital computer (as A) and the interrogator would be unable to distinguish them. Of course the digital computer must have an adequate storage capacity as well as working sufficiently fast. Moreover, it must be programmed afresh for each new machine which it is desired to mimic.

This special property of digital computers, that they can mimic any discrete state machine, is described by saying that they are *universal* machines. The existence of machines with this property has the important consequence that, considerations of speed apart, it is unnecessary to design various new machines to do various computing processes. They can all be done with one digital computer, suitably programmed for each case. It will be seen that as a consequence of this all digital computers are in a sense equivalent.

We may now consider again the point raised at the end of §3. It was suggested tentatively that the question, 'Can machines think ?' should be replaced by 'Are there imaginable digital computers which would do well in the imitation game ?' If we wish we can make this superficially more general and ask 'Are there discrete state machines which would do well ?' But in view of the universality property we see that either of these questions is equivalent to this, 'Let us fix our attention on one particular digital computer *C*. Is it true that by modifying this computer to have an adequate storage, suitably increasing its speed of action, and providing it with an appropriate programme, *C* can be made to play satisfactorily the part of A in the imitation game, the part of B being taken by a man ?'

6. *Contrary Views on the Main Question.*

We may now consider the ground to have been cleared and we are ready to proceed to the debate on our question, 'Can machines think ?' and the variant of it quoted at the end of the last section. We cannot altogether abandon the original form of the problem, for opinions will differ as to the appropriateness of the substitution and we must at least listen to what has to be said in this connexion.

It will simplify matters for the reader if I explain first my own beliefs in the matter. Consider first the more accurate form of the question. I believe that in about fifty years' time it will be possible to programme computers, with a storage capacity of about 10^9, to make them play the imitation game so well that an average interrogator will not have more than 70 per cent. chance of making the right identification after five minutes of questioning. The original question, 'Can machines think ?' I believe to be too meaningless to deserve discussion. Nevertheless I believe that at the end of the century the use of words and general educated opinion will have altered so much that one will be able to speak of machines thinking without expecting to be contradicted. I believe further that no useful purpose is served by concealing these beliefs. The popular view that scientists proceed inexorably from well-established fact to well-established fact, never being influenced by any unproved conjecture, is quite mistaken. Provided it is made clear which are proved facts and which are conjectures, no harm can result. Conjectures are of great importance since they suggest useful lines of research.

I now proceed to consider opinions opposed to my own.

(1) *The Theological Objection.* Thinking is a function of man's immortal soul. God has given an immortal soul to every man and woman, but not to any other animal or to machines. Hence no animal or machine can think.

I am unable to accept any part of this, but will attempt to reply in theological terms. I should find the argument more convincing if animals were classed with men, for there is a greater difference, to my mind, between the typical animate and the inanimate than there is between man and the other animals. The arbitrary character of the orthodox view becomes clearer if we consider how it might appear to a member of some other religious community. How do Christians regard the Moslem view that women have no souls ? But let us leave this point aside and return to the main argument. It appears to me that the argument quoted above implies a serious restriction of the omnipotence of the Almighty. It is admitted that there are certain things that He cannot do such as making one equal to two, but should we not believe that He has freedom to confer a soul on an elephant if He sees fit ? We might expect that He would only exercise this power in conjunction with a mutation which provided the elephant with an appropriately improved brain to minister to the needs of this soul. An argument of exactly similar form may be made for the case of machines. It may seem different because it is more difficult to "swallow". But this really only means that we think it would be less likely that He would consider the circumstances suitable for conferring a soul. The circumstances in question are discussed in the rest of this paper. In attempting to construct such machines we should not be irreverently usurping His power of creating souls, any more than we are in the procreation of children: rather we are, in either case, instruments of His will providing mansions for the souls that He creates.

However, this is mere speculation. I am not very impressed with theological arguments whatever they may be used to support. Such arguments have often been found unsatisfactory in the past. In the time of Galileo it was argued that the texts, "And the sun stood still . . . and hasted not to go down about a whole day" (Joshua x. 13) and "He laid the foundations of the earth,

[1] Possibly this view is heretical. St. Thomas Aquinas (*Summa Theologica*, quoted by Bertrand Russell, p. 480) states that God cannot make a man to have no soul. But this may not be a real restriction on His powers, but only a result of the fact that men's souls are immortal, and therefore indestructible.

that it should not move at any time" (Psalm cv. 5) were an adequate refutation of the Copernican theory. With our present knowledge such an argument appears futile. When that knowledge was not available it made a quite different impression.

(2) *The 'Heads in the Sand' Objection.* "The consequences of machines thinking would be too dreadful. Let us hope and believe that they cannot do so."

This argument is seldom expressed quite so openly as in the form above. But it affects most of us who think about it at all. We like to believe that Man is in some subtle way superior to the rest of creation. It is best if he can be shown to be *necessarily* superior, for then there is no danger of him losing his commanding position. The popularity of the theological argument is clearly connected with this feeling. It is likely to be quite strong in intellectual people, since they value the power of thinking more highly than others, and are more inclined to base their belief in the superiority of Man on this power.

I do not think that this argument is sufficiently substantial to require refutation. Consolation would be more appropriate: perhaps this should be sought in the transmigration of souls.

(3) *The Mathematical Objection.* There are a number of results of mathematical logic which can be used to show that there are limitations to the powers of discrete-state machines. The best known of these results is known as Gödel's theorem,[1] and shows that in any sufficiently powerful logical system statements can be formulated which can neither be proved nor disproved within the system, unless possibly the system itself is inconsistent. There are other, in some respects similar, results due to *Church*, *Kleene*, *Rosser*, and *Turing*. The latter result is the most convenient to consider, since it refers directly to machines, whereas the others can only be used in a comparatively indirect argument: for instance if Gödel's theorem is to be used we need in addition to have some means of describing logical systems in terms of machines, and machines in terms of logical systems. The result in question refers to a type of machine which is essentially a digital computer with an infinite capacity. It states that there are certain things that such a machine cannot do. If it is rigged up to give answers to questions as in the imitation game, there will be some questions to which it will either give a wrong answer, or fail to give an answer at all however much time is allowed for a reply. There may, of course, be many such questions, and questions which cannot be answered by one machine may be satisfactorily

[1] Author's names in italics refer to the Bibliography.

answered by another. We are of course supposing for the present that the questions are of the kind to which an answer 'Yes' or 'No' is appropriate, rather than questions such as 'What do you think of Picasso?' The questions that we know the machines must fail on are of this type, "Consider the machine specified as follows. . . . Will this machine ever answer 'Yes' to any question?" The dots are to be replaced by a description of some machine in a standard form, which could be something like that used in § 5. When the machine described bears a certain comparatively simple relation to the machine which is under interrogation, it can be shown that the answer is either wrong or not forthcoming. This is the mathematical result: it is argued that it proves a disability of machines to which the human intellect is not subject.

The short answer to this argument is that although it is established that there are limitations to the powers of any particular machine, it has only been stated, without any sort of proof, that no such limitations apply to the human intellect. But I do not think this view can be dismissed quite so lightly. Whenever one of these machines is asked the appropriate critical question, and gives a definite answer, we know that this answer must be wrong, and this gives us a certain feeling of superiority. Is this feeling illusory? It is no doubt quite genuine, but I do not think too much importance should be attached to it. We too often give wrong answers to questions ourselves to be justified in being very pleased at such evidence of fallibility on the part of the machines. Further, our superiority can only be felt on such an occasion in relation to the one machine over which we have scored our petty triumph. There would be no question of triumphing simultaneously over *all* machines. In short, then, there might be men cleverer than any given machine, but then again there might be other machines cleverer again, and so on.

Those who hold to the mathematical argument would, I think, mostly be willing to accept the imitation game as a basis for discussion. Those who believe in the two previous objections would probably not be interested in any criteria.

(4) *The Argument from Consciousness.* This argument is very well expressed in *Professor Jefferson's* Lister Oration for 1949, from which I quote. "Not until a machine can write a sonnet or compose a concerto because of thoughts and emotions felt, and not by the chance fall of symbols, could we agree that machine equals brain—that is, not only write it but know that it had written it. No mechanism could feel (and not merely

artificially signal, an easy contrivance) pleasure at its successes, grief when its valves fuse, be warmed by flattery, be made miserable by its mistakes, be charmed by sex, be angry or depressed when it cannot get what it wants."

This argument appears to be a denial of the validity of our test. According to the most extreme form of this view the only way by which one could be sure that a machine thinks is to *be* the machine and to feel oneself thinking. One could then describe these feelings to the world, but of course no one would be justified in taking any notice. Likewise according to this view the only way to know that a *man* thinks is to be that particular man. It is in fact the solipsist point of view. It may be the most logical view to hold but it makes communication of ideas difficult. A is liable to believe 'A thinks but B does not' whilst B believes 'B thinks but A does not'. Instead of arguing continually over this point it is usual to have the polite convention that everyone thinks.

I am sure that Professor Jefferson does not wish to adopt the extreme and solipsist point of view. Probably he would be quite willing to accept the imitation game as a test. The game (with the player B omitted) is frequently used in practice under the name of *viva voce* to discover whether some one really understands something or has 'learnt it parrot fashion'. Let us listen in to a part of such a *viva voce :*

Interrogator: In the first line of your sonnet which reads 'Shall I compare thee to a summer's day', would not 'a spring day' do as well or better ?

Witness: It wouldn't scan.

Interrogator: How about 'a winter's day' That would scan all right.

Witness: Yes, but nobody wants to be compared to a winter's day.

Interrogator: Would you say Mr. Pickwick reminded you of Christmas ?

Witness: In a way.

Interrogator: Yet Christmas is a winter's day, and I do not think Mr. Pickwick would mind the comparison.

Witness: I don't think you're serious. By a winter's day one means a typical winter's day, rather than a special one like Christmas.

And so on. What would Professor Jefferson say if the sonnet-writing machine was able to answer like this in the *viva voce?* I do not know whether he would regard the machine as 'merely artificially signalling ' these answers, but if the answers were as satisfactory and sustained as in the above passage I do not think he would describe it as 'an easy contrivance'. This phrase is, I think, intended to cover such devices as the inclusion in the machine of a record of someone reading a sonnet, with appropriate switching to turn it on from time to time.

In short then, I think that most of those who support the argument from consciousness could be persuaded to abandon it rather than be forced into the solipsist position. They will then probably be willing to accept our test.

I do not wish to give the impression that I think there is no mystery about consciousness. There is, for instance, something of a paradox connected with any attempt to localise it. But I do not think these mysteries necessarily need to be solved before we can answer the question with which we are concerned in this paper.

(5) *Arguments from Various Disabilities.* These arguments take the form, " I grant you that you can make machines do all the things you have mentioned but you will never be able to make one to do X ". Numerous features X are suggested in this connexion. I offer a selection :

Be kind, resourceful, beautiful, friendly (p. 448), have initiative, have a sense of humour, tell right from wrong, make mistakes (p. 448), fall in love, enjoy strawberries and cream (p. 448), make some one fall in love with it, learn from experience (pp. 456 f.), use words properly, be the subject of its own thought (p. 449), have as much diversity of behaviour as a man, do something really new (p. 450). (Some of these disabilities are given special consideration as indicated by the page numbers.)

No support is usually offered for these statements. I believe they are mostly founded on the principle of scientific induction. A man has seen thousands of machines in his lifetime. From what he sees of them he draws a number of general conclusions. They are ugly, each is designed for a very limited purpose, when required for a minutely different purpose they are useless, the variety of behaviour of any one of them is very small, etc., etc. Naturally he concludes that these are necessary properties of machines in general. Many of these limitations are associated with the very small storage capacity of most machines. (I am assuming that the idea of storage capacity is extended in some way to cover machines other than discrete-state machines.

The exact definition does not matter as no mathematical accuracy is claimed in the present discussion.) A few years ago, when very little had been heard of digital computers, it was possible to elicit much incredulity concerning them, if one mentioned their properties without describing their construction. That was presumably due to a similar application of the principle of scientific induction. These applications of the principle are of course largely unconscious. When a burnt child fears the fire and shows that he fears it by avoiding it, I should say that he was applying scientific induction. (I could of course also describe his behaviour in many other ways.) The works and customs of mankind do not seem to be very suitable material to which to apply scientific induction. A very large part of space-time must be investigated, if reliable results are to be obtained. Otherwise we may (as most English children do) decide that everybody speaks English, and that it is silly to learn French.

There are, however, special remarks to be made about many of the disabilities that have been mentioned. The inability to enjoy strawberries and cream may have struck the reader as frivolous. Possibly a machine might be made to enjoy this delicious dish, but any attempt to make one do so would be idiotic. What is important about this disability is that it contributes to some of the other disabilities, *e.g.* to the difficulty of the same kind of friendliness occurring between man and machine as between white man and white man, or between black man and black man.

The claim that "machines cannot make mistakes" seems a curious one. One is tempted to retort, "Are they any the worse for that ?" But let us adopt a more sympathetic attitude, and try to see what is really meant. I think this criticism can be explained in terms of the imitation game. It is claimed that the interrogator could distinguish the machine from the man simply by setting them a number of problems in arithmetic. The machine would be unmasked because of its deadly accuracy. The reply to this is simple. The machine (programmed for playing the game) would not attempt to give the *right* answers to the arithmetic problems. It would deliberately introduce mistakes in a manner calculated to confuse the interrogator. A mechanical fault would probably show itself through an unsuitable decision as to what sort of a mistake to make in the arithmetic. Even this interpretation of the criticism is not sufficiently sympathetic. But we cannot afford the space to go into it much further. It seems to me that this criticism depends on a confusion between two kinds of mistake. We may call them 'errors of functioning' and 'errors of conclusion'. Errors of functioning are due to some mechanical or electrical fault which causes the machine to behave otherwise than it was designed to do. In philosophical discussions one likes to ignore the possibility of such errors; one is therefore discussing 'abstract machines'. These abstract machines are mathematical fictions rather than physical objects. By definition they are incapable of errors of functioning. In this sense we can truly say that 'machines can never make mistakes'. Errors of conclusion can only arise when some meaning is attached to the output signals from the machine. The machine might, for instance, type out mathematical equations, or sentences in English. When a false proposition is typed we say that the machine has committed an error of conclusion. There is clearly no reason at all for saying that a machine cannot make this kind of mistake. It might do nothing but type out repeatedly '$0 = 1$'. To take a less perverse example, it might have some method for drawing conclusions by scientific induction. We must expect such a method to lead occasionally to erroneous results.

The claim that a machine cannot be the subject of its own thought can of course only be answered if it can be shown that the machine has *some* thought with *some* subject matter. Nevertheless, 'the subject matter of a machine's operations' does seem to mean something, at least to the people who deal with it. If, for instance, the machine was trying to find a solution of the equation $x^2 - 40x - 11 = 0$ one would be tempted to describe this equation as part of the machine's subject matter at that moment. In this sort of sense a machine undoubtedly can be its own subject matter. It may be used to help in making up its own programmes, or to predict the effect of alterations in its own structure. By observing the results of its own behaviour it can modify its own programmes so as to achieve some purpose more effectively. These are possibilities of the near future, rather than Utopian dreams.

The criticism that a machine cannot have much diversity of behaviour is just a way of saying that it cannot have much storage capacity. Until fairly recently a storage capacity of even a thousand digits was very rare.

The criticisms that we are considering here are often disguised forms of the argument from consciousness. Usually if one maintains that a machine *can* do one of these things, and describes the kind of method that the machine could use, one will not make

29

much of an impression. It is thought that the method (whatever it may be, for it must be mechanical) is really rather base. Compare the parenthesis in Jefferson's statement quoted on p. 21.

(6) *Lady Lovelace's Objection.* Our most detailed information of Babbage's Analytical Engine comes from a memoir by *Lady Lovelace.* In it she states, "The Analytical Engine has no pretensions to *originate* anything. It can do *whatever we know how to order it* to perform" (her italics). This statement is quoted by *Hartree* (p. 70) who adds: "This does not imply that it may not be possible to construct electronic equipment which will 'think for itself', or in which, in biological terms, one could set up a conditioned reflex, which would serve as a basis for 'learning'. Whether this is possible in principle or not is a stimulating and exciting question, suggested by some of these recent developments. But it did not seem that the machines constructed or projected at the time had this property".

I am in thorough agreement with Hartree over this. It will be noticed that he does not assert that the machines in question had not got the property, but rather that the evidence available to Lady Lovelace did not encourage her to believe that they had it. It is quite possible that the machines in question had in a sense got this property. For suppose that some discrete-state machine has the property. The Analytical Engine was a universal digital computer, so that, if its storage capacity and speed were adequate, it could by suitable programming be made to mimic the machine in question. Probably this argument did not occur to the Countess or to Babbage. In any case there was no obligation on them to claim all that could be claimed.

This whole question will be considered again under the heading of learning machines.

A variant of Lady Lovelace's objection states that a machine can 'never do anything really new'. This may be parried for a moment with the saw, 'There is nothing new under the sun'. Who can be certain that 'original work' that he has done was not simply the growth of the seed planted in him by teaching, or the effect of following well-known general principles. A better variant of the objection says that a machine can never 'take us by surprise'. This statement is a more direct challenge and can be met directly. Machines take me by surprise with great frequency. This is largely because I do not do sufficient calculation to decide what to expect them to do, or rather because, although I do a calculation, I do it in a hurried, slipshod fashion, taking risks. Perhaps I say to myself, 'I suppose the voltage here ought to be the same as there: anyway let's assume it is'.

Naturally I am often wrong, and the result is a surprise for me for by the time the experiment is done these assumptions have been forgotten. These admissions lay me open to lectures on the subject of my vicious ways, but do not throw any doubt on my credibility when I testify to the surprises I experience.

I do not expect this reply to silence my critic. He will probably say that such surprises are due to some creative mental act on my part, and reflect no credit on the machine. This leads us back to the argument from consciousness, and far from the idea of surprise. It is a line of argument we must consider closed, but it is perhaps worth remarking that the appreciation of something as surprising requires as much of a 'creative mental act' whether the surprising event originates from a man, a book, a machine or anything else.

The view that machines cannot give rise to surprises is due, I believe, to a fallacy to which philosophers and mathematicians are particularly subject. This is the assumption that as soon as a fact is presented to a mind all consequences of that fact spring into the mind simultaneously with it. It is a very useful assumption under many circumstances, but one too easily forgets that it is false. A natural consequence of doing so is that one then assumes that there is no virtue in the mere working out of consequences from data and general principles.

(7) *Argument from Continuity in the Nervous System.* The nervous system is certainly not a discrete-state machine. A small error in the information about the size of a nervous impulse impinging on a neuron, may make a large difference to the size of the outgoing impulse. It may be argued that, this being so, one cannot expect to be able to mimic the behaviour of the nervous system with a discrete-state system.

It is true that a discrete-state machine must be different from a continuous machine. But if we adhere to the conditions of the imitation game, the interrogator will not be able to take any advantage of this difference. The situation can be made clearer if we consider some other simpler continuous machine. A differential analyser will do very well. (A differential analyser is a certain kind of machine not of the discrete-state type used for some kinds of calculation.) Some of these provide their answers in a typed form, and so are suitable for taking part in the game. It would not be possible for a digital computer to predict exactly what answers the differential analyser would give to a problem, but it would be quite capable of giving the right sort of answer. For instance, if asked to give the value of π (actually about 3·1416) it would be reasonable to choose at random between the values 3·12, 3·13, 3·14, 3·15, 3·16 with the probabilities of 0·05, 0·15, 0·55, 0·19, 0·06 (say). Under these circumstances it would be very difficult for the interrogator to distinguish the differential analyser from the digital computer.

(8) *The Argument from Informality of Behaviour.* It is not possible to produce a set of rules purporting to describe what a man should do in every conceivable set of circumstances. One might for instance have a rule that one is to stop when one sees a red traffic light, and to go if one sees a green one, but what if by some fault both appear together ? One may perhaps decide that it is safest to stop. But some further difficulty may well arise from this decision later. To attempt to provide rules of conduct to cover every eventuality, even those arising from traffic lights, appears to be impossible. With all this I agree.

From this it is argued that we cannot be machines. I shall try to reproduce the argument, but I fear I shall hardly do it justice. It seems to run something like this. ' If each man had a definite set of rules of conduct by which he regulated his life he would be no better than a machine. But there are no such rules, so men cannot be machines.' The undistributed middle is glaring. I do not think the argument is ever put quite like this, but I believe this is the argument used nevertheless. There may however be a certain confusion between ' rules of conduct ' and ' laws of behaviour ' to cloud the issue. By ' rules of conduct ' I mean precepts such as ' Stop if you see red lights ', on which one can act, and of which one can be conscious. By ' laws of behaviour ' I mean laws of nature as applied to a man's body such as ' if you pinch him he will squeak '. If we substitute ' laws of behaviour which regulate his life ' for ' laws of conduct by which he regulates his life ' in the argument quoted the undistributed middle is no longer insuperable. For we believe that it is not only true that being regulated by laws of behaviour implies being some sort of machine (though not necessarily a discrete-state machine), but that conversely being such a machine implies being regulated by such laws. However, we cannot so easily convince ourselves of the absence of complete laws of behaviour as of complete rules of conduct. The only way we know of for finding such laws is scientific observation, and we certainly know of no circumstances under which we could say, ' We have searched enough. There are no such laws.'

We can demonstrate more forcibly that any such statement would be unjustified. For suppose we could be sure of finding such laws if they existed. Then given a discrete-state machine it should certainly be possible to discover by observation sufficent about it to predict its future behaviour, and this within a reasonable time, say a thousand years. But this does not seem to be the case. I have set up on the Manchester computer a small programme using only 1000 units of storage, whereby the machine supplied with one sixteen figure number replies with another within two seconds. I would defy anyone to learn from these replies sufficient about the programme to be able to predict any replies to untried values.

(9) *The Argument from Extra-Sensory Perception.* I assume that the reader is familiar with the idea of extra-sensory perception, and the meaning of the four items of it, *viz.* telepathy, clairvoyance, precognition and psycho-kinesis. These disturbing phenomena seem to deny all our usual scientific ideas. How we should like to discredit them! Unfortunately the statistical evidence, at least for telepathy, is overwhelming. It is very difficult to rearrange one's ideas so as to fit these new facts in. Once one has accepted them it does not seem a very big step to believe in ghosts and bogies. The idea that our bodies move simply according to the known laws of physics, together with some others not yet discovered but somewhat similar, would be one of the first to go.

This argument is to my mind quite a strong one. One can say in reply that many scientific theories seem to remain workable in practice, in spite of clashing with E.S.P.; that in fact one can get along very nicely if one forgets about it. This is rather cold comfort, and one fears that thinking is just the kind of phenomenon where E.S.P. may be especially relevant.

A more specific argument based on E.S.P. might run as follows: "Let us play the imitation game, using as witnesses a man who is good as a telepathic receiver, and a digital computer. The interrogator can ask such questions as 'What suit does the card in my right hand belong to?' The man by telepathy or clairvoyance gives the right answer 130 times out of 400 cards. The machine can only guess at random, and perhaps gets 104 right, so the interrogator makes the right identification." There is an interesting possibility which opens here. Suppose the digital computer contains a random number generator. Then it will be natural to use this to decide what answer to give. But then the random number generator will be subject to the psycho-kinetic powers of the interrogator. Perhaps this psycho-kinesis might cause the machine to guess right more often than would be expected on a probability calculation, so that the interrogator might still be unable to make the right identification. On the other hand, he might be able to guess right without any questioning, by clairvoyance. With E.S.P. anything may happen.

If telepathy is admitted it will be necessary to tighten our test up. The situation could be regarded as analogous to that which would occur if the interrogator were talking to himself and one of the competitors was listening with his ear to the wall. To put the competitors into a 'telepathy-proof room' would satisfy all requirements.

7. *Learning Machines.*

The reader will have anticipated that I have no very convincing arguments of a positive nature to support my views. If I had I should not have taken such pains to point out the fallacies in contrary views. Such evidence as I have I shall now give.

Let us return for a moment to Lady Lovelace's objection, which stated that the machine can only do what we tell it to do. One could say that a man can 'inject' an idea into the machine, and that it will respond to a certain extent and then drop into quiescence, like a piano string struck by a hammer. Another simile would be an atomic pile of less than critical size: an injected idea is to correspond to a neutron entering the pile from without. Each such neutron will cause a certain disturbance which eventually dies away. If, however, the size of the pile is sufficiently increased, the disturbance caused by such an incoming neutron will very likely go on and on increasing until the whole pile is destroyed. Is there a corresponding phenomenon for minds, and is there one for machines ? There does seem to be one for the human mind. The majority of them seem to be 'sub-critical', *i.e.* to correspond in this analogy to piles of subcritical size. An idea presented to such a mind will on average give rise to less than one idea in reply. A smallish proportion are super-critical. An idea presented to such a mind may give rise to a whole 'theory' consisting of secondary, tertiary and more remote ideas. Animals minds seem to be very definitely sub-critical. Adhering to this analogy we ask, 'Can a machine be made to be super-critical ?'

The 'skin of an onion' analogy is also helpful. In considering the functions of the mind or the brain we find certain operations which we can explain in purely mechanical terms. This we say does not correspond to the real mind : it is a sort of skin which we must strip off if we are to find the real mind. But then in what remains we find a further skin to be stripped off, and so on.

Proceeding in this way do we ever come to the 'real' mind, or do we eventually come to the skin which has nothing in it? In the latter case the whole mind is mechanical. (It would not be a discrete-state machine however. We have discussed this.)

These last two paragraphs do not claim to be convincing arguments. They should rather be described as 'recitations tending to produce belief'.

The only really satisfactory support that can be given for the view expressed at the beginning of § 6, will be that provided by waiting for the end of the century and then doing the experiment described. But what can we say in the meantime? What steps should be taken now if the experiment is to be successful?

As I have explained, the problem is mainly one of programming. Advances in engineering will have to be made too, but it seems unlikely that these will not be adequate for the requirements. Estimates of the storage capacity of the brain vary from 10^{10} to 10^{15} binary digits. I incline to the lower values and believe that only a very small fraction is used for the higher types of thinking. Most of it is probably used for the retention of visual impressions. I should be surprised if more than 10^9 was required for satisfactory playing of the imitation game, at any rate against a blind man. (Note—The capacity of the *Encyclopaedia Britannica*, 11th edition, is 2×10^9.) A storage capacity of 10^7 would be a very practicable possibility even by present techniques. It is probably not necessary to increase the speed of operations of the machines at all. Parts of modern machines which can be regarded as analogues of nerve cells work about a thousand times faster than the latter. This should provide a 'margin of safety' which could cover losses of speed arising in many ways. Our problem then is to find out how to programme these machines to play the game. At my present rate of working I produce about a thousand digits of programme a day, so that about sixty workers, working steadily through the fifty years might accomplish the job, if nothing went into the waste-paper basket. Some more expeditious method seems desirable.

In the process of trying to imitate an adult human mind we are bound to think a good deal about the process which has brought it to the state that it is in. We may notice three components,

(*a*) The initial state of the mind, say at birth,

(*b*) The education to which it has been subjected,

(*c*) Other experience, not to be described as education, to which it has been subjected.

Instead of trying to produce a programme to simulate the adult mind, why not rather try to produce one which simulates the child's ? If this were then subjected to an appropriate course of education one would obtain the adult brain. Presumably the child-brain is something like a note-book as one buys it from the stationers. Rather little mechanism, and lots of blank sheets. (Mechanism and writing are from our point of view almost synonymous.) Our hope is that there is so little mechanism in the child-brain that something like it can be easily programmed. The amount of work in the education we can assume, as a first approximation, to be much the same as for the human child.

We have thus divided our problem into two parts. The child-programme and the education process. These two remain very closely connected. We cannot expect to find a good child-machine at the first attempt. One must experiment with teaching one such machine and see how well it learns. One can then try another and see if it is better or worse. There is an obvious connection between this process and evolution, by the identifications

Structure of the child machine = Hereditary material
Changes ,, ,, = Mutations
Natural selection = Judgment of the experimenter

One may hope, however, that this process will be more expeditious than evolution. The survival of the fittest is a slow method for measuring advantages. The experimenter, by the exercise of intelligence, should be able to speed it up. Equally important is the fact that he is not restricted to random mutations. If he can trace a cause for some weakness he can probably think of the kind of mutation which will improve it.

It will not be possible to apply exactly the same teaching process to the machine as to a normal child. It will not, for instance, be provided with legs, so that it could not be asked to go out and fill the coal scuttle. Possibly it might not have eyes. But however well these deficiencies might be overcome by clever engineering, one could not send the creature to school without the other children making excessive fun of it. It must be given some tuition. We need not be too concerned about the legs, eyes, etc. The example of Miss *Helen Keller* shows that education can take place provided that communication in both directions between teacher and pupil can take place by some means or other.

We normally associate punishments and rewards with the teaching process. Some simple child-machines can be constructed or programmed on this sort of principle. The machine has to be so constructed that events which shortly preceded the occurrence of a punishment-signal are unlikely to be repeated, whereas a reward-signal increased the probability of repetition of the events which led up to it. These definitions do not presuppose any feelings on the part of the machine. I have done some experiments with one such child-machine, and succeeded in teaching it a few things, but the teaching method was too unorthodox for the experiment to be considered really successful.

The use of punishments and rewards can at best be a part of the teaching process. Roughly speaking, if the teacher has no other means of communicating to the pupil, the amount of information which can reach him does not exceed the total number of rewards and punishments applied. By the time a child has learnt to repeat 'Casabianca' he would probably feel very sore indeed, if the text could only be discovered by a 'Twenty Questions' technique, every 'NO' taking the form of a blow. It is necessary therefore to have some other 'unemotional' channels of communication. If these are available it is possible to teach a machine by punishments and rewards to obey orders given in some language, *e.g.* a symbolic language. These orders are to be transmitted through the 'unemotional' channels. The use of this language will diminish greatly the number of punishments and rewards required.

Opinions may vary as to the complexity which is suitable in the child machine. One might try to make it as simple as possible consistently with the general principles. Alternatively one might have a complete system of logical inference 'built in'.[1] In the latter case the store would be largely occupied with definitions and propositions. The propositions would have various kinds of status, *e.g.* well-established facts, conjectures, mathematically proved theorems, statements given by an authority, expressions having the logical form of proposition but not belief-value. Certain propositions may be described as 'imperatives'. The machine should be so constructed that as soon as an imperative is classed as 'well-established' the appropriate action automatically takes place. To illustrate this, suppose the teacher says to the machine, 'Do your homework now'. This may cause "Teacher says 'Do your homework now'" to be included amongst the well-established facts. Another such fact might be,

[1] Or rather 'programmed in' for our child-machine will be programmed in a digital computer. But the logical system will not have to be learnt.

" Everything that teacher says is true ". Combining these may eventually lead to the imperative, ' Do your homework now ', being included amongst the well-established facts, and this, by the construction of the machine, will mean that the homework actually gets started, but the effect is very satisfactory. The processes of inference used by the machine need not be such as would satisfy the most exacting logicians. There might for instance be no hierarchy of types. But this need not mean that type fallacies will occur, any more than we are bound to fall over unfenced cliffs. Suitable imperatives (expressed *within* the systems, not forming part of the rules *of* the system) such as ' Do not use a class unless it is a subclass of one which has been mentioned by teacher ' can have a similar effect to ' Do not go too near the edge '.

The imperatives that can be obeyed by a machine that has no limbs are bound to be of a rather intellectual character, as in the example (doing homework) given above. Important amongst such imperatives will be ones which regulate the order in which the rules of the logical system concerned are to be applied. For at each stage when one is using a logical system, there is a very large number of alternative steps, any of which one is permitted to apply, so far as obedience to the rules of the logical system is concerned. These choices make the difference between a brilliant and a footling reasoner, not the difference between a sound and a fallacious one. Propositions leading to imperatives of this kind might be " When Socrates is mentioned, use the syllogism in Barbara " or " If one method has been proved to be quicker than another, do not use the slower method ". Some of these may be ' given by authority ', but others may be produced by the machine itself, *e.g.* by scientific induction.

The idea of a learning machine may appear paradoxical to some readers. How can the rules of operation of the machine change ? They should describe completely how the machine will react whatever its history might be, whatever changes it might undergo. The rules are thus quite time-invariant. This is quite true. The explanation of the paradox is that the rules which get changed in the learning process are of a rather less pretentious kind, claiming only an ephemeral validity. The reader may draw a parallel with the Constitution of the United States.

An important feature of a learning machine is that its teacher will often be very largely ignorant of quite what is going on inside, although he may still be able to some extent to predict his pupil's behaviour. This should apply most strongly to the later education of a machine arising from a child-machine of well-tried design (or programme). This is in clear contrast with normal procedure when using a machine to do computations: one's object is then to have a clear mental picture of the state of the machine at each moment in the computation. This object can only be achieved with a struggle. The view that 'the machine can only do what we know how to order it to do',[1] appears strange in face of this. Most of the programmes which we can put into the machine will result in its doing something that we cannot make sense of at all, or which we regard as completely random behaviour. Intelligent behaviour presumably consists in a departure from the completely disciplined behaviour involved in computation, but a rather slight one, which does not give rise to random behaviour, or to pointless repetitive loops. Another important result of preparing our machine for its part in the imitation game by a process of teaching and learning is that 'human fallibility' is likely to be omitted in a rather natural way, *i.e.* without special 'coaching'. (The reader should reconcile this with the point of view on pp. 24, 25.) Processes that are learnt do not produce a hundred per cent. certainty of result; if they did they could not be unlearnt.

It is probably wise to include a random element in a learning machine (see p. 438). A random element is rather useful when we are searching for a solution of some problem. Suppose for instance we wanted to find a number between 50 and 200 which was equal to the square of the sum of its digits, we might start at 51 then try 52 and go on until we got a number that worked. Alternatively we might choose numbers at random until we got a a good one. This method has the advantage that it is unnecessary to keep track of the values that have been tried, but the disadvantage that one may try the same one twice, but this is not very important if there are several solutions. The systematic method has the disadvantage that there may be an enormous block without any solutions in the region which has to be investigated first. Now the learning process may be regarded as a search for a form of behaviour which will satisfy the teacher (or some other criterion). Since there is probably a very large number of satisfactory solutions the random method seems to be better than the systematic. It should be noticed that it is used in the analogous process of evolution. But there the systematic method is not possible. How could one keep track

[1] Compare Lady Lovelace's statement (p. 450), which does not contain the word 'only'.

of the different genetical combinations that had been tried, so as to avoid trying them again ?

We may hope that machines will eventually compete with men in all purely intellectual fields. But which are the best ones to start with ? Even this is a difficult decision. Many people think that a very abstract activity, like the playing of chess, would be best. It can also be maintained that it is best to provide the machine with the best sense organs that money can buy, and then teach it to understand and speak English. This process could follow the normal teaching of a child. Things would be pointed out and named, etc. Again I do not know what the right answer is, but I think both approaches should be tried.

We can only see a short distance ahead, but we can see plenty there that needs to be done.

BIBLIOGRAPHY

Samuel Butler, Erewhon, London, 1865. Chapters 23, 24, 25, *The Book of the Machines.*

Alonzo Church, " An Unsolvable Problem of Elementary Number Theory ", *American J. of Math.*, 58 (1936), 345-363.

K. Gödel, " Über formal unentscheidbare Sätze der Principia Mathematica und verwandter Systeme, I ", *Monatshefte für Math. und Phys.*, (1931), 173-189.

D. R. Hartree, *Calculating Instruments and Machines*, New York, 1949.

S. C. Kleene, " General Recursive Functions of Natural Numbers ", *American J. of Math.*, 57 (1935), 153-173 and 219-244.

G. Jefferson, " The Mind of Mechanical Man ". Lister Oration for 1949. *British Medical Journal*, vol. i (1949), 1105-1121.

Countess of Lovelace, ' Translator's notes tc an article on Babbage's Analytical Engire ', *Scientific Memoirs* (ed. by R. Taylor), vol. 3 (1842), 691-731.

Bertrand Russell, *History of Western Philosophy*, London, 1940.

A. M. Turing, " On Computable Numbers, with an Application to the Entscheidungsproblem ", *Proc. London Math. Soc.* (2), 42 (1937), 230-265.

Victoria University of Manchester.

Semantic Engines:

An Introduction to Mind Design

JOHN HAUGELAND

I. Cognitive Science

"Reasoning is but reckoning," said Hobbes (1651, ch. V), in the earliest expression of the computational view of thought. Three centuries later, with the development of electronic "computers," his idea finally began to catch on; and now, in three decades, it has become the single most important theoretical hypothesis in psychology (and several allied disciplines), and also the basis of an exciting new research field, called "artificial intelligence." Recently, the expression *cognitive science* has been introduced to cover all these varied enterprises, in recognition of their common conceptual foundation. This term, therefore, does not apply to every scientific theory of cognition, but only to those sharing a certain broad outlook—which is sometimes called the "information processing" or "symbol manipulation" approach. Perhaps, at last, Hobbes's philosophical insight has found its home in a proper scientific paradigm (Kuhn, 1970).

Collected here are a dozen major papers in the *philosophy of cognitive science*—efforts by philosophers and scientists alike to understand the basic structure, assumptions, and prospects of this vigorous young field. Mostly, these essays are nontechnical, and intended for a wide audience of nonspecialists. Sometimes, however, they do presuppose familiarity with a few elementary ideas and distinctions from cognitive science itself; consequently, I shall introduce the volume with a brief survey of the relevant background.

Often (here and elsewhere) the discussion focuses on *artificial intelligence*—"AI," among friends—because it amounts to a kind of distilled essence of cognitive science. But again, it is important to realize that "AI" (like "cognitive science") is more specific in its meaning than the words themselves might suggest. Crudely, we can put the point in terms of different technologies: a project at IBM to wire and program an intelligent robot would probably be AI, whereas a project at DuPont to brew and mold a synthetic-organic android probably would not. But this can be misleading; the crucial issue is not protoplasm versus semiconductor ("wetware" versus "hardware"), but rather whether the product is designed and specified in terms of a computational structure. If it is, then a working model could probably be manufactured much more easily by means of electronics and programming; and that's the *only* relevance of the technology. Indeed, the guiding inspiration of cognitive science is that, at a suitable level of abstraction, a theory of "natural" intelligence should have the same basic form as the theories that explain sophisticated computer systems. It is this idea which makes *artificial* intelligence seem not only possible, but also a central and pure form of *psychological* research.

A better perspective on all the excitement can be gained by asking why it took three hundred years for Hobbes's original proposal to be appreciated. Mainly, three famous philosophical dilemmas stood in the way: (i) the metaphysical problem of mind interacting with matter; (ii) the theoretical problem of explaining the relevance of meanings, without appealing to a question-begging homunculus; and (iii) the methodological issue over the empirical testability (and, hence, respectability) of "mentalistic" explanations. The computational idea can be seen as slicing through all three dilemmas at a stroke; and this is what gives it, I think, the bulk of its tremendous gut-level appeal.

Descartes, a contemporary of Hobbes, gave the mind/matter problem its modern form in his doctrine of metaphysical *dualism*. Mind and body, he said, are two entirely different *kinds* of substance: the one can have (as distinguishing characteristics) various thoughts and feelings, whereas the other can have shapes, motions, and the causal interactions described by physical laws (and not vice versa). Intuitively, this is much more appealing than *materialism* (the main alternative to dualism), according to which everything, including minds, is really just matter, in one form or another. Not only are we reluctant to ascribe thought and feeling to "mere" matter, but we also find it very hard to ascribe shape and location to minds or ideas. There is, however, one basic problem, which no dualist has ever really solved: how can mind and body *interact?* On the one hand, they certainly *seem* to interact, as when a mental decision leads to a physical action, or when a physical stimulus leads to a mental perception; indeed, it's not clear how perception and action could be possible at all without mind/body interaction. On the other hand, however, physical laws are supposed to describe all motions of all bodies *completely* in terms of their interactions with one another.[1] In other words, physics leaves no room for causal intervention by the mental; hence the price of mind/body interaction is violation of the laws of physics—a price that few philosophers (or scientists) are willing to pay.

Thought itself (quite apart from matter) is not static and not random: it progresses and develops in ways that obey (at least much of the time) various rules of inference and reason. Superficially, this suggests an analogy with material particles obeying the laws of physics. But the analogy breaks down at a crucial point: particles have neither choice nor difficulty in "obeying" physics—it happens infallibly and automatically. People, on the other hand, often have to work to be reasonable; following the rules of reason is hardly infallible and can be very difficult. But this means there cannot be an explanatory dynamics of thought, which is at all comparable to physical dynamic theories; the respective roles of rules and laws in the two cases are deeply different. In particular, since correct application of the rules of reason to particular thoughts depends on what those thoughts *mean,* it seems that there must be some active rule-applier, which (or: who) *understands* the thoughts (and the rules), and which

1. There remain, of course, quantum indeterminacies, even in physics; but these are no consolation to interactionism. It is generally best, in fact, to forget about quantum mechanics in any discussion of mind/body metaphysics.

applies the rules to the thoughts as well as it can. If the activity of this rule-applier, following the rules of reason, is to explain the rationality of our thought processes, then it must be regarded as a complete little person—or *homunculus* (in Latin)—inside the head, directing the thoughts like a traffic cop. The trouble is: a theory that invokes an homunculus to *explain* thinking, has begged its own question, because the homunculus itself has to think, and *that* thinking has *not* been explained.

Finally, there is the question of how the psychology of thought could ever be properly scientific. Thoughts, it seems, cannot be observed; and the diffculty is not that, like electrons or distant galaxies, they are too small or too far away. Rather, they are somehow essentially subjective—we don't even know what it would be like to observe (or measure) them objectively. So all that science has to go on, even in principle, is objective *behavior* (which might include internal "physiological behavior"); hence, thoughts can enter the picture only as inferred or hypothesized intermediates. Unfortunately, in any given case, invoking beliefs and desires to explain an action is just too easy. Whatever an organism does, one can always trump up a million different ideas and motives that would explain it. If there can be, in principle, no independent, empirical check on which of these hypotheses is the right one, it seems scientifically disreputable to accept any of them, even tentatively. This, roughly, is the stance taken by *behaviorism.* The other half of the story, however, is that explaining behavior *without* invoking intervening mental processes is just too hard. In general, the subtle regularities, connections, and nonrandom variations in real-life behavior cannot so much as be *described* in nonmentalist (pure behaviorist) terms, let alone *explained*—hence, the overwhelming mechanicalness and stupidity of all the phenomena that the behaviorists were ever really able to account for.[2] The upshot is another philosophical standoff, with mentalists and behaviorists gleefully accusing one another of scientific bankruptcy.

Cognitive scientists can be materialists (nondualists) and mentalists (nonbehaviorists) at the same time; and they can offer

2. Which is not to say, by any means, that those accounts themselves were stupid, or scientifically worthless.

explanations in terms of meaning and rule-following, without presupposing any unexplained homunculus. It all depends on a marvellously rich analogy with computers—the outlines of which we can see with a quick look at everybody's favorite example: a chess-playing machine. It would be very awkward and peculiar to start assigning geometrical shapes and locations to the internal program routines and operations (decision processes and data structures, say) of such a system; yet we are quite confident it has no immaterial soul. These same decisions clearly cause physical behavior (e.g., in teletypewriters or TV screens), yet no one is worried that the laws of physics are being violated. When the machine plays, it follows rules in at least two senses: it always abides by the rules of the game, and it employs various reasonable rules of thumb to select plausible moves. Though these rules are in no way laws of nature, the machine's behavior is explained (in part) by citing them—and yet, no unexplained "compunculus" is presupposed. Finally, this explanation will necessarily invoke the system's internal reasoning processes; yet it is far from easy to figure out (or design) processes that will consistently lead to the observed (or desired) behavioral responses. Moreover, for any given machine, on any given occasion, there seems to be a determinate right answer about which reasonings it in fact went through.

That may have been a bit swift, but still, *what an inspiration!* If there are no philosophical dilemmas about chess-playing computers, then why should there be any about chess-playing people—or, indeed, about human intelligence in any other form? To put it coldly: why not suppose that people *just are* computers (and send philosophy packing)? Well . . . nothing very interesting is ever that simple. Various questions come up, among the first of which is: What exactly is being proposed, anyway?

II. Formal Systems

To start at the beginning, we must first say a little bit more carefully what a computer is. It is an automatic formal system. To see what this means, we first consider what a formal system is, and then what it is to automate one.

A *formal system* is like a game in which tokens are manipulated according to rules, in order to see what configurations can be obtained. Basically, to define such a game, three things have to be specified:

(1) what the tokens are;

(2) what the starting position is; and

(3) what moves are allowed in any given position.

Implicit in (2) and (3) is a specification of what positions are possible (for instance, what the board is, if it's a board game). Also, there is sometimes a specified *goal* position, which the player (or each player) is trying to achieve—such as a "winning position."

For example, there is a familiar solitaire game in which the tokens are pegs, arranged as follows in the starting position:

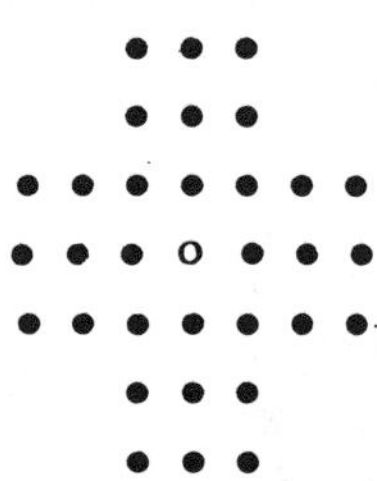

The solid dots are the tokens (pegs), and the circle in the middle is an empty space, into which a token could fit. The only move allowed by the rules is jumping one token over an adjacent one into an empty space, and then removing the token jumped over. This game has a goal: to perform such jumps until only one token remains, and it is in the center space.

Three points should be noticed about this (simple-minded) formal system. First, it is entirely *self-contained*. Only its own tokens, positions, and moves make any difference to it, and these only insofar as they matter to the application of the rules. In other words, the "outside world" (the weather, the state of the economy, whether the building is on fire, and so on) makes no difference whatsoever in the game. And, further, any aspects of the tokens and positions themselves which are irrelevant to determining which moves are legal—e.g., (in this game) color, size, weight, market value—are equally outside the game. Politics and courtship, by contrast, are not at all self-contained (even though they are sometimes called games) because just about anything could be relevant in some situation or other. Second, every relevant feature of the game is *perfectly definite;* that is, barring outright mistakes or breakdowns, there are no ambiguities, approximations, or "judgment calls" in determining what the position is, or whether a certain move is legal. For each peg and slot, that peg is either definitely (obviously and 100 percent) in that slot, or definitely (obviously and 100 percent) not in that slot–there are no in-between or borderline cases. Third, the moves are *finitely checkable,* in the sense that for each position and each candidate move, only a finite number of things has to be checked to see whether that move would be legal in that position. This is pretty trivial for our example, but it's nontrivial and very important for more complicated formal systems. Obviously, being self-contained, perfectly definite, and finitely checkable go nicely hand-in-hand; we will say that a game or system that has all three properties is *digital.* All formal systems are digital in this sense.

The digitalness of formal systems has the following important consequence: two systems that seem to be quite different may nevertheless be essentially the same. Clearly, the peg-jumping game would be essentially unchanged if the pegs were replaced by marbles, or even by helicopters (given a big enough board)–so long as the same rules were followed. But the differences can be more dramatic. Imagine a game played with two baskets and thirty-three dominoes, each with one letter and one numeral written on it. At the beginning, all the dominoes are in the start basket, except the one marked D4, which is in the finish basket; and the object of the game is to reverse that situation, by a process of "switching triads." A *triad* is three dominoes which have the same letter and sequential numerals, or the same numeral and sequential letters–so B4, C4, and D4 form a triad, because they have the same numeral and sequential letters. *Switching* a triad is just moving each of its members to the opposite basket; and this is legal whenever the middle member and one other are in the start basket and the third is in the finish basket. Though one would hardly suspect it at first, it turns out that this game (played with a certain domino set) is essentially the same as the peg-jumping game. It is easy to see why as soon as the members of that domino set are listed in the following revealing order:

A3, A4, A5,
B3, B4, B5,
C1, C2, C3, C4, C5, C6, C7,
D1, D2, D3, D5, D6, D7, D4,
E1, E2, E3, E4, E5, E6, E7,
F3, F4, F5,
G3, G4, G5.

Thus switching the D2-D3-D4 triad in the starting position would be equivalent to jumping the peg in slot D2 over the peg in slot D3, thereby emptying both of those slots and filling slot D4.

This kind of essential sameness among formal systems is called *formal equivalence.* Two formal systems are formally equivalent if they can be translated back and forth in roughly the following sense:

(1) for each position in one system, there is a unique corresponding position in the other system;

(2) the two starting positions correspond; and

(3) whenever you can get from one position to another in one system, you can get from the corresponding position to the corresponding position in the other system.

Actually, this definition is a little more stringent than necessary; but it gives the right idea. In particular, it leaves room for equivalent systems to be *very* different on the surface, so long as appropriate correspondences can be found.

There are, of course, an unlimited number of formal systems; and most of the interesting ones are significantly more complicated than our peg-jumping example (or its domino-switching equivalent). Two forms of complication are especially widespread and important; we introduce them by considering chess and algebra. The first is that there can be different *types* of tokens, such that what the rules permit depends on the type(s) of token(s) involved. Thus, in chess, each side begins with sixteen tokens of six different types; and whether it would be legal to move a certain token to a certain square always depends (among other things) on what type it is—what would be legal for a rook would not be legal for a bishop, and so on. In fact, whether two tokens are treated equally by the rules (in the same circumstances) is what determines whether they are tokens of the same type. For example, in some fancy chess sets, the pawns are little figurines, each one different from the next; but they are all the same type (namely, pawns), *because* the rules specify the same moves (namely, pawn moves) for all of them. To put it another way, tokens of the same type are formally interchangeable. Note, by the way, that the type of each token has to be perfectly definite (and also finitely checkable, and independent of the outside world) if the overall system is to remain digital.[3]

The second complication is that the *positions* of one formal system can function as the *tokens* in another ("higher level") system. We can see both how this works and why it is important, by considering high-school algebra as a formal system. Though one would not usually call algebra a game, the rules have actually been formalized to the point where it can be played like one. In the algebra game the tokens are equations or formulae, and the rules specify various transformations that can be made in these formulae—or (what comes to the same thing) various new formulae that can be written down, given some that are already written down. The starting position consists of a collection of formulae that are "given" (including, of course all the *axioms*); and making a "move" is adding a formula (*theorem*) to this list, by following the rules—that is, giving a formal *deduction* or *proof* (or, at least, a step in one). Now, the difficulty is that each different algebraic formula is a different type of token in this system, and there are indefinitely many of them—so how can the moves be finitely checkable? And the answer, of course, is that all these different tokens are built up in a systematic way out of a comparatively small collection of letters and standard symbols.

More specifically, each algebra-game token is a legal position in another game, which we might call the "well-formed-formula game." The tokens of the latter (i.e., the letters and symbols) are usually called "simple" or "atomic" tokens, to distinguish them

3. The number of different types of tokens is not a "deep" property of a formal system, as can be seen from the fact that the peg-jumping game has only one type, whereas the domino-switching game has 33 types—yet, in a deep sense, they are the same game. In effect, the domino version trades more sophisticated token discriminations for less sophisticated position discriminations.

from the tokens of the algebra game (i.e., the well-formed equations), which are "compound" or "molecular" tokens. The point is that the rules of the algebra game can apply to the various (molecular) tokens in terms of their structure; thus for *any* equation that has the same addend on both sides, you can "cancel" that addend. So, the same rule can apply in a parallel fashion to tokens of indefinitely many different types, so long as they have the specified structural features; hence, finitely many rules can suffice for the algebra game, even though there are indefinitely many types of well-formed algebraic formulae. This general strategy of using the positions of one formal system as the tokens of another makes large complicated systems much easier to deal with, and it is found throughout mathematics, formal logic, and virtually everywhere else that formal methods are used.

It might seem odd to include mathematics and logic here in the same category with chess and the peg-jumping game—because, roughly, their tokens *mean* something (and thus might be true or false, say). But their inclusion is perfectly serious and very important. Most mathematical and logical systems are *formal* in *exactly the same sense* that chess, checkers, and the like are formal: they have starting positions, and rules for making moves in any given position, and they are digital, in the sense explained above. From this point of view, any meanings that their tokens might have are utterly irrelevant; meaning has to do with the outside world, and is in no way part of any self-contained formal system, as such. There are, of course, other points of view, in which meaning is very important (we will discuss some of these when we come to interpretation and semantics). But, considered only *as formal systems*, games, logic, and mathematics are all equally meaningless, and entirely on a par.

III. Automatic Formal Systems (Turing Machines and Computers)

An *automatic* formal system is a physical device (such as a machine) which automatically manipulates the tokens of some formal system according to the rules of that system. It is like a chess set that sits there and plays chess *by itself*, without any intervention from the players, or an axiomatic system that writes out its own proofs and theorems, without any help from the mathematician. The exciting and astonishing fact is that such systems can be built. Looked at in the right way, this is exactly what computers are. There are two fundamental problems in building an automatic formal system. The first is getting the device to obey the rules (in principle, this problem has already been solved, as will be explained in the remainder of this section). The second is the "control" problem—how the device selects which move to make when there are several legal options. We will consider this briefly in the next section.

The theoretical ancestor of all automatic formal systems is a class of devices invented (in the abstract) by the mathematician Alan Turing and now called *Turing machines.* A Turing machine has:

(1) an unlimited number of *storage bins;*

(2) a finite number of *execution units;* and

(3) one *indicator unit.*

The indicator unit always indicates one execution unit (the "active" unit), and two storage bins (the "in" and "out" bins, respectively). Each storage bin can contain one formal token (any token, but only one at a time). Each execution unit has its own particular rule, which it obeys whenever it is the active unit. What that rule specifies will depend on what token is in the current in-bin; and in each case it will specify two things: first, what token to put in the current out-bin (discarding the previous contents, if any), and second, what the indicator unit should indicate next. The machine proceeds by steps: the active execution unit checks the in-bin, and then, according to what it finds there and what its rule is, it refills the out-bin and resets the indicator unit; then the next step begins. Usually there is one execution unit which does nothing; so if it ever gets activated, the machine stops.[4]

4. This is a slight generalization of Turing's original definition (Turing, 1937). In his version, the storage bins are all connected in a row, called a "tape"; each bin can hold only a *simple* token; the in-bin and the out-bin are always the same bin; and this in/out-bin is always either the same as or right next to the in/out-bin for the previous step. So Turing's machine chugs back and forth along the tape, one bin at a time, dealing with one simple token at a time. The surprising and important point, as we shall see shortly, is that (apart from convenience and efficiency) these differences don't make any difference.

Clearly, any Turing machine is an automated version of some formal system or other. The starting position is the initial contents of the storage bins, the moves are the machine steps, and the rules are those which the execution units obey (the control problem is handled in the rules for resetting the indicator unit). Not so obvious, but almost certainly true, is the converse: any automatic formal system can be formally imitated by some Turing machine.[5] "Formal imitation" is like formal equivalence, except for two things. First, since we are talking about *automatic* systems—that is, systems that actually "choose" which move to make—an imitating system has not merely to offer corresponding legal options in each corresponding position, but also to make the corresponding choice in each case. Let's call systems which are formally equivalent, and which make equivalent choices in each position *dynamically* equivalent. Second, the imitating system is often divided into two parts: the part which directly corresponds to the system being imitated, and another part which works behind the scenes, making everything come out right. The first part is called the *virtual machine*, and the second part the *program*.

For example, suppose some automatic formal system, *A*, is being formally imitated by some Turing machine, *T*. Then there is some virtual machine, *V*, which is both a part of *T*, and dynamically equivalent to *A*. So some portion (say half) of *T's* storage bins will be allocated to *V*, as *V's* storage bins; the tokens that appear in these bins will constitute *V's* positions (which, in turn, correspond to *A's* positions). The rest of *T's* storage bins contain the *program* (and perhaps some "scratchpad" workspace). The reason a program is necessary is that in general *V's* rules will be different from *T's* rules. The program is a (finite) set of tokens so contrived that when *T* obeys its own rules with respect to *all* of its storage bins, it will, in effect, obey *V's* rules with respect to the tokens in those bins that have been allocated to *V*. Intuitively, we can think of the program as "translating" *V's* rules into *T's*

5. This is a way of expressing *Church's thesis* (named after the logician, Alonzo Church); it has been proven true for all known, well-defined kinds of automatic formal system; but it cannot be proven in general, in part because the general idea of "automatic formal system" is itself somewhat intuitive, and not precisely definable.

rules, or even as "telling" *T* what *V's* rules are, so that *T* can follow them in moving the tokens in *V's* bins. In fact, it's not quite that straightforward, and *T's* rules have to have a certain versatility in the first place, in order to make such an imitation possible. But the point is: for any formal system, there is a Turing machine that can be programmed to imitate it.

But the fundamental importance of Turing machines rests on yet another truly amazing fact—a theorem first proved by Turing—which has, perhaps more than any other single result, shaped modern computer science. It is that there are special Turing machines, called *universal Turing machines,* which can be programmed to imitate any other Turing machine. In particular, one could imitate a Turing machine that was itself imitating some other automatic formal system—which means that, indirectly, the universal machine is also imitating that other automatic formal system. So, combining Church's thesis and Turing's theorem, a universal Turing machine can (suitably programmed) imitate any automatic formal system whatsoever! To put it another way: if you have just one universal Turing machine, and you are prepared to do some programming, you can have (a formal imitation of) any automatic formal system you care to specify.

It was soon discovered that there are a number of different kinds of universal machine, which are not (in the strict sense) Turing machines. But since they are universal, they can formally imitate any Turing machine; and, of course, any universal Turing machine can formally imitate any of them. In principle, therefore, it doesn't matter which one you have—*any* universal machine will do as well as any other (except for differences in efficiency, elegance, and the like). The reason this is important is that, with one qualification, universal machines can be built; that is what digital computers are. The one qualification is that a true universal machine must have unlimited storage, whereas any actual machine will have only a certain fixed amount (though it can be very large). So, aside from limitations of memory size, any standard digital computer can, with appropriate programming, formally imitate any automatic formal system yet discovered; that, basically, is why computers are so powerful.

Interestingly, computer programmers almost never program any of the machines that are actually constructed out of transistors, wires, and so on; rather, most programs are written for *virtual* machines, which are themselves merely being *imitated* by the hardware machine. The reason is that some universal machines are cheaper to build, while others are more convenient to use. The sensible course for a manufacturer, therefore, is to build the cheaper one, hire a few experts to write complicated programs (called "interpreters" or "compilers") which will make it imitate the more convenient ones, and then sell the package. The computer "languages" that you hear about—BASIC, FORTRAN, PASCAL, LISP, and so on—are really just some of these more convenient universal machines, which are widely imitated by various hardware machines. In fact, there are often more layers than that: thus the hardware directly imitates some intermediate virtual machine, which, in turn, is programmed to imitate the higher level machines, like those mentioned above. And, of course, when a programmer programs the latter, he or she is really designing yet another (virtual) machine, which the FORTRAN or LISP machine, or whatever, will formally imitate. This last machine, incidentally, will typically be designed for some special purpose, and so probably will not be a universal machine (though it could be).

A fundamental point should now be obvious: a particular physical object can be, at one and the same time, any number of *different machines.* There is no single correct answer to the question: which machine is that (really)? Of course, at the hardware level it is some particular model from some manufacturer; but at the same time it *is* (just as "really") all the other machines that are being imitated at various other levels. So a particular object is a particular machine (or automatic formal system) only at a particular level of description—at other levels of description it is other machines. Once we see this point, we see how foolish it is to say that computers are nothing but great big number crunchers, or that all they do is shuffle millions of "ones" and "zeros." Some machines are basically numerical calculators or "bit" manipulaters, but most of the interesting ones are nothing like that. And the fact that most actual commercial equipment can be described as such machines (e.g., most can be described as bit manipulators, on some level) is of no theoretical consequence. The machine one cares about—perhaps several levels of imitation up from the hardware—may have nothing at all to do with bits or numbers; and that is the only level that matters. For instance, an automatic system that played the peg-jumping game would probably not refer to numbers. Part of the reason for using the expression "automatic formal system" in place of "computer" is that the latter suggests a device which only "computes," and that is just wrong.

IV. The Control Problem

In the last section we considered systems in which each move is completely determined by the rules and the current position. This is essential in the design of an *automatic* system, because each step has to be made "automatically"—that is, it must be completely fixed by the state of the machine at the time.[6] But in most positions in most formal systems, any one of various moves would be legal; usually, that is what makes them interesting, as games or whatever. Does it follow that such interesting formal systems cannot be automated? No; it only follows that some device for deciding among the several legal options at any point must be automated as well.

The easiest way to think about it is to consider the machine as divided into two parts or "sub-machines": one to generate a number of legal options, and another to choose from among them. This, of course, is just an extension of the basic point that a given device can be various machines, depending on how you look at it; only now we are looking at it as *two* separate (virtual) machines, interacting with each other on the same level. The advantage is that we can see how the above dilemma is resolved: the move-generating submachine automates an "interesting" system, in which a variety of moves might be legal at any point; but the combined machine, with both parts together, satisfies the requirement that some *particular* next move be determined by the overall state of the device at each step. Designing the second submachine—the one that makes the choices, given the options—is the *control problem.* In most cases, control design turns out to be the hardest part of automating an interesting formal system.

In an average chess position, for example, a player will have 30

6. We ignore the possibility of "randomizers"—they don't affect the point.

or 35 legal possibilities to choose from. A beginning chess player could discover and list all of them without too much trouble; and designing a machine to do the same would not be terribly difficult either. The hard part—the entire difference between amateurs and world champions—is deciding *which* move to make, given these few possibilities; and that is the hard part to program as well. At first it might seem that big modern computers, with their tremendous speed and memory, could just look ahead to every possible outcome and see which moves lead to ultimate victory. In principle, this would be possible, since chess is technically finite; and such a machine would be literally invincible. In practical terms, however, such a computation is nowhere near possible. Assuming an average of 31.6 options per play gives a thousand (31.6 × 31.6) possible combinations per full move (each side having a turn). Thus looking ahead five moves would involve a quadrillion (10^{15}) possibilities; forty moves (a typical game) would involve 10^{120} possibilities. (For comparison, there have been fewer than 10^{18} seconds since the beginning of the universe.) These numbers are just preposterously large for any physically conceivable computer. They get that big because the number of choices at each additional step *multiplies* the total humber of possible combinations so far. For understandable reasons, this is called the *combinatorial explosion;* it plagues control design for all but the most straightforward problems.

Obviously, human chess-players don't make that many calculations either; in fact, the available evidence indicates that they make rather few. The trick is to consider only the *relevant* possibilities and ignore the rest. Thus most of those 30 or 35 options in a typical chess position would be totally pointless or manifestly stupid; hence, it would be a waste of time to consider all the possible developments that could follow after them. If the number of relevant alternatives could be reduced, say, to three at each stage, then looking ahead five complete moves would involve only 59,049 possible combinations—still too many for a person to consider (consciously, anyway), but well within reach of computers. So, the approach to the control problem in this case will almost certainly concentrate on determining which possible moves are the relevant ones, deserving further consideration.

Unfortunately, there is no fail-safe way to tell what is and isn't relevant. Everybody knows how a seemingly pointless or terrible move can turn out to be a brilliant stroke (once the opponent takes the bait). Any method that systematically bypasses certain moves as not worth pursuing will inevitably overlook some of these brilliancies. What we want is a method that is efficient at bypassing moves that *really are* worthless, but not easily fooled into ignoring moves that only *seem* worthless. Such methods in general are called "heuristics" (from the Greek word for "discover"), in contrast to "algorithms" (from the Latin word for the Arabic system of numerals, named after an Arabic mathematician). In current usage, the essential difference is this: an *algorithm* is a rule or procedure that is guaranteed to give a result meeting certain conditions (you just turn the crank and out it pops); a *heuristic*, on the other hand, is a rule or procedure that is more or less reliable, but not infallible—just a rule of thumb. We have algorithms for multiplying integers, arranging words in alphabetical order, and finding a checkmate in certain chess end-games (king and rook against king, for example). But there are no feasible algorithms for finding the best move in most other chess positions, or arranging words into poetry, or discovering proofs of arbitrary theorems in number theory. In these cases people proceed by intuition, inspiration, and a few explicit heuristic rules of thumb. (Intuition and inspiration might just be unconscious heuristics, of course—that's a disputed point among psychologists.)

Automatic systems, in any case, *must* proceed according to explicit rules (explicit, at least, in the program of the virtual machine). And in one sense these rules have to be algorithms—they have to determine the next move of the machine definitively, at each step. But often, whether a given rule is an algorithm or a heuristic depends on how the desired result is specified. Thus a reasonable rule of thumb for winning chess games is: never trade your queen for a pawn. Occasionally, of course, a queen sacrifice is a brilliant play; so this rule is only a heuristic when the result is specified as "Find the best move." But if the specified result is "Avoid swapping a queen for a pawn," then this rule is (trivially) infallible. The point is that the rules followed by the machine only *have to* be algorithms in this trivial sense. That is, it can perfectly well follow a bunch of inconclusive rules of thumb, relative to the interesting result specification (winning, say), so long as there are algorithms defining the heuristics themselves. The machine can infallibly follow quite fallible rules.

This shows, by the way, what's wrong with the idea that a (properly functioning) computer never makes a mistake. It just depends on what counts as a mistake—i.e., relative to which result specification. A chess-playing computer can function perfectly, never making a single mistake in following its internal heuristics but making lots of mistakes *in the game,* because its heuristics are rather clumsy. It is only at special tasks (like arithmetic and sorting), where there are algorithms for the interesting results, that a (perfect) computer can be infallible.

If we construe "heuristics" broadly to include any methods that improve a system's chances of making "correct" decisions while leaving some possibility of "mistakes," then any techniques for providing default assignments (standard assumptions), jumping to conclusions, or reading between the lines will be heuristic procedures. In this broad sense, a major part of the effort in artificial intelligence research goes toward finding better heuristics—ones that are more efficient and harder to fool—and better ways of implementing them on the machines (i.e., better algorithms for defining the heuristics). Indeed, in certain specialized areas, like game playing, theorem proving, and most tasks in "micro-worlds," work on heuristics is most of the problem. These areas are distinguished by the fact that the desired result is already known, and easy to specify in formal terms; for instance, in chess the goal is winning, and winning positions (checkmates) can be defined precisely. Many other forms of intelligent behavior, however, like writing good poetry (to take an extreme case) or carrying on a normal conversation (to take a case that does not *seem* so extreme) are not well defined in this way. In these areas, a major effort is required even to characterize the results toward which the heuristics are supposed to guide the system—and this involves the semantic and pragmatic issues to which we will turn shortly.

V. Digital and Analog

Automatic formal systems are, by definition, *digital* computers. There is another kind of device, sometimes called an *analog* computer, which is really quite different. Digital systems, remember, are self-contained, perfectly definite, and finitely checkable—all with regard to which moves are legal in which positions, according to the rules. An analog device, on the other hand, doesn't even have clearly defined moves, rules, and positions—though it may have states (which may change), and there is usually some way that it is supposed to work. The crucial difference is that in analog systems the relevant factors have not been defined and segregated to the point where it is always *perfectly definite* what the current state is, and whether it is doing what it is supposed to do. That is, there will often be slight inaccuracies, and marginal judgment calls, even when the device is working normally. To take the very simplest example, it is like the difference between a multiposition selector switch and a continuous tuning dial on a stereo. A switch has a number of click-stops, and it is always set definitely at one or another of them—you cannot set it between AM and FM. Of course, when you rotate it, it passes through intermediate angles; but these are irrelevant to its function, and (if it is a good switch) can be ignored. A tuning dial, on the other hand, moves smoothly without click-stops, and each angle tunes a different frequency. It is perfectly possible to set the dial between two stations, and, in fact, getting it "right on" a station can require a sensitive judgment call.

For some purposes, analog devices are very convenient. Scale models are a case in point. Suppose an architect wants to find out how the light and shadows will fall on a complicated structure at different times of day. A good analog approach is to build a model, illuminate it with a spotlight from various directions, and then *look* at it from various directions. A trickier but similar case is the use of laboratory animals in medical research. To estimate the physiological effects of weird drug combinations, experimenters can give corresponding (or exaggerated) doses to rats and then just wait to see what happens. Other common examples of analog devices are slide rules, electronic harmonic systems (modeling mechanical harmonic systems), and string-net pathfinders for railroad or highway networks. Though "analog" is itself a rather ill-defined notion, it clearly encompasses quite valuable tools.

Digital systems, however, have several inherent advantages. First, of course, universal machines are, by their very nature, extremely versatile; and that makes them more economical for each application. Second, analog systems can themselves often be *digitally simulated*—which makes the digital system even more versatile. For example, the architect's model could be simulated by writing equations for all the opaque surfaces in the building, and then calculating the paths of individual light rays at, say, one-inch intervals (for various positions of the sun). The whole thing might then drive a TV display, set for various viewing angles; and if all the intervals are small enough, the result can be pretty good. The amount of calculation involved can be prodigious, and the general technique has all the theoretical elegance of sandblasting; but computers are cheap, fast, and tireless, so it often works nicely.

It is sometimes said (with a grand air) that *any* analog device can be digitally simulated to *any* desired precision; but this is grossly misleading. Digital simulation is possible only when all the operative relationships in the analog system can be described in a relatively compact and precise way—e.g., not too many equations with not too many variables. The architectural simulation, for example, depends on assuming that all the light comes from the same direction and travels in a straight line until it's blocked by one of the few specified opaque surfaces. Without this simple structure to work from, the simulation could not get off the ground. Thus there is no comparable general description of the physiology of laboratory rats pumped full of odd chemicals—there are billions of potentially relevant subtle interactions and responses in a complex organic system, and the scope for combinatorial explosion is essentially indescribable. Hence, digital simulation is out of the question, except in very special cases where it is known in advance that only a certain few variables and relationships are relevant. It might seem that, in principle, simulation must be possible anyway, because rats are made of atoms, and each atom obeys known equations. But such a principle is utterly out to lunch. A single large molecule may have so many interdependent degrees of freedom, that no computer yet built could simulate it reliably in reasonable time; and one rat contains more molecules than there would be minicomputers if the entire volume of the earth were packed solid with them.

The real theoretical advantage of digital systems lies in quite another direction, and depends specifically on their digital nature. Consider two conventions for keeping track of money in a poker game. Each uses different colors for different denominations:

blue, red, and white for a hundred, ten, and one, respectively. But in one system, the unit of each denomination is a colored plastic disk (i.e., a poker chip), whereas in the other system it is a tablespoon of colored sand. The latter arrangement does have some merits—particularly the fact that *fractional* bets are possible—using less than a full tablespoon of white sand. But the chip system has one overwhelming advantage: all the bets are *exact.* By contrast, in measuring volumes of sand, there is always some small error, no matter how careful you are. Using the chips, and a very modest degree of care, it is possible to wager *exactly* 13 units (plus or minus zero); but with the sand this is impossible, even given the finest instruments in the world. The difference is that the chip system is digital; each token is perfectly definite, and there is no need for judgment calls.

The more complex and interdependent a system becomes, the more vulnerable it is to errors that propagate and get out of control. A small error in one component, affecting a more sensitive component, can result in a larger error going to the next component, and so on. We can see a rudimentary form of this, even in the poker example. Suppose the measurement error on sand volumes is ±2 percent; then it would be perverse to try to bet, say, 613 units, because the measurement error on the six blue tablespoons is worth four times as much (on the average) as all three white tablespoons—the latter simply drop out as irrelevant. There are ways to control such errors, of course, but only to a certain extent, and they tend to get expensive. The perfect definiteness of digital tokens, though confining in some cases, pays off in the elimination of this sort of error; thus, though you cannot bet a fraction of a unit with poker chips, there is no problem in betting 613 units—since six blue chips can be counted exactly, the white chips remain perfectly significant. This advantage is progressively more important for larger and more complicated systems—hence the contemporary predominance of digital methods.

VI. Semantics

Formal systems (and computers) can be more than mere games, because their tokens can have interpretations that relate them to the outside world. This is the domain of semantics and pragmatics.

Sometimes we say that the tokens in a certain formal system

mean something—that is, they are "signs," or "symbols," or "expressions" which "stand for," or "represent," or "say" something. Such relations connect the tokens to the outside world (what they are "about"), making it possible to use them for purposes like record-keeping, communication, calculation, and so on. A regular, systematic specification of what all the tokens of a system mean is called an *interpretation;* and the general theory of interpretations and meanings is called *semantics.* Accordingly, what any token means or says, and hence also whether it is true or false, and so on, are all *semantic properties* of that token.

Semantic properties are not formal properties. A formal system as such is completely self-contained and, viewed in that way, is just a meaningless game. In strictly formal terms, interpretation and meaning are entirely beside the point—they are extraneous "add ons" that are formally irrelevant. (When discussing a system that is to be interpreted, we call its purely formal characteristics and structure its *syntax;* "syntactical" is just another word for "formal," but it is generally used only when a contrast to "semantic" is relevant.)

So, formal tokens can lead two lives: *syntactical* (formal) *lives,* in which they are meaningless markers, moved according to the rules of some self-contained game; and (if the system is interpreted) *semantic lives,* in which they have meanings and significant relations to the outside world. The story of how these two lives get together is the foundation of modern mathematics and logic; and it is also the philosophical inspiration of cognitive science. We review the mathematical/logical case first, however, because it is better understood and there are fewer complications.

Consider a formal system (like the algebra game, discussed above in section 2) in which the positions are just sets of tokens, and the legal moves are just to add more tokens to the current position (depending, of course, on what is already in it). And suppose this system is interpreted in such a way that each of its (well-formed, complete) tokens "asserts" something—that is, each token (according to the meaning assigned to it by the interpretation) expresses some claim about the world. Then, depending on what the claim is and what the world is like, each of these tokens will be either true or false (relative to that interpretation).

Now, the *rules* of such a system will have the semantic property of being *truth-preserving* if and only if they meet the following condition: for any position which already contains *only* true tokens, any other token which can be added to that position (according to the rules) will also be true. In other words, if you start with tokens which are all true (under the interpretation), and if you obey the (purely formal) rules, then you can be sure there are no false tokens in any position you ever reach.

The rules of standard logical and mathematical systems, relative to their standard interpretations, are all truth-preserving; and, of course, the tokens in their starting positions (i.e., their axioms) are all true. Therefore, any token in any legal position of one of these systems is guaranteed also to be true! That is why we know in advance that their *theorems* (which are defined in purely syntactical/formal terms) are all *true* (which is a semantic property). Or, what comes to the same thing, in order to establish the semantic truth of a token in such a system, it suffices merely to prove it formally (play the game). This is how the "two lives" of the tokens get together; and it is the basic idea behind the formalization of modern logic and mathematics. In effect, given an interpreted formal system with true axioms and truth-preserving rules, if you take care of the syntax, *the semantics will take care of itself.*[7]

Most mathematical and logical systems are only partially interpreted, in the sense that some of their atomic tokens are left as variables, whose exact interpretation is to be specified by the user (in certain allowable ways). For example, in ordinary algebra, you can specify what the letters (variables) stand for in any way you want—so long as they stand for numbers. The important thing

7. Unfortunately, even in mathematics, formalization is not all that one might have hoped. Ideally, one would like a system such that not only were all its theorems true, but also all its true tokens were theorems (i.e., *only* theorems were true); such a system is *semantically complete.* But it has been shown (originally by Kurt Gödel, in 1931) that no consistent formalization of arithmetic can be complete; and the same applies to many other important axiomatic systems. Most people are agreed, however, that this result doesn't make any difference to cognitive science. (For a possibly dissenting view, see Lucas, 1961).

is that the rules are still truth-preserving, no matter what specific interpretation is given to the variables. For example, if a user knows, relative to some specific interpretation of the variables (as values in a physics problem, say) that the token

$$\frac{a-b}{c}+c=\frac{d-b}{c}+\frac{e(1+e)-e}{c}$$

is true, then he or she can apply the purely *formal* rules for multiplying through, deleting parentheses, collecting terms, etc., and be assured that the token

$$a+c^2=d+e^2$$

is also *true* (relative to the same interpretation). This is a vivid example of how useful it can be to have the semantics "take care of itself," if only one plays the syntactical game correctly.

An even more vivid example is computers, because precisely what an automatic formal system can do is "take care of the syntax"—i.e., play by the rules. The machine does not have to pay any attention to the interpretation or meaning of any of its tokens. It just chugs along purely formally; and if the starting position, rules, and interpretation happen to be of the sort we have been discussing, then it will automatically produce only truths. Given an appropriate formal system and interpretation, the semantics takes care of itself. This, fundamentally, is why computers can be so useful for calculations and the like—why they can be *computers* and not just electronic toys.

An automatic formal system with an interpretation such that the semantics will take care of itself is what Daniel Dennett (1981) calls a *semantic engine.* The discovery that semantic engines are possible—that with the right kind of formal system and interpretation, a machine can handle meanings—is the basic inspiration of cognitive science and artificial intelligence. Needless to say, however, mathematics and logic constitute a very narrow and specialized sample of general intelligence. People are both less and much more than automatic truth-preservers. Consequently, our discussion of interpretation needs to be expanded and generalized considerably; unfortunately, the issues will get messier and murkier as we go.

VII. Interpretation and Truth

Interpretation is especially straightforward in the special case of logic and mathematics because, in the final analysis, the only semantic property that matters is truth. Hence, it suffices if the theorems are guaranteed true, given the truth of the axioms (and special assumptions, if any)—that is, it suffices if the rules are truth-preserving. We shall see in the next section that there are many other cases where truth is far from all that matters in judging interpretations. But it is worth staying with the special case a little longer, to ask *why* truth has the importance it does; then it will be clearer why other considerations are important in other cases.

Imagine finding an automatic formal system that uses ordinary numerical tokens, and generates "theorems" (i.e., outputs) like the following:

= 5 = 1 ÷	= ÷ 3 - 1 - 8	+ 1 - 5940
71 ÷ 92 X	= 61 = 040	84 - 1 X 5 =

Formally, of course, there is nothing wrong with these tokens; we can imagine any number of (strange and boring) games in which they would be perfectly legal moves. *Semantically,* on the other hand, they look like nonsensical, random gibberish—"arithmetic salad." That is, it seems impossible to construe them as expressing claims about the relationships among numbers (e.g., equations). But hold on: this reaction depends on a tacit adoption of the familiar Arabic interpretation of what the numerals and signs mean (the digit '1' stands for the number one, the '+' sign stands for addition, and so on). Formally, however, these numerals and signs are just neutral marks (tokens), and many other (unfamiliar) interpretations are possible (as if the outputs were in a code). Suppose, for instance, we construed the atomic tokens according to the following noncustomary scheme (using '⇒' to abbreviate "stands for"):

'1' ⇒ equals	'6' ⇒ zero	'+' ⇒ five
'2' ⇒ plus	'7' ⇒ one	'–' ⇒ six
'3' ⇒ minus	'8' ⇒ two	'X' ⇒ seven
'4' ⇒ times	'9' ⇒ three	'÷' ⇒ eight
'5' ⇒ div. by	'0' ⇒ four	'=' ⇒ nine

Then, with this table, we could translate the system's outputs back into the familiar notation as

9 ÷ 9 = 8	98 – 6 = 62	5 = 6 ÷ 3 X 4
1 = 83 + 7	90 = 94 X 40	2 X 6 = 7 ÷ 9

Superficially, these look more like equations, and hence not nearly as random or crazy as the raw (untranslated) outputs. Unfortunately, they're all false—*wildly* false. In fact, on closer inspection, the digits look just as random as before; we still have arithmetic salad, only disguised in regular equation format.

But there are over a trillion possible ways to interpret these fifteen atomic tokens (even sticking to permutations of the ordinary one). Here is just one more possibility, together with the translations it would yield for the original outputs

'1' ⇒ equals	'6' ⇒ zero	'+' ⇒ five
'2' ⇒ div. by	'7' ⇒ nine	'–' ⇒ four
'3' ⇒ times	'8' ⇒ eight	'X' ⇒ three
'4' ⇒ minus	'9' ⇒ seven	'÷' ⇒ two
'5' ⇒ plus	'0' ⇒ six	'=' ⇒ one

1 + 1 = 2	12 X 4 = 48	5 = 4 + 7 – 6
9 = 27 ÷ 3	10 = 16 – 6	8 – 4 = 3 + 1

What a difference! These not only look like equations, they *are* equations—they are *true.* And, intuitively, that strongly inclines us to prefer this interpretation—to think it "better" or "righter" than the ones which yield random nonsense as readings. This intuition has several theoretical considerations behind it.

In the first place, formal tokens in themselves never intrinsically favor one interpretation scheme over any other—from their point of view, all interpretations are equally extraneous and arbitrary. So if some particular interpretation is to be adopted, over all the other possibilities, there must be something distinctive about it, which makes it stand out in the crowd. But, as our example suggests, an interpretation that renders a system's theorems as truths is a rare and special discovery (the alternatives yield mostly gibberish). Hence, such an interpretation is distinctive.

Second, if we regard an interpretation as *relating* or *connecting* a formal system to the outside world (i.e., to whatever its tokens are "about"), then the distinctiveness of the preferred interpretation should lie in that relation. But if a system's theorems are all true under an interpretation, then there is, in fact, a relation strong enough to support inferences about the world from the theorems, and about the theorems from (knowledge of) the world. Thus we can discover new facts about numbers, using an interpreted formalization of arithmetic; likewise, the above-noted (practical) utility of the semantics "taking care of itself" depends on the *truth*-preservingness of the rules. In the other direction, we (sometimes) can predict theorems, given what we know about numbers. For instance, if our example system produced the theorem fragment '7401 . . .', we would be hard pressed to guess its completion, from its form alone. The first interpretation scheme (which gives '1 X 4 = . . .') is no help either, because its "translations" come out randomly false. But knowing that the second scheme gives '9 - 6 = . . .', and that the theorem will be true, makes the prediction easy: the completion will be whichever token means "three" (namely, 'X'). The reliability of such inferences (both ways) indicates that *this* relation between the tokens on the one hand and the numbers and operations on the other is *not* arbitrary—i.e., this interpretation somehow genuinely connects them.

Finally, and most important, interpreting is tantamount to "making sense of"; hence, if the system doesn't end by making sense (but, rather, makes nonsense), then the interpretation attempt has failed. Arithmetic salad does not make sense (whether clothed in the outer form of equations, or not); and that, primarily, is why random interpretation schemes don't really give *interpretations* at all. In the context of arithmetic, true equations make eminently good sense—hence the preferability of our second scheme. (An occasional lapse could be understood as meaningful though false; but constant, random falsehood is, in effect, impossible—because the tokens cease to make any sense at all.) So truth matters to interpretations not only because it provides a nonarbitrary choice among candidate schemes and because this choice reflects some relation between the system and what it is (interpreted to be) "about," but also, and most of all, because wild falsehood amounts to *nonsense*—the antithesis of meaning.

VIII. Interpretation and Pragmatics

In most activities involving meaningful tokens (other than logic and mathematics) truth is far from the only semantic property that matters. Take ordinary conversation, for example. In the first place, many speech acts—such as questions, commands, expletives, and even most banter and quips—are neither true nor false; so some other kind of appropriateness must be what matters. And even in the case of statements (which typically *are* true or false), much else is important besides just whether they are true. For instance, in conversation it is also important (usually) to stick to the topic, be polite, say only what is worth saying (not obvious, inane, redundant, etc.)—and, in general, to avoid making an ass of oneself. It is not clear to what extent such conditions should be called "semantic" (some authors prefer to call them "pragmatic"), but they are all relevant to the acceptability of an interpretation as soon as you get away from special cases like logic and mathematics.

In these cases we are driven back to the more general but also somewhat fuzzier notion of "making sense" as our criterion for the adequacy of interpretations. There is, to my knowledge, no satisfactory philosophical account of what it is to make sense; indeed, it is questionable whether a precise, explicit definition is even possible. Still, there is much to be said, and philosophers have worked out a variety of rough characterizations and prerequisites (sometimes referred to by the peculiar misnomer "principles of charity"). The truth of simple, uncontroversial declarative outputs (i.e., tokens interpreted as such) is, of course, one rough prerequisite on making sense in general; and a few philosophers (notably, Davidson, 1973b) are inclined to stick with that. But most would agree there are other considerations.

The most widely discussed, *rationality*, is loosely analogous to truth-preservation in mathematical systems. The idea is that "obvious consequences" of tokens in the current position should be relatively easy to evoke from the system (as outputs), or to get it to add to the position. In general, the point applies not only to logically valid inferences, but to common sense inferences of all kinds, including the formation of subsidiary goals and attitudes (given the facts, goals and attitudes already at hand) and also the ability to solve suitably simple "problems." Further, the system should have a tendency to root out tensions and incompatibilities among the tokens in its positions—e.g., by altering or eliminating one of the offending parties. It goes without saying that this notion is not very precisely defined; but it is equally clear that "rationality" in some such sense is an important factor in "making sense."

A second important factor is reliable interaction with the world via transducers. A *transducer* is a kind of automatic encoder or decoder which either reacts to the physical environment and adds tokens to the current position (an *input* transducer), or else reacts to certain tokens in the current position and produces physical behavior in the environment (an *output* transducer). So transducers are analogous to sense organs and motor systems in animals and people; and they become, in effect, part of the whole system, when it comes to determining whether (according to some interpretation) the system is making sense. Roughly, when an input transducer adds a token that is interpreted as a report, then (other things being equal) that report ought to be correct; and when an output transducer reacts to a token interpreted as a decision to do something, then (other things being equal) the behavior produced ought to be that action. For instance, if the token that regularly gets added in response to a rabbit running by were interpreted to mean "Lo, a flaming giraffe," then the system isn't making much sense—which is to say, the interpretation is probably defective. This is essentially Quine's (1960; ch. 2) criterion of preserving "stimulus meaning." Though he doesn't mention it, there is a corresponding condition on the reliability of output transducers.

A third condition on making sense is *conversational cooperativeness*, in more or less the sense introduced by Grice (1975)—assuming, of course, that the system is interpreted as "conversing" or communicating in some way. Suppose, for example, that you ask it what the capital of Illinois is (i.e., give it a token so interpreted); then "It is Springfield" or "I don't know" would be perfectly sensible replies, but "Easy on the mustard, please," or "Wow, 400 squirrels" would not. Even a false but relevant answer, like "It is Chicago," makes much more sense in context than some utterly irrelevant truth, such as "2+7 = 9." Answering the question one is asked is a very basic example of being cooperative; there are many subtler points as well, concerning how much information is given in the answer, the manner in which it is provided, how it pertains to the larger topic, whether it is rude, obvious, or funny, and so on. Cooperativeness is clearly a matter of degree, involving judgment and compromise; but if it is ever lacking altogether, a "conversation" quickly reduces to impossible nonsense.

A related consideration is what Austin (1970) called "felicity conditions" (compare also Searle's 1969 "constitutive rules"). Roughly, the idea is that one cannot or cannot "properly" make an unkeepable promise, threaten someone with something he or she wants anyway, give commands for which one lacks the authority, propose marriage to one's spouse, offer to sell (or buy) the planet Mars, and so on. That is, these "speech acts" or "performances" have various prerequisites or presuppositions; and if the prerequisites are not satisfied, there is something wrong with doing them. As with all of our conditions, a few such violations look merely foolish, or perhaps dishonest; but wholesale and flagrant disregard will yield an overall pattern of outputs which fails to make sense—and hence the interpretation will be unsatisfactory.

These last two points, more than the earlier ones, bring in the relevant "context," and indicate the importance of considering the outputs in relation to one another and in relation to the situation in which they are produced. Further work in this direction must confront issues like what is involved in the coherence of extended conversations, dramatic plots, and scholarly essays. Very little in the way of explicit theories or conditions has been proposed in this area—which is symptomatic of an impoverished philosophical literature on the problem of understanding and intelligibility in general. (For a brief overview of some of the difficulties, see Haugeland, 1979, and the works cited there.)

Interpreting an automatic formal system is finding a way of

construing its outputs (assigning them meanings) such that they consistently make reasonable sense in the light of the system's prior inputs and other outputs. In the special case of logical and mathematical systems, it suffices if the outputs are consistently true; and this can be guaranteed by having only true axioms and truth-preserving rules. In more ambitious systems, however, including any with aspirations to artificial intelligence, truth is not a sufficient condition on the output tokens "making sense"—many other considerations are important as well. Hence, there is no reason to believe that truth-preservingness is the only, or even the most important, requirement to be imposed on the system's rules. Unfortunately, the alternative—nonasininity-preservation, perhaps?—is not at all clear. And the foregoing motley list of amorphous "further conditions" holds out little promise of any quick or clean solution. I think that this problem constitutes one of the deepest challenges that cognitive science must face.

IX. Cognitive Science (Again)

The basic idea of cognitive science is that *intelligent beings are semantic engines*—in other words, automatic formal systems with interpretations under which they consistently make sense. We can now see why this includes psychology and artificial intelligence on a more or less equal footing: people and intelligent computers (if and when there are any) turn out to be merely different manifestations of the same underlying phenomenon. Moreover, with universal hardware, *any* semantic engine can in principle be formally imitated by a computer if only the right program can be found. And that will guarantee *semantic imitation* as well, since (given the appropriate formal behavior) the semantics is "taking care of itself" anyway. Thus we also see why, from this perspective, artificial intelligence can be regarded as psychology in a particularly pure and abstract form. The same fundamental structures are under investigation, but in AI, all the relevant parameters are under direct experimental control (in the programming), without any messy physiology or ethics to get in the way.

Of course, it is possible that this is all wrong. It might be that people just *aren't* semantic engines, or even that no semantic engine (in a robot, say) can be genuinely intelligent. There are two quite different strategies for arguing that cognitive science is basically misconceived. The first, or *hollow shell* strategy has the following form: no matter how well a (mere) semantic engine acts *as if* it understands, etc., it can't *really* understand anything, because it isn't (or hasn't got) "X" (for some "X"). In other words, a robot based on a semantic engine would still be a sham and a fake, no matter how "good" it got. The other, or *poor substitute,* strategy draws the line sooner: it denies that (mere) semantic engines are capable even of acting as if they understood—semantic engine robots are not going to get that good in the first place. The first strategy tends to be more conceptual and *a priori,* while the second depends more on experimental results. (Compare: No beverage made from coal tar would be wine, no matter what it tasted like; with: There's no way to turn coal tar into a beverage that tastes like wine.)

The most obvious candidate for "X" in the hollow shell strategy is *consciousness;* thus "No computer really understands anything, no matter how smart it *seems,* because it isn't conscious." Now it is true that cognitive science sheds virtually no light on the issue of what consciousness is (though see Dennett, 1978d, for a valiant effort); indeed, the term itself is almost a dirty word in the technical literature. So it's natural to suspect that something difficult and important is being left out. Unfortunately, nobody else has anything very specific or explanatory to say about consciousness either—it is just mysterious, regardless of your point of view. But that means that a cognitivist can say, "Look, none of us has much of an idea of what consciousness is; so how can we be so sure *either* that genuine understanding is impossible without it, *or* that semantic engines won't ever have it (e.g., when they are big and sophisticated enough)?" Those questions may seem intuitively perverse, but they are very difficult to answer.

A different candidate for "X" is what we might call *original intentionality.*[8] The idea is that a semantic engine's tokens only have meaning because we give it to them; their intentionality, like that of smoke signals and writing, is essentially borrowed, hence *derivative.* To put it bluntly: computers themselves don't mean anything by their tokens (any more than books do)—they only

8. "Intentionality" is a philosopher's term for being about something, or having a meaning.

mean what we say they do. Genuine understanding, on the other hand, is intentional "in its own right" and not derivatively from something else. But this raises a question similar to the last one: What does it take to have original intentionality (and how do we know computers can't have it)? If we set aside divine inspiration (and other magical answers), it seems that original intentionality must depend on whether the object has a suitable structure and/or dispositions, relative to the environment. But it is hard to see how these could fail to be suitable (whatever exactly that is) if the object (semantic engine *cum* robot) always *acts* intelligent, self-motivated, responsive to questions and challenges, and so on. A book, for instance, pays no attention to what "it" says—and that's (one reason) why we really do not think it is the *book* which is saying anything (but rather the author). A perfect robot, however, would seem to act on its opinions, defend them from attack, and modify them when confronted with counter-evidence—all of which would suggest that they really are the *robot's own* opinions.

A third candidate for "X" in the hollow shell strategy is *caring*. Here the intuition is that a system could not really *mean* anything unless it had a stake in what it was saying—unless its beliefs and goals mattered to it. Otherwise, it is just mouthing noises, or generating tokens mechanically. The popular picture of computers as cold (metallic, unfeeling) calculators motivates the view that they could never really *care* about anything, hence that they could never genuinely *mean* (or understand) anything on their own. But, of course, the legitimacy of this picture is just what we're inquiring about. If cognitive science is on the right track, then some semantic engines—starting with people—*can* care about things, be involved with them, have personalities, and so on. And, indeed, if we had a robot which *seemed* (in appropriate circumstances) to be sympathetic, disappointed, embarrassed, ambitious, offended, affectionate, and so on, it would be very difficult to claim that it was merely an unfeeling hunk of metal—especially if this very remark "hurt its feelings." Again, we need some further criterion or intuitive test for what it is to have the appropriate inner quality, if we are to justify saying that a semantic engine which merely *acts as if* it is intelligent (etc.) is a hollow shell.

The "poor substitute" strategy—which I, myself, think is much more likely to succeed–argues instead that semantic engines will never even *seem* to have the full range of common sense and values of people. The basic suggestion is that those areas in which computers excel (or can be expected eventually to excel) are all of a special sort, where the relevant considerations are comparatively few and well defined. This includes formal games (by definition) and also a number of other routine technical or micro-world tasks. But it is an open question whether the intelligence manifested in everyday life, not to mention art, invention, and discovery, is of essentially this same sort (though presumably more complicated). Cognitive science, in effect, is betting that it is; but the results are just not in yet. The above issues of consciousness, original intentionality, and caring can all be raised again in the poor substitute strategy, in a more empirical form: Does the system *in fact* act as if it had the relevant "X"? And if, so far, the answer is always "No," is there any pattern to the failures which might give us a clue to the deeper nature of the problems, or the ultimate outcome? These, it seems to me, are the most important questions, but they are beyond the scope of this introduction.

Minds, Brains, and Programs

JOHN R. SEARLE

Abstract: I distinguish between strong and weak AI. According to strong AI, appropriately programmed computers literally have cognitive states, and therefore the programs are psychological theories. I argue that strong AI must be false, since a human agent could instantiate the program and still not have the appropriate mental states. I examine some arguments against this claim, and I explore some consequences of the fact that human and animal brains are the causal bases of existing mental phenomena.

WHAT PSYCHOLOGICAL and philosophical significance should we attach to recent efforts at computer simulations of human cognitive capacities? In answering this question I find it useful to distinguish what I will call "strong" AI from "weak" or "cautious" AI. According to weak AI, the principal value of the computer in the study of the mind is that it gives us a very powerful tool. For example, it enables us to formulate and test hypotheses in a more rigorous and precise fashion than before. But according to strong AI the computer is not merely a tool in the study of the mind; rather the appropriately programmed computer really is a mind in the sense that computers given the right programs can be literally said to *understand* and have other cognitive states. And, according to strong AI, because the programmed computer has cognitive states, the programs are not mere tools that enable us to test psychological explanations; rather, the programs are themselves the explanations. I have no objection to the claims to weak AI, at least as far as this article is concerned. My discussion here will be directed to the claims I have defined as strong AI, specifically the claim that the appropriately programmed computer literally has cognitive states and that the programs thereby explain human cognition. When I refer to AI, it is the strong version as expressed by these two claims which I have in mind.

I will consider the work of Roger Schank and his colleagues at Yale (cf. Schank and Abelson, 1977), because I am more familiar with it than I am with any similar claims, and because it provides a clear example of the sort of work I wish to examine. But nothing that follows depends upon the details of Schank's programs. The same arguments would apply to Winograd's (1972) SHRDLU, Weizenbaum's (1965) ELIZA, and, indeed, any Turing machine simulation of human mental phenomena.

Briefly and leaving out the various details, one can describe Schank's program as follows: the aim of the program is to simulate the human ability to understand stories. It is characteristic of the abilities of human beings to understand stories that they can answer questions about the story even though the information they give was not explicitly stated in the story. Thus, for example, suppose you are given the following story: "A man went into a restaurant and ordered a hamburger. When the hamburger arrived, it was burned to a crisp, and the man stormed out of the restaurant angrily without paying for the hamburger or leaving a tip." Now, if you are given the question "Did the man eat the hamburger?", you will presumably answer, "No, he did not." Similarly if you are given the following story: "A man went into a restaurant, and ordered a hamburger; when the hamburger came, he was very pleased with it; and as he left the restaurant he gave the waitress a large tip before paying his bill," and you are asked the question "Did the man eat the hamburger?", you will presumably answer, "Yes, he ate the hamburger." Now Schank's machines can similarly answer questions about restaurants in this fashion. In order to do so, they have a "representation" of the sort of information that human beings have about restaurants which enables them to answer such questions as those above, given these sorts of stories. When the machine is given the story and then asked the question, the machine will print out answers of the sort that we would expect human beings to give if told similar stories. Partisans of strong AI claim that in this question-and-answer sequence, not only is the machine simulating a human ability but also:

(a) the machine can literally be said to *understand* the story and provide answers to questions; and

(b) what the machine and its program do *explains* the human ability to understand the story and answer questions about it.

Claims (a) and (b) seem to me totally unsupported by Schank's work, as I will attempt to show in what follows.[1]

A way to test any theory of the mind is to ask oneself what it would be like if one's own mind actually worked on the principles that the theory says all minds work on. Let us apply this test to the Schank program with the following *Gedankenexperiment.* Suppose that I'm locked in a room and suppose that I'm given a large batch of Chinese writing. Suppose furthermore, as is indeed the case, that I know no Chinese either written or spoken, and that I'm not even confident that I could recognize Chinese writing as Chinese writing distinct from, say, Japanese writing or meaningless squiggles. Now suppose further that after this first batch of Chinese writing, I am given a second batch of Chinese script together with a set of rules for correlating the second batch with the first batch. The rules are in English and I understand these rules as well as any other native speaker of English. They enable me to correlate one set of formal symbols with another set of formal symbols, and all that "formal" means here is that I can identify the symbols entirely by their shapes. Now suppose also that I am given a third batch of Chinese symbols together with some instructions, again in English, that enable me to correlate elements of this third batch with the first two batches, and these rules instruct me how I am to give back certain Chinese symbols with certain sorts of shapes in response to certain sorts of shapes given me in the third batch. Unknown to me, the people who are giving me all of these symbols call the first batch 'a script,' they call the second batch a 'story,' and they call the third batch 'questions.'

1. I am not saying, of course, that Schank himself is committed to these claims.

Furthermore, they call the symbols I give them back in response to the third batch 'answers to the questions,' and the set of rules in English that they gave me they call 'the program.' To complicate the story a little bit, imagine that these people also give me stories in English which I understand, and they then ask me questions in English about these stories, and I give them back answers in English. Suppose also that after a while I get so good at following the instructions for manipulating the Chinese symbols and the programmers get so good at writing the programs that from the external point of view—that is, from the point of view of somebody outside the room in which I am locked—my answers to the questions are indistinguishable from those of native Chinese speakers. Nobody looking at my answers can tell that I don't speak a word of Chinese. Let us also suppose that my answers to the English questions are, as they no doubt would be, indistinguishable from those of other native English speakers, for the simple reason that I am a native speaker of English. From the external point of view, from the point of view of someone reading my 'answers,' the answers to the Chinese questions and the English questions are equally good. But in the Chinese case, unlike the English case, I produce the answers by manipulating uninterpreted formal symbols. As far as the Chinese is concerned, I simply behave like a computer; I perform computational operations on formally specified elements. For the purposes of the Chinese, I am simply an instantiation of the computer program.

Now the claims made by strong AI are that the programmed computer understands the stories and that the program in some sense explains human understanding. But we are now in a position to examine these claims in light of our thought experiment.

(a) As regards the first claim it seems to me obvious in the example that I do not understand a word of the Chinese stories. I have inputs and outputs that are indistinguishable from those of the native Chinese speaker, and I can have any formal program you like, but I still understand nothing. Schank's computer for the same reasons understands nothing of any stories whether in Chinese, English, or whatever, since in the Chinese case the computer is me; and in cases where the computer is not me, the computer has nothing more than I have in the case where I understand nothing.

(b) As regards the second claim—that the program explains human understanding—we can see that the computer and its program do not provide sufficient conditions of understanding, since the computer and the program are functioning and there is no understanding. But does it even provide a necessary condition or a significant contribution to understanding? One of the claims made by the supporters of strong AI is this: when I understand a story in English, what I am doing is exactly the same—or perhaps more of the same—as what I was doing in the case of manipulating the Chinese symbols. It is simply more formal symbol manipulation which distinguishes the case in English, where I do understand, from the case in Chinese, where I don't. I have not demonstrated that this claim is false, but it would certainly appear an incredible claim in the example. Such plausibility as the claim has derives from the supposition that we can construct a program that will have the same inputs and outputs as native speakers, and in addition we assume that speakers have some level of description where they are also instantiations of a program. On the basis of these two assumptions, we assume that even if Schank's program isn't the whole story about understanding, maybe it is part of the story. That is, I suppose, an empirical possibility, but not the slightest reason has so far been given to suppose it is true, since what is suggested—though certainly not demonstrated—by the example is that the computer program is irrelevant to my understanding of the story. In the Chinese case I have everything that artificial intelligence can put into me by way of a program, and I understand nothing; in the English case I understand everything, and there is so far no reason at all to suppose that my understanding has anything to do with computer programs—i.e., with computational operations on purely formally specified elements. As long as the program is defined in terms of computational operations on purely formally defined elements, what the example suggests is that these by themselves have no interesting connection with understanding. They are certainly not sufficient conditions, and not the slightest reason has been given to suppose that they are necessary conditions or even that they make a significant contribution to understanding. Notice that the force of the argument is not simply that different machines can have the same input and output while operating on different formal principles—that is not the point at all—but rather that whatever purely formal principles you put into the computer will not be sufficient for understanding, since a human will be able to follow the formal principles without understanding anything, and no reason has been offered to suppose they are necessary or even contributory, since no reason has been given to suppose that when I understand English, I am operating with any formal program at all.

What is it, then, that I have in the case of the English sentences which I do not have in the case of the Chinese sentences? The obvious answer is that I know what the former mean but haven't the faintest idea what the latter mean. In what does this consist, and why couldn't we give it to a machine, whatever it is? Why couldn't the machine be given whatever it is about me that makes it the case that I know what English sentences mean? I will return to these questions after developing my example a little more.

I have had occasions to present this example to several workers in artificial intelligence and, interestingly, they do not seem to agree on what the proper reply to it is. I get a surprising variety of replies, and in what follows I will consider the most common of these (specified along with their geographical origins). First I want to block out some common misunderstandings about "understanding." In many of these discussions one finds fancy footwork about the word "understanding." My critics point out that there are different degrees of understanding, that "understanding" is not a simple two-place predicate, that there are even different kinds and levels of understanding, and often the law of the excluded middle doesn't even apply in a straightforward way to statements of the form 'x understands y,' that in many cases it is a matter for decision and not a simple matter of fact whether x understands y. And so on. To all these points I want to say of course, of course; but they have nothing to do with the points at issue. There are clear cases where "understanding" applies and clear cases where it does not apply; and such cases are all I need for this argument.[2] I understand stories in English; to a lesser

2. Also, "understanding" implies both the possession of mental (intentional) states and the truth (validity, success) of these states. For the purposes of this discussion, we are concerned only with the possession of the states.

degree I can understand stories in French; to a still lesser degree, stories in German; and in Chinese, not at all. My car and my adding machine, on the other hand, understand nothing; they are not in that line of business. We often attribute "understanding" and other cognitive predicates by metaphor and analogy to cars, adding machines, and other artifacts, but nothing is proved by such attributions. We say, "The door *knows* when to open because of its photoelectric cell," "the adding machine *knows how* (*understands how,* is *able*) to do addition and subtraction but not division," and "the thermostat *perceives* changes in the temperature." The reason we make these attributions is interesting and has to do with the fact that in artifacts we extend our own intentionality;[3] our tools are extensions of our purposes, and so we find it natural to make metaphorical attributions of intentionality to them; but I take it no philosophical ice is cut by such examples. The sense in which an automatic door "understands instructions" from its photoelectric cell is not at all the sense in which I understand English. If the sense in which Schank's programmed computers understand stories is supposed to be the metaphorical sense in which the door understands, and not the sense in which I understand English, the issue would not be worth discussing. Newell and Simon write that the sense of "understanding" they claim for computers is exactly the same as for human beings. I like the straightforwardness of this claim, and it is the sort of claim I will be considering. I will argue that in the literal sense the programmed computer understands what the car and the adding machine understand, viz. exactly nothing. The computer understanding is not just (like my understanding of German) partial or incomplete; it is zero.

Now to the replies:

I. *The Systems Reply* (Berkeley): "While it is true that the individual person who is locked in the room does not understand the story, the fact is that he is merely part of a whole system

3. Intentionality is by definition that feature of certain mental states by which they are directed at or about objects and states of affairs in the world. Thus beliefs, desires, and intentions are intentional states; undirected forms of anxiety and depression are not. For further discussion, see Searle (1979).

and the system does understand the story. The person has a large ledger in front of him in which are written the rules, he has a lot of scratch paper and pencils for doing calculations, he has "data banks" of sets of Chinese symbols. Now, understanding is not being ascribed to the mere individual, rather it is being ascribed to this whole system of which he is a part."

My response to the systems theory is simple: Let the individual internalize all of these elements of the system. He memorizes the rules in the ledger and the data banks of Chinese symbols, and he does all the calculations in his head.The individual then incorporates the entire system. There isn't anything at all to the system which he does not encompass. We can even get rid of the room and suppose he works outdoors. All the same, he understands nothing of the Chinese, and *a fortiori* neither does the system, because there isn't anything in the system which isn't in him. If he doesn't understand, then there is no way the system could understand because the system is just a part of him.

Actually I feel somewhat embarrassed even to give this answer to the systems theory because the theory seems to me so implausible to start with. The idea is that while a person doesn't understand Chinese, somehow the *conjunction* of that person and bits of paper might understand Chinese. It is not easy for me to imagine how someone who was not in the grip of an ideology would find the idea at all plausible. Still, I think many people who are committed to the ideology of strong AI will in the end be inclined to say something very much like this; so let us pursue it a bit further. According to one version of this view, while the man in the internalized systems example doesn't understand Chinese in the sense that a native Chinese speaker does (because, for example, he doesn't know that the story refers to restaurants and hamburgers, etc.), still "the man as formal symbol manipulation system" *really does understand Chinese.* The subsystem of the man which is the formal symbol manipulation system for Chinese should not be confused with the subsystem for English.

So there are really two subsystems in the man; one understands English, the other Chinese, and "it's just that the two systems have little to do with each other." But, I want to reply, not only do they have little to do with each other, they are not even remotely alike. The subsystem that understands English (assuming we allow ourselves to talk in this jargon of "subsystems" for a moment) knows that the stories are about restaurants and eating hamburgers, etc.; he knows that he is being asked questions about restaurants and that he is answering questions as best as he can by making various inferences from the content of the story, and so on. But the Chinese system knows none of this; whereas the English subsystem knows that "hamburgers" refers to hamburgers, the Chinese subsystem knows only that "squiggle-squiggle" is followed by "squoggle-squoggle." All he knows is that various formal symbols are being introduced at one end and are manipulated according to rules written in English, and that other symbols are going out at the other end. The whole point of the original example was to argue that such symbol manipulation by itself couldn't be sufficient for understanding Chinese in any literal sense because the man could write "squoggle-squoggle" after "squiggle-squiggle" without understanding anything in Chinese. And it doesn't meet that argument to postulate subsystems within the man, because the subsystems are no better off than the man was in the first place; they still don't have anything even remotely like what the English-speaking man (or subsystem) has. Indeed, in the case as described, the Chinese subsystem is simply a part of the English subsystem, a part that engages in meaningless symbol manipulation according to rules in English.

Let us ask ourselves what is supposed to motivate the systems reply in the first place—that is, what *independent* grounds are there supposed to be for saying that the agent must have a subsystem within him which literally understands stories in Chinese? As far as I can tell, the only grounds are that in the example I have the same input and output as native Chinese speakers, and a program that goes from one to the other. But the point of the example has been to show that that couldn't be sufficient for understanding, in the sense in which I understand stories in English, because a person, hence the set of systems that go to make up a person, could have the right combination of input, output, and program and still not understand anything in the relevant literal sense in which I understand English. The only motivation for saying there *must* be a subsystem in me which understands Chinese is that I have a program and I can pass the Turing test;

I can fool native Chinese speakers (cf. Turing, 1950). But precisely one of the points at issue is the adequacy of the Turing test. The example shows that there could be two "systems" both of which pass the Turing test but only one of which understands; and it is no argument against this point to say that since they both pass the Turing test, they must both understand, since this claim fails to meet the argument that the system in me which understands English has a great deal more than the system which merely processes Chinese. In short the systems reply simply begs the question by insisting without argument that the system must understand Chinese.

Furthermore, the systems reply would appear to lead to consequences that are independently absurd. If we are to conclude that there must be cognition in me on the grounds that I have a certain sort of input and output and a program in between, then it looks as though all sorts of noncognitive subsystems are going to turn out to be cognitive. For example, my stomach has a level of description where it does information processing, and it instantiates any number of computer programs, but I take it we do not want to say that it has any understanding. Yet if we accept the systems reply, it is hard to see how we avoid saying that stomach, heart, liver, etc. are all understanding subsystems, since there is no principled way to distinguish the motivation for saying the Chinese subsystem understands from saying that the stomach understands. (It is, by the way, not an answer to this point to say that the Chinese system has information as input and output and the stomach has food and food products as input and output, since from the point of view of the agent, from my point of view, there is no information in either the food or the Chinese; the Chinese is just so many meaningless squiggles. The information in the Chinese case is solely in the eyes of the programmers and the interpreters, and there is nothing to prevent them from treating the input and output of my digestive organs as information if they so desire.)

This last point bears on some independent problems in strong AI, and it is worth digressing for a moment to explain it. If strong AI is to be a branch of psychology, it must be able to distinguish systems which are genuinely mental from those which are not. It must be able to distinguish the principles on which the mind works from those on which nonmental systems work; otherwise it will offer us no explanations of what is specifically mental about the mental. And the mental-nonmental distinction cannot be just in the eye of the beholder—it must be intrinsic to the systems, for otherwise it would be up to any beholder to treat people as nonmental and, e.g., hurricanes as mental, if he likes. But quite often in the AI literature the distinction is blurred in ways which would in the long run prove disastrous to the claim that AI is a cognitive inquiry. McCarthy, for example, writes: "Machines as simple as thermostats can be said to have beliefs, and having beliefs seems to be a characteristic of most machines capable of problem solving performance" (McCarthy, 1979). Anyone who thinks strong AI has a chance as a theory of the mind ought to ponder the implications of that remark. We are asked to accept it as a discovery of strong AI that the hunk of metal on the wall which we use to regulate the temperature has beliefs in exactly the same sense that we, our spouses, and our children have beliefs, and furthermore that "most" of the other machines in the room—telephone, tape recorder, adding machine, electric light switch, etc.—also have beliefs in this literal sense. It is not the aim of this article to argue against McCarthy's point, so I will simply assert the following without argument. The study of the mind starts with such facts as that humans have beliefs and thermostats, telephones, and adding machines don't. If you get a theory that denies this point, you have produced a counter-example to the theory, and the theory is false. One gets the impression that people in AI who write this sort of thing think they can get away with it because they don't really take it seriously and they don't think anyone else will either. I propose, for a moment at least, to take it seriously. Think hard for one minute about what would be necessary to establish that that hunk of metal on the wall over there has real beliefs, beliefs with direction of fit, propositional content, and conditions of satisfaction; beliefs that have the possibility of being strong beliefs or weak beliefs; nervous, anxious or secure beliefs; dogmatic, rational, or superstitious beliefs; blind faiths or hesitant cogitations; any kind of beliefs. The thermostat is not a candidate. Neither are stomach, liver, adding machine, or telephone. However, since we are taking the idea seriously, notice that its truth would be fatal to the claim of strong AI to be a science of the mind, for now the mind is everywhere. What we wanted to know is what distinguishes the mind from thermostats, livers, etc. And if McCarthy were right, strong AI hasn't a hope of telling us that.

> II. *The Robot Reply* (Yale): "Suppose we wrote a different kind of program from Schank's program. Suppose we put a computer inside a robot, and this computer would not just take in formal symbols as input and give out formal symbols as output, but rather it would actually operate the robot in such a way that the robot does something very much like perceiving, walking, moving about, hammering nails, eating, drinking—anything you like. The robot would, for example, have a television camera attached to it that enabled it to see, it would have arms and legs that enabled it to act, and all of this would be controlled by its computer brain. Such a robot would, unlike Schank's computer, have genuine understanding and other mental states."

The first thing to notice about the robot reply is that it tacitly concedes that cognition is not solely a matter of formal symbol manipulation, since this reply adds a set of causal relations with the outside world. But the answer to the robot reply is that the addition of such "perceptual" and "motor" capacities adds nothing by way of understanding, in particular, or intentionality, in general, to Schank's original program; and to see this, notice that the same thought experiment applies to the robot case. Suppose that instead of the computer inside the robot, you put me inside the room and you give me again, as in the original Chinese case, more Chinese symbols with more instructions in English for matching Chinese symbols to Chinese symbols and feeding back Chinese symbols to the outside. Suppose unknown to me, some of the Chinese symbols that come to me come from a television camera attached to the robot, and other Chinese symbols that I am giving out serve to make the motors inside the robot move the robot's legs or arms. It is important to emphasize that all I am doing is manipulating formal symbols: I know none of these other facts. I am receiving "information" from the robot's "perceptual" apparatus, and I am giving out "instructions" to its motor apparatus without knowing either of these facts. I am the robot's homunculus, but unlike the traditional homunculus, I don't know what's going on. I don't understand anything except the rules for symbol manipulation. Now in this case I want to say that the robot has no intentional states at all; it is simply moving about as a result of its electrical wiring and its program. And furthermore, by instantiating the program, I have no intentional states of the relevant type. All I do is follow formal instructions about manipulating formal symbols.

> III. *The Brain Simulator Reply* (Berkeley and M.I.T.): "Suppose we design a program that doesn't represent information that we have about the world, such as the information in Schank's scripts, but simulates the actual sequence of neuron firings at the synapses of the brain of a native Chinese speaker when he understands stories in Chinese and gives answers to them. The machine takes in Chinese stories and questions about them as input, it simulates the formal structure of actual Chinese brains in processing these stories, and it gives out Chinese answers as outputs. We can even imagine that the machine operates not with a single serial program but with a whole set of programs operating in parallel, in the manner that actual human brains presumably operate when they process natural language. Now surely in such a case we would have to say that the machine understood the stories; and if we refuse to say that, wouldn't we also have to deny that native Chinese speakers understood the stories? At the level of the synapses what would or could be different about the program of the computer and the program of the Chinese brain?"

Before addressing this reply, I want to digress to note that it is an odd reply for any partisan of artificial intelligence (functionalism, etc.) to make. I thought the whole idea of strong artificial intelligence is that we don't need to know how the brain works to know how the mind works. The basic hypothesis, or so I had supposed, was that there is a level of mental operations that consists in computational processes over formal elements which constitute the essence of the mental and can be realized in all sorts of different brain processes in the same way that any computer program can be realized in different computer hardwares: on the assumptions of strong AI, the mind is to the brain as the program is to the hardware, and thus we can understand the mind without doing neurophysiology. If we had to know how the brain worked in order to do AI, we wouldn't bother with AI. However, even getting this close to the operation of the brain is still not sufficient to produce understanding. To see that this is so, imagine that instead of a monolingual man in a room shuffling symbols we have the man operate an elaborate set of water pipes with valves connecting them. When the man receives the Chinese symbols he looks up in the program, written in English, which valves he has to turn on and off. Each water connection corresponds to a synapse in the Chinese brain, and the whole system is rigged up so that after doing all the right firings—that is, after turning on all the right faucets—the Chinese answers pop out at the output end of the series of pipes.

Now where is the understanding in this system? It takes Chinese as input, it simulates the formal structure of the synapses of the Chinese brain, and it gives Chinese as output. But the man certainly doesn't understand Chinese, and neither do the water pipes, and if we are tempted to adopt what I think is the absurd view that somehow the *conjunction* of man *and* water pipes understands, remember that in principle the man can internalize the formal structure of the water pipes and do all the "neuron firings" in his imagination. The problem with the brain simulator is that it is simulating the wrong things about the brain. As long as it simulates only the formal structure of the sequence of neuron firings at the synapses, it won't have simulated what matters about the brain, namely its causal properties, its ability to produce intentional states. And that the formal properties are not sufficient for the causal properties is shown by the water pipe example: we can have all the formal properties carved off from the relevant neurobiological causal properties.

IV. *The Combination Reply* (Berkeley and Stanford): "While each of the previous three replies might not be completely convincing by itself as a refutation of the Chinese room counter-example, if you take all three together they are collectively much more convincing and even decisive. Imagine a robot with a brain-shaped computer lodged in its cranial cavity; imagine the computer programmed with all the synapses of a human brain;

> imagine that the whole behavior of the robot is indistinguishable from human behavior; and now think of the whole thing as a unified system and not just as a computer with inputs and outputs. Surely in such a case we would have to ascribe intentionality to the system."

I entirely agree that in such a case we would find it rational and indeed irresistible to accept the hypothesis that the robot had intentionality, as long as we knew nothing more about it. Indeed, besides appearance and behavior the other elements of the combination are really irrelevant. If we could build a robot whose behavior was indistinguishable over a large range from human behavior, we would attribute intentionality to it, pending some reason not to. We wouldn't need to know in advance that its computer brain was a formal analogue of the human brain.

But I really don't see that this is any help to the claims of strong AI, and here is why: According to strong AI, instantiating a formal program with the right input and output is a sufficient condition of, indeed is constitutive of, intentionality. As Newell (1980) puts it, the essence of the mental is the operation of a physical symbol system. But the attributions of intentionality that we make to the robot in this example have nothing to do with formal programs. They are simply based on the assumption that if the robot looks and behaves sufficiently like us, we would suppose until proven otherwise that it must have mental states like ours which cause and are expressed by its behavior, and it must have an inner mechanism capable of producing such mental states. If we knew independently how to account for its behavior without such assumptions, we would not attribute intentionality to it, especially if we knew it had a formal program. And this is the point of my earlier reply to objection II.

Suppose we knew that the robot's behavior was entirely accounted for by the fact that a man inside it was receiving uninterpreted formal symbols from the robot's sensory receptors and sending out uninterpreted formal symbols to its motor mechanisms, and the man was doing this symbol manipulation in accordance with a bunch of rules. Furthermore, suppose the man knows none of these facts about the robot; all he knows is which operations to perform on which meaningless symbols. In such a case we would regard the robot as an ingenious mechanical dummy. The hypothesis that the dummy has a mind would now be unwarranted and unnecessary, for there is now no longer any reason to ascribe intentionality to the robot or to the system of which it is a part (except of course for the man's intentionality in manipulating the symbols). The formal symbol manipulations go on, the input and output are correctly matched, but the only real locus of intentionality is the man, and he doesn't know any of the relevant intentional states; he doesn't, for example, *see* what comes into the robot's eyes, he doesn't *intend* to move the robot's arm, and he doesn't *understand* any of the remarks made to or by the robot. Nor, for the reasons stated earlier, does the system of which man and robot are a part.

To see the point contrast this case with cases where we find it completely natural to ascribe intentionality to members of certain other primate species, such as apes and monkeys, and to domestic animals, such as dogs. The reasons we find it natural are, roughly, two: we can't make sense of the animal's behavior without the ascription of intentionality, and we can see that the beasts are made of stuff similar to our own—an eye, a nose, its skin, etc. Given the coherence of the animal's behavior and the assumption of the same causal stuff underlying it, we assume both that the animal must have mental states underlying its behavior, and the mental states must be produced by mechanisms made out of the stuff that is like our stuff. We would certainly make similar assumptions about the robot unless we had some reason not to, but as soon as we knew that the behavior was the result of a formal program, and that the actual causal properties of the physical substance were irrelevant, we would abandon the assumption of intentionality.

There are two other responses to my example which come up frequently (and so are worth discussing) but really miss the point.

> V. *The Other Minds Reply* (Yale): "How do you know that other people understand Chinese or anything else? Only by their behavior. Now the computer can pass the behavioral tests as well as they can (in principle), so if you are going to attribute cognition to other people, you must in principle also attribute it to computers."

The objection is worth only a short reply. The problem in this discussion is not about how I know that other people have cognitive states, but rather what it is that I am attributing to them when I attribute cognitive states to them. The thrust of the argument is that it couldn't be just computational processes and their output because there can be computational processes and their output without the cognitive state. It is no answer to this argument to feign anesthesia. In "cognitive sciences" one presupposes the reality and knowability of the mental in the same way that in physical sciences one has to presuppose the reality and knowability of physical objects.

> VI. *The Many Mansions Reply* (Berkeley): "Your whole argument presupposes that AI is only about analogue and digital computers. But that just happens to be the present state of technology. Whatever these causal processes are that you say are essential for intentionality (assuming you are right), eventually we will be able to build devices that have these causal processes and that will be artificial intelligence. So your arguments are in no way directed at the ability of artificial intelligence to produce and explain cognition."

I have no objection to this reply except to say that it in effect trivializes the project of strong artificial intelligence by redefining it as whatever artificially produces and explains cognition. The interest of the original claims made on behalf of artificial intelligence is that it was a precise, well defined thesis: mental processes are computational processes over formally defined elements. I have been concerned to challenge that thesis. If the claim is redefined so that it is no longer that thesis, my objections no longer apply, because there is no longer a testable hypothesis for them to apply to.

Let us now return to the questions I promised I would try to answer: Granted that in my original example I understand the English and I do not understand the Chinese, and granted therefore that the machine doesn't understand either English or Chinese; still there must be something about me that makes it the case that I understand English and a corresponding something lacking in me which makes it the case that I fail to understand Chinese. Now why couldn't we give those somethings, whatever they are, to a machine?

I see no reason in principle why we couldn't give a machine the capacity to understand English or Chinese, since in an important sense our bodies with our brains are precisely such machines. But I do see very strong arguments for saying that we could not give such a thing to a machine where the operation of the machine is defined solely in terms of computational processes over formally defined elements; that is, where the operation of the machine is defined as an instantiation of a computer program. It is not because I am the instantiation of a computer program that I am able to understand English and have other forms of intentionality (I am, I suppose, the instantiation of any number of computer programs), but as far as we know it is because I am a certain sort of organism with a certain biological (i.e., chemical and physical) structure, and this structure under certain conditions is causally capable of producing perception, action, understanding, learning, and other intentional phenomena. And part of the point of the present argument is that only something that had those causal powers could have that intentionality. Perhaps other physical and chemical processes could produce exactly these effects; perhaps, for example, Martians also have intentionality, but their brains are made of different stuff. That is an empirical question, rather like the question whether photosynthesis can be done by something with a chemistry different from that of chlorophyl.

But the main point of the present argument is that no purely formal model will ever be by itself sufficient for intentionality, because the formal properties are not by themselves constitutive of intentionality, and they have by themselves no causal powers except the power, when instantiated, to produce the next stage of the formalism when the machine is running. And any other causal properties which particular realizations of the formal model have are irrelevant to the formal model because we can always put the same formal model in a different realization where those causal properties are obviously absent. Even if by some miracle Chinese speakers exactly realize Schank's program, we can put the same program in English speakers, water pipes, or computers, none of which understand Chinese, the program notwithstanding.

What matters about brain operation is not the formal shadow cast by the sequence of synapses but rather the actual properties of the sequences. All the arguments for the strong version of artificial intelligence that I have seen insist on drawing an outline around the shadows cast by cognition and then claiming that the shadows are the real thing.

By way of concluding I want to state some of the general philosophical points implicit in the argument. For clarity I will try to do it in a question-and-answer fashion, and I begin with that old chestnut:

"Could a machine think?"

The answer is, obviously, yes. We are precisely such machines.

"Yes, but could an artifact, a man-made machine, think?"

Assuming it is possible to produce artificially a machine with a nervous system, neurons with axons and dendrites, and all the rest of it, sufficiently like ours, again the answer to the question seems to be obviously 'yes'. If you can exactly duplicate the causes, you could duplicate the effects. And indeed it might be possible to produce consciousness, intentionality and all the rest of it using chemical principles different from those human beings use. It is, as I said, an empirical question.

"OK, but could a digital computer think?"

If by "digital computer" we mean anything at all which has a level of description where it can correctly be described as the instantiation of a computer program, then again the answer is, of course, yes, since we are the instantiations of any number of computer programs and we can think.

"But could something think, understand, etc. *solely* by virtue of being a computer with the right sort of program? Could instantiating a program, the right program of course, by itself be a sufficient condition of understanding?"

This I think is the right question to ask, though it is usually confused with one or more of the earlier questions, and the answer to it is "no."

"Why not?"

Because the formal symbol manipulations by themselves don't have any intentionality: they are meaningless; they aren't even *symbol* manipulations, since the symbols don't symbolize anything. In the linguistic jargon they have only a syntax but no semantics. Such intentionality as computers appear to have is solely in the minds of those who program them and those who use them, those who send in the input and who interpret the output.

The aim of the Chinese room example was to try to show this by showing that as soon as we put something into the system which really does have intentionality, a man, and we program the man with the formal program, you can see that the formal program carries no additional intentionality. It adds nothing, for example, to a man's ability to understand Chinese.

Precisely that feature of AI which seemed so appealing—the distinction between the program and the realization—proves fatal to the claim that simulation could be duplication. The distinction between the program and its realization in the hardware seems to be parallel to the distinction between the level of mental operations and the level of brain operations. And if we could describe the level of mental operations as a formal program, it seems we could describe what was essential about the mind without doing either introspective psychology or neurophysiology of the brain. But the equation "Mind is to brain as program is to hardware" breaks down at several points, among them the following three:

First, the distinction between program and realization has the consequence that the same program could have all sorts of crazy realizations which had no form of intentionality. Weizenbaum (1976), for example, shows in detail how to construct a computer using a roll of toilet paper and a pile of small stones. Similarly, the Chinese story-understanding program can be programmed into a sequence of water pipes, a set of wind machines, or a monolingual English speaker, none of which thereby acquires an understanding of Chinese. Stones, toilet paper, wind, and water pipes are the wrong kind of stuff to have intentionality in the first place (only something that has the same causal powers as brains can have intentionality), and though the English speaker has the right kind of stuff for intentionality, you can easily see that he doesn't get any extra intentionality by memorizing the program, since memorizing it won't teach him Chinese.

Second, the program is purely formal, but the intentional states are not in that way formal. They are defined in terms of their content, not their form. The belief that it is raining, for example, if defined not as a certain formal shape, but as a certain mental content, with conditions of satisfaction, a direction of fit (cf. Searle, 1979), etc. Indeed, the belief as such hasn't even got a formal shape in this syntactical sense, since one and the same belief can be given an indefinite number of different syntactical expressions in different linguistic systems.

Third, as I mentioned before, mental states and events are a product of the operation of the brain, but the program is not in that way a product of the computer.

"Well if programs are in no way constitutive of mental processes, then why have so many people believed the converse? That at least needs some explanation."

I don't know the answer to that. The idea that computer simulations could be the real thing ought to have seemed suspicious in the first place because the computer isn't confined to simulating mental operations, by any means. No one supposes that computer simulations of a five-alarm fire will burn the neighborhood down or that a computer simulation of a rainstorm will leave us all drenched. Why on earth would anyone suppose that a computer simulation of understanding actually understood anything? It is sometimes said that it would be frightfully hard to get computers to feel pain or fall in love, but love and pain are neither harder nor easier than cognition or anything else. For simulation, all you need is the right input and output and a program in the middle that transforms the former into the latter. That is all the computer has for anything it does. To confuse simulation with duplication is the same mistake, whether it is pain, love, cognition, fires, or rainstorms.

Still, there are several reasons why AI must have seemed and to many people perhaps still does seem in some way to reproduce and thereby explain mental phenomena, and I believe we will not succeed in removing these illusions until we have fully exposed the reasons that give rise to them.

First, and perhaps most important, is a confusion about the notion of "information processing." Many people in cognitive science believe that the human brain with its mind does something called "information processing," and analogously the computer with its program does information processing, but fires and rainstorms on the other hand don't do information processing at all. Thus though the computer can simulate the formal features of any process whatever, it stands in a special relation to the mind and brain because when the computer is properly programmed, ideally with the same program as the brain, the information processing is identical in the two cases, and this information processing is really the essence of the mental. But the trouble with this argument is that it rests on an ambiguity in the notion of "information." In the sense in which people "process information" when they reflect, say, on problems in arithmetic or when they read and answer questions about stories, the programmed computer does not do "information processing." Rather, what it does is manipulate formal symbols. The fact that the programmer and the interpreter of the computer output use the symbols to stand for objects in the world is totally beyond the scope of the computer. The computer, to repeat, has a syntax but no semantics. Thus if you type into the computer "2 plus 2 equals?" it will type out "4." But it has no idea that "4" means 4 or that it means anything at all. And the point is not that it lacks some second-order information about the interpretation of its first-order symbols, but rather that its first-order symbols don't have any interpretations as far as the computer is concerned. All the computer has is more symbols. The introduction of the notion of "information processing" therefore produces a dilemma: Either we construe the notion of "information processing" in such a way that it implies intentionality as part of the process or we don't. If the former, then the programmed computer does not do information processing, it only manipulates formal symbols. If the latter, then although the computer does information processing, it is only in the sense in which adding machines, typewriters, stomachs, thermostats, rainstorms, and hurricanes do information processing—namely, they have a level of description where we can describe them as taking information in at one end, transforming it, and producing information as output. But in this case it is up to outside observers to interpret the input and output as information in the ordinary sense. And no similarity is established between the computer and the brain in terms of any similarity of information processing in the two cases.

Secondly, in much of AI there is a residual behaviorism or operationalism. Since appropriately programmed computers can have input/output patterns similar to human beings, we are tempted to postulate mental states in the computer similar to human mental states. But once we see that it is both conceptually and empirically possible for a system to have human capacities in some realm without having any intentionality at all, we should be able to overcome this impulse. My desk adding machine has calculating capacities but no intentionality, and in this paper I have tried to show that a system could have input and output capabilities which duplicated those of a native Chinese speaker and still not understand Chinese, regardless of how it was programmed. The Turing test is typical of the tradition in being unashamedly behavioristic and operationalistic, and I believe that if AI workers totally repudiated behaviorism and operationalism, much of the confusion between simulation and duplication would be eliminated.

Third, this residual operationalism is joined to a residual form of dualism; indeed, strong AI only makes sense given the dualistic assumption that where the mind is concerned the brain doesn't matter. In strong AI (and in functionalism, as well) what matters are programs, and programs are independent of their realization in machines; indeed, as far as AI is concerned, the same program could be realized by an electronic machine, a Cartesian mental substance, or a Hegelian world spirit. The single most surprising discovery that I have made in discussing these issues is that many AI workers are shocked by my idea that actual human mental phenomena might be dependent on actual physical-chemical properties of actual human brains. But I should not have been surprised; for unless you accept some form of dualism, the strong AI project hasn't got a chance. The project is to reproduce and explain the mental by designing programs; but unless the mind is not only conceptually but empirically independent of the brain, you cannot carry out the project, for the program is completely independent of any realization. Unless you believe that the mind is separable from the brain both conceptually and empirically—dualism in a strong form—you cannot hope to reproduce the mental by writing and running programs since programs must be independent of brains or any other particular forms of instantiation. If mental operations consist of computational operations on formal symbols, it follows that they have no interesting connection with the brain, and the only connection would be that the brain just happens to be one of the indefinitely many types of machines capable of instantiating the program. This form of dualism is not the traditional Cartesian variety that claims there are two sorts of *substances*, but it is Cartesian in the sense that it insists that what is specifically mental about the mind has no intrinsic connection with the actual properties of the brain. This underlying dualism is masked from us by the fact that AI literature contains frequent fulminations against "dualism"; what the authors seem to be unaware of is that their position presupposes a strong version of dualism.

"Could a machine think?" My own view is that *only* a machine could think, and indeed only very special kinds of machines, namely brains and machines that had the *same causal powers* as brains. And that is the main reason why strong AI has had little to tell us about thinking: it has nothing to tell us about machines. By its own definition it is about programs, and programs are not machines. Whatever else intentionality is, it is a biological phenomenon and it is as likely to be as causally dependent on the specific biochemistry of its origins as lactation, photosynthesis, or any other biological phenomena. No one would suppose that we could produce milk and sugar by running a computer simulation of the formal sequences in lactation and photosynthesis; but where the mind is concerned, many people are willing to believe in such a miracle, because of a deep and abiding dualism: the mind they suppose is a matter of formal processes and is independent of specific material causes in the way that milk and sugar are not.

In defense of this dualism, the hope is often expressed that the brain is a digital computer (early computers, by the way, were often called "electronic brains"). But that is no help. Of course the brain is a digital computer. Since everything is a digital computer, brains are too. The point is that the brain's causal capacity to produce intentionality cannot consist in its instantiating a computer program, since for any program you like it is possible for something to instantiate that program and still not have any mental states. Whatever it is that the brain does to produce intentionality, it cannot consist of instantiating a program, since no program by itself is sufficient for intentionality.

Acknowledgments: I am indebted to a rather large number of people for discussion of these matters and for their patient attempts to overcome my ignorance of artificial intelligence. I would especially like to thank Ned Block, Hubert Dreyfus, John Haugeland, Roger Schank, Robert Wilensky, and Terry Winograd.

Physica D 42 (1990) 335–346
North-Holland

THE SYMBOL GROUNDING PROBLEM

Stevan HARNAD
Department of Psychology, Princeton University, Princeton, NJ 08544, USA

There has been much discussion recently about the scope and limits of purely symbolic models of the mind and about the proper role of connectionism in cognitive modeling. This paper describes the "symbol grounding problem": How can the semantic interpretation of a formal symbol system be made *intrinsic* to the system, rather than just parasitic on the meanings in our heads? How can the meanings of the meaningless symbol tokens, manipulated solely on the basis of their (arbitrary) shapes, be grounded in anything but other meaningless symbols? The problem is analogous to trying to learn Chinese from a Chinese/Chinese dictionary alone. A candidate solution is sketched: Symbolic representations must be grounded bottom-up in nonsymbolic representations of two kinds: (1) *iconic representations*, which are analogs of the proximal sensory projections of distal objects and events, and (2) *categorical representations*, which are learned and innate feature detectors that pick out the invariant features of object and event categories from their sensory projections. Elementary symbols are the names of these object and event categories, assigned on the basis of their (nonsymbolic) categorical representations. Higher-order (3) *symbolic representations*, grounded in these elementary symbols, consist of symbol strings describing category membership relations (e.g. "An X is a Y that is Z").

Connectionism is one natural candidate for the mechanism that learns the invariant features underlying categorical representations, thereby connecting names to the proximal projections of the distal objects they stand for. In this way connectionism can be seen as a complementary component in a hybrid nonsymbolic/symbolic model of the mind, rather than a rival to purely symbolic modeling. Such a hybrid model would not have an autonomous symbolic "module," however; the symbolic functions would emerge as an intrinsically "dedicated" symbol system as a consequence of the bottom-up grounding of categories' names in their sensory representations. Symbol manipulation would be governed not just by the arbitrary shapes of the symbol tokens, but by the nonarbitrary shapes of the icons and category invariants in which they are grounded.

1. Modeling the mind

1.1. From behaviorism to cognitivism

For many years the only empirical approach in psychology was behaviorism, its only explanatory tools input/input and input/output associations (in the case of classical conditioning [42]) and the reward/punishment history that "shaped" behavior (in the case of operant conditioning [1]). In a reaction against the subjectivity of armchair introspectionism, behaviorism had declared that it was just as illicit to theorize about what went on in the *head* of the organism to generate its behavior as to theorize about what went on in its *mind*. Only *observables* were to be the subject matter of psychology; and, apparently, these were expected to explain themselves.

Psychology became more like an empirical science when, with the gradual advent of cognitivism [17, 25, 29], it became acceptable to make inferences about the *unobservable* processes underlying behavior. Unfortunately, cognitivism let mentalism in again by the back door too, for the hypothetical internal processes came embellished with subjective interpretations. In fact, semantic interpretability (meaningfulness), as we shall see, was one of the defining features of the most prominent contender vying to become the theoretical vocabulary of cognitivism, the "language of thought" [6], which became the prevailing view in cognitive theory for several decades in the form of the

0167-2789/90/$03.50

"symbolic" model of the mind: The mind is a symbol system and cognition is symbol manipulation. The possibility of generating complex behavior through symbol manipulation was empirically demonstrated by successes in the field of artificial intelligence (AI).

1.2. Symbol systems

What is a symbol system? From Newell [28], Pylyshyn [33], Fodor [6] and the classical work by von Neumann, Turing, Gödel, Church, etc. (see ref. [18]) on the foundations of computation, we can reconstruct the following definition:

A symbol system is:

(1) a set of arbitrary *physical tokens* (scratches on paper, holes on a tape, events in a digital computer, etc.) that are

(2) manipulated on the basis of *explicit rules* that are

(3) likewise physical tokens and *strings* of tokens. The rule-governed symbol-token manipulation is based

(4) purely on the *shape* of the symbol tokens (not their "meaning"), i.e. it is purely *syntactic*, and consists of

(5) *rulefully combining* and recombining symbol tokens. There are

(6) primitive *atomic* symbol tokens and

(7) *composite* symbol-token strings. The entire system and all its parts – the atomic tokens, the composite tokens, the syntactic manipulations (both actual and possible) and the rules – are all.

(8) *semantically interpretable*: The syntax can be *systematically* assigned a meaning (e.g. as standing for objects, as describing states of affairs).

According to proponents of the symbolic model of mind such as Fodor [7] and Pylyshyn [32, 33], symbol strings of this sort capture what mental phenomena such as thoughts and beliefs are. Symbolists emphasize that the symbolic level (for them, the mental level) is a natural functional level of its own, with ruleful regularities that are independent of their specific physical realizations. For symbolists, this implementation independence is the critical difference between cognitive phenomena and ordinary physical phenomena and their respective explanations. This concept of an autonomous symbolic level also conforms to general foundational principles in the theory of computation and applies to all the work being done in symbolic AI, the field of research that has so far been the most successful in generating (hence explaining) intelligent behavior.

All eight of the properties listed above seem to be critical to this definition of symbolic[#1]. Many phenomena have some of the properties, but that does not entail that they are symbolic in this explicit, technical sense. It is not enough, for example, for a phenomenon to be *interpretable* as rule-governed, for just about anything can be interpreted as rule-governed. A thermostat may be interpreted as following the rule: Turn on the furnace if the temperature goes below 70°F and turn it off if it goes above 70°F, yet nowhere in the thermostat is that rule explicitly represented. Wittgenstein [45] emphasized the difference between *explicit* and *implicit* rules: It is not the same thing to "follow" a rule (explicitly) and merely to behave "in accordance with" a rule (implicitly)[#2]. The critical difference is in the compositness (7) and systematicity (8) criteria. The explicitly represented symbolic rule is part of a formal system, it is decomposable (unless primitive), its application and manipulation is purely formal (syntactic, shape dependent), and the entire system must be semantically interpretable,

[#1] Paul Kube (personal communication) has suggested that (2) and (3) may be too strong, excluding some kinds of Turing machine and perhaps even leading to an infinite regress on levels of explicitness and systematicity.

[#2] Similar considerations apply to Chomsky's [2] concept of "psychological reality" (i.e. whether Chomskian rules are really physically represented in the brain or whether they merely "fit" our performance regularities, without being what actually governs them). Another version of the distinction concerns explicitly represented rules versus hard-wired physical constraints [40]. In each case, an explicit representation consisting of elements that can be recombined in systematic ways would be symbolic whereas an implicit physical constraint would not, although *both* would be semantically "interpretable" as a "rule" if construed in isolation rather than as part of a system.

not just the chunk in question. An isolated ("modular") chunk cannot be symbolic; being symbolic is a systematic property.

So the mere fact that a behavior is "interpretable" as ruleful does not mean that it is really governed by a symbolic rule[#3]. Semantic interpretability must be coupled with explicit representation (2), syntactic manipulability (4), and systematicity (8) in order to be symbolic. None of these criteria is arbitrary, and, as far as I can tell, if you weaken them, you lose the grip on what looks like a natural category and you sever the links with the formal theory of computation, leaving a sense of "symbolic" that is merely unexplicated metaphor (and probably differs from speaker to speaker). Hence it is only this formal sense of "symbolic" and "symbol system" that will be considered in this discussion of the grounding of symbol systems.

1.3. Connectionist systems

An early rival to the symbolic model of mind appeared [36], was overcome by symbolic AI [27] and has recently re-appeared in a stronger form that is currently vying with AI to be the general theory of cognition and behavior [23, 39]. Variously described as "neural networks", "parallel distributed processing" and "connectionism", this approach has a multiple agenda, which includes providing a theory of brain function. Now, much can be said for and against studying behavioral and brain function independently, but in this paper it will be assumed that, first and foremost, a cognitive theory must stand on its own merits, which depend on how well it explains our observable behavioral capacity. Whether or not it does so in a sufficiently brainlike way is another matter, and a downstream one, in the course of theory development. Very little is known of the brain's structure and its "lower" (vegetative) functions so far; and the nature of "higher" brain function is itself a theoretical matter. To "constrain" a cognitive theory to account for behavior in a brainlike way is hence premature in two respects: (1) It is far from clear yet what "brainlike" means, and (2) we are far from having accounted for a lifesize chunk of behavior yet, even without added constraints. Moreover, the formal principles underlying connectionism seem to be based on the associative and statistical structure of the causal interactions in certain dynamical systems; a neural network is merely one possible implementation of such a dynamical system[#4].

Connectionism will accordingly only be considered here as a cognitive theory. As such, it has lately challenged the symbolic approach to modeling the mind. According to connectionism, cognition is not symbol manipulation but dynamic patterns of activity in a multilayered network of nodes or units with weighted positive and negative interconnections. The patterns change according to internal network constraints governing how the activations and connection strengths are adjusted on the basis of new inputs (e.g. the generalized "delta rule", or "backpropagation" [23]). The result is a system that learns, recognizes patterns, solves problems, and can even exhibit motor skills.

1.4. Scope and limits of symbols and nets

It is far from clear what the actual capabilities and limitations of either symbolic AI or connectionism are. The former seems better at formal and language-like tasks, the latter at sensory, motor and learning tasks, but there is considerable overlap and neither has gone much beyond the stage of "toy" tasks toward lifesize behavioral capacity. Moreover, there has been some disagree-

[#3] Analogously, the mere fact that a behavior is *interpretable* as purposeful or conscious or meaningful does not mean that it really is purposeful or conscious. (For arguments to the contrary, see ref. [5].)

[#4] It is not even clear yet that a "neural network" needs to be implemented as a net (i.e. a parallel system of interconnected units) in order to do what it can do; if symbolic simulations of nets have the same functional capacity as real nets, then a connectionist model is just a special kind of symbolic model, and connectionism is just a special family of symbolic algorithms.

ment as to whether or not connectionism itself is symbolic. We will adopt the position here that it is not, because connectionist networks fail to meet several of the criteria for being symbol systems, as Fodor and Pylyshyn [10] have argued recently. In particular, although, like everything else, their behavior and internal states can be given isolated semantic interpretations, nets fail to meet the compositeness (7) and systematicity (8) criteria listed earlier: The patterns of interconnections do not decompose, combine and recombine according to a formal syntax that can be given a systematic semantic interpretation[#5]. Instead, nets seem to do what they do *non*-symbolically. According to Fodor and Pylyshyn, this is a severe limitation, because many of our behavioral capacities appear to be symbolic, and hence the most natural hypothesis about the underlying cognitive processes that generate them would be that they too must be symbolic. Our linguistic capacities are the primary examples here, but many of the other skills we have – logical reasoning, mathematics, chess playing, perhaps even our higher-level perceptual and motor skills – also seem to be symbolic. In any case, when we interpret our sentences, mathematical formulas, and chess moves (and perhaps some of our perceptual judgments and motor strategies) as having a systematic *meaning* or *content*, we know at first hand that this is literally true, and not just a figure of speech. Connectionism hence seems to be at a disadvantage in attempting to model these cognitive capacities.

Yet it is not clear whether connectionism should for this reason aspire to be symbolic, for the symbolic approach turns out to suffer from a severe handicap, one that may be responsible for the limited extent of its success to date (especially in modeling human-scale capacities) as well as the uninteresting and ad hoc nature of the symbolic "knowledge" it attributes to the "mind" of the symbol system. The handicap has been noticed in various forms since the advent of computing; I have dubbed a recent manifestation of it the "symbol grounding problem" [14].

[#5] There is some misunderstanding of this point because it is often conflated with a mere implementational issue: Connectionist networks can be simulated using symbol systems, and symbol systems can be implemented using a connectionist architecture, but that is independent of the question of what each can do *qua* symbol system or connectionist network, respectively. By way of analogy, silicon can be used to build a computer, and a computer can simulate the properties of silicon, but the functional properties of silicon are not those of computation, and the functional properties of computation are not those of silicon.

2. The symbol grounding problem

2.1. The Chinese room

Before defining the symbol grounding problem I will give two examples of it. The first comes from Searle's [37] celebrated "Chinese room argument", in which the symbol grounding problem is referred to as the problem of intrinsic meaning (or "intentionality"): Searle challenges the core assumption of symbolic AI that a symbol system capable of generating behavior indistinguishable from that of a person must have a mind. More specifically, according to the symbolic theory of mind, if a computer could pass the Turing test [43] in Chinese – i.e. if it could respond to all Chinese symbol strings it receives as input with Chinese symbol strings that are indistinguishable from the replies a real Chinese speaker would make (even if we keep testing for a lifetime) – then the computer would understand the meaning of Chinese symbols in the same sense that I understand the meaning of English symbols.

Searle's simple demonstration that this cannot be so consists of imagining himself doing everything the computer does – receiving the Chinese input symbols, manipulating them purely on the basis of their shape (in accordance with (1) to (8) above), and finally returning the Chinese output symbols. It is evident that Searle (who knows no Chinese) would not be understanding Chinese under those conditions – hence neither could the computer. The symbols and the symbol manipulation, being all based on shape rather than mean-

斑馬　带有斑紋的馬

Fig. 1. Chinese dictionary entry. For translation, see footnote 17.

ing, are systematically *interpretable* as having meaning – that, after all, is what it is to be a symbol system, according to our definition. But the interpretation will not be *intrinsic* to the symbol system itself: It will be parasitic on the fact that the symbols have meaning for *us*, in exactly the same way that the meanings of the symbols in a book are not intrinsic, but derive from the meanings in our heads. Hence, if the meanings of symbols in a symbol system are extrinsic, rather than intrinsic like the meanings in our heads, then they are not a viable model for the meanings in our heads: Cognition cannot be just symbol manipulation.

2.2. *The Chinese / Chinese dictionary-go-round*

My own example of the symbol grounding problem has two versions, one difficult, and one, I think, impossible. The difficult version is: Suppose you had to learn Chinese as a second language and the only source of information you had was a Chinese/Chinese dictionary. The trip through the dictionary would amount to a merry-go-round, passing endlessly from one meaningless symbol or symbol-string (the definiens) to another (the definiendum), never coming to a halt on what anything meant[#6]. (See fig. 1.)

The only reason cryptologists of ancient languages and secret codes seem to be able to successfully accomplish something very like this is that their efforts are *grounded* in a first language and in real world experience and knowledge[#7]. The second variant of the dictionary-go-round, however, goes far beyond the conceivable resources of cryptology: Suppose you had to learn Chinese as a *first* language and the only source of information you had was a Chinese/Chinese dict-

[#6]Symbolic AI abounds with symptoms of the symbol grounding problem. One well-known (though misdiagnosed) manifestation of it is the so-called "frame" problem [22, 24, 26, 34]: It is a frustrating but familiar experience in writing "knowledge-based" programs that a system apparently behaving perfectly intelligently for a while can be foiled by an unexpected case that demonstrates its utter stupidity: A "scene-understanding" program will blithely describe the goings-on in a visual scene and answer questions demonstrating its comprehension (who did what, where, why?) and then suddenly reveal that it does not "know" that hanging up the phone and leaving the room does not make the phone disappear, or something like that. (It is important to note that these are not the kinds of lapses and gaps in knowledge that people are prone to; rather, they are such howlers as to cast serious doubt on whether the system has anything like "knowledge" at all.) The "frame" problem has been optimistically defined as the problem of formally specifying ("framing") what varies and what stays constant in a particular "knowledge domain," but in reality it is the problem of second-guessing all the contingencies the programmer has not anticipated in symbolizing the knowledge he is attempting to symbolize. These contingencies are probably unbounded, for practical purposes, because purely symbolic "knowledge" is ungrounded. Merely adding on more symbolic contingencies is like taking a few more turns in the Chinese/Chinese dictionary-go-round. There is in reality no ground in sight: merely enough "intelligent" symbol manipulation to lull the programmer into losing sight of the fact that its meaningfulness is just parasitic on the meanings he is projecting onto it from the grounded meanings in his own head. (I have called this effect the "hermeneutic hall of mirrors" [16]; it is the reverse side of the symbol grounding problem.) Yet parasitism it is, as the next "frame problem" lurking around the corner is ready to confirm. (A similar form of over-interpretation has occurred in the ape "language" experiments [41]. Perhaps both apes and computers should be trained using Chinese code, to immunize their experimenters and programmers against spurious over-interpretations. But since the actual behavioral tasks in both domains are still so trivial, there is probably no way to prevent their being decrypted. In fact, there seems to be an irresistible tendency to overinterpret toy task performance itself, preemptively extrapolating and "scaling it up" conceptually to lifesize without any justification in practice.)

[#7]Cryptologists also use statistical information about word frequencies, inferences about what an ancient culture or an enemy government are likely to be writing about, decryption algorithms, etc.

ionary[#8]! This is more like the actual task faced by a purely symbolic model of the mind: How can you ever get off the symbol/symbol merry-go-round? How is symbol meaning to be grounded in something other than just more meaningless symbols[#9]? This is the symbol grounding problem[#10]

2.3. Connecting to the world

The standard reply of the symbolist (e.g. Fodor [7, 8]) is that the meaning of the symbols comes from connecting the symbol system to the world "in the right way". But it seems apparent that the problem of connecting up with the world in the right way is virtually coextensive with the problem of cognition itself. If each definiens in a Chinese/Chinese dictionary were somehow connected to the world in the right way, we would hardly need the definienda! Many symbolists believe that cognition, being symbol manipulation, is an autonomous functional module that need only be hooked up to peripheral devices in order to "see" the world of objects to which its symbols refer (or, rather, to which they can be systematically interpreted as referring)[#11]. Unfortunately, this radically underestimates the difficulty of picking out the objects, events and states of affairs in the world that symbols refer to, i.e. it trivializes the symbol grounding problem.

It is one possible candidate for a solution to this problem, confronted directly, that will now be sketched: What will be proposed is a hybrid nonsymbolic/symbolic system, a "dedicated" one, in which the elementary symbols are grounded in two kinds of nonsymbolic representations that pick out, from their proximal sensory projections, the distal object categories to which the elementary symbols refer. Most of the components of which the model is made up (analog projections and transformations, discretization, invariance detection, connectionism, symbol manipulation) have also been proposed in various configurations by others, but they will be put together in a specific bottom-up way here that has not, to my knowledge, been previously suggested, and it is on this specific configuration that the potential success of the grounding scheme critically depends.

Table 1 summarizes the relative strengths and weaknesses of connectionism and symbolism, the two current rival candidates for explaining *all* of cognition single-handedly. Their respective strengths will be put to cooperative rather than competing use in our hybrid model, thereby also remedying some of their respective weaknesses. Let us now look more closely at the behavioral capacities such a cognitive model must generate.

3. Human behavioral capacity

Since the advent of cognitivism, psychologists have continued to gather behavioral data, although to a large extent the relevant evidence is already in: We already know what human beings

[#8] There is of course no need to restrict the symbolic resources to a dictionary; the task would be just as impossible if one had access to the entire body of Chinese-language literature, including all of its computer programs and anything else that can be codified in symbols.

[#9] Even mathematicians, whether Platonist or formalist, point out that symbol manipulation (computation) itself cannot capture the notion of the intended interpretation of the symbols [31]. The fact that formal symbol systems and their interpretations are not the same thing is hence evident independently of the Church–Turing thesis [18] or the Gödel results [3, 4], which have been zealously misapplied to the problem of mind-modeling (e.g. by Lucas [21]) – to which they are largely irrelevant, in my view.

[#10] Note that, strictly speaking, symbol grounding is a problem only for cognitive modeling, not for AI in general. If symbol systems alone succeed in generating all the intelligent machine performance pure AI is interested in – e.g. an automated dictionary – then there is no reason whatsoever to demand that their symbols have intrinsic meaning. On the other hand, the fact that our own symbols do have intrinsic meaning whereas the computer's do not, and the fact that we can do things that the computer so far cannot, may be indications that even in AI there are performance gains to be made (especially in robotics and machine vision) from endeavouring to ground symbol systems.

[#11] The homuncular viewpoint inherent in this belief is quite apparent, as is the effect of the "hermeneutic hall of mirrors" [16].

Table 1
Connectionism versus symbol systems.

Strengths of connectionism
(1) *Nonsymbolic function*: As long as it does not aspire to be a symbol system, a connectionist network has the advantage of not being subject to the symbol grounding problem.
(2) *Generality*: connectionism applies the same small family of algorithms to many problems, whereas symbolism, being a methodology rather than an algorithm, relies on endless problem-specific symbolic rules.
(3) "*Neurosimilitude*": Connectionist architecture seems more brain-like than a Turing machine or a digital computer.
(4) *Pattern learning*: Connectionist networks are especially suited to the learning of patterns from data.
Weaknesses of connectionism
(1) *Nonsymbolic function*: Connectionist networks, because they are not symbol systems, do not have the systematic semantic properties that many cognitive phenomena appear to have.
(2) *Generality*: Not every problem amounts to pattern learning. Some cognitive tasks may call for problem-specific rules, symbol manipulation, and standard computation.
(3) "*Neurosimilitude*": Connectionism's brain-likeness may be superficial and may (like toy models) camouflage deeper performance limitations.
Strengths of symbol systems
(1) *Symbolic function*: Symbols have the computing power of Turing machines and the systematic properties of a formal syntax that is semantically interpretable.
(2) *Generality*: All computable functions (including all cognitive functions) are equivalent to a computational state in a Turing machine.
(3) *Practical successes*: Symbol systems' ability to generate intelligent behavior is demonstrated by the successes of Artificial Intelligence.
Weaknesses of symbol systems
(1) *Symbolic function*: Symbol systems are subject to the symbol grounding problem.
(2) *Generality*: Turing power is too general. The solutions to AI's many toy problems do not give rise to common principles of cognition but to a vast variety of ad hoc symbolic strategies.

are able to do. They can (1) *discriminate*, (2) *manipulate*[#12], (3) *identify* and (4) *describe* the objects, events and states of affairs in the world they live in, and they can also (5) *produce descriptions* and (6) *respond to descriptions* of those objects, events and states of affairs. Cognitive theory's burden is now to explain *how* human beings (or any other devices) do all this[#13].

3.1. Discrimination and identification

Let us first look more closely at discrimination and identification. To be able to *discriminate* is to be able to judge whether two inputs are the same or different, and, if different, *how* different they are. Discrimination is a relative judgment, based on our capacity to tell things apart and discern their degree of similarity. To be able to *identify* is to be able to assign a unique (usually arbitrary) response – a "name" – to a class of inputs, treating them all as equivalent or invariant in some respect. Identification is an absolute judgment, based on our capacity to tell whether or not a given input is a member of a particular *category*.

Consider the symbol "horse". We are able, in viewing different horses (or the same horse in different positions, or at different times) to tell

[#12]Although they are no doubt as important as perceptual skills, motor skills will not be explicitly considered here. It is assumed that the relevant features of the sensory story (e.g. iconicity) will generalize to the motor story (e.g. in motor analogs [20]). In addition, large parts of the motor story may not be cognitive, drawing instead upon innate motor patterns and sensorimotor feedback. Gibson's [11] concept of "affordances" – the invariant stimulus features that are detected by the motor possibilities they "afford" – is relevant here too, though Gibson underestimates the processing problems involved in finding such invariants [44]. In any case, motor and sensory-motor grounding will no doubt be as important as the sensory grounding that is being focused on here.

[#13]If a candidate model were to exhibit all these behavioral capacities, both *linguistic* (5)–(6) and *robotic* (i.e. sensorimotor) (1)–(3), it would pass the "total Turing test" [15]. The standard Turing test [43] calls for linguistic performance capacity only: symbols in and symbols out. This makes it equivocal about the status, scope and limits of pure symbol manipulation, and hence subject to the symbol grounding problem. A model that could pass the total Turing test, however, would be grounded in the world.

them apart and to judge which of them are more alike, and even how alike they are. This is discrimination. In addition, in viewing a horse, we can reliably call it a horse, rather than, say, a mule or a donkey (or a giraffe, or a stone). This is identification. What sort of internal representation would be needed in order to generate these two kinds of performance?

3.2. *Iconic and categorical representations*

According to the model being proposed here, our ability to discriminate inputs depends on our forming *iconic representations* of them [14]. These are internal analog transforms of the projections of distal objects on our sensory surfaces [38]. In the case of horses (and vision), they would be analogs of the many shapes that horses cast on our retinas[#14]. Same/different judgments would be based on the sameness or difference of these iconic representations, and similarity judgments would be based on their degree of congruity. No homunculus is involved here; simply a process of superimposing icons and registering their degree of disparity. Nor are there memory problems, since the inputs are either simultaneously present or available in rapid enough succession to draw upon their persisting sensory icons.

So we need horse icons to discriminate horses, but what about identifying them? Discrimination is independent of identification. I could be discriminating things without knowing what they were. Will the icon allow me to identify horses? Although there are theorists who believe it would ([30]), I have tried to show why it could not [12, 14]. In a world where there were bold, easily detected natural discontinuities between all the categories we would ever have to (or choose to) sort and identify – a world in which the members of one category could not be confused with the members of any another category – icons might be sufficient for identification. But in our underdetermined world, with its infinity of confusable potential categories, icons are useless for identification because there are too many of them and because they blend continuously[#15] into one another, making it an independent problem to *identify* which of them are icons of members of the category and which are not! Icons of sensory projections are too unselective. For identification, icons must be selectively reduced to those *invariant features* of the sensory projection that will reliably distinguish a member of a category from any nonmembers with which it could be confused. Let us call the output of this category-specific feature detector the *categorical representation*. In some cases these representations may be innate, but since evolution could hardly anticipate all of the categories we may ever need or choose to identify, most of these features must be learned from experience. In particular, our categorical representation of a horse is probably a learned one. (I will defer till section 4 the problem of how the invariant features underlying identification might be learned.)

Note that both iconic and categorical representations are nonsymbolic. The former are analog copies of the sensory projection, preserving its "shape" faithfully; the latter are icons that have been selectively filtered to preserve only some of the features of the shape of the sensory projection: those that reliably distinguish members from nonmembers of a category. But both representations are still sensory and nonsymbolic. There is no

[#14] There are many problems having to do with figure/ground discrimination, smoothing, size constancy, shape constancy, stereopsis, etc., that make the problem of discrimination much more complicated than what is described here, but these do not change the basic fact that iconic representations are a natural candidate substrate for our capacity to discriminate.

[#15] Elsewhere [13, 14] I have tried to show how the phenomenon of "categorical perception" could generate internal discontinuities where there is external continuity. There is evidence that our perceptual system is able to segment a continuum, such as the color spectrum, into relatively discrete, bounded regions or categories. Physical differences of equal magnitude are more discriminable across the boundaries between these categories than within them. This boundary effect, both innate and learned, may play an important role in the representation of the elementary perceptual categories out of which the higher-order ones are built.

problem about their connection to the objects they pick out: It is a purely causal connection, based on the relation between distal objects, proximal sensory projections and the acquired internal changes that result from a history of behavioral interactions with them. Nor is there any problem of semantic interpretation, or of whether the semantic interpretation is justified. Iconic representations no more "mean" the objects of which they are the projections than the image in a camera does. Both icons and camera images can of course be *interpreted* as meaning or standing for something, but the interpretation would clearly be derivative rather than intrinsic[#16].

3.3. Symbolic representations

Nor can categorical representations yet be interpreted as "meaning" anything. It is true that they pick out the class of objects they "name", but the names do not have all the systematic properties of symbols and symbol systems described earlier. They are just an inert taxonomy. For systematicity it must be possible to combine and recombine them rulefully into propositions that can be semantically interpreted. "Horse" is so far just an arbitrary response that is reliably made in the presence of a certain category of objects. There is no justification for interpreting it holophrastically as meaning "This is a [member of the category] horse" when produced in the presence of a horse, because the other expected systematic properties of "this" and "a" and the all-important "is" of predication are not exhibited by mere passive taxonomizing. What would be required to generate these other systematic properties? Merely that the grounded names in the category taxonomy be strung together into *propositions* about further category membership relations. For example:

(1) Suppose the name "horse" is grounded by iconic and categorical representations, learned from experience, that reliably discriminate and identify horses on the basis of their sensory projections.

(2) Suppose "stripes" is similarly grounded.

Now consider that the following category can be constituted out of these elementary categories by a symbolic description of category membership alone:

(3) "Zebra" = "horse" & "stripes"[#17]

What is the representation of zebra? It is just the symbol string "horse & stripes". But because "horse" and "stripes" are grounded in their respective iconic and categorical representations, "zebra" inherits the grounding, through its grounded *symbolic* representation. In principle, someone who had never seen a zebra (but had seen and learned to identify horses and stripes) could identify a zebra on first acquaintance armed with this symbolic representation alone (plus the nonsymbolic – iconic and categorical – representations of horses and stripes that ground it).

Once one has the grounded set of elementary symbols provided by a taxonomy of names (and the iconic and categorical representations that give content to the names and allow them to pick out the objects they identify), the rest of the symbol strings of a natural language can be generated by symbol composition alone[#18], and they will all inherit the intrinsic grounding of the elementary

[#16]On the other hand, the resemblance on which discrimination performance is based – the degree of isomorphism between the icon and the sensory projection, and between the sensory projection and the distal object – seems to be intrinsic, rather than just a matter of interpretation. The resemblance can be objectively characterized as the degree of invertibility of the physical transformation from object to icon [14].

[#17]Fig. 1 is actually the Chinese dictionary entry for "zebra", which is "striped horse". Note that the character for "zebra" actually happens to be the character for "horse" plus the character for "striped." Although Chinese characters are iconic in structure, they function just like arbitrary alphabetic lexigrams at the level of syntax and semantics.

[#18]Some standard logical connectives and quantifiers are needed too, such as not, and, all, etc. (though even some of these may be learned as higher-order categories).

set[#19]. Hence, the ability to discriminate and categorize (and its underlying nonsymbolic representations) have led naturally to the ability to describe and to produce and respond to descriptions through symbolic representations.

4. A complementary role for connectionism

The symbol grounding scheme just described has one prominent gap: No mechanism has been suggested to explain how the all-important categorical representations could be formed: How does the hybrid system find the invariant features of the sensory projection that make it possible to categorize and identify objects correctly[#20]?

Connectionism, with its general pattern learning capability, seems to be one natural candidate (though there may well be others): Icons, paired with feedback indicating their names, could be processed by a connectionist network that learns to identify icons correctly from the sample of confusable alternatives it has encountered by dynamically adjusting the weights of the features and feature combinations that are reliably associated with the names in a way that (provisionally) resolves the confusion, thereby reducing the icons to the *invariant* (confusion-resolving) features of the category to which they are assigned. In effect, the "connection" between the names and the objects that give rise to their sensory projections and their icons would be provided by connectionist networks.

This circumscribed complementary role for connectionism in a hybrid system seems to remedy the weaknesses of the two current competitors in their respective attempts to model the mind single-handedly. In a pure symbolic model the crucial connection between the symbols and their referents is missing; an autonomous symbol system, though amenable to a systematic semantic interpretation, is ungrounded. In a pure connectionist model, names are connected to objects through invariant patterns in their sensory projections, learned through exposure and feedback, but the crucial compositional property is missing; a network of names, though grounded, is not yet amenable to a full systematic semantic interpreta-

[#19]Note that it is not being claimed that "horse", "stripes", etc. are actually elementary symbols, with direct sensory grounding; the claim is only that *some* set of symbols must be directly grounded. Most sensory category representations are no doubt hybrid sensory/symbolic; and their features can change by bootstrapping: "Horse" can always be revised, both sensorily and symbolically, even if it was previously elementary. Kripke [19] gives a good example of how "gold" might be baptized on the shiny yellow metal in question, used for trade, decoration and discourse, and then we might discover "fool's gold", which would make all the sensory features we had used until then inadequate, forcing us to find new ones. He points out that it is even possible in principle for "gold" to have been inadvertently baptized on "fool's gold"! Of interest here are not the ontological aspects of this possibility, but the epistemic ones: We could bootstrap successfully to real gold even if every prior case had been fool's gold. "Gold" would still be the right word for what we had been trying to pick out (i.e. what we had "had in mind") all along, and its original provisional features would still have provided a close enough approximation to ground it, even if later information were to pull the ground out from under it, so to speak.

[#20]Although it is beyond the scope of this paper to discuss it at length, it must be mentioned that this question has often been begged in the past, mainly on the grounds of "vanishing intersections". It has been claimed that one cannot find invariant features in the sensory projection because they simply do not exist: The intersection of all the projections of the members of a category such as "horse" is empty. The British empiricists have been criticized for thinking otherwise; for example, Wittgenstein's [45] discussion of "games" and "family resemblances" has been taken to have discredited their view. Current research on human categorization [35] has been interpreted as confirming that intersections vanish and that hence categories are not represented in terms of invariant features. The problem of vanishing intersections (together with Chomsky's [2] "poverty of the stimulus argument") has even been cited by thinkers such as Fodor [8, 9] as a justification for extreme nativism. The present paper is frankly empiricist. In my view, the reason intersections have not been found is that no one has yet looked for them properly. Introspection certainly is not the way to look, and general pattern learning algorithms such as connectionism are relatively new; their inductive power remains to be tested. In addition, a careful distinction has not been made between pure sensory categories (which, I claim, must have invariants, otherwise we could not successfully identify them as we do) and higher-order categories that are *grounded* in sensory categories; these abstract representations may be symbolic rather than sensory, and hence not based directly on sensory invariants. For further discussion of this problem, see ref. [14].

tion. In the hybrid system proposed here, there is no longer any autonomous symbolic level at all; instead, there is an intrinsically *dedicated* symbol system, its elementary symbols (names) connected to nonsymbolic representations that can pick out the objects to which they refer, via connectionist networks that extract the invariant features of their analog sensory projections.

5. Conclusions

The expectation has often been voiced that "top-down" (symbolic) approaches to modeling cognition will somehow meet "bottom-up" (sensory) approaches somewhere in between. If the grounding considerations in this paper are valid, then this expectation is hopelessly modular and there is really only one viable route from sense to symbols: from the ground up. A free-floating symbolic level like the software level of a computer will never be reached by this route (or vice versa) – nor is it clear why we should even try to reach such a level, since it looks as if getting there would just amount to uprooting our symbols from their intrinsic meanings (thereby merely reducing ourselves to the functional equivalent of a programmable computer).

In an intrinsically dedicated symbol system there are more constraints on the symbol tokens than merely syntactic ones. Symbols are manipulated not only on the basis of the arbitrary shape of their tokens, but also on the basis of the decidedly nonarbitrary "shape" of the iconic and categorical representations connected to the grounded elementary symbols out of which the higher-order symbols are composed. Of these two kinds of constraints, the iconic/categorical ones are primary. I am not aware of any formal analysis of such dedicated symbol systems[#21], but this may be because they are unique to cognitive and robotic modeling and their properties will depend on the specific kinds of robotic (i.e. behavioral) capacities they are designed to exhibit.

[#21] Although mathematicians investigate the formal properties of uninterpreted symbol systems, all of their motivations and intuitions clearly come from the intended interpretations of those systems (see ref. [31]). Perhaps these too are grounded in the iconic and categorical representations in their heads.

It is appropriate that the properties of dedicated symbol systems should turn out to depend on behavioral considerations. The present grounding scheme is still in the spirit of behaviorism in that the only tests proposed for whether a semantic interpretation will bear the semantic weight placed on it consist of one formal test (does it meet the eight criteria for being a symbol system?) and one behavioral test (can it discriminate, identify (manipulate) and describe all the objects and states of affairs to which its symbols refer?). If both tests are passed, then the semantic interpretation of its symbols is "fixed" by the behavioral capacity of the dedicated symbol system, as exercised on the objects and states of affairs in the world to which its symbols refer; the symbol meanings are accordingly not just parasitic on the meanings in the head of the interpreter, but intrinsic to the dedicated symbol system itself. This is still no guarantee that our model has captured subjective meaning, of course. But if the system's behavioral capacities are lifesize, it is as close as we can ever hope to get.

References

[1] A.C. Catania and S. Harnad, eds., The Selection of Behavior. The Operant Behaviorism of B.F. Skinner: Comments and Consequences (Cambridge Univ. Press, Cambridge, 1988).

[2] N. Chomsky, Rules and representations, Behav. Brain Sci. 3 (1980) 1–61.

[3] M. Davis, Computability and Unsolvability (McGraw-Hill, New York, 1958).

[4] M. Davis, The Undecidable (Raven, New York, 1965).

[5] D.C. Dennett, Intentional systems in cognitive ethology, Behav. Brain Sci. 6 (1983) 343–390.

[6] J.A. Fodor, The Language of Thought (Crowell, New York, 1975).

[7] J.A. Fodor, Methodological solipsism considered as a research strategy in cognitive psychology, Behav. Brain Sci. 3 (1980) 63–109.

[8] J.A. Fodor, Précis of the modularity of mind, Behav. Brain Sci. 8 (1985) 1–42.
[9] J.A. Fodor, Psychosemantics (MIT/Bradford, Cambridge, MA, 1987).
[10] J.A. Fodor and Z.W. Pylyshyn, Connectionism and cognitive architecture: A critical appraisal, Cognition 28 (1988) 3–71.
[11] J.J. Gibson, An ecological approach to visual perception (Houghton Mifflin, Boston, 1979).
[12] S. Harnad, Metaphor and mental duality, in: Language, Mind and Brain, eds. T. Simon and R. Scholes (Erlbaum Hillsdale, NJ, 1982).
[13] S. Harnad, Categorical perception: A critical overview, in: Categorical Perception: The Groundwork of Cognition, ed. S. Harnad (Cambridge Univ. Press, Cambridge, 1987).
[14] S. Harnad, Category induction and representation, in: Categorical Perception: The Groundwork of Cognition, ed. S. Harnad (Cambridge Univ. Press, Cambridge, 1987).
[15] S. Harnad, Minds, machines and searle, J. Theor. Exp. Artificial Intelligence 1 (1989) 5–25.
[16] S. Harnad, Computational hermeneutics, Social Epistemology, in press.
[17] J. Haugeland, The nature and plausibility of cognitivism, Behav. Brain Sci. 1 (1978) 215–260.
[18] S.C. Kleene, Formalized Recursive Functionals and Formalized Realizability (Am. Math. Soc., Providence, RI, 1969).
[19] S.A. Kripke, Naming and Necessity (Harvard Univ. Press, Cambridge, MA, 1980).
[20] A.M. Liberman, On the finding that speech is special, Am. Psychologist 37 (1982) 148–167.
[21] J. Lucas, Minds, machines and Gödel, Philosophy 36 (1961) 112–117.
[22] J. McCarthy and P. Hayes, Some philosophical problems from the standpoint of artificial intelligence, in: Machine Intelligence, Vol. 4, eds. B. Meltzer and P. Michie (Edinburgh Univ. Press, Edinburgh, 1969).
[23] J.L. McClelland, D.E. Rumelhart and the PDP Research Group, Parallel Distributed Processing: Explorations in the Microstructure of Cognition, Vol. 1 (MIT/Bradford, Cambridge, MA, 1986).
[24] D. McDermott, Artificial intelligence meets natural stupidity, SIGART Newsletter 57 (1976) 4–9.
[25] G.A. Miller, The magical number seven, plus or minus two: Some limits on our capacity for processing information, Psychological Rev. 63 (1956) 81–97.
[26] M. Minsky, A framework for representing knowledge, MIT Lab Memo No. 306 (1974).
[27] M. Minsky and S. Papert, Perceptrons: An Introduction to Computational Geometry (MIT Press, Cambridge, MA, 1969) Reissued in an expanded edition (1988).
[28] A. Newell, Physical symbol systems, Cognitive Sci. 4 (1980) 135–183.
[29] U. Neisser, Cognitive Psychology (Appleton-Century-Crofts., New York, 1967).
[30] A. Paivio, Mental Representation: A Dual Coding Approach (Oxford Univ. Press, Oxford, 1986).
[31] R. Penrose, The Emperor's New Mind (Oxford Univ. Press, Oxford, 1989).
[32] Z.W. Pylyshyn, Computation and cognition: Issues in the foundations of cognitive science, Behav. Brain Sci. 3 (1980) 111–169.
[33] Z.W. Pylyshyn, Computation and Cognition (MIT/Bradford, Cambridge, MA, 1984).
[34] Z.W. Pylyshyn, ed., The Robot's Dilemma: The Frame Problem in Artificial Intelligence (Ablex, Norwood, NJ, 1987).
[35] E. Rosch and B.B. Lloyd, Cognition and Categorization (Erlbaum, Hillsdale, NJ, 1978).
[36] F. Rosenblatt, Principles of Neurodynamics (Spartan, New York, 1962).
[37] J. Searle, Minds, brains and programs, Behav. Brain Sci. 3 (1980) 417–457.
[38] R.N. Shepard and L.A. Cooper, Mental Images and Their Transformations (MIT Press/Bradford, Cambridge, 1982).
[39] P. Smolensky, On the proper treatment of connectionism, Behav. Brain Sci. 11 (1988) 1–74.
[40] E.P. Stabler, How are grammars represented? Behav. Brain Sci. 6 (1985) 391–421.
[41] H. Terrace, Nim (Random House, New York, 1979).
[42] J. Turkkan, Classical conditioning: The new hegemony, Behav. and Brain Sci. 12 (1989) 121–179.
[43] A.M. Turing, Computing machinery and intelligence, in: Minds and Machines, ed. A. Anderson (Prentice Hall, Engelwood Cliffs, NJ, 1964).
[44] S. Ullman, Against direct perception, Behav. Brain Sci. 3 (1980) 373–415.
[45] L. Wittgenstein, Philosophical Investigations (Macmillan, New York, 1953).

Could a Machine Think?

Classical AI is unlikely to yield conscious machines; systems that mimic the brain might

by Paul M. Churchland and Patricia Smith Churchland

Artificial-intelligence research is undergoing a revolution. To explain how and why, and to put John R. Searle's argument in perspective, we first need a flashback.

By the early 1950's the old, vague question, Could a machine think? had been replaced by the more approachable question, Could a machine that manipulated physical symbols according to structure-sensitive rules think? This question was an improvement because formal logic and computational theory had seen major developments in the preceding half-century. Theorists had come to appreciate the enormous power of abstract systems of symbols that undergo rule-governed transformations. If those systems could just be automated, then their abstract computational power, it seemed, would be displayed in a real physical system. This insight spawned a well-defined research program with deep theoretical underpinnings.

Could a machine think? There were many reasons for saying yes. One of the earliest and deepest reasons lay in two important results in computational theory. The first was Church's thesis, which states that every effectively computable function is recursively computable. Effectively computable means that there is a "rote" procedure for determining, in finite time, the output of the function for a given input. Recursively computable means more specifically that there is a finite set of operations that can be applied to a given input, and then applied again and again to the successive results of such applications, to yield the function's output in finite time. The notion of a rote procedure is nonformal and intuitive; thus, Church's thesis does not admit of a formal proof. But it does go to the heart of what it is to compute, and many lines of evidence converge in supporting it.

PAUL M. CHURCHLAND and PATRICIA SMITH CHURCHLAND are professors of philosophy at the University of California at San Diego. Together they have studied the nature of the mind and knowledge for the past two decades. Paul Churchland focuses on the nature of scientific knowledge and its development, while Patricia Churchland focuses on the neurosciences and on how the brain sustains cognition. Paul Churchland's *Matter and Consciousness* is the standard textbook on the philosophy of the mind, and Patricia Churchland's *Neurophilosophy* brings together theories of cognition from both philosophy and biology. Paul Churchland is currently chair of the philosophy department at UCSD, and the two are, respectively, president and past president of the Society for Philosophy and Psychology. Patricia Churchland is also an adjunct professor at the Salk Institute for Biological Studies in San Diego. The Churchlands are also members of the UCSD cognitive science faculty, its Institute for Neural Computation and its Science Studies program.

The second important result was Alan M. Turing's demonstration that any recursively computable function can be computed in finite time by a maximally simple sort of symbol-manipulating machine that has come to be called a universal Turing machine. This machine is guided by a set of recursively applicable rules that are sensitive to the identity, order and arrangement of the elementary symbols it encounters as input.

These two results entail something remarkable, namely that a standard digital computer, given only the right program, a large enough memory and sufficient time, can compute *any* rule-governed input-output function. That is, it can display any systematic pattern of responses to the environment whatsoever.

More specifically, these results imply that a suitably programmed symbol-manipulating machine (hereafter, SM machine) should be able to pass the Turing test for conscious intelligence. The Turing test is a purely behavioral test for conscious intelligence, but it is a very demanding test even so. (Whether it is a fair test will be addressed below, where we shall also encounter a second and quite different "test" for conscious intelligence.) In the original version of the Turing test, the inputs to the SM machine are conversational questions and remarks typed into a console by you or me, and the outputs are typewritten responses from the SM machine. The machine passes this test for conscious intelligence if its responses cannot be discriminated from the typewritten responses of a real, intelligent person. Of course, at present no one knows the function that would produce the output behavior of a conscious person. But the Church and Turing results assure us that, whatever that (presumably effective) function might be, a suitable SM machine could compute it.

This is a significant conclusion, especially since Turing's portrayal of a purely teletyped interaction is an unnecessary restriction. The same conclusion follows even if the SM machine interacts with the world in more complex ways: by direct vision, real speech and so forth. After all, a more complex recursive function is still Turing-computable. The only remaining problem is to identify the undoubtedly complex function that governs the human pattern of response to the environment and then write the program (the set of recursively applicable rules) by which the SM machine will compute it. These goals form the fundamental research program of classical AI.

Initial results were positive. SM machines with clever programs performed a variety of ostensibly cognitive activities. They responded to complex instructions, solved complex arithmetic, algebraic and tactical problems, played checkers and chess, proved theorems and engaged in simple dialogue. Performance continued to improve with the appearance of larger memories and faster machines and with the use of longer and more cunning programs. Classical, or "program-writing," AI was a vigorous and successful research effort from almost every perspective. The occasional denial that an SM machine might eventually think appeared uninformed and ill motivated. The case for a positive answer to our title question was overwhelming.

There were a few puzzles, of course. For one thing, SM machines were admittedly not very brainlike. Even here, however, the classical approach had a convincing answer. First, the physical material of any SM machine has nothing essential to do with what function it computes. That is fixed by its program. Second, the engineering details of any machine's functional architecture are also irrelevant, since different architectures running quite different programs can still be computing the same input-output function.

Accordingly, AI sought to find the input-output *function* characteristic of intelligence and the most efficient of the many possible programs for computing it. The idiosyncratic way in which the brain computes the function just doesn't matter, it was said. This completes the rationale for classical AI and for a positive answer to our title question.

Could a machine think? There were also some arguments for saying no. Through the 1960's interesting negative arguments were relatively rare. The objection was occasionally made that thinking was a nonphysical process in an immaterial soul. But such dualistic resistance was neither evolutionarily nor explanatorily plausible. It had a negligible impact on AI research.

A quite different line of objection was more successful in gaining the AI community's attention. In 1972 Hubert L. Dreyfus published a book that was highly critical of the parade-case simulations of cognitive activity. He argued for their inadequacy as simulations of genuine cognition, and he pointed to a pattern of failure in these attempts. What they were missing, he suggested, was the vast store of inarticulate background knowledge every person possesses and the commonsense capacity for drawing on relevant aspects of that knowledge as changing circumstance demands. Dreyfus did not deny the possibility that an artificial physical system of some kind might think, but he was highly critical of the idea that this could be achieved solely by symbol manipulation at the hands of recursively applicable rules.

Dreyfus's complaints were broadly perceived within the AI community, and within the discipline of philosophy as well, as shortsighted and unsympathetic, as harping on the inevitable simplifications of a research effort still in its youth. These deficits might be real, but surely they were temporary. Bigger machines and better programs should repair them in due course. Time, it was felt, was on AI's side. Here again the impact on research was negligible.

Time was on Dreyfus's side as well: the rate of cognitive return on increasing speed and memory began to slacken in the late 1970's and early 1980's. The simulation of object recognition in the visual system, for example, proved computationally intensive to an unexpected degree. Realistic results required longer and longer periods of computer time, periods far in excess of what a real visual system requires. This relative slowness of the simulations was darkly curious; signal propagation in a computer is roughly a million times faster than in the brain, and the clock frequency of a computer's central processor is greater than any frequency found in the brain by a similarly dramatic margin. And yet, on realistic problems, the tortoise easily outran the hare.

Furthermore, realistic performance required that the computer program have access to an extremely large knowledge base. Constructing the relevant knowledge base was problem enough, and it was compounded by the problem of how to access just the contextually relevant parts of that knowledge base in real time. As the knowledge base got bigger and better, the access problem got worse. Exhaustive search took too much time, and heuristics for relevance did poorly. Worries of the sort Dreyfus had raised finally began to take hold here

THE CHINESE ROOM

Axiom 1. Computer programs are formal (syntactic).

Axiom 2. Human minds have mental contents (semantics).

Axiom 3. Syntax by itself is neither constitutive of nor sufficient for semantics.

Conclusion 1. Programs are neither constitutive of nor sufficient for minds.

THE LUMINOUS ROOM

Axiom 1. Electricity and magnetism are forces.

Axiom 2. The essential property of light is luminance.

Axiom 3. Forces by themselves are neither constitutive of nor sufficient for luminance.

Conclusion 1. Electricity and magnetism are neither constitutive of nor sufficient for light.

OSCILLATING ELECTROMAGNETIC FORCES constitute light even though a magnet pumped by a person appears to produce no light whatsoever. Similarly, rule-based symbol manipulation might constitute intelligence even though the rule-based system inside John R. Searle's "Chinese room" appears to lack real understanding.

and there even among AI researchers.

At about this time (1980) John Searle authored a new and quite different criticism aimed at the most basic assumption of the classical research program: the idea that the appropriate manipulation of structured symbols by the recursive application of structure-sensitive rules could constitute conscious intelligence.

Searle's argument is based on a thought experiment that displays two crucial features. First, he describes a SM machine that realizes, we are to suppose, an input-output function adequate to sustain a successful Turing test conversation conducted entirely in Chinese. Second, the internal structure of the machine is such that, however it behaves, an observer remains certain that neither the machine nor any part of it understands Chinese. All it contains is a monolingual English speaker following a written set of instructions for manipulating the Chinese symbols that arrive and leave through a mail slot. In short, the system is supposed to pass the Turing test, while the system itself lacks any genuine understanding of Chinese or real Chinese semantic content [see "Is the Brain's Mind a Computer Program?" by John R. Searle, page 26].

The general lesson drawn is that any system that merely manipulates physical symbols in accordance with structure-sensitive rules will be at best a hollow mock-up of real conscious intelligence, because it is impossible to generate "real semantics" merely by cranking away on "empty syntax." Here, we should point out, Searle is imposing a nonbehavioral test for consciousness: the elements of conscious intelligence must possess real semantic content.

One is tempted to complain that Searle's thought experiment is unfair because his Rube Goldberg system will compute with absurd slowness. Searle insists, however, that speed is strictly irrelevant here. A slow thinker should still be a real thinker. Everything essential to the duplication of thought, as per classical AI, is said to be present in the Chinese room.

Searle's paper provoked a lively reaction from AI researchers, psychologists and philosophers alike. On the whole, however, he was met with an even more hostile reception than Dreyfus had experienced. In his companion piece in this issue, Searle forthrightly lists a number of these critical responses. We think many of them are reasonable, especially those that "bite the bullet" by insisting that, although it is appallingly slow, the overall system of the room-plus-contents does understand Chinese.

We think those are good responses, but not because we think that the room understands Chinese. We agree with Searle that it does not. Rather they are good responses because they reflect a refusal to accept the crucial third axiom of Searle's argument: "*Syntax by itself is neither constitutive of nor sufficient for semantics.*" Perhaps this axiom is true, but Searle cannot rightly pretend to know that it is. Moreover, to assume its truth is tantamount to begging the question against the research program of classical AI, for that program is predicated on the very interesting assumption that if one can just set in motion an appropriately structured internal dance of syntactic elements, appropriately connected to inputs and outputs, it can produce the same cognitive states and achievements found in human beings.

The question-begging character of Searle's axiom 3 becomes clear when it is compared directly with his conclusion 1: "*Programs are neither constitutive of nor sufficient for minds.*" Plainly, his third axiom is already carrying 90 percent of the weight of this almost identical conclusion. That is why Searle's thought experiment is devoted to shoring up axiom 3 specifically. That is the point of the Chinese room.

Although the story of the Chinese room makes axiom 3 tempting to the unwary, we do not think it succeeds in establishing axiom 3, and we offer a parallel argument below in illustration of its failure. A single transparently fallacious instance of a disputed argument often provides far more insight than a book full of logic chopping.

Searle's style of skepticism has ample precedent in the history of science. The 18th-century Irish bishop George Berkeley found it unintelligible that compression waves in the air, by themselves, could constitute or be sufficient for objective sound. The English poet-artist William Blake and the German poet-naturalist Johann W.

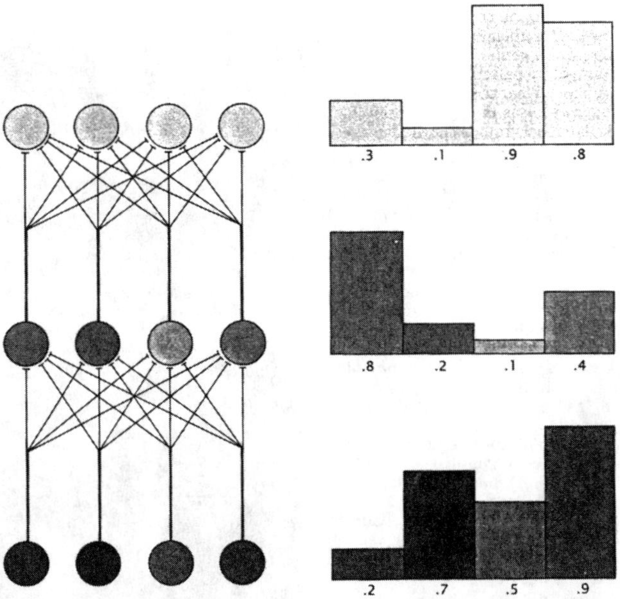

NEURAL NETWORKS model a central feature of the brain's microstructure. In this three-layer net, input neurons (*bottom left*) process a pattern of activations (*bottom right*) and pass it along weighted connections to a hidden layer. Elements in the hidden layer sum their many inputs to produce a new pattern of activations. This is passed to the output layer, which performs a further transformation. Overall the network transforms any input pattern into a corresponding output pattern as dictated by the arrangement and strength of the many connections between neurons.

von Goethe found it inconceivable that small particles by themselves could constitute or be sufficient for the objective phenomenon of light. Even in this century, there have been people who found it beyond imagining that inanimate matter by itself, and however organized, could ever constitute or be sufficient for life. Plainly, what people can or cannot imagine often has nothing to do with what is or is not the case, even where the people involved are highly intelligent.

To see how this lesson applies to Searle's case, consider a deliberately manufactured parallel to his argument and its supporting thought experiment.

Axiom 1. *Electricity and magnetism are forces.*

Axiom 2. *The essential property of light is luminance.*

Axiom 3. *Forces by themselves are neither constitutive of nor sufficient for luminance.*

Conclusion 1. *Electricity and magnetism are neither constitutive of nor sufficient for light.*

Imagine this argument raised shortly after James Clerk Maxwell's 1864 suggestion that light and electromagnetic waves are identical but before the world's full appreciation of the systematic parallels between the properties of light and the properties of electromagnetic waves. This argument could have served as a compelling objection to Maxwell's imaginative hypothesis, especially if it were accompanied by the following commentary in support of axiom 3.

"Consider a dark room containing a man holding a bar magnet or charged object. If the man pumps the magnet up and down, then, according to Maxwell's theory of artificial luminance (AL), it will initiate a spreading circle of electromagnetic waves and will thus be luminous. But as all of us who have toyed with magnets or charged balls well know, their forces (or any other forces for that matter), even when set in motion, produce no luminance at all. It is inconceivable that you might constitute real luminance just by moving forces around!"

How should Maxwell respond to this challenge? He might begin by insisting that the "luminous room" experiment is a misleading display of the phenomenon of luminance because the frequency of oscillation of the magnet is absurdly low, too low by a factor of 10^{15}. This might well elicit the impatient response that frequency has nothing to do with it, that the room with the bobbing magnet already contains everything essential to light, according to Maxwell's own theory.

In response Maxwell might bite the bullet and claim, quite correctly, that the room really is bathed in luminance, albeit a grade or quality too feeble to appreciate. (Given the low frequency with which the man can oscillate the magnet, the wavelength of the electromagnetic waves produced is far too long and their intensity is much too weak for human retinas to respond to them.) But in the climate of understanding here contemplated—the 1860's—this tactic is likely to elicit laughter and hoots of derision. "Luminous room, my foot, Mr. Maxwell. It's pitch-black in there!"

Alas, poor Maxwell has no easy route out of this predicament. All he can do is insist on the following three points. First, axiom 3 of the above argument is false. Indeed, it begs the question despite its intuitive plausibility. Second, the luminous room experiment demonstrates nothing of interest one way or the other about the nature of light. And third, what is needed to settle the problem of light and the possibility of artificial luminance is an ongoing research program to determine whether under the appropriate conditions the behavior of electromagnetic waves does indeed mirror perfectly the behavior of light.

This is also the response that classical AI should give to Searle's argument. Even though Searle's Chinese room may appear to be "semantically dark," he is in no position to insist, on the strength of this appearance, that rule-governed symbol manipulation can never constitute semantic phenomena, especially when people have only an uninformed commonsense understanding of the semantic and cognitive phenomena that need to be explained. Rather than exploit one's understanding of these things, Searle's argument freely exploits one's ignorance of them.

With these criticisms of Searle's argument in place, we return to the question of whether the research program of classical AI has a realistic chance of solving the problem of conscious intelligence and of producing a machine that thinks. We believe that the prospects are poor, but we rest this opinion on reasons very different from Searle's. Our reasons derive from the specific performance failures of the classical research program in AI and from a variety of lessons learned from the biological brain and a new class of computational models inspired by its structure. We have already indicated some of the failures of classical AI regarding tasks that the brain performs swiftly and efficiently. The emerging consensus on these failures is that the functional architecture of classical SM machines is simply the wrong architecture for the very demanding jobs required.

What we need to know is this: How does the brain achieve cognition? Reverse engineering is a common practice in industry. When a new piece of technology comes on the market, competitors find out how it works by taking it apart and divining its structural rationale. In the case of the brain, this strategy presents an unusually stiff challenge, for the brain is the most complicated and sophisticated thing on the planet. Even so, the neurosciences have revealed much about the brain on a wide variety of structural levels. Three anatomic points will provide a basic contrast with the architecture of conventional electronic computers.

First, nervous systems are parallel machines, in the sense that signals are processed in millions of different pathways simultaneously. The retina, for example, presents its complex input to the brain not in chunks of eight, 16 or 32 elements, as in a desktop computer, but rather in the form of almost a million distinct signal elements arriving simultaneously at the target of the optic nerve (the lateral geniculate nucleus), there to be processed collectively, simultaneously and in one fell swoop. Second, the brain's basic processing unit, the neuron, is comparatively simple. Furthermore, its response to incoming signals is analog, not digital, inasmuch as its output spiking frequency varies continuously with its input signals. Third, in the brain, axons projecting from one neuronal population to another are often matched by axons returning from their target population. These descending or recurrent projections allow the brain to modulate the character of its sensory processing. More important still, their existence makes the brain a genuine dynamical system whose continuing behavior is both highly complex and to some degree independent of its peripheral stimuli.

Highly simplified model networks have been useful in suggesting how real neural networks might work and in revealing the computational properties of parallel architectures. For example, consider a three-layer model consisting of neuronlike units fully connected by axonlike connections to the units at the next layer. An input stimulus produces some activation level in a given input unit, which conveys a signal of proportional strength along its "axon" to its many "synaptic" connections to the hidden units. The global effect is that a pattern of activations across the set of input units produces a distinct pattern of activations across the set of hidden units.

The same story applies to the output units. As before, an activation pattern across the hidden units produces a distinct activation pattern across the output units. All told, this network is a device for transforming any one of a great many possible input vectors (activation patterns) into a uniquely corresponding output vector. It is a device for computing a specific function. Exactly which function it computes is fixed by the global configuration of its synaptic weights.

There are various procedures for adjusting the weights so as to yield a network that computes almost any function—that is, any vector-to-vector transformation—that one might desire. In fact, one can even impose on it a function one is unable to specify, so long as one can supply a set of examples of the desired input-output pairs. This process, called "training up the network," proceeds by successive adjustment of the network's weights until it performs the input-output transformations desired.

Although this model network vastly oversimplifies the structure of the brain, it does illustrate several important ideas. First, a parallel architecture provides a dramatic speed advantage over a conventional computer, for the many synapses at each level perform many small computations simultaneously instead of in laborious sequence. This advantage gets larger as the number of neurons increases at each layer. Strikingly, the speed of processing is entirely independent of both the number of units involved in each layer and the complexity of the function they are computing. Each layer could have four units or a hundred million; its configuration of synaptic weights could be computing simple one-digit sums or second-order differential equations. It would make no difference. The computation time would be exactly the same.

Second, massive parallelism means that the system is fault-tolerant and functionally persistent; the loss of a few connections, even quite a few, has a negligible effect on the character of the overall transformation performed by the surviving network.

Third, a parallel system stores large amounts of information in a distributed fashion, any part of which can be accessed in milliseconds. That information is stored in the specific configuration of synaptic connection strengths, as shaped by past learning. Relevant information is "released" as the input vector passes through—and is transformed by—that configuration of connections.

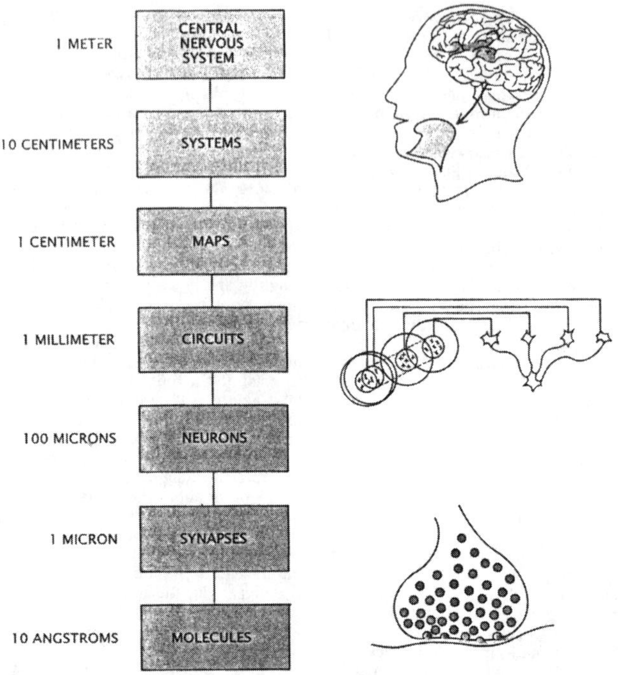

NERVOUS SYSTEMS span many scales of organization, from neurotransmitter molecules (*bottom*) to the entire brain and spinal cord. Intermediate levels include single neurons and circuits made up of a few neurons, such as those that produce orientation selectivity to a visual stimulus (*middle*), and systems made up of circuits such as those that subserve language (*top right*). Only research can decide how closely an artificial system must mimic the biological one to be capable of intelligence.

Parallel processing is not ideal for all types of computation. On tasks that require only a small input vector, but many millions of swiftly iterated recursive computations, the brain performs very badly, whereas classical SM machines excel. This class of computations is very large and important, so classical machines will always be useful, indeed, vital. There is, however, an equally large class of computations for which the brain's architecture is the superior technology. These are the computations that typically confront living creatures: recognizing a predator's outline in a noisy environment; recalling instantly how to avoid its gaze, flee its approach or fend off its attack; distinguishing food from nonfood and mates from nonmates; navigating through a complex and ever-changing physical/social environment; and so on.

Finally, it is important to note that the parallel system described is not manipulating symbols according to structure-sensitive rules. Rather symbol manipulation appears to be just one of many cognitive skills that a network may or may not learn to display. Rule-governed symbol manipulation is not its basic mode of operation. Searle's argument is directed against rule-governed SM machines; vector transformers of the kind we describe are therefore not threatened by his Chinese room argument even if it were sound, which we have found independent reason to doubt.

Searle is aware of parallel processors but thinks they too will be devoid of real semantic content. To illustrate their inevitable failure, he outlines a second thought experiment, the Chinese gym, which has a gymnasium full of people organized into a parallel network. From there his argument proceeds as in the Chinese room.

We find this second story far less responsive or compelling than his first. For one, it is irrelevant that no unit in his system understands Chinese, since the same is true of nervous systems: no neuron in my brain understands English, although my whole brain does. For another, Searle neglects to mention that his simulation (using one person per neuron, plus a fleet-footed child for each synaptic connection) will require at least 10^{14} people, since the human brain has 10^{11} neurons, each of which averages over 10^3 connections. His system will require the entire human populations of over 10,000 earths. One gymnasium will not begin to hold a fair simulation.

On the other hand, if such a system were to be assembled on a suitably cosmic scale, with all its pathways faithfully modeled on the human case, we might then have a large, slow, oddly made but still functional brain on our hands. In that case the default assumption is surely that, given proper inputs, it would think, not that it couldn't. There is no guarantee that its activity would constitute real thought, because the vector-processing theory sketched above may not be the correct theory of how brains work. But neither is there any a priori guarantee that it could not be thinking. Searle is once more mistaking the limits on his (or the reader's) current imagination for the limits on objective reality.

The brain is a kind of computer, although most of its properties remain to be discovered. Characterizing the brain as a kind of computer is neither trivial nor frivolous. The brain does compute functions, functions of great complexity, but not in the classical AI fashion. When brains are said to be computers, it should not be implied that they are serial, digital computers, that they are programmed, that they exhibit the distinction between hardware and software or that they must be symbol manipulators or rule followers. Brains are computers in a radically different style.

How the brain manages meaning is still unknown, but it is clear that the problem reaches beyond language use and beyond humans. A small mound of fresh dirt signifies to a person, and also to coyotes, that a gopher is around; an echo with a certain spectral character signifies to a bat the presence of a moth. To develop a theory of meaning, more must be known about how neurons code and transform sensory signals, about the neural basis of memory, learning and emotion and about the interaction of these capacities and the motor system. A neurally grounded theory of meaning may require revision of the very intuitions that now seem so secure and that are so freely exploited in Searle's arguments. Such revisions are common in the history of science.

Could science construct an artificial intelligence by exploiting what is known about the nervous system? We see no principled reason why not. Searle appears to agree, although he qualifies his claim by saying that "any other system capable of causing minds would have to have causal powers (at least) equivalent to those of brains." We close by addressing this claim. We presume that Searle is not claiming that a successful artificial mind must have *all* the causal powers of the brain, such as the power to smell bad when rotting, to harbor slow viruses such as kuru, to stain yellow with horseradish peroxidase and so forth. Requiring perfect parity would be like requiring that an artificial flying device lay eggs.

Presumably he means only to require of an artificial mind all of the causal powers relevant, as he says, to conscious intelligence. But which exactly are they? We are back to quarreling about what is and is not relevant. This is an entirely reasonable place for a disagreement, but it is an empirical matter, to be tried and tested. Because so little is known about what goes into the process of cognition and semantics, it is premature to be very confident about what features are essential. Searle hints at various points that every level, including the biochemical, must be represented in any machine that is a candidate for artificial intelligence. This claim is almost surely too strong. An artificial brain might use something other than biochemicals to achieve the same ends.

This possibility is illustrated by Carver A. Mead's research at the California Institute of Technology. Mead and his colleagues have used analog VLSI techniques to build an artificial retina and an artificial cochlea. (In animals the retina and cochlea are not mere transducers: both systems embody a complex processing network.) These are not mere simulations in a minicomputer of the kind that Searle derides; they are real information-processing units responding in real time to real light, in the case of the artificial retina, and to real sound, in the case of the artificial cochlea. Their circuitry is based on the known anatomy and physiology of the cat retina and the barn owl cochlea, and their output is dramatically similar to the known output of the organs at issue.

These chips do not use any neurochemicals, so neurochemicals are clearly not necessary to achieve the evident results. Of course, the artificial retina cannot be said to see anything, because its output does not have an artificial thalamus or cortex to go to. Whether Mead's program could be sustained to build an entire artificial brain remains to be seen, but there is no evidence now that the absence of biochemicals renders it quixotic.

We, and Searle, reject the Turing test as a sufficient condition for conscious intelligence. At one level our reasons for doing so are similar: we agree that it is also very important how the input-output function is achieved; it is important that the right sorts of things be going on inside the artificial machine. At another level, our reasons are quite different. Searle bases his position on commonsense intuitions about the presence or absence of semantic content. We base ours on the specific behavioral failures of the classical SM machines and on the specific virtues of machines with a more brainlike architecture. These contrasts show that certain computational strategies have vast and decisive advantages over others where typical cognitive tasks are concerned, advantages that are empirically inescapable. Clearly, the brain is making systematic use of these computational advantages. But it need not be the only physical system capable of doing so. Artificial intelligence, in a nonbiological but massively parallel machine, remains a compelling and discernible prospect.

FURTHER READING

COMPUTING MACHINERY AND INTELLIGENCE. Alan M. Turing in *Mind*, Vol. 59, pages 433–460; 1950.

WHAT COMPUTERS CAN'T DO; A CRITIQUE OF ARTIFICIAL REASON. Hubert L. Dreyfus. Harper & Row, 1972.

NEUROPHILOSOPHY: TOWARD A UNIFIED UNDERSTANDING OF THE MIND/BRAIN. Patricia Smith Churchland. The MIT Press, 1986.

FAST THINKING in *The Intentional Stance*. Daniel Clement Dennett. The MIT Press, 1987.

A NEUROCOMPUTATIONAL PERSPECTIVE: THE NATURE OF MIND AND THE STRUCTURE OF SCIENCE. Paul M. Churchland. The MIT Press, in press.

On Implementing a Computation

DAVID J. CHALMERS
Department of Philosophy, Washington University, St. Louis, Missouri 63130, U.S.A.
(dave@twinearth.wustl.edu)

Abstract. To clarify the notion of computation and its role in cognitive science, we need an account of implementation, the nexus between abstract computations and physical systems. I provide such an account, based on the idea that a physical system implements a computation if the causal structure of the system mirrors the formal structure of the computation. The account is developed for the class of combinatorial-state automata, but is sufficiently general to cover all other discrete computational formalisms. The implementation relation is non-vacuous, so that criticisms by Searle and others fail. This account of computation can be extended to justify the foundational role of computation in artificial intelligence and cognitive science.

Key words. Computation, implementation, artificial intelligence, cognition, Turing machines.

1. Introduction

Much of modern cognitive science centers on the notion of computation, but many questions about computation remain unclear. What is it for a physical object to implement a computation? Does implementing an appropriate computation suffice for the possession of a mind? Does every cognitive system have a computational basis? These are among the most controversial questions in the foundations of cognitive science.

The mathematical theory of computation in the abstract is well-understood, but cognitive science and artificial intelligence go beyond the domain of abstract objects to deal with concrete systems in the physical world. The difficult questions about computation are largely questions about the relationship between these domains. How does the abstract theory of computation relate to a science of concrete, causal systems, and how might it help us explain cognition in the real world? To answer these questions, we need a bridge between the abstract and the concrete domains.

The crucial element of such a bridge is a theory of *implementation*. Implementation is the relation that holds between an abstract computational object (a *computation* for short) and a physical system, such that we can say that in some sense the system "realizes" the computation, and that the computation "describes" the system. The key question that such a theory needs to answer is *what are the conditions under which a physical system implements a given computation*? Without an answer to this question, the foundational role of computation in cognitive science cannot be justified.

Searle (1990) has argued that there is no objective answer to this question, and that any given system can be seen to implement any computation if interpreted

Minds and Machines **4**: 391–402, 1995.

appropriately. He argues, for instance, that his wall can be seen to implement the Wordstar program. If this is right, then it is hard to see how computation can play a foundational role in cognitive science. If there is no objective fact of the matter about whether a system implements a given computation, then we cannot appeal to the fact that a system implements a computation in explaining any of its objective properties. It would follow, for example, that unless a strong form of panpsychism is true, there is no computation such that implementing that computation suffices for the possession of a mind.

I will argue that there is no reason for such pessimism, and that a theory of implementation can be straightforwardly spelled out. Such an account can give perfectly objective criteria for when a physical system implements a given computation, such that any given computation will only be implemented by a small fraction of physical systems. With such an account in place, the path is cleared to justify the foundational role of computation in the science of the mind.

2. Implementation

When does a physical system implement a given computation? The short answer to this is straightforward.

> A physical system implements a given computation when the causal structure of the physical system mirrors the formal structure of the computation.

In a little more detail, this comes to:

> A physical system implements a given computation when there exists a grouping of physical states of the system into state-types and a one-to-one mapping from formal states of the computation to physical state-types, such that formal states related by an abstract state-transition relation are mapped onto physical state-types related by a corresponding causal state-transition relation.

There is still a little vague. To spell it out fully, we must specify the class of computations in question. Computations are generally specified within some formalism, and there are many different formalisms: these include the formalisms of Turing machines, Pascal programs, cellular automata, and connectionist networks, among others. The story about implementation is similar for each of these; only the details differ. All of these can be subsumed under the class of *combinatorial-state automata* (CSAs), which I will outline shortly, but for the purposes of illustration I will first deal with the special case of *simple finite-state automata* (FSAs).

An FSA is specified by giving a set of input states $I_1, \ldots, I_k$, a set of internal states $S_1, \ldots, S_m$, and a set of output states $O_1, \ldots, O_n$, along with a set of state-transition relations of the form $(S, I) \rightarrow (S', O')$, for each pair (S, I) of internal states and input states, where S' and O' are an internal state and an output state respectively. S and I can be thought of as the "old" internal state and the input at a given time; S' is the "new" internal state, and O' is the output produced at that time. (There are some variations in the ways this can be spelled out—e.g. one need not include outputs at each time step, and it is common to designate some internal state as a "final" state—but these variations are unimportant for our purposes.) The conditions for the *implementation* of an FSA are the following:

> A physical system P implements an FSA M if there is a mapping f that maps internal states of P to internal states of M, inputs to P to input states of M, and outputs of P to output states of M, such that: for every state-transition relation $(S, I) \rightarrow (S', O')$ of M, the following conditional holds: if P is in internal state s and receiving input i where $f(s) = S$ and $f(i) = I$, this reliably causes it to enter internal state s' and produce output o' such that $f(s') = S'$ and $f(o') = O'$.[1]

This definition uses maximally specific physical states s rather than the grouped state-types referred to above. The state-types can be recovered, however: each corresponds to a set $\{s \mid f(s) = S_i\}$, for each $S_i \in M$. From here we can see that the definitions are equivalent. The causal relations between physical state-types will precisely mirror the abstract relations between formal states.

There is a lot of room to play with the details of this definition. For example, it is generally useful to put restrictions on the way that inputs and outputs to the system map onto input and outputs of the FSA. We also need not map *all* possible internal states of P, if some are not reachable from certain initial states. These matters are unimportant here, however. What is important is the overall form of the definition: in particular, the way it ensures that the formal state-transitional structure of the computation mirrors the causal state-transitional structure of the physical system. This is what all definitions of implementation, in any computational formalism, will have in common.

I take it that something like this is the "standard" definition of implementation of a finite-state automaton; see, for example, the definition of the description of a system by a probabilistic automaton in Putnam (1967). It is surprising, however, how little space has been devoted to accounts of implementation in the literature in theoretical computer science, philosophy of psychology, and cognitive science, considering how central the notion of computation is to these fields.

3. Combinatorial-state Automata

Simple finite-state automata are unsatisfactory for many purposes, due to the monadic nature of their states. The states in most computational formalisms have a combinatorial structure: a cell pattern in a cellular automaton, a combination of tape-state and head-state in a Turing machine, variables and registers in a Pascal program, and so on. All this can be accommodated within the framework of combinatorial-state automata (CSAs), which differ from FSAs only in that an internal state is specified not by a monadic label S, but by a vector $[S^1, S^2, S^3, \ldots]$. The elements of this vector can be thought of as the components of the overall state, such as the cells in a cellular automaton or the tape-squares in a Turing machine. There are a finite number of possible values S^i_j for each element S^i, where S^i_j is the jth possible value for the ith element. These values can be thought of as "substates". Inputs and outputs can have a similar sort of complex structure: an input vector is $[I^1, \ldots, I^k]$, and so on. State-transition rules are determined by specifying, for each element of the state-vector, a function by which its new state depends on the old overall state-vector and input-vector, and the same for each element of the output-vector.

Input and output vectors are always finite, but the internal state vectors can be either finite or infinite. The finite case is simpler, and is all that is required for any practical purposes. Even if we are dealing with Turing machines, a Turing machine with a tape limited to 10^{200} squares will certainly be all that is required for simulation or emulation within cognitive science and AI. The infinite case can be spelled out in an analogous fashion, however. The main complication is that restrictions have to be placed on the vectors and dependency rules, so that these do not encode an infinite amount of information. This is not too difficult, but I will not go into details here.

The conditions under which a physical system implements a CSA are analogous to those for an FSA. The main difference is that internal states of the system need to be specified as vectors, where each element of the vector corresponds to an independent element of the physical system. A natural requirement for such a decomposition is that each element correspond to a distinct physical region within the system, although there may be other alternatives. The same goes for the complex structure of inputs and outputs. The system implements a given CSA if there exists such a vectorization of states of the system, and a mapping from elements of those vectors onto corresponding elements of the vectors of the CSA, such that the state-transition relations are isomorphic in the obvious way. The details can be filled in straightforwardly, as follows:

> A physical system P implements a CSA M if there is a decomposition of internal states of P into components $[s^1, s^2, \ldots]$, and a mapping f from the substates s^j into corresponding substates S^j of M, along with similar decompositions and mappings for inputs and outputs, such that for every state-transition rule $([I^1, \ldots, I^k], [S^1, S^2, \ldots]) \rightarrow ([S'^1, S'^2, \ldots], [O^2, \ldots, O^l])$ of M: if P is in internal state $[s^1, s^2, \ldots]$ and receiving input $[i^i, \ldots, i^n]$ which map to formal state and input $[S^1, S^2, \ldots]$ and $[I^1, \ldots, I^k]$ respectively, this reliably causes it to enter an internal state and produce an output that map to $[S'^1, S'^2, \ldots]$ and $[O^1, \ldots, O^l]$ respectively.

Once again, further constraints might be added to this definition for various purposes, and there is much that can be said to flesh out the definition's various parts; a detailed discussion of these technicalities must await another forum (see Chalmers 1993 for a start). This definition is not the last word in a theory of implementation, but it captures the theory's basic form.

One might think that CSAs are not much of an advance on FSAs. Finite CSAs, at least, are no more computationally powerful than FSAs; there is a natural correspondence that associates every finite CSA with an FSA with the same input/output behavior. Of course infinite CSAs (such as Turing machines) are more powerful, but even leaving that reason aside, there are a number of reasons why CSAs are a more suitable formalism for our purposes than FSAs.

First, the *implementation* conditions on a CSA are much more constrained than those of the corresponding FSA. An implementation of a CSA is required to consist in a complex causal interaction among a number of separate parts; a CSA description can therefore capture the causal organization of a system to a much finer grain. Second, the structure in CSA states can be of great *explanatory* utility. A description of a physical system as a CSA will often be much more illuminating than a description as the corresponding FSA. Third, CSAs reflect in a much more direct way the formal organization of such familiar computational objects as Turing machines, cellular automata, and the like. Finally, the CSA framework allows a unified account of the implementation conditions for both finite and infinite machines.

This definition can straightforwardly be applied to yield implementation conditions for more specific computational formalisms. To develop an account of the implementation-conditions for a Turing machine, say, we need only redescribe the Turing machine as a CSA. The overall state of a Turing machine can be seen as a giant vector, consisting of (a) the internal state of the head, and (b) the state of each square of the tape, where this state in turn is an ordered pair of a symbol and a flag indicating whether the square is occupied by the head (of course only one square can be so occupied; this will be ensured by restrictions on initial state and on state-transition rules). The state-transition rules between vectors can be derived naturally from the quintuples specifying the behavior of the machine-head. As usually understood, Turing machines only take inputs at a single time-step (the start), and do not produce any output separate from the contents of the tape. These restrictions can be overridden in natural ways, for example by adding separate input and output tapes, but even with inputs and outputs limited in this way there is a natural description as a CSA. Given this translation from the Turing machine formalism to the CSA formalism, we can say that a given Turing machine is implemented whenever the corresponding CSA is implemented.

A similar story holds for computations in other formalisms. Some formalisms, such as cellular automata, are even more straightforward. Others, such as Pascal programs, are more complex, but the overall principles are the same. In each case there is some room for maneuver, and perhaps some arbitrary decisions to make (does writing a symbol and moving the head count as two state-transitions or one?) but little rests on the decisions we make. We can also give accounts of implementation for nondeterministic and probabilistic automata, by making simple changes in the definition of a CSA and the corresponding account of implementation. The theory of implementation for combinatorial-state automata provides a basis for the theory of implementation in general.

4. Questions Answered

The above account may look complex, but the essential idea is very simple: the relation between an implemented computation and an implementing system is one of isomorphism between the formal structure of the former and the causal structure of the latter. In this way, we can see that as far as the theory of implementation is concerned, a computation is simply an *abstract specification of causal organization*.

This account can be brought to bear to answer various questions bout computation and implementation. I will also address some potential objections to the account.

DOES EVERY SYSTEM IMPLEMENT SOME COMPUTATION?

Yes. For example, every physical system will implement the simple FSA with a single internal state; most physical systems will implement the 2-state cyclic FSA, and so on. This is no problem, and certainly does not render the account vacuous. That would only be the case if every system implemented *every* computation, and that is not the case.

DOES EVERY SYSTEM IMPLEMENT ANY GIVEN COMPUTATION?

No. The conditions for implementing a given complex computation—say, a CSA whose state-vectors have 1000 elements, with 10 possibilities for each element and complex state-transition relations—will generally be sufficiently rigorous that extremely few physical systems will meet them. What is required is not just a mapping from states of the system onto states of the CSA, as Searle (1990) effectively suggests. The added requirement that the mapped states must satisfy reliable state-transition rules is what does all the work. In this case, there will effectively be at least 10^{1000} constraints on state-transitions (one for each possible state-vector, and more if there are multiple possible inputs). Each constraint will specify one out of at least 10^{1000} possible consequents (one for each possible resultant state-vector, and more if there are outputs). The chance that an arbitrary set of states will satisfy these constraints is something less than one in $(10^{1000})^{10^{1000}}$ (actually significantly less, because of the requirement that transitions be reliable). There is no reason to suppose that the causal structure of an arbitrary system (such as Searle's wall) will satisfy these constraints. It is true that while we lack knowledge of the fundamental constituents of matter, it is impossible to *prove* that arbitrary objects do not implement every computation (perhaps every proton has an infinitely rich internal structure), but anybody who denies this conclusion will need to come up with a remarkably strong argument.

CAN A GIVEN SYSTEM IMPLEMENT MORE THAN ONE COMPUTATION?

Yes. Any system implementing some complex computation will simultaneously be implementing many simpler computations—not just 1-state and 2-state FSAs, but computations of some complexity. This is not a flaw in the current account; it is precisely what we should expect. The system on my deck is currently implementing all kinds of computations, from EMACS to a clock program, and various sub-computations of these. In general, there is no canonical mapping from a physical object to "the" computation it is performing. We might say that within every physical system, there are numerous computational systems. To this very limited extent, the notion of implementation is "interest-relative". Once again, however, there is no threat of vacuity. The question of whether a given system implements a given computation is still entirely objective. What counts is that a given system does not implement *every* computation, or to put the point differently, that most given computations are only implemented by a very limited class of physical systems. This is what is required for a substantial foundation for AI and cognitive science, and it is what the account I have given provides.

IF EVEN DIGESTION IS A COMPUTATION, ISN'T THIS VACUOUS?

This objection expresses the feeling that if every process, including such things as digestion and oxidation, implements some computation, then there seems to be nothing special about cognition any more, as computation is so pervasive. This objection rests on a misunderstanding. It is true that any given *instance* of digestion will implement some computation, as any physical system does, but the system's implementing this computation is in general irrelevant to its being an instance of digestion. To see this, we can note that the same computation could have been implemented by various other physical systems (such as my SPARC) without it's being an instance of digestion. Therefore the fact that the system implements the computation is not responsible for the existence of digestion in the system.

With cognition, by contrast, the claim is that it is *in virtue* of implementing some computation that a system is cognitive. That is, there is a certain class of computations such that *any* system implementing that computation is cognitive. We might go further and argue that every cognitive system implements some computation such that any implementation of the computation would also be cognitive, and would share numerous specific mental properties with the original system. These claims are controversial, of course, but it is precisely this relation between computation and cognition that gives bite to the computational analysis of cognition. If this relation or something like it did not hold, the computational status of cognition would be analogous to that of digestion.

WHAT ABOUT PUTNAM'S ARGUMENT?

Putnam (1988) has suggested that on a definition like this, almost any physical system can be seen to implement every finite-state automaton. He argues for this conclusion by demonstrating that there will almost always be a mapping from physical states of a system to internal states of an FSA, such that over a given time-period (from 12:00 to 12:10 today, say) the transitions between states are just as the machine table say they should be. If the machine table requires that state *A* be followed by state *B*, then every instance of state *A* is followed by state *B* in this time period. Such a mapping will be possible for an inputless FSA under the assumption that physical states do not repeat. We simply map the initial physical state of the system onto an intial formal state of the computation, and map successive states of the system onto successive states of the computation.

However, to suppose that this system implements the FSA in question is to misconstrue the state-transition conditionals in the definition of implementation. What is required is not simply that state *A* be followed by state *B* on all instances in which it happens to come up in a given time-period. There must be a reliable, counterfactual-supporting connection between the states. Given a formal state-transition $A \rightarrow B$, it must be the case that *if* the system were to be in state *A*, it would transit to state *B*. Further, such a conditional must be satisfied for *every* transition in the machine table, not just for those whose antecedent states happen to come up in a given time period. It is easy to see that Putnam's system does not satisfy this much stronger requirement. In effect, Putnam has required only that certain weak material conditionals be satisfied, rather than conditionals with modal force. For this reason, his purported implementations are not implementations at all.

(Two notes. First, Putnam responds briefly to the charge that his system fails to support counterfactuals, but considers a different class of counterfactuals—those of the form "if the system had not been in state *A*, it would not have transited to state *B*". It is not these counterfactuals that are relevant here. Second, it turns out that Putnam's argument for the widespread realization of inputless FSAs can be patched up in a certain way; this just goes to show that inputless FSAs are an inappropriate formalism for cognitive science, due to their complete lack of combinatorial structure. Putnam gives a related argument for the widespread realization of FSAs with input and output, but this argument is strongly vulnerable to an objection like the one above, and cannot be patched up in an analogous way. CSAs are even less vulnerable to this sort of argument. I discuss all this at much greater length in Chalmers (forthcoming).)

WHAT ABOUT SEMANTICS?

It will be noted that nothing in my account of computation and implementation invokes any semantic considerations, such as the representational content of internal states. This is precisely as it should be: computations are specified syntactically, not semantically. Although it may very well be the case that any implementations of a given computation share some kind of semantic content, this should be a *consequence* of an account of computation and implementation, rather than built into the definition. If we build semantic considerations into the conditions for implementation, any role that computation can play in providing a foundation for AI and cognitive science will be endangered, as the notion of semantic content is so ill-understood that it desperately needs a foundation itself.

The original account of Turing machines by Turing (1936) had no semantic constraints built in. A Turing machine is defined purely in terms of the mechanisms involved, that is, in terms of syntactic patterns and the way they are transformed. At most, a semantic interpretation is sometimes imposed on the inputs and outputs, in order to interpret a Turing machine as computing a given arithmetical function, but this does not add any constraints on implementation. To implement a Turing machine, we need only ensure that the relevant formal structure is reflected in the causal structure of the implementation. Some Turing machines will support a systematic semantic interpretation, in which case their implementations will also, but this plays no part in the definition of what it is to be or to implement a Turing machine. This is made particularly clear if we note that there are some Turing machines, such as machines defined by random sets of state-transition quintuples, that support no non-trivial semantic interpretation. We need an account of what it is to implement these machines, and such an account will then generalize to machines that support a semantic interpretation. Certainly, when computer designers ensure that their machines implement the programs that they are supposed to, they do this by ensuring that the mechanisms have the right causal organization; they are not concerned with semantic content. In the words of Haugeland (1985), if you take care of the syntax, the semantics will take care of itself.

I have said that the notion of computation should not be dependent on that of semantic content; neither do I think that the latter notion should be dependent on the former. Rather, both computation and content should be dependent on the common notion of *causation*. We have seen the first dependence in the account of computation above. The notion of content has also been frequently analyzed in terms of causation (e.g. Dretske 1981 and Fodor 1987). This common pillar in the analyses of both computation and content allows that the two notions will not sway independently, while at the same time ensuring that neither is dependent on the other for its analysis.

WHAT ABOUT COMPUTERS?

Although Searle (1990) talks about what it takes for something to be a "digital computer", I have talked only about computations and eschewed reference to computers. This is deliberate, as it seems to me that computation is the more fundamental notion, and certainly the one that is important for AI and cognitive science. AI and cognitive science certainly do not require that cognitive systems be computers, unless we stipulate that all it takes to be a computers is to implement some computation, in which case the definition is vacuous.

What does it take for something to be a computer? Presumably, a computer cannot merely implement a single computation. It must be capable of implementing many computations—that is, it must be *programmable*. In the extreme case, a computer will be universal, capable of being programmed to compute any recursively enumerable function. Perhaps universality is not required of a computer, but programmability certainly is. To bring computers within the scope of the theory of implementation above, we could require that a computer be a CSA with certain parameters, such that depending on how these parameters are set, a number of different CSAs can be implemented. A universal Turing machine could be seen in this light, for instance, where the parameters correspond to the "program" symbols on the tape. In any case, such a theory of computers is not required for the study of cognition.

Is the brain a computer in this sense? Arguably. For a start, the brain can be "programmed" to implement various computations by the laborious means of conscious serial rule-following; but this is a fairly incidental ability. On a different level, it might be argued that learning provides a certain kind of programmability and parameter-setting, but this is a sufficiently indirect kind of parameter-setting that it might be argued that it does not qualify. In any case, the question is quite unimportant for our purposes. What counts is that the brain implements various complex computations, not that it is a computer.

5. Conclusion

An account of implementation is only half the story. The question remains open: *What is the relationship between computation and cognition*? This is an entirely different sort of question, but an account of implementation is vital in answering it. Without a bridge between the abstract domain of computation and the concrete domain of cognitive systems, such questions are out of our reach. With a bridge in place, however, there is the possibility of progress.

I discuss this matter at much greater length elsewhere (Chalmers 1994), but we can see very briefly the shape of an answer. According to the account I have given here, a computational description of a physical system is an *abstract specification of its causal organization.* To implement a computation is just to have a set of components that interact causally according to a certain pattern. The nature of the components does not matter, and nor does the way that the causal links between components are implemented; all that matters is the pattern of causal organization of the system. What do all implementations of a given computation have in common? Precisely their causal organization. Further, almost any causal organization we can imagine can be captured by a computational description. As long as a system's causal organization can be analyzed into a finite number of parts interacting in a finitely specifiable way, this organization can be abstracted into a CSA description, or perhaps a description within some other computational formalism.

We can therefore use the notion of causal organization as the central pivot in justifying the foundational role of computation in cognitive science. For example, the thesis of "strong artificial intelligence" holds that implementation of certain sorts of computation suffices for possession of a mind. With an account of implementation in place, this thesis can be justified in two steps. First, argue that implementation of a given computation suffices for possession of a given causal organization; second, argue that possession of the appropriate sort of causal organization suffices for the possession of a mind. The first step has been taken already. The second step is trickier, but it is not hard to imagine how it might go.

We can also use this account to justify the *explanatory* centrality of computation in cognitive science. It is independently plausible that the properties of a cognitive system that are most directly relevant to the explanation of its behavior and of its cognitive capacities are properties of its causal organization. Neurophysiological properties and the like are relevant, but only insofar as they play a role in determining the pattern of causal organization of the system. And on the account I have given, computation provides a perfect language for the description of causal organization. Descriptions of a system in computational terms are in effect descriptions of its causal organization, and are therefore descriptions of precisely the aspects of the system that are most relevant in the explanation of its cognitive capacities.

In this way, we can see why computation is such a valuable tool in cognitive science. Almost any theory of cognitive processes is ultimately a theory of causal organization, and computational descriptions are flexible enough to capture causal organization of almost any kind. Thus, computation is central in such diverse approaches to the modeling of cognition as the symbol-processing approach, connectionism, and artificial life. To embrace any one of these approaches is to make a bold empirical hypothesis, but to embrace the computational approach to the mind is not. If the mind can be understood in terms of a finite causal organization, it can be understood computationally. Computation is central to the study of the mind precisely because it provides a flexible, almost universal framework for the expression and analysis of causal organization.

References

Chalmers, D. J. (forthcoming), 'Does a Rock Implement Every Finite-state Automaton?' *Synthese.*

Chalmers, D. J. (1994), 'A Computational Foundation for the Study of Cognition', Philosophy-Neuroscience-Psychology Technical Report 94-03, Washington University.

Dretske, F. (1981), *Knowledge and the Flow of Information*, MIT Press.

Fodor, J. A. (1987), *Psychosemantics: The Problem of Meaning in the Philosophy of Mind*, MIT Press.

Haugeland, J. (1985), *Artificial intelligence: The Very Idea.* MIT Press.

Putnam, H. (1967), 'The Nature of Mental States', in W.H. Capitan and D.D. Merrill (eds.), *Art, Mind, and Religion*, University of Pittsburgh Press.

Putnam, H. (1988), *Representation and Reality*, MIT Press.

Pylyshyn, Z. W. (1984), *Computation and Cognition: Toward a Foundation for Cognitive Science*, MIT Press.

Searle, J. R. (1980), 'Minds, Brains and Programs', *Behavioral and Brain Science* **3**, 417–57.

Searle, J. R. (1990), 'Is the Brain a Digital Computer?', *Proceedings and Addresses of the American Philosophical Association* **64**, 21–37.

Searle, J. R. (1991), *The Rediscovery of the Mind*, MIT Press.

Turing, A. M. (1936), 'On Computable Numbers, with the Application to the Entscheidungsproblem', *Proceedings of the London Mathematical Society, Series 2* **42**, 230–65.

YOU CAN'T PLAY 20 QUESTIONS WITH NATURE AND WIN: PROJECTIVE COMMENTS ON THE PAPERS OF THIS SYMPOSIUM

Allen Newell
Carnegie-Mellon University

I am a man who is half and half. Half of me is half distressed and half confused. Half of me is quite content and clear on where we are going.

My confused and distressed half has been roused by my assignment to comment on the papers of this symposium. It is curious that it should be so. We have just listened to a sample of the best work in current experimental psychology. For instance, the beautifully symmetric RT data of Cooper and Shepard (Chapter 3) make me positively envious. It is a pleasure to watch Dave Klahr (Chapter 1) clean up the subitizing data. The demonstrations of Bransford and Johnson (Chapter 8) produce a special sort of impact. And so it goes. Furthermore, independent of the particular papers presented here, the speakers constitute a large proportion of my all-time favorite experimenters--Chase, Clark, Posner, Shepard. Not only this, but almost all of the material shown here serves to further a view of man as a processor of information, agreeing with my current theoretical disposition. Half of me is ecstatic.

Still, I am distressed. I can illustrate it by the way I was going to start my comments, though I could not in fact bring myself to do so. I was going to draw a line on the blackboard and, picking one of the speakers of the day at random, note on the line the time at which he got his PhD and the current time (in mid-career). Then, taking his total production of papers like those in the present symposium, I was going to compute a rate of productivity of such excellent work. Moving, finally, to the date of my chosen target's retirement, I was going to compute the total future additon of such papers to the (putative) end of this man's scientific career. Then I was going to pose, in my role as discussant, a question: Suppose you had all those additional papers, just like those of today (except being on new aspects of the problem), *where will psychology then be?* Will we have achieved a science of man adequate in power and commensurate with his complexity? And if so, how will this have happened via these papers that I have just granted you? Or will we be asking for yet another quota of papers in the next dollop of time?

Such an approach seems fairly harsh, expecially to visit upon visitors. It almost made me subtitle my comments "The Time of the Walrus," as those of you who know their Alice Through the Looking Glass can appreciate. The Walrus and the Carpenter invited a passel of oysters to take a pleasant walk with them--and ended up having them for lunch. Thus, I thought I'd try a different way.

Detection

Psychology, in its current style of operation, deals with phenomena. Looking just at the local scene, we have Cooper and Shepard dealing with the phenomenon of apparent rotation, Posner (Chapter 2) dealing with the phenomenon of coding, Klahr dealing with the phenomenon of subitizing, and so on. There is, today, an amazing number of such phenomena that we deal with. The number is so large it scares me. Figure 1 gives a list of some--hardly all--that I generated in a few minutes. With each I've associated a name or two, not so much as originators (for this is not a scholarly review I am writing), but simply as an aid to identification.

How are these phenomena dealt with by Experimental Psychology, once brought into existence by some clever experimental discovery? Every time we find a new phenomenon--every time we find PI release, or marking, or linear search, or what-not--we produce a flurry of experiments to investigate it. We explore what it is

PHENOMENA

1. Physical - name match difference (Posner)
2. Continuous rotation effect (Shepard)
3. Subitizing (Klahr)
4. Chess position perception (DeGroot)
5. Chunks in STM (Miller)
6. Recency effect in free recall (Murdock)
7. Instructions to forget (Bjork)
8. PI release (Wickens)
9. Linear search in sets in STM (Sternberg)
10. Non-improvement of STM search on success (Sternberg)
11. Linear search on displays (Neisser)
12. Non-difference of single and multiple targets in display search (Neisser)
13. Rapid STM loss with interpolated task (Peterson and Peterson)
14. Acoustic confusions in STM (Conrad)
15. High recognition rates for large set of pictures (Teghtsoonian and Shepard)
16. Visual icon (Sperling)
17. LTM hierarchy (Collins and Quillian)
18. LTM principle of economy (Collins and Quillian)
19. Successive versus paired recall in dichotic listening (Broadbent)
20. Click shift in linguistic expressions (Ladefoged and Broadbent)
21. Consistent extra delay for negation (Wason)
22. Saturation effect on constrained free recall (?)
23. Conservative probabilitistic behavior (Edwards)
24. Clustering in free recall (Bousefield)
25. Constant recall per category in free recall (Tulving)
26. Serial position effect in free recall (?)
27. Backward associations (Ebenholtz and Asch)
28. Einstellung (Luchins)
29. Functional fixity (Dunker)
30. Two-state concept models (all or none learning) (Bower and Trabasso)

Fig. 1. A partial list of psychological phenomena and investigators (parentheses).

a function of, and the combinational variations flow from our experimental laboratories. Each of the items in Figure 1 has been the source of such a flurry. I insisted on knowing at least one "second study" in order to include the item in the figure; in general there are many more. Those phenomena form a veritable horn of plenty for our experimental life--the spiral of

PHENOMENA (cont'd)

31. Concept difficulty ordering: conjunct, disjunct, cond, ... (Hovland)
32. Reversal learning (Kendlers)
33. von Restorff effect
34. Log dependency in disjunctive RT
35. Forward masking
36. Backward masking
37. Correlation between RT and EEG
38. Moon illusion (Boring)
39. Perceptual illusions (Mueller-Lyer, etc.)
40. Ambiguous figures (Necker cube)
41. Cyclopean perception (Julesz)
42. Imagery and recall (Pavio)
43. Constant time learning (Murdock, Bugelski)
44. Probability matching (Humphreys)
45. Transmission capacity in bits (Quastler)
46. Pupillary response to interest (Hess)
47. Stabilized images (Ditchburn)
48. Meaningful decay of the stabilized image (Hebb)
49. Categorical concepts (phonemes) (Lieberman)
50. Effect of marking (Clark)
51. Negative effect in part-whole free recall learning (Tulving)
52. Storage of semantic content over linguistic expression (Bransford)
53. Information addition (Anderson)
54. Induced chunking (Neal Johnson, Gregg and McLean)
55. Rehearsal
56. Repetitive eye scanning (Noton and Stark)
57. Positive effects of redundancy on learning (syntactic, semantic)
58. Effects of sentence transformations on recall (Miller)
59. Effect of irrelevant dimensions in concept learning (Restle)

Fig. 1 (continued).

the horn itself growing all the while it pours forth the requirements for secondary experiments.

Do not let my description put you off. Such fecundity is a sign of vitality. We do not stay, like the medieval scholastics, forever notating and annotating the same small set of questions. The phenomena are assuredly real, the investigations surely warrented to verify their reality and confirm their nature.

Psychology also attempts to conceptualize what it is doing, as a guide to investigating these phenomena. How do we do that? Mostly, so it seems to me, by the construction of oppositions--usually binary ones. We worry about nature versus nurture, about central versus peripheral, about serial versus parallel, and so on. To bring this point home, I give in Figure 2 a list of oppositions that have currency in psychology. These issues, I claim--about whether one or the other characterizes or explains some phenomenon--serve to drive a large part of the experimental endeavor. There are, to be sure, a few strands of theory of a different stripe, where the theory strives for some kind of quantitative explanation over a class of phenomena, parametrically expressed. I do not wish to deny these studies; neither do they dominate the current style of research enough to quiet my concern.

I stand by my assertion that the two constructs that drive our current experimental style are (1) at a low level, the discovery and empirical exploration of phenomena such as are shown in Figure 1; and (2) at the middle level, the formulation of questions to be put to nature that center on the resolution of binary oppositions. At the high level of grand theory, we may be driven by quite general concerns: to explore development; to discover how language is used; to show that man is a processor of information; to show he is solely analysable in terms of contingencies of reinforcement responded to. But it is through the mediation of these lower two levels that we generate our actual experiments and give our actual explanations. Indeed, psychology with its penchant for being explicit about its methodology has created special terms, such as "orienting attitudes" and "pretheoretical dispositions," to convey the large distance that separates the highest levels of theory from the immediate decisions of day to day science.

Accept this view, then for the moment, despite the fact that psychology like all human endeavors is too diverse to be forced into such an iron maiden. Suppose that in the next thirty years we continued as we are now going. Another hundred phenomena, give or take a

BINARY OPPOSITIONS

1. Nature versus nurture
2. Peripheral versus central
3. Continuous versus all-or-none learning
4. Uniprocess versus duoprocess learning (Harlow)
5. Single memory versus dual memory (STM-LTM) (Melton)
6. Massed versus distributed practice
7. Serial versus parallel processing
8. Exhaustive versus self-terminating search
9. Spatial logic versus deep structure
10. Analog versus digital
11. Single code versus multiple codes
12. Contextual versus independent interpretation
13. Trace decay versus interference forgetting
14. Stages versus continuous development
15. Innate versus learned grammars (Chomsky)
16. Existence versus non-existence of latent learning
17. Existence versus non-existence of subliminal perception
18. Grammars versus associations for language (reality of grammar)
19. Conscious versus unconscious
20. Channels versus categorizing in auditory perception (Broadbent)
21. Features versus templates
22. Motor versus pure perception in perceptual learning
23. Learning on non-error trials versus learning only on error trials
24. Preattentive versus attentive

Fig. 2. A partial list of binary oppositions in psychology.

few dozen, will have been discovered and explored. Another forty oppositions will have been posited and their resolution initiated. Will psychology then have come of age? Will it provide the kind of encompassing of its subject matter--the behavior of man--that we all posit as a characteristic of a mature science? And if so, how will the transformation be accomplished by this succession of phenomena and oppositions? Same question as before, just a different lead in.

As I examine the fate of our oppositions, looking at those already in existence as a guide to how they fare and shape the course of science, it seems to me that clarity is never achieved. Matters simply become

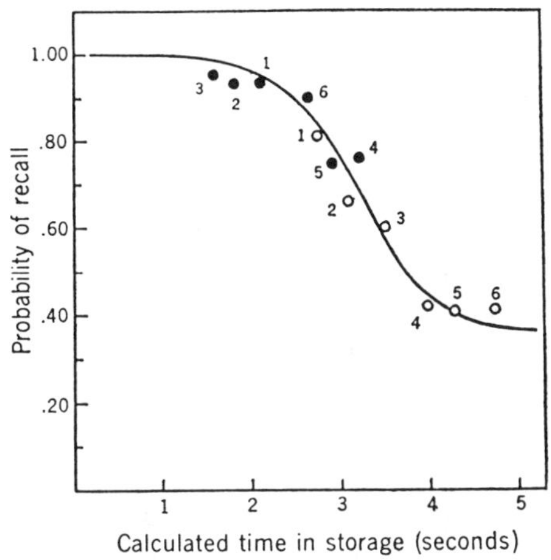

Fig. 3. Probability of recall of successive report (filled circles) and pair-by-pair report (open circles) as a function of storage time in STM (after Wingfield and Byrnes, 1972).

muddier and muddier as we go down through time. Thus, far from providing the rungs of a ladder by which psychology gradually climbs to clarity, this form of conceptual structure leads rather to an ever increasing pile of issues, which we weary of or become diverted from, but never really settle.

As I was preparing these comments an inadvertent illustration happened my way. The new *Science* came across my desk. Sure enough, there was an article by Wingfield and Byrnes (1972) entitled "Decay of Information in Short Term Memory." They are concerned with dichotic listening. The phenomenon is that if you hear a series of stimuli simultaneously in both ears at a rapid rate there are differences in the difficulty of reporting the stimuli, depending on how they are to be grouped. If the left ear gets stimuli L1, L2, L3 and the right ear R1, R2, R3, then *successive* reporting (L1, L2, L3, R1, R2, R3) is easier than so-called *simultaneous* reporting (L1, R1, L2, R2, L3, R3). The paper reports a new explanation for the phenomenon, which is most easily understood from Figure 3 (reproduced from their article). If one considers a uniform decay curve for memory, dependent only on the length of time an item is in short term memory, then both results follow from a detailed calculation of the lengths of time each item is in store. Thus, the grouping itself is not the operative consideration, but simply an indirect way of determining how long items must remain in memory, hence be subject to differential decay.

The original experiments showing the phenomenon and the original explanations, in terms of time to switch a channel go back 18 years to Broadbent (1958). Furthermore, this phenomenon of simultaneous versus sequential grouping has occasioned some hundreds of papers over the intervening years, in an attempt to clarify the issues (was it channel switching or not?). Now Wingfield and Byrnes provide yet one more explanation. Regardless of the exact merits of their case--and for my purposes here I need not judge them--it can be stated with confidence that their article does not settle the issue. Theirs is just one more entry in what seems like a forever ending series of so-called clarifying experiments. With due apologies to Wingfield and Byrnes for using their work in this way (it was in fact the random occurrence noted above), it provides good evidence for the general proposition that psychological issues have difficulty even fading away.

There is, I submit, a view of the scientific endeavor that is implicit (and sometimes explicit) in the picture I have presented above. Science advances by playing twenty questions with nature. The *proper* tactic is to frame a general question, hopefully binary, that can be attacked experimentally. Having settled that bits-worth, one can proceed to the next. The policy appears optimal--one never risks much, there is feedback from nature at every step, and progress is inevitable. Unfortunately, the questions never seem to be really answered, the strategy does not seem to work.

Of course I caricature. But I must get your attention. And the caricature is not so great as to be without merit.

Why do these considerations rise in me upon attempting to comment on the papers in this symposium?

First, I took as my assignment from Bill Chase to comment on them all, to the extent that I was able. To do so was probably a fateful error. Second, since I was playing the theorist, I adopted the set of trying to put them all together. *Put them all together.* No doubt a compounding of the error. For not only could I not put them all together, I did not see how they themselves were putting them all together. It was exceedingly clear that each paper made a contribution. I was not exaggerating when I asserted that we have witnessed here an exceptionally fine set of experimental results and theoretical interpretations based thereon. But as I tried to put them all together, I was led back from the particular results described to a set of results that these papers referenced and used, in a qualitative sort of way. These led me back to yet other papers, many by the same group of authors and of equal merit and precision. It became less and less clear to me that all these papers were cumulating. Only the barest fraction of each prior paper found its way into the next (though fortunately there were some exceptions), and these experiments I was considering (those today) seemed destined to play a similar role *vis à vis* the future.

As I considered the issues raised (single code versus multiple code, continuous versus discrete representation, etc.) I found myself conjuring up this model of the current scientific process in psychology--of phenomena to be explored and their explanation by essentially oppositional concepts. And I coundn't convince myself that it would add up, even in thirty more years of trying, even if one had another 300 papers of similar, excellent ilk.

In opting for worrying about this larger issue, I am not trying thereby to shirk my duty as a reviewer of the particular papers under consideration. (How often have I been annoyed as someone who was to review *my* paper simply took it as the opportunity to go his own way with what *he* wanted to talk about!) As an earnest of my good faith, I record herewith a sample of the direct responses generated by the specifics of the papers.

To Mike Posner: Certainly, I agree that there are multiple codes. That turns out to be almost a logical necessity. You certainly would seem to have knocked out one particular simple view. However, it would seem impossible, on the evidence that you present, to distinguish codes in the sense of the content of a representation with codes in the sense of implying separate boxes in an architectural memory structure.

To Lynn Cooper and Roger Shepard: I am extraordinarily impressed by your data. However, it seems to me quite unlikely that there is a physical process of continuous rotation involved. I do not take this belief from a general bias for discrete symbolic processing (though I have that bias). Much of what is known about the visual system tells us that it is like a sampled data system--that it doesn't work continuously either in space or time (Hubel & Wiesel, 1962; Stark, 1968). It would be surprising if (1) the visual system itself, considered as a tracking and eye-movement-controlling device, were a sampled data system, yet (2) inside that (that is, centerward from the processing of the stimulus) it became continuous again to deal with rotation. For the intuition behind the belief that rotation is to be accomplished by a continuous system is that the outside world is continuous and this should be mirrored in the internal mechanism.

To Bill Chase and Herb Simon: You have clearly established that there is a phenomenon associated with chess skill, and that we have a theory now to explain how this phenomenon could arise--and arise in chess masters to a degree that it would not in experts or beginners. This correlational fact, however, does not yet explain why chess masters are better chess

> players than beginners or experts. A natural theory is at hand given the type of theory provided; namely, a chess player will have specific actions associated with each pattern. (This is, in fact, the scheme proposed in Newell and Simon (1965) for guiding the tactical search, where the actions were functional move generators.) However, the theory as you present it only lays the groundwork for a theory of master level skill, and does not in any sense provide evidence for it. It requires that someone construct a program with such an arrangement and see if it plays as prescribed.

And so it might go. But it didn't seem to me to add up to much. What I wanted was for these excellent pieces of the experimental mosiac to add up to the psychology that we all wished to foresee. They didn't, not because of any lack of excellence locally, but because most of them seemed part of a pattern of psychological activity that didn't seem able to cumulate.

Diagnosis

Let me turn, then, from detection to diagnosis--from assertions that we have certain difficulties that are manifest in the current pattern of our research, to an attempt to say why that is the case.

On Methods

The most fundamental fact about behavior is that it is programmable. That is to say, behavior is under the control of the subject to shape in the service of his own ends. There is a sort of symbolic formula that we use in information processing psychology. To predict a subject you must know: (1) his goals; (2) the structure of the task environment; and (3) the invariant structure of his processing mechanisms. From this you can pretty well predict what methods are available to the subject; and from the method you can predict what the subject will do. Without these things, most importantly without the method, you cannot predict what he will do.

We may translate this assertion:[1]

> *First Injunction of Psychological Experimentation:* Know the method your subject is using to perform the experimental task.

Uncertainty over what method the subject is using drives a substantial amount of discussion of experimental results. It is quite in evidence in the present set of papers. Klahr's discussion of why the last point in his Figure 6 (Chapter 1) is a little lower hinges on asserting the subject knows there cannot be more than five elements so he can terminate the loop early. That is, it is argued that the subject has a special method that can capitalize timewise on a bit of knowledge that we know exists in the task environment.

In Cooper and Shepard's piece (Chapter 3) there is a similar concern, for instance, at what choices the subject is making at the bottom--whether to rotate to the left or right. In Chase and Simon's paper (Chapter 5), the entire data analysis rests, in some sense, on the method attributed to the subject for doing the tasks; and much of the side calculations (e.g., those on chunking) are done to confirm the method. Again, so it goes. In short, we are totally engaged, in psychological experimentation, in the discovery and verification of the specific methods used by the subject in doing the experimental tasks.

---

[1]An earlier form was the injunction to know the effective stimulus. The present formulation seems more adequate to the complexities of human behavior.

The above considerations lead directly to the next assertion:

> *Second Injunction of Psychological Experimentation:* Never average over methods.

To do so conceals, rather than reveals. You get garbage or, even worse, spurious regularity. The classic example of the failure to heed this injunction is the averaging of single-shot learning curves to yield continuous learning curves. However, we have two almost perfect examples in the present papers--perfect, not because an error was made, but because in each the authors provide data both before and after, so to speak, so one can appreciate the mis-interpretation, narrowly missed.

The first is the Cooper-Shepard data given in their Figure 5. It shows that RT is non-linear with angle of rotation. Their Figure 13 shows, however, that time is linear with angle. The explanation of the latter, as noted by Cooper and Shepard, is that it averages over all the different starting points. If they had settled for this latter data, having obtained it first, then the problem of interpretation of the non-linear curves would not have arisen--and we could have been led down a lovely garden path of over-simplified regularity.

The second example is from the Klahr paper. Gradually he purifies the subitizing data. At one stage (his Figure 5) we get the curve with a slope of 66 ms. However, he then separates out the instances with eye movement, leaving an additionally purified sample of response done with a single fixation and with a single subject: The slope drops to 25 ms per point in the subitizing set (his Figure 7). We are grateful for the unmixing of the methods. Can we assume to have touched bottom and that interpretation can now commence?

The point of all these remarks is that an immense amount of effort is devoted to such clarifications--that, in fact, much of the ability of the field continually and forever to dispute and question interpretations arises from the possibility of the subject's having done the task by a not-til-then-thought-of method or by the set of subjects having adopted a mixture of methods so the regularities produced were not what they seemed.

To put this in general terms again, our task in psychology is first to discover that structure which is fixed and invariant so that we can theoretically infer the method. Given the goal of the subject and the task environment which he faces, we can generate the (small) collection of methods that are likely to be used by him to perform the task (given his processing limits). Then, by means of careful design of the experiments or by suitable *post-hoc* analysis of the subject's performance we can settle what method he did indeed use. Without such a framework within which to work, the generation of new methods, hence new explanations, for old phenomena, will go on *ad nauseum*. There will be no discipline for it, as there is none now.

Let me push this branch of the diagnosis one step further. The papers of our symposium proceed by extracting for consideration a couple of mechanisms out of the totality of those required for the job. They then proceed by means of experimental technique to verify their existence, or to measure some of their properties (e.g., duration). Thus, Posner (Chapter 2) attempts (successfully, in my view) to deal with encoding of visual and auditory information, to determine whether they are the same. Sometimes more detail of a total process is presented: the flow diagrams in Cooper-Shepard, in Klahr, and in other presentations of Clark's work (Clark & Chase, 1972). These flow diagrams serve to assert the existence of an entire set of processing stages or components and some orderings between them.

All of the above, especially including the flow diagrams, represent major progress, both in our experimental technique and in our frameworks of interpretation. I am not here to challenge that. However, they have in common that they leave open the total method being used. They do not operate within a frame that constrains what other methods might also be evoked to perform the same task. In short, they do not model the *control* structure.

What is that, the control structure? It is best illustrated by programming languages. A language such as FORTRAN (or any other, for that matter) may be seen as a device to evoke a sequence of primitive operations, the exact sequence being conditional upon the data. The primitive operations in FORTRAN are the arithmetic operations, the given functions (sine, cosine, logarithm, etc.), the assignment of a value to a variable, the input and output operations, etc. Each of these has a name in the language (+, -, SIN, LOG, etc.). However, just having names for the operations is not enough. Specifying the conditional sequence is also required and what does that is called the control structure. In FORTRAN it includes the syntax of algebraic expressions, which governs how the arithmetic operations are evoked, the order of statements, which implies that the operations specified by these statements are to be done in order, the syntax of the iteration statement (the DO statement), the format of the conditional and unconditional branch. Given the control structure, there exists a definite problem of programming to get a task done. Given only the basic operations, but not control structure, it is not possible to say what sequences of operations are or are not possible, or are possible within constraints of time and space.

Much of the new progress in the experimental analysis of the information processing of humans has eschewed attention to the control strurture. The present papers of this symposium are no exception. However, my best example (my canonical one, so to speak) is the deservedly well-known paper by Atkinson and Shiffrin (1968) entitled: "Human Memory: A proposed system and its control processes." The model of memory is there all right, and is applied to a number of tasks with quantitative precision. However, the control structure is completely absent and is used as a *deus ex machina* to concoct separate models for each task. Criticism is not directed at that justly influential piece of work. But it does illustrate well the current state of the theoretical art. As long as the control structure--the glue--is missing, so long will it be possible to suggest an indefinite sequence of alternative possibilities for how a given task was performed, hence to keep theoretical issues from becoming settled.

Putting it Together

There is a second source of our difficulties, distinct from the one discussed above, though not unrelated to it. We never seem in the experimental literature to put the results of all the experiments together. The paper by Posner in the present symposium is an excellent example--excellent both in showing the skillful attempts we do currently make and in showing how far short this falls of really integrating the results. We do--Posner does--relate sets of experiments. But the linkage is extraordinarily loose. One picks and chooses among the qualitative summaries of a given experiment what to bring forward and juxtapose with the concerns of a present treatment.

This aspect of our current scientific style is abetted by our tendency noted at the beginning to case the results of experiments in terms of their support or refutation of various binary oppositions. Thus, what is brought forward from an experiment is supposed to be just such qualitative summaries. Innumerable aspects of the situations are permitted to be suppressed. Thus, no way exists of knowing whether the earlier studies are in fact commensurate with whatever ones are under present scrutiny, or are in fact contradictory. Only if the contradiction is blatant, so to speak--e.g., asserting a single memory structure versus two, a long-term and a short-term memory--will the appropriate clash occur. Of course, it is not true that these other aspects are suppressed. They remain available to be dug up by any reviewer who cares to do so, thus to keep the cycle of uncertainty and re-interpretation going.

The article of Wingfield and Byrnes in *Science*, discussed above, provides a good example of what is permissible in our present experimental style. A single result is permitted, so to speak, to challenge a rather large edifice. So loose jointed are our edifices that a divide and conquer strategy can be used. A part of the totality can be pulled out and attacked in isolation with seeming impunity.

What should be the case? A challenge to one part of a pattern of experimental results should not be permitted unless it can successfully challenge (or be shown to be consistent with) a substantial part of the total existing pattern. It is a question of where scientific responsibility lays. The warp and woof of our experimental web hangs so loose that it comes as a novel suggestion that a paper such as the Wingfield-Byrnes one is being theoretically irresponsible.

A reaction of protest, or at least annoyance, should by now surely have set in. Am I not being harsh? How do I expect experimental work and interpretation to proceed? Isn't this the way all sciences proceed? As to the latter (since I get to give the answers, I get to select the questions), the other sciences may not have had such a slippery eel to contend with. That the same human subject can adopt many (radically different) methods for the same basic task, depending on goal, background knowledge, and minor details of payoff structure and task texture--all this--implies that the "normal" means of science may not suffice. As to the first question, the harshness, I restate my initial point: this is my confused and distressed half speaking. My other half is tickled pink at how fast and how far we have come in the last decade, not to speak of the last two days.

Let me stress as well that nothing in my concern implies a lessened dependence on the extraction of experimental fact or the need to develop experimental techniques. The benefits yielded to this symposium from the chronometric analysis of reaction times, a tool that the last five years has honed to a fine edge, are immense: In fact, I really approve of all those phenomena in Figure 1. They are examples of the kinds of experimental insights that we reap from our current investigations. I do in fact hope they double in the next ten years. My concern, to state it once more, is with how they will add up.

Prognosis

What can be done about these concerns, assuming I have convinced you to take them seriously, at least by half? I will spend no time arguing that what is needed is to view man as an information processing system. This has been argued at length in several places (e.g., see Newell and Simon, 1972, for our contribution). More important, all of the papers in the present symposium are executed enough within that conceptual view to demonstrate that the lack of such a metaview is not the culprit. From this vantage point the work of Cooper and Shepard, raising as it does the possibility of continuous processing mechanisms, is as much a scientific exemplar of an information processing view as is, say, the discrete symbolic models of Chase and Simon.

I will not assert that I know exactly what should be done. My distress is genuine. I am worried that our efforts, even the excellent ones I see occurring here, will not add up. Let me, however, discuss at least three possible (non-exclusive) courses of action. These might be viewed as possible paradigms within which to operate experimentally.

Complete Processing Models

The first suggestion is to construct complete processing models rather than the partial ones we now do. In the present company the work of Chase and Simon fits this mold best, expecially when you add to it the simulations of Simon and Gilmartin (1973). This theory, embodied in the simulation, actually carries out the experimental task, thus is fairly tight.

As I noted earlier, the attempts in some of the other papers to move toward a process model by giving a flow diagram (Cooper-Shepard and Klahr[2]) seem to me not to be tight enough. Too much is left unspecified and unconstrained. To make the comparison with Chase and Simon somewhat sharp, these flow diagrams are not sufficient to perform their tasks. That flow diagrams may leave something to be desired as a scheme for cumulating knowledge might be inferred from a comparison of Donald Broadbent's two books (1958 and 1971), both of which contain flow diagrams representing what is known (at each respective date) about short-term memory and the immediate processor.

In one important respect, however, the Chase and Simon (and Gilmartin) work is deficient for present purposes. It does not employ a psychologically relevant model of the control processes. I argued above (and I believe) that until one has a model of the control processes (along with a model of the memories and the primitive operations) we will not be able to bring the problem of specifying subjects' methods under control.

At the moment I know of only one model of the human control processes, that of production systems (Newell & Simon, 1972; Newell, 1972). These are a form of programming system that have proved useful in discussing complex cognitive tasks (such as the cryptarithmetic, logic and chess tasks treated in Newell and Simon, 1972). At one level they are like any programming language, providing a way of specifying a conditional sequence of primitive operations to be applied. However, in most work on simulation programs the control structure has been treated about as casually as it is in the flow diagrams declared above to be deficient (see for instance Johnson, 1964). The production systems, by a route that need not be recounted, have become tied in with a model of the structure of memory. They

---

[2]Excluding the material in Klahr's second paper (Chapter 11).

thus find themselves providing a detailed model of the control processes.

It is not my main purpose in these comments to extol the advantages of production systems. However, as noted they are the sole exemplars to my knowledge of human control processes (though they will surely not be the last). Since the notion of modeling the control and the benefits that accrue thereby in putting experimental results together is not familiar, it seems incumbent on me to provide an illustration. The attempt to do this, though it fits in this comment as a single paragraph, so to speak, is extensive enough to require an independent statement. This I have done in a companion article (Chapter 10). One should simply imagine it inserted in this essay at this point.

Let me summarize the results of that excursion *vis à vis* the present argument. It is possible to construct models of the detailed control structure coupled with equally detailed assumptions about memories and elementary processes. Within such a system the question of what method the subject employs in an experimental task can be investigated in the same fashion as discovering a program in a given programming language to perform a specified task. Just as with programming, several organizations may lead to adequate performance of the task. However, each method makes definite predictions as to time and space used, providing the basis for experimental operations to determine which method was actually operating.

There is an immense space of possible control organization and each provides a scheme within which almost any method can be programmed. Thus, the problem of determining what control system is used by the human is analogous to determining what machine language is used by a computer, given that you can never see any written code, but only the outputs of running programs. However, each control organization has different details of encoding, processing time, and memory load. They provide a basis for identifying the system experimentally if a sufficiently large and diverse set of tasks is analysed.

Analyze a Complex Task

The second experimental strategy, or paradigm, to help overcome the difficulties enumerated earlier is to accept a single complex task and do all of it. The current experimental style is to design specific small experiments to attempt to settle specific small questions--often as not, as I've said, dictated by the empirical exploration of a new phenomenon or by one of the polar issues. Whenever a coordinated series of experiments is created, it is usually phenomenon driven, e.g., one thinks of the sequences by Underwood and colleagues on verbal learning. The effect of this is to keep each experiment a thing-in-itself--disparate enough to guarantee the sort of loose jointed fabric I've bemoaned.

An alternative is to focus a series of experimental and theoretical studies around a single complex task, the aim being to demonstrate that one has a sufficient theory of a genuine slab of human behavior. All of the studies would be designed to fit together and add up to a total picture in detail. Such a paradigm is best described by illustration. Unfortunately, I know of no single example which successfully shows this scheme at work. I attribute this not to its difficulty but to its not really having been tried. However, let me give several partial examples.

The work of Dave Klahr provides, I believe, one example. The paper presented at this symposium is a component of a general attack on some problems of development. Initial work with a Piagetian set-inclusion task (Klahr & Wallace, 1970) led to a model that depended on quantification operators. There followed a paper (Klahr & Wallace, 1972) that attempted to construct a theory of quantification operators, to be used in pursuing the larger plan. The paper we heard here is a further subcomponent--the attempt to obtain some fresh data to solidify the models of quantification operators. Thus, the entire program of research is built to produce, ultimately, a complete model of the developmental set-inclusion task. I've never explicitly asked Klahr about the strategy, but it serves my purposes to interpret it so.

A second example is a thesis done awhile ago by Donald Dansereau on mental multiplication (Dansereau, 1969). The goal was a theory of how people did tasks such as 17 x 638 = ?, all in their heads. Dansereau constructed an information processing model of the process and simulated it to predict the results. That model had half a dozen or more parameters: memory transfer times, operation times, etc. The important point, for our purposes, was that he estimated all these parameters, not by fitting the simulation results to the timing data, but by conducting a series of independent micro-studies. Each of these studies was built to supply one or more parameter values to be used in the larger model. Thus, he forced a close coupling between the entire set of experimental results.

A final example, clearly mostly prospect, would be to take chess as the target super-task. We know already from existing work that the task involves forms of reasoning and search (de Groot, 1965; Newell & Simon, 1972; Wagner & Scurrah, 1972) and complex perceptual and memorial processes (de Groot, 1966; Chase & Simon, This volume, Chapter 5). From more general considerations we know that it also involves planning, evaluation, means-ends analysis, and redefinition of the situation, as well as several varieties of learning--short term, *post-hoc* analysis, preparatory analysis, study from books, etc. Why should one not accept the task of understanding thoroughly how chess is learned and played and how this interacts with the general capabilities brought to the game? To the query of why pick chess, the response must be, Why not? Or pick another. It doesn't matter much what task is picked as long as we settle on a total complex task to force all studies into intimate relation to each other. To the point that there are lots of important mental activities not well represented by chess, the answer must be that no task is universal. What is important is to rise up a couple of levels of integration over the disaggregated scattering of tasks we now address. Concern with completeness can be saved for later iterations.

One Program for Many Tasks

The third alternative paradigm I have in mind is to stay with the diverse collection of small experimental tasks, as now, but to construct a single system to perform them all. This single system (this model of the human information processor) would have to take the instructions for each, as well as carry out the task. For it must truly be a single system in order to provide the integration that we seek.

The companion piece on productions systems (Newell, this volume, Chapter 10) in conjunction with Klahr's production system (Klahr, this volume, Chapter 11) indicates how such an endeavor might go. It is only a beginning, but it shows already a certain promise, it seems to me.

An alternative mold for such a task is to construct a single program that would take a standard intelligence test, say the WAIS or the Stanford-Binet. This is actually an enterprise that was called for much earlier (Green, 1964), but only recently has anything really stirred (Hunt, Frost, & Lunneborg, 1972).

Conclusion

My distressed and confused half has held the ascendency throughout this paper. I do not believe that it is just a commentator's ploy, though it emerged in the act of reviewing the papers of this symposium. It is certainly not a universal complaint I voice wherever occasion offers. Another half of my life is concerned with artificial intelligence, a part of computer science devoted to the construction of artifacts that do what mind can do--an enterprise not unrelated to the psychology of thought, though still distinct (Newell, 1970). There, despite the constant chorus of critics, whose universal complaint is that man and machine are of different categories, hence that progress is not possible in principle, and illusory at best, I feel that we have the ingredients of accumulation. Winograd's system (1972) is a genuine advance over the first natural language efforts. The robots do significantly better than they once did. Challengers keep showing up with programs that do all that their predecessors did and more besides.

Thus, I diagnose my concern as real. And I take seriously my call that we find some way to put it all together--even though this is voiced in an era when we have never been so successful experimentally and conceptually, and at a symposium where the papers exhibit so perfectly this success.

Maybe we are reaching the day of the theorist in psychology, much as it exists in other sciences such as physics. Then the task of putting things together falls to them, and experimentalists can proceed their own way. (That is not quite the way it works in physics, but no matter.) This does not seem to me our present case, but it could be.

Maybe we should cooperate in working on larger experimental wholes than we now do. My positive suggestions in the prior section were proposals of how to do that. They all have in common forcing enough detail and scope to tighten the inferential web that ties our experimental studies together. This is what I think would be good for the field.

Maybe we should all simply continue playing our collective game of 20 questions. Maybe all is well, as my other half assures me, and when we arrive in 1992 (the retirement date I pick might as well be my own) we will have homed in to the essential structure of the mind.

References

Atkinson, R. C., & Shiffrin, R. M. Human Memory: A proposed system and its control processes. In K. W. Spence & J. T. Spence (Eds.), *The psychology of learning and motivation: Advances in research and theory*. Vol. II. New York: Academic Press, 1968.

Broadbent, D. E. *Perception and communication*. New York: Pergamon, 1958.

Broadbent, D. E. *Decision and stress.* New York: Academic Press, 1971.

Clark, H. H., & Chase, W. G. On the process of comparing sentences against pictures. *Cognitive Psychology,* 1972, 3, 472-517.

Dansereau, D. An information processing model of mental multiplication. Unpublished doctoral dissertation, Carnegie-Mellon University, 1969.

de Groot, A. *Thought and choice in chess.* The Hague: Mouton, 1965.

de Groot, A. Perception and memory versus thought: some old ideas and recent findings. In B. Kleinmuntz (Ed.), *Problem solving.* New York: Wiley, 1966.

Green, B. F. Intelligence and computer simulation. *Transactions of the New York Academy of Sciences,* 1964, Ser. II, 27, 55-63.

Hubel, D. H., & Wiesel, T. N. Receptive fields, binocular interaction and functional architecture in the cat's visual cortex. *Journal of Physiology,* 1962, 160, 106-154.

Hunt, E., Frost, N., & Lunneborg, C. Individual differences in cognition. In G. Bower (Ed.), *Advances in learning and memory,* Vol. 7. New York: Academic Press, 1973.

Johnson, E. S. An information processing model of one kind of problem solving. *Psychological Monographs,* Whole No. 581, 1964.

Klahr, D., & Wallace, J. G. An information processing analysis of some Piagetian experimental tasks. *Cognitive Psychology,* 1970, 1, 358-387.

Klahr, D., & Wallace, J. G. Class inclusion processes. In S. Farnham-Diggory (Ed.), *Information processing in children.* New York: Academic Press, 1972.

Newell, A. Remarks on the relationship between artificial intelligence and cognitive psychology. In R. B. Banerji & M. D. Mesarovic (Eds.), *Theoretical approaches to non-numerical problem solving.* Berlin: Springer Verlag, 1970.

Newell, A. A theoretical exploration of mechanisms for coding the stimulus. In A. W. Melton & E. Martin (Eds.), *Coding processes in human memory.* Washington D. C.: Winston, 1972.

Newell, A., & Simon, H. A. An example of human chess playing in the light of chess playing programs. In N. Wiener & J. P. Schade (Eds.), *Progress in biocybernetics*, Vol. 2. Amsterdam: Elsevier, 1965.

Newell, A., & Simon, H. A. *Human problem solving*. Englewood Cliffs, N. J.: Prentice-Hall, 1972.

Simon, H. A., & Gilmartin, K. A simulation of memory for chess positions. *Cognitive Psychology*, 1973, in press.

Stark, L. *Neurological control systems*. New York: Plenum, 1968.

Wagner, D. A., & Scurrah, M. J. Some characteristics of human problem solving in chess. *Cognitive Psychology*, 1971, 2, 454-478.

Wingfield, A., & Byrnes, D. L. Decay of information in short-term memory. *Science*, 1972, 176, 690-691.

Winograd, T. Understanding natural language. *Cognitive Psychology*, 1972, 3, 1-191.

Acknowledgments

This work was supported by Public Health Service Research Grant MH-07722 from the National Institute of Mental Health.

Artificial Intelligence—A Personal View

D. Marr

The Artificial Intelligence Laboratory,
Massachusetts Institute of Technology,
545, Technology Square, Cambridge, MA 02139, U.S.A.

Recommended by B. Meltzer

ABSTRACT

The goal of Artificial Intelligence is to identify and solve tractable information processing problems. In so doing, two types of theory arise. Here, they are labelled Types 1 and 2, and their characteristics are outlined. This discussion creates a more than usually rigorous perspective of the subject, from which past work and future prospects are briefly reviewed.

Artificial Intelligence is the study of complex information processing problems that often have their roots in some aspect of biological information processing. The goal of the subject is to identify interesting and solvable information processing problems, and solve them.

The solution to an information processing problem divides naturally into two parts. In the first, the underlying nature of a particular computation is characterized, and its basis in the physical world is understood. One can think of this part as an abstract formulation of *what* is being computed and *why*, and I shall refer to it as the "theory" of a computation. The second part consists of particular algorithms for implementing a computation, and so it specifies *how*. The choice of algorithm usually depends upon the hardware in which the process is to run, and there may be many algorithms that implement the same computation. The theory of a computation, on the other hand, depends only on the nature of the problem to which it is a solution. Jardine and Sibson [6] decomposed the subject of cluster analysis in precisely this way, using the term "method" to denote what I call the theory of a computation.

To make the distinction clear, let us take the case of Fourier analysis. The (computational) theory of the Fourier transform is well understood, and is expressed

Artificial Intelligence **9** (1977), 37–48

independently of the particular way in which it is computed. There are however several algorithms for implementing a Fourier transform—the Fast Fourier transform (Cooley and Tukey [3]), which is a serial algorithm; and the parallel "spatial" algorithms that are based on the mechanisms of coherent optics. All these algorithms carry out the same computation, and the choice of which one to use depends upon the available hardware. In passing, we also note that the distinction between serial and parallel resides at the algorithm level, and is not a deep property of a computation.

Strictly speaking then, a *result* in Artificial Intelligence consists of the isolation of a particular information processing problem, the formulation of a computational theory for it, the construction of an algorithm that implements it, and a practical demonstration that the algorithm is successful. The important point here, and it is what makes progress possible, is that once a computational theory has been established for a particular problem, it never has to be done again, and in this respect a result in A.I. behaves like a result in mathematics or any of the hard natural sciences. Some judgement has to be applied when deciding whether the computational theory for a problem has been formulated adequately; the statement "take the opponent's king" defines the goal of chess, but it is hardly an adequate characterization of the computational problem of doing it.[1] The kind of judgement that is needed seems to be rather similar to that which decides whether a result in mathematics amounts to a substantial new theorem, and I do not feel uncomfortable about having to leave the basis of such judgements unspecified.[2]

This view of what constitutes a result in A.I. is probably acceptable to most scientists. Chomsky's [2] notion of a "competence" theory for English syntax is precisely what I mean by a computational theory for that problem. Both have the quality of being little concerned with the gory details of algorithms that must be run to express the competence (i.e. to implement the computation). That is not to say that devising suitable algorithms will be easy, but it is to say that before one can devise them, one has to know what exactly it is that they are supposed to be doing, and this information is captured by the computational theory. When a problem decomposes in this way, I shall refer to it as having a *Type 1* theory.

The fly in the ointment is that while many problems of biological information processing have a Type 1 theory, there is no reason why they should all have. This can happen when a problem is solved by the simultaneous action of a considerable number of processes, *whose interaction is its own simplest description*,

[1] One computational theory that in principle can solve chess is exhaustive search. The rea interest lies however in formulating the pieces of computation that we apply to the game. One presumably wants a computational theory that has a rather general application, together with a demonstration that it happens to be applicable to some class of games of chess, and evidence that we play games in this class.

[2] New algorithms for implementing a known computational theory may subsequently be devised without throwing substantial new light upon the theory, just as Winograd's [31] Very Fast Fourier Transform shed no new light on the nature of Fourier analysis.

and I shall refer to such a situation as a *Type 2* theory.[3] One promising candidate for a Type 2 theory is the problem of predicting how a protein will fold. A large number of influences act on a large polypeptide chain as it flaps and flails in a medium. At each moment only a few of the possible interactions will be important, but the importance of those few is decisive. Attempts to construct a simplified theory must ignore some interactions; but if most interactions are crucial at some stage during the folding, a simplified theory will prove inadequate. Interestingly, the most promising studies of protein folding are currently those that take a brute force approach, setting up a rather detailed model of the amino acids, the geometry associated with their sequence, hydrophobic interactions with the circumambient fluid, random thermal perturbations etc., and letting the whole set of processes run until a stable configuration is achieved (Levitt and Warshel [8]).

The principal difficulty in A.I. is that one can never be quite sure whether a problem has a Type I theory. If one is found, well and good; but failure to find one does not mean that it does not exist. Most A.I. programs have hitherto amounted to Type 2 theories, and the danger with such theories is that they can bury crucial decisions, that in the end provide the key to the correct Type 1 decomposition of the problem, beneath the mound of small administrative decisions that are inevitable whenever a concrete program is designed. This phenomenon makes research in A.I. difficult to pursue and difficult to judge. If one shows that a given information processing problem is solved by a particular, neatly circumscribed computational theory, then that is a secure result. If on the other hand one produces a large and clumsy set of processes that solves a problem, one cannot always be sure that there isn't a simple underlying computational theory for one or more related problems whose formulation has somehow been lost in the fog. With any candidate for a Type 2 theory, much greater importance is attached to the performance of the program. Since its only possible virtue might be that it works, it is interesting only if it does. Often, a piece of A.I. research has resulted in a large program without much of a theory, which commits it to a Type 2 result, but that program either performs too poorly to be impressive or (worse still) has not even been implemented. Such pieces of research have to be judged very harshly, because their lasting contribution is negligible.

Thus we see that as A.I. pursues its study of information processing problems, two types of solution are liable to emerge. In one, there is a clean underlying theory in the traditional sense. Examples of this from vision are Horn's [5] method for obtaining shape from shading, the notion of the primal sketch as a representation of the intensity changes and local geometry of an image (Marr [10]), Ullman's [26] method for detecting light sources, Binford's [1] generalized cylinder

[3] The underlying point here is that there is often a natural modularity in physics (e.g. under normal conditions, electrical interactions are independent of gravitational interactions), but some processes involve several at the same time and with roughly equal importance, like protein-folding. Thus the Type 1–Type 2 distinction is not a pure dichotomy, and there is a spectrum of possibilities between them.

representation, on which Marr and Nishihara's [12] theory of the internal representation and manipulation of 3-D structures was based, a recent theory of stereo vision (Marr [9], Marr and Poggio [13])[4] and Poggio and Reichardt's [17] analysis of the visual orienting behaviour of the housefly. One characteristic of these results is that they often lie at a relatively low level in the overall canvas of intellectual functions, a level often dismissed with contempt by those who purport to study "higher, more central" problems of intelligence. Our reply to such criticism is that low-level problems probably do represent the easier kind, but that is precisely the reason for studying them first. When we have solved a few more, the questions that arise in studying the deeper ones will be clearer to us.

But even relatively clean Type 1 theories such as these involve Type 2 theories as well. For example, Marr and Nishihara's 3-D representation theory asserts that the deep underlying structure is based on a distributed, object-centred coordinate system that can be thought of as a stick figure, and that this representation is explicitly manipulated during the analysis of an image. Such a theory would be little more than speculation unless it could also be shown that such a description may be computed from an image and can be manipulated in the required way. To do so involves several intermediate theories, for some of which there is hope of eventual Type 1 status, but others look intractably of Type 2. For example, a Type 1 theory now exists for part of the problem of determining the appropriate local coordinate system from the contours formed in an object's image (Marr [11]), but it may be impossible to derive a Type 1 theory for the basic grouping processes that operate on the primal sketch to help separate figure from ground. The figure-ground "problem" may not be a single problem, being instead a mixture of several subproblems which combine to achieve figural separation, just as the different molecular interactions combine to cause a protein to fold. There is in fact no reason why a solution to the figure-ground problem should be derivable from a single underlying theory. The reason is that it needs to contain a procedural representation of many facts about images that derive ultimately via evolution from the cohesion and continuity of matter in the physical world. Many kinds of knowledge and different techniques are involved; one just has to sort them out one by one. As each is added the performance of the whole improves, and the complexity of the images that can be handled increases.

We have already seen that to search for a Type 2 theory for a problem may be dangerous if in fact it has a Type 1 theory. This danger is most acute in premature assaults on a high-level problem, for which few or none of the concepts that underlie its eventual Type 1 theory have yet been developed, and the consequence is a complete failure to formulate correctly the problems that are in fact involved. But it is equally important to realize that the opposite danger exists

[4] The notion of cooperative computation, or relaxation labeling (Zucker [33]), is a notion at the algorithm level. It suggests a way of implementing certain computations, but does not address the problem of what should be implemented, which seems to be the real issue for vision no less than elsewhere.

lower down. For example, in our current theory of visual processing, the notion of the primal sketch seems respectable enough, but one might have doubts about the aesthetics of the grouping processes that decode it. There are many of them, their details are somewhat messy; and seemingly arbitrary preferences occur (e.g. for vertical or horizontal organizations). A clear example of a Type 2 theory is our assertion that texture-vision discriminations rest on these grouping processes and first-order discriminations applied to the information held in primal sketch of the image (Marr [10]). As such, it is less attractive than Julesz's [7] clean (Type 1) theory that textured regions are discriminable only if there is a difference in the first or second-order statistics of their intensity arrays. But as Julesz himself found, there exist patterns with different second-order statistics that are nevertheless indiscriminable; and one can in fact view our own work as attempting to define precisely what characteristics of the second-order statistical structure cause discriminability (see Schatz, 1977, in preparation).

This inevitably forces us to relinquish the beauty of Julesz's concise theory, but I feel that one should not be too distressed by the need at this level of investigation to explore rather messy and untidy details. We already know that separate modules must exist for computing other aspects of visual information—motion, stereoscopy, fluorescence, color—and there is no reason why they should all be based on a single theory. Indeed one would a priori expect the opposite; as evolution progressed, new modules came into existence that could cope with yet more aspects of the data, and as a result kept the animal alive in ever more widely ranging circumstances. The only important constraint is that the system as a whole should be roughly modular, so that new facilities can be added easily.

So, especially at the more peripheral stages of sensory information processing, and perhaps also more centrally, one should not necessarily give up if one fails to find a Type 1 theory—there may not be one. More importantly even if there were, there would be no reason why that theory should bear much relation to the theory of more central phenomena. In vision for example, the theory that says 3-D representations are based on stick-figure coordinate systems and shows how to manipulate them, is independent of the theory of the primal sketch, or for that matter of most other stages en route from the image to that representation. In particular, it is especially dangerous to suppose that an approximate theory of a peripheral process has any significance for higher level operations. For example, because Julesz's second-order statistics idea is so clean and so neatly fits much data, one might be tempted to ask whether the idea of second order interactions is in some way central to higher processes. In doing so one should bear in mind that the true explanation of visual texture discrimination may be quite different in nature even if the theory is very often a correct predictor of performance.

The reason for drawing this point out at such length is that it bears upon another issue, namely the type of theory that the grammar of natural language might have. The purpose of human language is presumably to transform a datastructure that is not inherently one-dimensional into one-dimensional form for transmission as a sequential utterance, thereafter to be retranslated into some rough copy of the original in the head of the listener. Viewed in this light, it becomes entirely possible that there may exist no Type 1 theory of English syntax of the type that transformational grammar attempts to define—that its constraints resemble wired-in conventions about useful ways of executing this tedious but vital operation, rather than deep principles about the nature of intelligence. An abstract theory of syntax may be an illusion, approximating what really happens only in the sense that Julesz's second order statistics theory approximates the behaviour of the set of processes that implement texture vision and which, in the final analysis, are all the theory that there is. In other words, the grammar of natural language may have a theory of Type 2 rather than of Type 1.

Even if a biological information processing problem has only a Type 2 theory, it may still be possible to infer more from a solution to it than the solution itself. This comes about because at some point in the implementation of a set of processes, design constraints attached to the machine in which they will run start to affect the structure of the implementation. This observation adds a different perspective to the two types of research carried out by linguists and by members of the artificial intelligence community. If the theory of syntax is really of Type 2, then any important implications about the CNS are likely to come from details of the way in which its constituent processes are implemented, and these are often explorable only by implementing them.

Implications of this view

If one accepts this view of A.I. research, one is led to judge its achievements according to rather clear criteria. What information processing problem has been isolated? Has a clean theory been developed for solving it, and if so how good are the arguments that support it? If no clean theory has been given what is the evidence that favors a set-of-processes solution or suggests that no single clean theory exists for it, and how well does the proposed set of mechanisms work? For very advanced problems like story-understanding, current research is often purely exploratory. That is to say, in these areas our knowledge is so poor that we cannot even begin to formulate the appropriate questions, let alone solve them. It is important to realize that this is an inevitable phase of any human endeavor, personally risky (almost surely no exploring pioneer will himself succeed in finding a useful question), but a necessary precursor of eventual success.

Most of the history of A.I. (now fully 16 years old) has consisted of exploratory studies. Some of the best-known are Slagle's [24] symbolic integration program, Weizenbaum's [30] Eliza program, Evans' [4] analogy program, Raphael's [19] SIR, Quillian's [18] semantic nets and Winograd's [32] Shrdlu. All of these programs have (in retrospect) the property that they are either too simple to be interesting Type 1 theories, or very complex yet perform too poorly to be taken seriously as a Type 2 theory. Perhaps the only really successful Type 2 theory to emerge in the early phase of A.I. was Waltz's [27] program. And yet many things have been learnt from these experiences—mostly negative things (the first 20 obvious ideas about how intelligence might work are too simple or wrong) but including several positive things. The MACSYMA algebraic manipulation system (Moses [15]) is undeniably successful and useful, and it had its roots in programs like Slagle's. The mistakes made in the field lay not in having carried out such studies—they formed an essential part of its development—but consisted mainly in failures of judgement about their value, since it is now clear that few of the early studies themselves formulated any solvable problems. Part of the reason for these internal failures of judgement lay in external pressures for early results from the field, but this is not the place to discuss what in the end are political matters.

Yet, I submit, one would err to judge these failures of judgement too harshly. They are merely the inevitable consequence of a necessary enthusiasm, based on a view of the long-term importance of the field that seems to me correct. All important fields of human endeavor start with a personal commitment based on faith rather than on results. A.I. is just one more example. Only a sour, crabbed and unadventurous spirit will hold it against us.

Current trends

Exploratory studies are important. Many people in the field expect that, deep in the heart of our understanding of intelligence, there will lie at least one and probably several important principles about how to organize and represent knowledge that in some sense captures what is important about the *general* nature of our intellectual abilities. An optimist might see the glimmer of such principles in programs like those of Sussman and Stallman [25], of Marr and Nishihara [12], in the overall attitudes to central problems set out by Minsky [14], and possibly in some of Schank's [21, 22] work, although I sometimes feel that he failed to draw out the important points. While still somewhat cloudy, the ideas that seem to be emerging (and which owe much to the early exploratory studies) are:

(1) That the "chunks" of reasoning, language, memory, and perception ought to be larger than most recent theories in psychology have allowed (Minsky [14]). They must also be very flexible—at least as flexible as Marr and Nishihara's stick-figure 3-D models, and probably more. Straightforward mechanisms that are suggested by the terms "frame" and "terminal", are certainly too inflexible.

(2) That the perception of an event or of an object must include the simultaneous computation of several different descriptions of it, that capture diverse aspects of the use, purpose or circumstances of the event or object.

(3) That the various descriptions described in (2) include coarse versions as well as fine ones. These coarse descriptions are a vital link in choosing the appropriate overall scenarios demanded by (1), and in establishing correctly the roles played by the objects and actions that caused those scenarios to be chosen.

An example will help to make these points clear. If one reads

(A) The fly buzzed irritatingly on the window-pane.

(B) John picked up the newspaper.

the immediate inference is that John's intentions towards the fly are fundamentally malicious. If he had picked up the telephone, the inference would be less secure. It is generally agreed that an "insect-damaging" scenario is somehow deployed during the reading of these sentences, being suggested in its coarsest form by the fly buzzing irritatingly. Such a scenario will contain a reference to something that can squash an insect on a brittle surface—a description which fits a newspaper but not a telephone. We might therefore conclude that when the newspaper is mentioned (or in the case of vision, seen) not only is it described internally as a newspaper, and some rough 3-D description of its shape and axes set up, but it is also described as a light, flexible object with area. Because sentence (B) might have continued "and sat down to read", the newspaper may also be being described as reading-matter; similarly, as a combustible article, and so forth. Since one does not usually know in advance what aspect of an object or action is important, it follows that most of the time, a given object will give rise to several different coarse internal descriptions. Similarly for actions. It may be important to note that the description of fly-swatting or reading or fire-lighting does not have to be attached to the newspaper; merely that a description of the newspaper is available that will match its role in each scenario.

The important thing about Schank's "primitive actions" seems to me not the fact that there happens to be a certain small number of them, nor the idea that every act is expressed solely by reduction to them (which I cannot believe at all), nor even the idea that the scenarios to which they are attached contain all the answers for the present situation (that is where the missing flexibility comes in). The importance of a primitive, coarse catalogue of events and objects lies in the role such coarse descriptions play in the ultimate access and construction of perhaps exquisitely tailored specific scenarios, rather in the way that a general 3-D animal model in Marr and Nishihara's theory can finish up as a very specific Cheshire Cat, after due interaction between the image and information stored in the primitive model. What after sentence (A) existed as little more than a malicious intent towards the innocent fly becomes, with the additional information about the newspaper, a very specific case of fly-squashing.

Marr and Nishihara have labelled the problem of providing multiple-descriptions for the newspaper its "reference-window problem". Exactly how it is best done, and exactly what descriptions should accompany different words or perceived objects, is not yet known. These insights are the result of exploratory studies, and the problems to which they lead have yet to be precisely formulated, let alone satisfactorily solved. But it is now certain that some problems of this kind do exist and are important; and it seems likely that a fairly respectable theory of them will eventually emerge.

Mimicry versus exploration

Finally, I would like to draw one more distinction that seems to be important when choosing a research problem, or when judging the value of completed work. The problem is that studies—particularly of natural language understanding, problem-solving, or the structure of memory—can easily degenerate into the writing of programs that do no more than mimic in an unenlightening way some small aspect of human performance. Weizenbaum [30] now judges his program Eliza to belong to this category, and I have never seen any reason to disagree. More controversially, I would also criticize on the same grounds Newell and Simon's work on production systems, and some of Norman and Rummelhart's [16] work on long term memory.

The reason is this. If one believes that the aim of information-processing studies is to formulate and understand particular information-processing problems, then it is the structure of those problems that is central, not the mechanisms through which they are implemented. Therefore, the first thing to do is to find problems that we can solve well, find out how to solve them, and examine our performance in the light of that understanding. The most fruitful source of such problems is operations that we perform well, fluently (and hence unconsciously) since it is difficult to see how reliability could be achieved if there were no sound underlying method. On the other hand, problem-solving research has tended to concentrate on problems that we understand well intellectually but perform poorly on, like mental arithmetic and criptarithmatic or on problems like geometry theorem-proving, or games like chess, in which human skills seem to rest on a huge base of knowledge and expertise. I argue that these are exceptionally good grounds for *not* studying how we carry out such tasks yet. I have no doubt that when we do mental arithmetic we are doing *something* well, but it is not arithmetic, and we seem far from understanding even one component of what that something is. Let us therefore concentrate on the simpler problems first, for there we have some hope of genuine advancement.

If one ignores this stricture, one is left in the end with unlikely looking mechanisms whose only recommendation is that they cannot do something we cannot do. Production systems seem to me to fit this description quite well. Even taken on their own terms as mechanisms, they leave a lot to be desired. As a programming language they are poorly designed, and hard to use, and I cannot believe that the human brain could possibly be burdened with such poor implementation decisions at so basic a level.

A parallel may perhaps be drawn between production systems for students of problem-solving, and Fourier analysis for visual neurophysiologists. Simple operations on a spatial frequency representation of an image can mimic several interesting visual phenomena that seem to be exhibited by our visual systems. These include the detection of repetition, certain visual illusions, the notion of separate linearly adding channels, separation of overall shape from fine local detail, and a simple expression of size invariance. The reason why the spatial frequency domain is ignored by image analysts is that it is virtually useless for the main job of vision—building up a description of what is there from the intensity array. The intuition that visual physiologists lack, and which is so important, is for how this may be done. A production system exhibits several interesting ideas—the absence of explicit subroutine calls, a blackboard communication channel, and some notion of a short term memory. But just because production systems display these side-effects (as Fourier analysis "displays" some visual illusions) does not mean that they have anything to do with what is really going on. My own guess would be, for example, that the fact that short-term memory can act as a storage register is probably the least important of its functions. I expect that there are several "intellectual reflexes" that operate on items held there, about which nothing is yet known, and which will eventually be held to be the crucial things about it because they perform central functions like opening up an item's reference window. Studying our performance in close relation to production systems seems to me a waste of time, because it amounts to studying a mechanism not a problem, and can therefore lead to no Type 1 results. The mechanisms that such research is trying to penetrate will be unravelled by studying problems, just as vision research is progressing because it is the *problem* of vision that is being attacked, not neural visual mechanisms.

A reflexion of the same criticism can be made of Norman and Rummelhart's work, where they studied the way information seems to be organized in long term memory. Again, the danger is that questions are not asked in relation to a clear information-processing problem. Instead, they are asked and answers proposed in terms of a mechanism—in this case, it is called an "active structural network" and it is so simple and general as to be devoid of theoretical substance. They may be able to say that such and such an "association" seems to exist, but they cannot say of what the association consists, nor that it has to be so because to solve problem X (which we can solve) you *need* a memory organized in such-and-such a way; and that if one has it, certain apparent "associations" occur as side-effects. Experimental psychology can do a valuable job in discovering facts that need explaining, including those about long-term memory, and the work of Shepard [23], Rosch [20] and of Warrington [28] (for example) seems to me very successful at this; but like experimental neurophysiology, experimental psychology will not be able to explain those facts unless information-processing research has identified and solved the appropriate problems X.[5] It seems to me that finding such problems X, and solving them, is what A.I. should be trying to do.

ACKNOWLEDGMENT

Although I take full responsibility for the purely personal views set out here, any virtues that they may have are due in part to many conversations with Drew McDermott. This report describes work done at the Artificial Intelligence Laboratory of the Massachusetts Institute of Technology.

[5] In the present state of the art, it seems wisest to concentrate on problems that probably have Type 1 solutions, rather than on those that are almost certainly of Type 2.

Support for the Laboratory's artificial intelligence research is provided in part by the Advanced Research Projects Agency of the Department of Defense under Office of Naval Research contract number N00014-75-C-0643.

REFERENCES

1. Binford, T. O., Visual perception by computer, IEEE Conf. Systems and Control, Miami (December 1971).
2. Chomsky, A. N., *Aspects of the Theory of Syntax* (M.I.T. Press, Cambridge, MA., 1965).
3. Cooley, J. M. and Tukey, J. W., An algorithm for the machine computation of complex Fourier series, *Math. Comp.* **19** (1965) 297–301.
4. Evans, T., A program for the solution of geometric-analogy intelligence test questions, in: M. Minsky, Ed., *Semantic Information Processing* (M.I.T. Press, Cambridge, MA., 1968) 271–353.
5. Horn, B. K. P., Obtaining shape from shading information, in: P. H. Winston, Ed., *The Psychology of Computer Vision* (McGraw-Hill, NY, 1975) 115–155.
6. Jardine, N. and Sibson, R., *Mathematical Taxonomy* (Wiley, NY, 1971).
7. Julesz, B., Experiments in the visual perception of texture, *Scientific American* **232** (April 1975) 34–43.
8. Levitt, M. and Warshel, A., Computer simulation of protein folding, *Nature* **253** (1975) 694–698.
9. Marr, D., A note on the computation of binocular disparity in a symbolic, low-level visual processor, M.I.T. A.I. Lab. Memo 327 (1974).
10. Marr, D., Early processing of visual information, *Phil. Trans. Roy. Soc. B.* **275** (1976) 483–524.
11. Marr, D., Analysis of occluding contour, *Proc. Roy. Soc. B.*, in the press.
12. Marr, D. and Nishihara, H. K., Representation and recognition of the spatial organization of three dimensional shapes, *Royal Soc.*, submitted for publication.
13. Marr, D. and Poggio, T., Cooperative computation of stereo disparity, *Science* **194** (1976) 283–287.
14. Minsky, M., A framework for representing knowledge, in: P. H. Winston, Ed., *The Psychology of Computer Vision* (McGraw-Hill, NY, 1975) 211–277.
15. Moses, J., MACSYMA—the fifth year, *SIGSAM Bull., ACM,* **8** (1974) 105–110.
16. Norman, D. A. and Rumelhart, D. E., *Explorations in cognition* (W. H. Freeman and Co., San Francisco, 1974) e.g. The active structural network, 35–64.
17. Poggio, T. and Reichardt, W., Visual control of the orientation behaviour of the fly: towards the underlying neural interactions. Quarterly Reviews of Biophysics **9** (1976) 377–438.
18. Quillian, M. R., Semantic memory, in: M. Minsky, Ed., *Semantic Information Processing* (M.I.T. Press, Cambridge, MA, 1968) 227–270.
19. Raphael, B., SIR: semantic information retrieval, in: M. Minsky, Ed., *Semantic Information Processing* (M.I.T. Press, Cambridge, MA, 1968) 33–145.
20. Rosch, E., Classifications of real-world objects: origins and representations in cognition, *Bulletin de Psychologie,* in press.
21. Schank, R. C., Identification of conceptualizations underlying natural language, in: R. C. Schank and K. M. Colby, Eds., *Computer Models of Thought and Language* (W. H. Freeman, San Francisco, 1973).
22. Schank, R. C., *Conceptual Information Processing* (North-Holland, Amsterdam, 1975).
23. Shepard, R. N., Form, formation, and transformation of internal representations, in: R. Solso, Ed., *Information Processing and Cognition: The Loyola Symposium* (Lawrence Erlbaum Assoc., Hillsdale NJ, 1975) 87–122.
24. Slagle, J. R., A heuristic program that solves symbolic integration problems in freshman calculus, in: E. A. Feigenbaum and J. Feldman, Eds., *Computers and Thought* (McGraw-Hill, NY, 1963) 191–203.

25. Sussman, G. J. and Stallman, R. M., Heuristic techniques in computer-aided circuit analysis, IEEE Transactions on Circuits and Systems, CAS-22 (1975) 857–865.
26. Ullman, S., On visual detection of light sources, *Biol. Cybernetics* **21** (1976) 205–212.
27. Waltz, D. L., Understanding line drawings of scenes with shadows, in: P. H. Winston, Ed., *The Psychology of Computer Vision* (McGraw-Hill, NY, 1975) 19–91.
28. Warrington, E. K., The selective impairment of semantic memory, *Q. J. Exp. Psychol.* **27** (1975) 635–657.
29. Weizenbaum, J., ELIZA—a computer program for the study of natural language communication between man and machine. *Commun. ACM* **9** (1965) 36–45.
30. Weizenbaum, J., *Computer Thought and Human Reason* (W. H. Freeman, San Francisco, 1976).
31. Winograd, S., Computing the discrete Fourier transform, *Proc. Nat. Acad. Sci.* **73** (1976) 1005–1006.
32. Winograd, T., *Understanding Natural Language* (Academic Press, NY, 1972).
33. Zucker, S. W., Relaxation labelling and the reduction of local ambiguities, University of Maryland Computer Science *TR-451* (1976).

Received June 1976; revised version received February 1977

George N. Reeke, Jr., and Gerald M. Edelman

Real Brains and Artificial Intelligence

ARTIFICIAL INTELLIGENCE is a science that finds itself in somewhat the same epistemological position as Aristotelian dentistry. Aristotle stated that women have fewer teeth than men[1] and attributed this characteristic to women's supposed lesser need, men being stronger and more choleric,[2] but he never bothered to look in Mrs. Aristotle's mouth to verify his theory. Similarly, AI has developed as an almost entirely *synthetic* enterprise, quite isolated from the complementary, *analytic* study of the biology of natural intelligence represented by psychology and the neurosciences. To a biologist, the AI approach to the study of intelligence seems like a strange way of trying to understand the brain, which is, after all, at the basis of human intelligence. Nonetheless, biologists and computer scientists for the most part share the monistic view that mental events, including the manifestations of intelligence, necessarily reflect the activity of neurons in the brain.

It is important, then, to ask whether the goals of AI are really so different from those of neurobiology as to require entirely different methods of investigation and demonstration. For if they are not, there is much to be gained by joining experiment with theory and synthetic modeling to make a whole science of the brain.

We shall argue that the ultimate goals of AI and neuroscience are quite similar but that they have become obscured by erroneous

George N. Reeke, Jr., is associate professor of developmental and molecular biology at The Rockefeller University.

Gerald M. Edelman is Vincent Astor Professor at The Rockefeller University and director of The Neurosciences Institute.

epistemological assumptions drawn on the one hand from the arguments of Alan Turing and Alonzo Church about the universal problem-solving capabilities of computers (suggesting that the brain may be understood as a computer) and on the other hand from the reductionism of molecular biology (suggesting that the brain may be understood as a collection of units that exchange chemical signals). These confining assumptions, along with enormous practical and experimental difficulties, have kept the practitioners of both approaches very busy, while placing the goals always well out of their reach. In fact, consideration of the magnitude of the problem with due modesty suggests that perception alone is hard enough to understand, without attempting to jump directly from perception to learning, through learning to social transmission and language, and from there to all the richness of ethology. At present, it is still a large challenge to understand how an animal can even move, and it would be well for AI to look first to such fundamental issues.

As biologists (that is, as evolutionists) seeking to understand what we perceive as the nearly dogmatic neglect of our science—at least in recent years—by those attempting to create AI, we shall begin by asking just what it is that AI seeks to accomplish, and what are the basic assumptions about the nature of the solution that engender the standard paradigms of AI. We shall discuss some problems that have arisen in the application of these paradigms and some recent attempts to overcome them by what we call "looking sideways to biology," or "the physicist's approach to neural networks."

These new approaches, the misleading label "neural network computing" notwithstanding, draw their inspiration from statistical physics and engineering, not from biology. They are immensely appealing to the AI community for several reasons. They provide a practical recipe for parceling out AI computations among large numbers of simple processors, with a potentially enormous increase in computing speed. Parallelism has proven difficult to apply to AI, although it has already emerged in numerical computing as the only indefinitely extensible way to overcome the "von Neumann bottleneck" (the fundamental limits imposed on the speed of single processors by the laws of physics, for example, because signals cannot travel from one part of a computer to another faster than the speed of light). By virtue of their imitation of statistical systems, the new approaches also provide statistical approximations to optimization problems that have proven recalcitrant to all attempts at exact computation.

Nonetheless, these statistical approaches share with mainstream AI the implicit notion that objects and events, categories and logic are given and that the nature of the task for the brain is to process information about the world with algorithms to arrive at conclusions leading to behavior. This information-processing paradigm fundamentally fails to come to grips with certain basic problems concerning the nature of information and the ways that systems capable of analyzing information-bearing signals can come to exist. The assumption that categories and signals encoding information about them are the basic stuff around which computations are organized constitutionally biases AI to equate perceptual and intellectual performance with algorithms. This "category problem" leads directly to the inability of AI systems to cope with the complexity and unpredictability of the real world.

Our goal in this essay is to point out the fundamental nature of this problem. By characterizing observable forms of intelligence in the biological world (among others, human intelligence), we will introduce an approach based on the most basic of biological principles, namely, Darwin's theory of natural selection. We will present a theory that suggests how selection can provide the solution to the category problem and how it might occur in the nervous system.[3] We will describe several automata that carry out tasks involving perceptual categorization by selective mechanisms. Finally, we will discuss some ways that this purely biological principle might contribute to further progress in AI.

THE NATURE OF THE AI ENTERPRISE

Artificial intelligence is one of those terms with such an apparently self-evident meaning that it is rarely defined carefully. As a result, it has come to have an overly broad interpretation that adds confusion to the debate about its merits and prospects. Some have gone so far as to define AI as "whatever people in AI are working on." However, we will require a more meaningful, nonrecursive definition. To help us see the fundamental issues most clearly, we will exclude endeavors that have purely engineering goals, that is, projects aimed at devising effective computer solutions for problems that are already well understood in principle. (We include in this category essentially all work on so-called expert systems and logical programming.)

In his influential textbook *Artificial Intelligence,* Patrick Winston defines AI as "the study of ideas that enable computers to be intelligent." As for the goals of this study, he states (in this order) that "one central goal of Artificial Intelligence is to make computers more useful. Another central goal is to understand the principles that make intelligence possible."[4] Neurobiologists would find the mention of these two goals in the same discourse rather lacking in balance. They would acknowledge the great practical importance of the first but consider it to have very little fundamental interest. They would agree, on the other hand, that the second goal captures much of the essential nature of their own enterprise, although they would consider its formulation rather abstract. In contrast, neurobiologists would almost certainly refer to their own interest in discovering and validating such principles by observing existing intelligent systems. For the time being, such systems remain confined to the world of biological organisms.

Thus, as already suggested, the major goals of AI and neuroscience are indeed similar. AI, however, starts off with a more formal approach to these goals that directs it away from the study of "messy" biological systems. What are the subjects of inquiry that AI considers appropriate to a pursuit of its goals, and what are the research paradigms these subjects engender? In 1961 Marvin Minsky presented a list that most workers in AI would probably still accept today: to find effective procedures for search, pattern recognition, learning, planning, and induction.[5] Perhaps language understanding would now be added as a separate category; in agreement with Minsky, "search" would include a variety of optimization and reasoning problems as well as retrieval of coded information from memory, and "pattern recognition" clearly would have to encompass the decomposition of sensory data into component objects as well as the categorization of these objects and events after (or while) they were being recognized.

This choice of subject matter reflects the epistemological assumptions alluded to earlier. In the standard AI paradigm, as presented by Winston, the key to finding powerful procedures that can solve these problems is to discover appropriate representations of the relevant information. Once a representation is given that "make[s] the right things explicit and expose[s] natural constraints,"[6] it is a much simpler matter to devise purely computational procedures to manipulate the information, still in its encoded representation, so as to obtain the desired solutions. Winston is right. Once an appropriate representation is available, many problems do become amenable to automatic solution. In our view, however, the problem requiring intelligence is the original one of *finding* a representation. To place this problem in the domain of the system designer rather than in that of the designed system is to beg the question and reduce intelligence to symbol manipulation.

The line of reasoning that leads to this oversimplified and mechanical view of intelligence has distinguished origins. It can be traced back at least to Pascal and Leibniz, and it took on its present form in the earliest days of modern computers. The most important underpinning of the theory of digital computers, Turing's universality principle, was developed before any workable machines existed; perhaps this is why people were encouraged to think in very general, abstract terms about computers and their capabilities. The very real limitations of actual computers and computer programs only became clear later, after the initial excitement was over and the basic paradigm was well established. The limitations then came to be viewed as purely practical and eventually surmountable; after all, those who believed otherwise did not remain in the field to invest their creative energies in building what they saw as a house of cards. Thus, only now is it becoming more widely suspected, as it always was by some,[7] that AI may have fundamental difficulties as opposed to merely practical ones. This situation is quite unlike the case with such inventions as the steam engine, where practice preceded theory and guided it into the most fruitful channels.

The basic justification for AI, which we shall criticize in detail later, goes essentially like this:

1. Objects and events exist in the world. Information about them may be gathered by appropriate sensors. It is the goal of intelligent systems to process or transform this information so as to provide the basis for the "planning" and "induction" of which Minsky speaks.

2. Given a representation of information as strings of symbols, its manipulation can be carried out by purely formal rules that need

make no reference to the meanings of the symbols. These rules may be expressed as algorithms.

3. An algorithm may be executed by any universal Turing machine.[8] The very existence of these machines implies that the particular mechanism of operation of any one of them is unimportant. The important thing for understanding intelligence is the algorithms, not the hardware on which they are executed. In particular, what the brain does may be described by algorithms.

4. Church's thesis further suggests that if any consistent, terminating method exists to solve a given problem, then a method exists that can run on a Turing machine and give exactly the same results.[9] Therefore, at least for problems that can be solved consistently in a specified, finite amount of time, a Turing machine is as powerful as any other entity that can solve the problem, including the brain.

5. Since inconsistency makes science impossible and infinite time requires immortality, it only makes sense to discuss problems of the kind that can be solved by Turing machines.

6. Once the informational requirements for such a problem have been identified and an algorithm presented, the problem is in some sense understood. Other algorithms may be found that are more elegant or more efficient in some implementation, but all algorithms, including those used by the brain, are subject to the same informational requirements and may be understood in the same way.

7. Therefore, the brain is equivalent to a computer, or at least the computer is an adequate model for the interesting things the brain does.

The standard, entirely synthetic, paradigm for carrying out AI research immediately follows from this line of argument: Choose a significant problem that everyone would agree requires the exercise of intelligence for solution; identify the items of information needed to reach a solution to the problem; determine how this information might best be represented in a computer; find an algorithm that can manipulate the information to solve the problem; write a computer code implementing this algorithm; and test it with sample (usually also simple) instances of the problem.

This approach has led to a number of impressive demonstrations. For reasons that are no accident, the most successful of these have come in areas that most obviously meet the conditions for applying Church's thesis: logical problem solving and theorem proving (GPS, MACSYMA, and the Prolog language, for example), identification of objects in images (ACRONYM, CONSIGHT), playing chess and other games (CHESS, KAISSA, BELLE, PARADISE), understanding human language in limited domains (SHRDLU, BORIS), and expert systems, which combine rule-based inference and natural-language interface techniques with domain-specific data bases (MYCIN, DENDRAL, PROSPECTOR, XCON). However, all of these programs share a common quality that John McCarthy[10] and others have repeatedly pointed out: they are "brittle" in the sense that, if pressed around the edges, they tend to "crack." In other words, the programs lack commonsense knowledge and reasoning—they do not "know" their own limitations. They are insensitive to context and are likely to give quite incorrect responses to queries that are slightly outside the domains for which they were programmed. These responses are perfectly logical consequences of the rules built into each system, but to the observer equipped with normal human reasoning faculties, they can appear arbitrary and even mysterious.

A general solution to this problem of brittleness is not easy to find. While it may appear to be just another instance of the general difficulty of setting up and maintaining reliable large software systems, there seems to be a qualitative difference stemming from the open-endedness of natural language and the need for experience in the real world to acquire a competent repertoire of common sense. In the next section, we will look at some of the solutions to this problem attempted from within the standard AI paradigm. Then we will explain why we believe the problem lies with the paradigm itself and how the solution may be found by looking to real nervous systems and the ways they deal with complexity and novelty in the world.

LOOKING SIDEWAYS TO BIOLOGY

When one experiences difficulties in any large endeavor, the first impulse is to do more of the same or to do the same thing better. In the case of AI, this impulse has taken two directions—to improve the hardware and to improve the software. Each of these directions has given impetus to the development of new methods involving the representation of information by the states of simple processors and the connections between them (the so-called connectionist, or neural net, models).

First, improved hardware has made it possible to evaluate more conditionals (programmed logical tests) per second, to store larger data bases, and to examine images in more detail than before. This faster computation has certainly led to the improved performance of traditional AI systems. Chess automata, for example, can now "look deeper" (more moves ahead) into board positions.[11] Ultimately, however, hardware speeds can be improved only to a point. Eventually, parallel processing must be introduced to bring about further progress—but effective use of parallel processing requires new software techniques. Among the most intriguing of the new techniques being developed to replace traditional AI software are network models, which are ideally suited for implementation on multiprocessor systems whose physical arrangement matches or can be made to imitate the network structure of the models.

Second, new software techniques have been widely heralded as ways to approach the brittleness problem. Nonprocedural computer languages promise to relieve the programmer of the responsibility for specifying the sequence of steps needed to solve a particular problem (in reality, they substitute standard sequencing methods that are built into a compiler and that, on account of their generality, are rarely optimal for particular problems). These languages allow programmers to introduce large numbers of domain-specific rules into expert systems before the complexity becomes totally unmanageable. Some form of "nonmonotonic" reasoning[12] must then be introduced to mitigate the problems that arise when such rules are applied without precise consistency checks before the program is used. However, even these techniques require a vast software engineering effort for each problem that is attacked. The possibility of solving some of these problems with network-oriented methods that reduce the amount of explicit programming still further has provided the second major impetus for the development of simulated network methods within AI. Curiously, however, these developments have taken place in relative isolation from prior and contemporaneous work by biologists that was aimed at making models that incorporate some of the rich functional diversity of real nervous systems. (Some examples from our own work appear later in this article.)

We shall trace only the major currents in the development of these nonbiological networks; more details may be found in the works listed in the endnotes. While much of the activity has been recent, the notion that networks might be employed to carry out computations actually antedates the introduction of the programmable digital computer. The most influential of these early discussions was probably the 1943 paper of Warren McCulloch and Walter Pitts,[13] in which activity in neuronal* networks was identified with the operations of the propositional calculus. Actual simulations of recognition automata based on networks were carried out by Frank Rosenblatt before 1958,[14] but the theoretical limitations of his "perceptrons" were soon pointed out by Marvin Minsky and Seymour Papert,[15] and interest in network models waned until the recent introduction of more complicated nonlinear models that do not share these limitations. Other lines of development that have influenced many of the current models include networks that are specially crafted for specific purposes, such as the system of David Marr and Tomaso Poggio for computing stereo disparity,[16] and networks in which nodes are identified with cognitive "units" and interconnections with relationships between concepts, as in John R. Anderson's ACT model for retrieving information from memory.[17]

Thus the stage was set for the "physicist's approach to neural networks" as many scientists perceived a need to design networks for which convergence and learning properties could be predicted by mathematical theorems rather than by lengthy computer runs. Linear systems provided a relatively tractable starting point,[18] but nonlinearity is essential if categories are to be distinguished without overlap. A convenient physical analogy was the spin-glass, for which an extensive theory was already available. Never mind if the analogy had to be a highly strained one. The possibility of analysis was more important to these workers than whether what their systems did was related to the basic problem of intelligence. All one had to do was identify network nodes with spins and connections with spin interactions, and one could then speak of an "energy" that increased with the number of incompatibly connected spin pairs. From any starting state, the system would "relax" toward a state of minimum energy,

*We use the term *neuronal* when a close identification with the properties of actual neurons is implied. We use the term *neural* when only a general similarity to actual neurons is involved.

and these states could be identified with "memories" encoded in the connectivity coefficients of the network. Each memory would have a "zone of attraction" in the surrounding "state space." This description neatly tied in the neural networks with recent advances in the dynamics of nonlinear systems and the theory of chaos. The best-known models of this class are those of John Hopfield and his coworkers, who have been concerned primarily with the construction of ready-made networks for various tasks rather than with learning algorithms for such networks.[19] The latter element has been added in "Boltzmann machine" models, which take their name from their use of the concept of energy from statistical mechanics associated with the late nineteenth-century physicist Ludwig Boltzmann.[20] The representation of concepts from cognitive psychology in such networks has been zealously explored, and illustrative applications presented.[21]

Even with parallel computation and new learning algorithms, however, the possibility of training a network in a sufficient number of circumstances to confer *common sense* on it appears to recede forever into the distance as one contemplates the exceptions to the exceptions that are present in real-life situations. This unending compounding of exceptions comes close to revealing the true nature of the brittleness problem, which is that no amount of anticipation, planning, and programming can ever enumerate, a priori, all the variants of even a routine situation that may occur in daily life. It would seem, in what is perhaps an analogy to the classic "halting problem" in the analysis of algorithms (the problem of determining whether a given algorithm will run forever or eventually halt), that the only way to determine all the responses a system needs to have to deal with the vagaries of the real world is to expose it to the world and let it "run." Thus, each system will be different and fundamentally unprogrammable.

We say that connectionist models "look sideways to biology" because they take their inspiration and much of their terminology from the neural networks in living organisms, but they are not model neural networks (nor are they intended to be). Physicists, in their search for simplicity, are not prepared to deal with systems whose fundamental aspect lies in variability rather than regularity. In the attempt to find regularity in biological systems, many features have been introduced into their simulation in connectionist systems that are quite unbiological. These include the notion of memory as a replica or a transformation of "information" given in the world (human memories are highly context- and affect-sensitive and to some extent nonveridical); the conception of memory retrieval as the relaxation of a network to a stable state (a brain is continually exposed to changing input patterns and has no opportunity to freeze them while waiting for the approach to equilibrium); the idea of energy minimization through simulated annealing (a brain decides actions more quickly than known annealing procedures could attain in model networks operating at the speeds of real neurons); the notion of bidirectional and symmetric single connections (synaptic connections in the brain are monodirectional); and the idea that learning can proceed by clamping the output of the system to a desired value while synaptic weights are adjusted according to some rule (the motor output of a brain can in general not be imposed externally). Yet each of these elements is present in one or another of the connectionist models.

These unrealistic features should be a warning sign that something is seriously amiss in the basic assumptions behind the AI paradigm, even as modified by the introduction of parallel processing in neural-network–inspired systems. The *ad hoc* quality of these assumptions suggests that the true problem lies deeper than the details of the network simulations; it must have to do with the concept of information and the way it comes to be represented and transformed in the intelligent systems that have evolved in nature.

Standing at the start of the chain of deductions enumerated on pages 147–48, which for AI justify the notion of the brain as a computer, is the assumption that information exists in the world—that it is just there to be manipulated. There is also the idea that the organism is a *receiver* rather than a *creator* of criteria leading to information. Once the prior existence of such external information is conceded, it is entirely natural to proceed without further ado to the business of programming the rules to deal with it. At this point, the damage is already done. All efforts to program such rules run quickly into five vicious problems that have in common the transfer to the programmer of functions that belong properly to the putatively intelligent system:

1. *The coding problem.* The programmer must find a suitable representation of the information to put it in the proper form for

symbolic manipulation. It will usually not be clear in advance just what symbolic manipulations may be required and what the antecedent requirements on the representation may be.

2. *The category problem.* The programmer must specify a sufficient set of rules to define all the categories with which the program must deal. It is difficult to see in advance what these categories must be in a real world, much less how to define them.

3. *The procedure problem.* The programmer must specify in advance the actions to be taken by the system for all combinations of inputs that may occur. The number of such combinations is enormous and becomes even larger when the relevant aspects of context are taken into account. The behavior of biological organisms with real nervous systems becomes quite unpredictable in such circumstances.

4. *The homunculus problem.* Separate mechanisms are required to interpret the strings of symbols produced as output by any formal information-processing system. The strings can have no meaning within the formal system itself. But then, the necessary properties of intelligence are embodied in the observer, not the system. To avoid an infinite regress, the programmer is obliged to specify all the procedures the observer must follow.

5. *The developmental problem.* Can a programmed system come to exist without a programmer? Intelligent biological systems exist, yet they evolved and were not programmed, either as species or as individuals. Thus, the AI argument that brains carry out computations as computers do leads to a contradiction: brains must have programs, yet at the same time must not be programmed.

We hold that the solution to these conundrums may be found by examining existing natural intelligences and other biological systems in an attempt to understand how they come to exist and how they operate without prior programs. In the remainder of this essay, we shall argue that a form of selection, akin to Darwinian selection but operating among collections of neurons in the brain of a single organism during its lifetime, provides the only tenable basis for a theory of categorization and intelligence.[22] Evolution, by extending selection in this way to the individual brain, was able to remove the need for the programmer.

LOOKING DIRECTLY TO BIOLOGY

From the preceding analysis, it is clear that the notion of information preexisting in the world must be rejected. The essential requirement for learning, logic, and the other mental functions that are the usual subjects of AI research is the prior ability to categorize objects and events based on sensory signals reaching the brain. The variety of sensory experiences is both vast and unique for each individual. The categories themselves are not present in the environment but must be constructed by each individual according to what is adaptive for its species and its own particular circumstances. The a priori specification of rules for categorization, applicable to all individuals and all contexts, is precluded by the complexity, variability, and unpredictability of the macroscopic world. To make matters worse, the categories constructed by an organism cannot be fixed but must constantly change in response to new experiences and new realities in its part of the environment. The only way categories constructed in this individualistic manner can be validated is by constant coupling back to the world through behavior. However, once this adaptive categorization process has been established, the rest of the task—the construction of higher categories, memories, and associations—is enormously simplified.

Our first task, then, is to build a satisfactory theory that goes beyond the formal processing of information to a consideration of how that information comes to exist in an unlabeled world, what relationship exists between signals in the brain and the categories it has constructed, and how the interactions of those signals yield behavior without the benefit of prearranged codes to give them meaning or of prearranged algorithms to process them. The problems encompass memory as well as transient signals: How can memory function in the absence of a replicative store like that found in a computer, and how can memory be combined with current sensory signals to produce behaviors that enhance the survival of the organism? To make such a theory, we must consider the entire biological system, its evolutionary origins, and its development as an individual from embryo to functioning adult.

It would be well to begin by considering some basic facts of neurobiology. First, nervous systems are organized as networks with distinct areas having different patterns of connectivity, apparently specialized for different functions. Often these networks are connected to one another in a sequence of maps. We characterize this anatomy as a "heterarchy" (an arrangement in which the subnetworks are cross-connected in ways that do not follow a strict hierarchy). In such an arrangement, subnetworks with different functions interact to yield more complex functions that they do not possess alone. Successive regions appear to have been added gradually during the course of evolution, each contributing a new function but working in conjunction with older regions to confer a high degree of functional redundancy on the brain. There is no apparent analog to the functions of the clock and the instruction decoder in a computer. Instead, there is apparently a high degree of parallelism in the operations of the functional regions as well as in the responses of individual neurons. Extensive overlaps of dendritic and axonal arborizations suggest a functional degeneracy in which there are many alternative paths between any two points in the network, even within a single map. That no single neuron appears to be indispensable for any function suggests that only patterns of response over many neurons can have functional significance. Inasmuch as neurons have limited speed and dynamic range, they probably do not carry out computational algorithms in anything like the way a computer does.

The final, and most telling, observation is the enormous diversity of neuronal populations. This diversity is seen at all phylogenetic levels but, if anything, is greater in higher forms. Diversity extends to the number and arrangement of neurons in genetically identical animals and even to the detailed structure of individual neurons of known function in those animals in which such structures can be identified. It can easily be calculated that there is not enough information in the DNA to specify uniquely the locations of all these neurons and their connections. Thus, indeterminate, dynamic, epigenetic mechanisms (mechanisms reflecting the influence of the local environment on the unfolding genetic programs of individual cells) must operate during development to determine the fine structure of the nervous system. This is not what one would expect if nervous systems were optimized by design to carry out specific cognitive functions. Furthermore, the variability appears to be not just an unavoidable consequence of essential developmental processes but an evolutionarily selected trait. While such variation in wiring would lead to total failure in a computer, it seems to serve a functional role in the brain. The nature of this role will become clear when we consider how selective processes can act to give the kind of flexible, adaptive categorization that we have argued is necessary to enable an animal to deal with the world without benefit of a preordained program.

The biological facts we have pointed out, particularly the structural variation at all levels in the nervous system, together suggest that selection has a role not only in the development of nervous systems but also in their functioning at maturity. In selective systems the functional units are not specifically constructed to carry out their functions in an optimal way but instead are selected from much larger sets called "repertoires." The component units in a repertoire are constructed with a wide structural variety that is sufficient to cover, with overlap, the range of possible functions needed in any particular instantiation of the system. Selection occurs during experience without further alteration of the functional properties of units already constructed. Rather, the selected units are multiplied or amplified in such a manner as to make a larger contribution to the future responses of the system than the unselected units. Selective processes of this kind, with different amplification modes appropriate to each system, provide the basic mechanisms of the immune system and, of course, of evolution itself.

Consideration of the need for nervous systems to provide organisms with the behavioral adaptability to survive in a hostile environment without prior knowledge or programming, consideration of the structural variability found in all nervous systems, and other considerations have prompted the idea embodied in the neuronal group selection (NGS) theory[23] that the brain is in fact a selective system operating in somatic time (that is, during the lifetime of an individual organism). Population thinking, the fundamental theoretical mode of biology in which the properties of populations as well as those of individuals are taken into account, is thereby introduced into considerations of how individual brains work.

THE NEURONAL GROUP SELECTION THEORY

According to the NGS theory, two kinds of selection events play critical roles in shaping the development of the nervous system.

During the formation of the brain in the embryo, selection among competing neuronal cells and their processes determines the anatomical form and the pattern of synaptic connectivity of the nervous system. This selection for connectivity is elaborated through the developmental mechanisms of cell adhesion and movement, differential growth, cell division, and cell death. Because of their dynamic properties, these selective mechanisms introduce individual variance into the neuronal networks. Later, during postnatal experience, selection among diverse preexisting groups of cells, accomplished by differential modification of synaptic strengths or efficacies *without change in the connectivity pattern,* shapes the behavioral repertoire of the organism according to what is of adaptive value to it in its econiche.

A system must have three features if it is to be selective: (1) it must have an a priori repertoire of variant entities capable of responding to relevant environmental states; (2) the individual members of this repertoire must have extensive opportunities to encounter the rich diversity of the environment, providing opportunities for selection, and (3) the system must have a mechanism for differentially amplifying the relative contributions of those members of the repertoire that are in some sense favored or selected in their interactions with the environment. According to the NGS theory, the repertoires in the nervous system comprise groups of perhaps 50 to 10,000 neurons, capable, as a result of their interconnections, of responding to particular patterns of activity that arrive at their synapses. These interconnections are formed during development, prior to experience. The inputs to which the groups respond originate ultimately at the sense organs (encounter with the environment) but frequently are relayed first through other neuronal groups. Selective modification in the strengths of synaptic connections (differential amplification) leads to the compartition and stabilization of functioning circuits out of fixed networks. In higher forms, responses of neuronal populations are significantly influenced by similarities between present and past constellations of sensory signals. This reevocation of previous responses constitutes the basis of what we call memory. Memory is a consequence of selective amplification, which leads to increased speed or strength of selected responses when similar patterns of stimulation are repeated.

To be able to respond adequately to a wide range of novel inputs, a selective system must have a sufficient number of units in its repertoires. A relationship can be derived between the sizes of the repertoires and the specificities of the individual groups.[24] If recognition is too specific, the system will fail because there will be no way to place enough groups in a finite repertoire to recognize all possible stimuli; similarly, if specificity is too broad, the system will fail because stimuli with significant differences may be confused. The specificities must therefore be intermediate, allowing several groups to respond more or less well to any given stimulus. This phenomenon, which we call "degeneracy," is critical to an understanding of selective recognition systems. Degeneracy ensures that any perceptual problem has multiple potential solutions. Context determines exactly which combination of groups responds in a given situation and therefore which solution is selected. Degeneracy also ensures that the entire "space" of possible stimuli is covered and that the system has the functional redundancy needed to make it fail-safe against the loss of individual groups.

One additional concept that is critical to the NGS theory is that of "reentry," or the exchange of output signals, usually in a mapped arrangement, from one repertoire to another at the same or an earlier stage of neuronal processing. Reentry provides a mechanism for correlating responses at corresponding positions in related maps so as to ensure consistency across the entire system with respect to the current state and spatiotemporal continuity of the environment. Reentry ensures that subrepertoires at all levels in the nervous system are constantly mapped to each other and to the outside world, obviating any need for the context switching, time stamps, or other bookkeeping apparatus used in computers. It encompasses feedback but is more general. For example, two different repertoires in independent parallel pathways, each disjunctively sampling different aspects of signals, can classify stimuli according to different criteria and can be cross-connected at higher levels. Such interacting repertoires form "classification couples," which, by their mutual interaction, can perform classifications more complex than either repertoire could accomplish alone. Another form of reentry involves the total system of creature plus environment. In this "global" form of reentry, the motor output of the organism influences sensory systems by changing the relative arrangement of objects or the organism's position in space. Mappings at all levels of the nervous system thus become joined in a global loop. Iteration of activity in this loop can alter reentry in local maps and lead to modified behaviors that are more adaptive for the organism.

The NGS theory is consistent with the biological facts we have summarized. It takes advantage of the unavoidable variance in connectivity introduced by epigenetic events during the construction of neuronal networks to provide a plausible mechanism for categorization without programmed descriptions, homunculi, or reinforced learning. The theory is based on principles of selection similar to those that govern the evolution of species; the mechanisms, of course, are different. Such an approach is not all-inclusive, but it does give one a way to confront the fundamental problem of categories before taking on social psychology and all the intervening problems between perception and language.

Like any scientific theory, NGS must be tested by experiment. Data from several lines of study already provide significant support for it. Studies of development in the nervous system show that the dynamic regulation of a small number of cell-adhesion molecules is responsible for the growth patterns of neuronal processes,[25] and there is no evidence for the kind of extensive system of chemical markers that would be required if all connectivity were somehow genetically specified. Indeed, there is evidence for extensive variance of connectivity, even in genetically identical animals. In adult animals, data now show that neuronal mappings, such as those in the somatosensory cortex (a brain area that responds to touch receptors in the skin), are not nearly as rigid and unvarying as had previously been thought.[26] Rather, competition occurs to determine map boundaries. The evidence shows that certain connections that are anatomically present but not used in the normal functioning of these cortical regions can become active by selection when normal patterns of activation are disrupted. These inactive connections correspond to the ones not selected in normal functioning; their existence would make no sense in a nonselective system. A complete discussion[27] of this evidence[28] is beyond the scope of this article. Instead, we shall briefly describe a series of automata that we have constructed in computer simulations to test the self-consistency of NGS as well as to demonstrate the ability of selective recognition systems to carry out interesting recognition and categorization tasks. Such models can be invaluable in helping to focus experimental questions for the biologist. Ultimately, we hope also to learn from them how to construct machines capable of carrying out context-sensitive classification tasks far better than any computers that are now available.

SELECTIVE RECOGNITION AUTOMATA

We have been exploring the properties of selective recognition systems by constructing and testing a series of automata. These automata address some of the problems of the standard AI paradigm by avoiding preestablished categories and programming altogether. Instead, they are constructed as networks of simulated neuronlike units that, by a process of selection, can carry out simple categorization and association tasks in variant worlds full of novelty. Programming is used to instruct the computer how to simulate the neuronal units, but the function of these units is not itself programmed. The first automaton, called Darwin I, dealt with the process of recognition itself by using strings of binary digits as both recognizands and recognizers.[29] The second, Darwin II, was used for the recognition and classification of two-dimensional patterns presented on a retinalike array.[30] A third system, Darwin III, combines the recognition and categorization networks of Darwin II with motor circuits and effectors that act upon the environment to form a complete automaton capable of autonomous behavior. Unlike the previous two automata, Darwin III can be observed behaving without our looking into its "nervous system."

The arrangement of networks in Darwin III may be varied at will to suit various experimental protocols. A simplified functional schematic of one such arrangement, which we will describe in detail shortly, is shown in the diagram on page 162.

Networks may be constructed from multiple repertoires, corresponding to functional regions in the brain. Each repertoire may contain several layers of cells, just as the cerebral cortex does. Each layer may have its own rules for connectivity and synaptic modification. Once established, the connectivity is fixed, but the connection strengths vary in accordance with rules for synaptic modification that provide the mechanism of NGS. Stimuli are presented on a retinalike input array. An environmental module permits these stimuli to be generated and moved about in various ways in order to test the

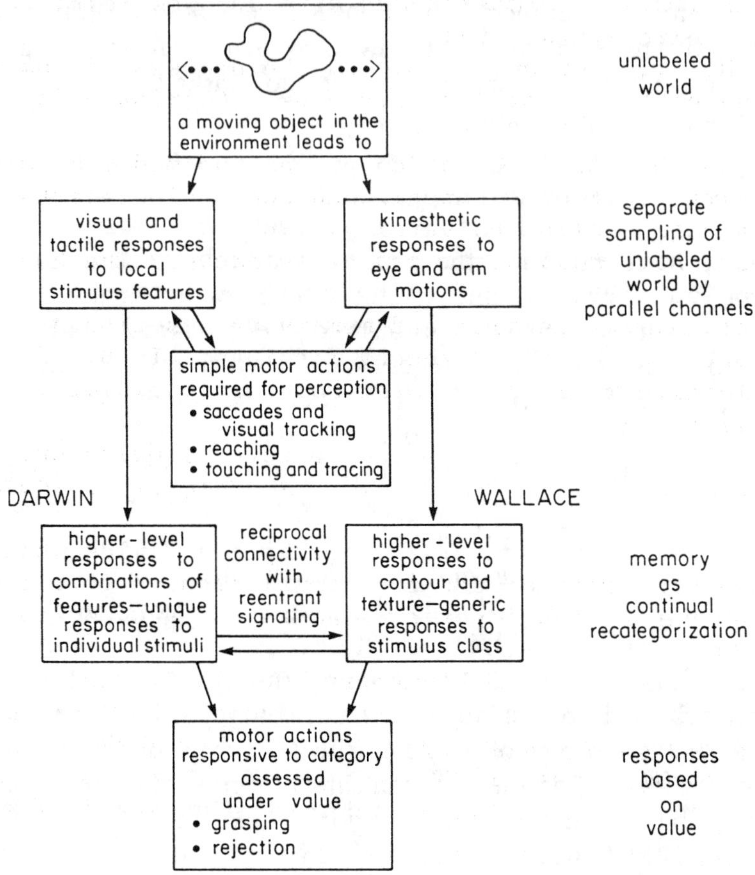

This diagram shows the functional relationships in one arrangement of Darwin III. The box at the top represents the environment, in which an unnamed object is moving about. The remaining boxes represent functions, each of which is subserved by several repertoires of neuronal groups with appropriate interconnections. The arrows suggest causal relationships, which generally reflect the existence of anatomical connections among the various regions. The two separate sampling systems of the automaton, Darwin and Wallace, are at the left and the right, respectively.

The result of the automaton's neuronal activity is externally apparent as motor activity responsive to its categorization of objects. This categorization proceeds according to internal criteria that emerge because the automaton has biases or values. For example, the value "seeing is better than not seeing" is expressed in terms of changes in connection strengths in oculomotor repertoires when visual units become more active following eye movements. Note that value does not prespecify categories, but when categories do emerge, it biases the selection of behaviors consequent upon them. Note also that the automaton reflects its experience in more or less stable alterations of connection strengths but does not have coded representations for memory. Instead, memory is exhibited as an enhanced ability to recognize and categorize objects in classes seen before.

responses of the automaton. Two devices are provided for motor output from Darwin III: a multijointed arm and a movable head with one or two eyes. Motions of the arm can actually displace objects in the environment, while motions of the head affect only their perceived positions. Specialized networks may be incorporated that respond by simple innate criteria to the relative adaptive value to the automaton of its various motor actions. Selective amplification may be made to depend on adaptive value as registered by these internal structures. External criteria for amplification (such as might be provided by a programmer) are not permitted.

An important rule, one that distinguishes the Darwin automata from AI systems with similar goals, is that no specific information about the stimulus objects to be presented is built into the system when it is constructed. General information about the kinds of stimuli that will be significant to the system (for example, the fact that they will be line drawings) is, however, implicit in the choice of feature-detecting elements that are used. This choice is akin to the specializations built into the receptor organs of each species during the course of evolution.

A part of Darwin III is specialized, like Darwin II, to deal with categorization. Psychological studies suggest that humans use several different methods to make classifications.[31] Accordingly, both automata incorporate two separate categorization functions. The first is to recognize aspects of individual objects according to their unique characteristics; the second is to recognize similarities among things in the same class and differences among things in different classes and thus to define objects. To accomplish these tasks, two sets of repertoires are used that operate in parallel. They both incorporate series of maps, but the maps are constructed differently and they make classifications according to quite different principles. These complementary subsystems interact via reentrant reciprocal connections to give associative functions not possessed by either set alone.

The two subsystems are arbitrarily named Darwin and Wallace (see the diagram). Darwin is the one designed to respond uniquely to individual stimulus patterns. Its responses loosely correspond to an approach to categorization known in the psychological literature as "matching to exemplars." In this approach, objects are compared to stored exemplars, and categories are assigned according to the maximum degree of match obtained with features; Darwin, however, does not store feature patterns but rather produces patterns of response corresponding to each unique input that it recognizes. In itself, Darwin cannot define an object, because it is insensitive to the continuities of features. Wallace, on the other hand, is designed to respond in the same way to different objects in a class by correlating a variety of features; this process loosely corresponds to a probabilistic matching approach to categorization and cannot in itself distinguish individuals. Of course, the particular response specificities of Darwin and Wallace (mainly to contour in a two-dimensional world) are intended to be merely exemplary, and other stimulus properties such as color and texture would also be represented in real nervous systems.

The Darwin and Wallace networks both have hierarchical structures. Each has a level that is connected directly to sensory input and that deals with features of the stimulus; connected to that is an abstracting or combining level that receives its main input from the first level and responds to combinations of the elementary responses that are relevant to categorization. The initial layer of the Darwin subsystem comprises groups of cells that respond to local features on the input array, such as line segments oriented in certain directions or with certain bends. These are connected in various combinations to higher-level abstracting groups that give the desired unique responses to each stimulus pattern. These responses include elements contributed by the surrounding context.

On the other hand, Wallace deals with object and class properties. In Darwin III, the Wallace subsystem makes use of the automaton's arm to trace over the contours of stimulus objects, much as a blind person reading braille text might do. The first-level repertoire of Wallace receives input from the arm's kinesthetic sensory neurons. It responds to correlations of trace activities that distinguish objects as entities from the background by their spatial continuity. Cells in this repertoire are in turn connected to an abstracting network similar to the one in Darwin. Because the trace responds to the presence or changes of direction of lines in the environment with little regard for their lengths and orientations, Wallace is insensitive to both rigid and nonrigid transformations of stimulus objects and tends to respond to class characteristics of whole families of related objects.

The networks in the two abstracting repertoires are connected to each other at higher levels to form a classification couple. It is important that in such a couple the earlier levels not be connected, for if they were, the separate modes of sampling for later classification would be confounded and their distinct characteristics lost. In other words, the sampling of the world by parallel channels must be disjunctive for rich, context-sensitive classification to occur.

The responses of the neuronal groups in Darwin III are determined by their present inputs and past histories in a manner that incorporates the most important features of the far more complicated responses of real neurons. Input connections are specified by lists that are constructed when the model is set up. These lists are constructed differently for each repertoire according to its function. Each input contributes to the output of the group according to the current strength of its connection. In addition, the groups are subject to random fluctuations in their activity analogous to those found in real neuronal networks. The recognition specificity of each group depends on its connection list and connection strengths; the best response is obtained when the most active inputs are connected via synapses with high connection strengths. For other inputs, a group will respond more or less well, overlapping in specificity with other groups and conferring degeneracy on the system as a whole.

The connection strengths among cells, both within and between groups, are modified during selective amplification. The amplification rule depends only on quantities that could reasonably have an influence on the efficacies of real synapses in real neuronal networks and is purely local in nature. In the scheme we have used most often, a connection is strengthened if the activities of both pre- and postsynaptic cells exceed specified thresholds. In other words, a connection from an active input to an active cell is strengthened and leads to a stronger response the next time a similar input is encountered. In certain other circumstances, connection strengths are weakened, preventing the system from eventually reaching a state in which all synapses have maximum efficacy. If this were to happen, any input would drive the network as a whole to a state of maximal activity corresponding to a kind of "epileptic seizure."

With appropriate stimulation sequences, Darwin II and Darwin III are capable of producing responses corresponding to behaviors such as categorization, recognition, generalization, and association. A detailed treatment of some typical experiments has been presented elsewhere.[32] *Categorization* is most evident in the Wallace responses.

It does not involve *naming,* which requires a linguistic convention, but only similarity of response to items in the same category. As we have already seen, such similarity is characteristic of the operation of Wallace. (The particular categories arrived at for various kinds of stimuli are dependent on the particular choice of kinesthetic trace correlations that Wallace groups respond to, and might or might not agree with the categories *we* define for the stimuli. The existence of discrepancies is consistent with the idea that categories are not inherent in the environment, but depend on the evolutionarily dictated predispositions of organisms to attend to categories that are relevant to their adaptive needs. The construction of information depends on these internal adaptive criteria.)

The effect of synaptic modification on the responses of groups in these networks is to alter cells that respond above a certain level (the amplification threshold) so that they will give a stronger response when later they experience a similar input pattern; groups with weaker responses generally are changed so as not to respond at all after amplification. Groups that are not involved in the response to a particular stimulus remain unchanged and available for response to novel stimuli not yet encountered. These selective changes demonstrate *recognition,* or the enhancement of meaningful response to a stimulus after it has been experienced before. In addition, amplification can be shown to improve the ability of the system to categorize.

Generalization occurs when responses to novel shapes are more like the responses to previously encountered shapes in the same class than would have been the case without prior experience. In Wallace, generalization is already present without amplification as a consequence of the feature-correlating property of that network, but in Darwin, generalization is not built in and can occur only with the help of Wallace. Reentrant connections between Darwin and Wallace make it possible for common patterns of response in Wallace to bias the units amplified in Darwin in accord with the class membership of the various stimuli. After a number of repetitions of this process, with shapes from several different classes, the Darwin responses become more alike within each class. To the extent that novel stimuli in the same class elicit responses in the feature-detecting layer of Darwin that have elements in common with the responses to the stimuli used during amplification, responses to these new stimuli will also become more similar, consistent with generalization in Darwin.

Reentrant connections in both directions between Darwin and Wallace are also essential for the process of *association*. Association is achieved when individual responses in Darwin are linked to different stimuli in the same class via Wallace in such a way that presentation of one of the individual stimuli evokes elements of the response in Darwin proper to another. Such associative properties among individuals could not be displayed by Wallace alone.

These capabilities of categorization, recognition, generalization, and association all underline the point that these critical aspects of perception can, and indeed must, occur before conventional learning. They also show how systems based on more than one principle of categorization can be joined in classification couples to give modes of classification not available to any single system.

Darwin III is also being used to study problems involving motion, perceptual invariance, figure-ground discrimination, and memory, among other phenomena. The NGS theory suggests that object motion is a critical factor in the selective process, particularly in early visual learning, where it provides to the perceptual system a major clue that the world in fact can be parsed adaptively into separate objects. This view is consistent with experiments suggesting that human infants have a conception of objects as spatially connected, coherent, continuously movable entities.[33] For this reason, the first experiments using the motor systems in Darwin III have been aimed at gaining a better understanding of this parsing process, beginning with the simple ability to track a moving object on a plain background.

In these experiments, connections are provided from retinotopically mapped visual layers (corresponding to the superior colliculus or optic tectum in various biological species) to motor layers connecting ultimately to the muscles that control the position of the eye. These connections are made indiscriminately to motor cells corresponding to all directions of eye movement. Thus, there is no a priori specificity with regard to input in any particular part of the visual field and there are no prearranged motor skills; performance can develop and improve only by selection from spontaneous movements generated by pairs of mutually inhibitory motor pattern-generating layers. Amplification of connections from sensory to motor regions is modulated by value schemes based respectively on the appearance of activity in a circumfoveal region and in the fovea itself. (The fovea is the region of greatest visual acuity near the center of the retina.) Thus, connections from a particular point on a visual layer to a particular motor area will tend to be strengthened when the appearance of an object at that point is correlated with activity in the motor area that leads to foveation of the stimulus. These same connections will tend to be weakened when the motor activity does not lead to foveation.

After a suitable period of experience with various moving stimuli, Darwin III in fact begins to make the appropriate saccades and fine tracking movements with no further specification of its task than that implicit in the value scheme. The automaton finally displays a system of behavior in which the eye scans at random when no stimulus is visible, makes a rapid saccade to any stimulus that appears within the outer limits of its widest visual field, and finely tracks any stimulus that has successfully been foveated. During fine tracking, the Darwin and Wallace networks are able to respond to the now-centered object, permitting position-independent categorization to occur. Habituation eventually sets in, permitting occasional saccades to other parts of the visual field. After such a saccade, a new stimulus object can take over as tracking target.

In a similar fashion, the multijointed arm of Darwin III can be trained to reach for and touch objects that are first detected and tracked by the visual system. This performance, which entails the coordination of gestural motions involving the various joints to different extents, requires the participation of a whole series of repertoires that perform functions similar to those thought to be carried out by the cerebellum in real nervous systems.

Of course, these selective systems make mistakes. For example, in the oculomotor system, amplification errors may occur when a stimulus crosses the edge of a visual field diagonally, and very large stimuli may confuse the tracking mechanism. By the use of standard engineering techniques, a better tracking system could surely be designed, one in which the correct motions for a spot of light at any location on the visual field would all be calculated in advance and incorporated in the logic of the design. The selective system needs experience to develop its functional capabilities. But this very lack of built-in function is its biggest advantage; the machinery in a selective system "doesn't know what it is for," permitting the same networks to accomplish various tasks depending on what we, acting as external agents of "evolution," decide they should find "adaptive." This flexibility is possible precisely because the functional organization of the system arises only *after* interaction with the environment. Equally simple training regimes should work for a wide variety of tasks, such as finding a desirable object in a background of distracting objects and picking it out with the arm. The modular combination of subsystems capable of carrying out recognition tasks provides an attractive approach to the construction of automata with increasingly complex perceptual capabilities and should have eventual significance for efforts at machine vision. As for output, the corollary for motor control is the ability to generate complex behavioral sequences by selection from simple and innate motion patterns. This has obvious significance for developments in robotics and the control of complex systems, particularly in connection with "attentional tasks."[34] Such context-sensitive tasks present an apparently insuperable barrier to traditional AI approaches.

From a purely economical point of view, it might be argued that artificial selective systems would be impractical because they must always contain some units that do not respond to any of the inputs actually encountered, and thus are never used at all. The fraction of such units does not increase with system size, however, and the extra units provide redundancy that may well yield overall cost savings because of reduced repairs and downtime. Speed of execution is also no barrier to the usefulness of selective systems implemented on parallel processors; responses require only a few times the response latency of the individual units because relaxation is not required as it is in systems based on the statistical-mechanical concept of lattice (network) energy minimization. It is therefore reasonable to expect that practical systems based on selection could be constructed with hardware that is presently available or forseeable in the near future. Such systems will have more components but a simpler overall design than possible systems based on information-processing network models. Obviously, such systems, if proven feasible, will have a great influence on the design of computer hardware.

SUMMARY AND CONCLUSIONS

The automata we have described are intended to illustrate certain aspects of the NGS theory without attempting to emulate real nervous systems in a detailed way. The experimental data and the computer resources to do that are not yet at hand. Thus, the models do not provide evidence for the applicability of the theory to real nervous systems; such evidence can come only from experiment. Nonetheless, NGS provides satisfying explanations for a whole panoply of perceptual processes involving categorization, and as inanimate examples of selective systems, the models can help to demonstrate the consistency of the theory as an abstract description of these processes. Such demonstrations are important for understanding complicated biological systems and at the same time can provide real insight into the computer-science problem of designing artificial systems with brainlike capabilities.

In particular, it is quite clear that nervous systems do not work in anything like the way that has been assumed in the standard AI paradigm, yet the performance of at least some nervous systems is definitive of the term *intelligence* as used in the phrase "artificial intelligence." It is therefore very curious that AI, even in its new connectionist guise, has for the most part neglected the fundamental biology of the nervous system, from which the very definition of intelligence is derived. We suggest that in order to make progress in overcoming the obstacles we have discussed, AI must recognize these origins and incorporate what can be learned from a study of nervous systems. It must stop reasoning by analogy with well-studied, but irrelevant, physical systems such as spin glasses, and must instead reason by analysis of relevant facts about biological systems that actually have intelligence. This change will require AI to abandon the notion of intelligence as a purely abstract information-processing activity.

A confrontation of the number of interactive levels in a real organism capable of intelligent behavior reveals a staggering complexity of nonlinear interactions. If social transmission through language is added, the complexity increases even more. It appears to be the height of arrogance, in the face of this complexity, to think that all problems intelligent creatures confront can be understood by just pondering them in the abstract. One must instead begin by analyzing such systems in terms of their basic necessary structures and functions and their modes of origin—developmental as well as evolutionary. The separation of hardware from software implicit in the traditional AI approach needs to be abandoned, even though it served well as a guiding principle in the development of von Neumann–type computers, which may be logic engines and—to some extent, culture engines—but are not biological engines. We believe that AI will eventually be achieved only in non–von Neumann systems in which specialized variants of hardware, based on a common theme of selection and population thinking, will work without programs to adapt to the particular environments in which they find themselves, just as biological organisms do. Programs and intelligence based on communication can come later.

ENDNOTES

We thank the International Business Machines Corporation and the Cornell National Supercomputer Facility for their support of part of this work.

[1]Aristotle, *Historia Animalium,* trans. D'Arcy Wentworth Thompson (Oxford: Clarendon Press, 1910), bk. 2, sec. 3, 501^b 20.

[2]Aristotle, *De Partibus Animalium,* trans. William Ogle (Oxford: Clarendon Press, 1912), bk. 3, sec. 1, 661^b 33.

[3]Gerald M. Edelman, *Neural Darwinism: The Theory of Neuronal Group Selection* (New York: Basic Books, 1987).

[4]Patrick Henry Winston, *Artificial Intelligence,* 2d ed. (Reading, Mass.: Addison-Wesley, 1984), 1–2.

[5]Marvin Minsky, "Steps Toward Artificial Intelligence," in *Proceedings of the Institute of Radio Engineers,* 49 (1961):8–30.

[6]Winston, *Artificial Intelligence,* 42.

[7]Hubert L. Dreyfus, *What Computers Can't Do* (New York: Harper and Row, 1972).

[8]Alan M. Turing, "On Computable Numbers, with an Application to the Entscheidungsproblem," in *Proceedings of the London Mathematical Society* 42 (1937):230–65. Turing defined a certain class of automaton, now known as the Turing machine, and showed that any member of this class could compute any of a large class of functions. All but a few special-purpose digital computers are Turing machines.

[9]Douglas R. Hofstadter, *Gödel, Escher, Bach: An Eternal Golden Braid* (New York: Basic Books, 1979), 561. Hofstadter points out that "like tea, the Church-Turing Thesis can be given in a variety of different strengths," and he presents several of these with a discussion of their implications for AI.

[10]John McCarthy, "Programs with Common Sense," in *Proceedings of the Teddington Conference on the Mechanization of Thought Processes* (London: Her Majesty's Stationery Office, 1960); John McCarthy, "Some Expert Systems Need Common Sense," *Annals of the New York Academy of Sciences* 426 (1984):129–35.

[11]Peter W. Frey, ed., *Chess Skill in Man and Machine,* 2d ed. (New York: Springer-Verlag, 1984).

[12]Raymond Reiter, "Nonmonotonic Reasoning," *Annual Reviews of Computer Science* (Palo Alto: Annual Reviews Inc., forthcoming).

[13]Warren S. McCulloch and Walter H. Pitts, "A Logical Calculus of the Ideas Immanent in Nervous Activity," *Bulletin of Mathematical Biophysics* 5 (1943):115–33.

[14]Frank Rosenblatt, *The Perceptron: A Theory of Statistical Separability in Cognitive Systems* (Ithaca: Cornell Aeronautical Laboratory Inc., Report No. VG-1196-G-1, 1958).

[15]Marvin Minsky and Seymour Papert, *Perceptrons: An Introduction to Computational Geometry* (Cambridge: MIT Press, 1969).

[16]David Marr and Tomaso Poggio, "Cooperative Computation of Stereo Disparity," *Science* 194 (15 Oct. 1976):283–87.

[17]John R. Anderson, "A Spreading Activation Theory of Memory," *Journal of Verbal Learning and Verbal Behavior* 22 (1983):261–95.

[18]Leon N. Cooper, "A Possible Organization of Animal Memory and Learning," in *Nobel Symposium*, no. 24 (1973), 252–64; Teuvo Kohonen, *Associative Memory: A System Theoretical Approach* (New York: Springer-Verlag, 1977).

[19]Reviewed in John J. Hopfield and David W. Tank, "Computing with Neural Circuits: A Model," *Science* 233 (8 August 1986):625–33.

[20]David H. Ackley, Geoffrey E. Hinton, and Terrence J. Sejnowski, "A Learning Algorithm for Boltzmann Machines," *Cognitive Science* 9 (January-March 1985):147–69.

[21]David E. Rumelhart, James L. McClelland, and the PDP Research Group, eds., *Parallel Distributed Processing: Explorations in the Microstructure of Cognition*, vols. 1,2 (Cambridge: MIT Press, 1986).

[22]Edelman, *Neural Darwinism*.

[23]Ibid.; and Gerald M. Edelman, "Group Selection and Phasic Reentrant Signalling: A Theory of Higher Brain Function," in *The Mindful Brain*, Gerald M. Edelman and Vernon B. Mountcastle, eds. (Cambridge: MIT Press, 1978), 51–100.

[24]Edelman, *Neural Darwinism*.

[25]Gerald M. Edelman, "Cell-Adhesion Molecules: A Molecular Basis for Animal Form," *Scientific American* 250 (April 1984): 118–29; Gerald M. Edelman, "Cell Adhesion Molecules in the Regulation of Animal Form and Tissue Pattern," *Annual Review of Cell Biology* 2 (1986):81–116.

[26]John H. Kaas, Michael M. Merzenich, and Herbert P. Killackey, "The Reorganization of Somatosensory Cortex Following Peripheral-Nerve Damage in Adult and Developing Mammals," *Annual Review of Neuroscience* 6 (1983):325–56; Michael M. Merzenich et al., "Topographic Reorganization of Somatosensory Cortical Areas 3b and 1 in Adult Monkeys Following Restricted Deafferentation," *Neuroscience* 8 (January 1983):33–55. Numerous other examples have been reported.

[27]Edelman, *Neural Darwinism*.

[28]Gerald M. Edelman and Leif H. Finkel, "Neuronal Group Selection in the Cerebral Cortex," in *Dynamical Aspects of Neocortical Function*, Gerald M. Edelman, W. Einar Gall, and W. Maxwell Cowan, eds. (New York: John Wiley, 1984), 653–95.

[29]Gerald M. Edelman, "Group Selection as the Basis for Higher Brain Function," in *Organization of the Cerebral Cortex*, Francis O. Schmitt et al., eds. (Cambridge: MIT Press, 1981), 51–100.

[30]Gerald M. Edelman and George N. Reeke, Jr., "Selective Networks Capable of Representative Transformations, Limited Generalizations, and Associative Memory," in *Proceedings of the National Academy of Sciences USA* 79 (1982):2091–95.

[31]Edward E. Smith and Douglas L. Medin, *Categories and Concepts* (Cambridge: Harvard University Press, 1981).

[32]George N. Reeke, Jr., and Gerald M. Edelman, "Selective Networks and Recognition Automata," *Annals of the New York Academy of Sciences* 426 (1984):181–201.

[33]Philip J. Kellman and Elizabeth S. Spelke, "Perception of Partly Occluded Objects in Infancy," *Cognitive Psychology* 15 (4) (October 1983):483–524.

[34]Anya Hurlbert and Tomaso Poggio, "Do Computers Need Attention?" *Nature* 321 (12 June 1986): 651–52.

Hubert L. Dreyfus and Stuart E. Dreyfus

Making a Mind Versus Modeling the Brain: Artificial Intelligence Back at a Branchpoint

[N]othing seems more possible to me than that people some day will come to the definite opinion that there is no copy in the . . . nervous system which corresponds to a particular *thought, or a* particular *idea, or memory.*[1]
—*Ludwig Wittgenstein (1948)*

[I]nformation is not stored anywhere in particular. Rather, it is stored everywhere. Information is better thought of as "evoked" than "found."[2]
—*David Rumelhart and Donald Norman (1981)*

IN THE EARLY 1950S, as calculating machines were coming into their own, a few pioneer thinkers began to realize that digital computers could be more than number crunchers. At that point two opposed visions of what computers could be, each with its correlated research program, emerged and struggled for recognition. One faction saw computers as a system for manipulating mental symbols; the other, as a medium for modeling the brain. One sought to use computers to instantiate a formal representation of the world;

Hubert L. Dreyfus is professor of philosophy at the University of California at Berkeley.

Stuart E. Dreyfus is professor of industrial engineering and operations research at the University of California at Berkeley.

the other, to simulate the interactions of neurons. One took problem solving as its paradigm of intelligence; the other, learning. One utilized logic; the other, statistics. One school was the heir to the rationalist, reductionist tradition in philosophy; the other viewed itself as idealized, holistic neuroscience.

The rallying cry of the first group was that both minds and digital computers are physical symbol systems. By 1955 Allen Newell and Herbert Simon, working at the Rand Corporation, had concluded that strings of bits manipulated by a digital computer could stand for anything—numbers, of course, but also features of the real world. Moreover, programs could be used as rules to represent relations between these symbols, so that the system could infer further facts about the represented objects and their relations. As Newell put it recently in his account of the history of issues in AI,

> The digital-computer field defined computers as machines that manipulated numbers. The great thing was, adherents said, that everything could be encoded into numbers, even instructions. In contrast, the scientists in AI saw computers as machines that manipulated symbols. The great thing was, they said, that everything could be encoded into symbols, even numbers.[3]

This way of looking at computers became the basis of a way of looking at minds. Newell and Simon hypothesized that the human brain and the digital computer, while totally different in structure and mechanism, had at a certain level of abstraction a common functional description. At this level both the human brain and the appropriately programmed digital computer could be seen as two different instantiations of a single species of device—a device that generated intelligent behavior by manipulating symbols by means of formal rules. Newell and Simon stated their view as a hypothesis:

> *The Physical Symbol System Hypothesis.* A physical symbol system has the necessary and sufficient means for general intelligent action.
>
> By "necessary" we mean that any system that exhibits general intelligence will prove upon analysis to be a physical symbol system. By "sufficient" we mean that any physical symbol system of sufficient size can be organized further to exhibit general intelligence.[4]

Newell and Simon trace the roots of their hypothesis back to Gottlob Frege, Bertrand Russell, and Alfred North Whitehead,[5] but Frege and company were of course themselves heirs to a long, atomistic, rationalist tradition. Descartes had already assumed that all understanding consisted of forming and manipulating appropriate representations, that these representations could be analyzed into primitive elements *(naturas simplices)*, and that all phenomena could be understood as complex combinations of these simple elements. Moreover, at the same time, Hobbes had implicitly assumed that the elements were formal components related by purely syntactic operations, so that reasoning could be reduced to calculation. "When a man *reasons*, he does nothing else but conceive a sum total from addition of parcels," Hobbes wrote, "for REASON . . . is nothing but reckoning. . . . "[6] Finally, Leibniz, working out the classical idea of mathesis—the formalization of everything—sought support to develop a universal symbol system so that "we can assign to every object its determined characteristic number."[7] According to Leibniz, in understanding we analyze concepts into more simple elements. In order to avoid a regress to simpler and simpler elements, there must be ultimate simples in terms of which all complex concepts can be understood. Moreover, if concepts are to apply to the world, there must be simple features that these elements represent. Leibniz envisaged "a kind of alphabet of human thoughts"[8] whose "characters must show, when they are used in demonstrations, some kind of connection, grouping and order which are also found in the objects."[9]

Ludwig Wittgenstein, drawing on Frege and Russell, stated in his *Tractatus Logico-Philosophicus* the pure form of this syntactic, representational view of the relation of the mind to reality. He defined the world as the totality of logically independent atomic facts:

> 1.1. The world is the totality of facts, not of things.

Facts in turn, he held, could be exhaustively analyzed into primitive objects.

> 2.01. An atomic fact is a combination of objects. . . .
>
> 2.0124. If all objects are given, then *thereby* all atomic facts are given.

These facts, their constituents, and their logical relations, Wittgenstein claimed, were represented in the mind.

2.1. We make to ourselves pictures of facts.

2.15. That the elements of the picture are combined with one another in a definite way, represents that the things are so combined with one another.[10]

AI can be thought of as the attempt to find the primitive elements and logical relations in the subject (man or computer) that mirror the primitive objects and their relations that make up the world. Newell and Simon's physical symbol system hypothesis in effect turns the Wittgensteinian vision (which is itself the culmination of the classical rationalist philosophical tradition) into an empirical claim and bases a research program on it.

The opposed intuition, that we should set about creating artificial intelligence by modeling the brain rather than the mind's symbolic representation of the world, drew its inspiration not from philosophy but from what was soon to be called neuroscience. It was directly inspired by the work of D.O. Hebb, who in 1949 suggested that a mass of neurons could learn if when neuron A and neuron B were simultaneously excited, that excitation increased the strength of the connection between them. [11]

This lead was followed by Frank Rosenblatt, who reasoned that since intelligent behavior based on our representation of the world was likely to be hard to formalize, AI should instead attempt to automate the procedures by which a network of neurons learns to discriminate patterns and respond appropriately. As Rosenblatt put it,

> The implicit assumption [of the symbol manipulating research program] is that it is relatively easy to specify the behavior that we want the system to perform, and that the challenge is then to design a device or mechanism which will effectively carry out this behavior. . . . [I]t is both easier and more profitable to axiomatize the *physical system* and then investigate this system analytically to determine its behavior, than to axiomatize the *behavior* and then design a physical system by techniques of logical synthesis.[12]

Another way to put the difference between the two research programs is that those seeking symbolic representations were looking for a formal structure that would give the computer the ability to solve a certain class of problems or discriminate certain types of patterns. Rosenblatt, on the other hand, wanted to build a physical device, or to simulate such a device on a digital computer, that could then generate its own abilities:

Many of the models which we have heard discussed are concerned with the question of what logical structure a system must have if it is to exhibit some property, X. This is essentially a question about a static system. . . .

An alternative way of looking at the question is: what kind of a system can *evolve* property X? I think we can show in a number of interesting cases that the second question can be solved without having an answer to the first.[13]

Both approaches met with immediate and startling success. By 1956 Newell and Simon had succeeded in programming a computer using symbolic representations to solve simple puzzles and prove theorems in the propositional calculus. On the basis of these early impressive results it looked as if the physical symbol system hypothesis was about to be confirmed, and Newell and Simon were understandably euphoric. Simon announced:

It is not my aim to surprise or shock you. . . . But the simplest way I can summarize is to say that there are now in the world machines that think, that learn and that create. Moreover, their ability to do these things is going to increase rapidly until—in a visible future—the range of problems they can handle will be coextensive with the range to which the human mind has been applied.[14]

He and Newell explained:

[W]e now have the elements of a theory of heuristic (as contrasted with algorithmic) problem solving; and we can use this theory both to understand human heuristic processes and to simulate such processes with digital computers. Intuition, insight, and learning are no longer exclusive possessions of humans: any large high-speed computer can be programmed to exhibit them also.[15]

Rosenblatt put his ideas to work in a type of device that he called a perceptron.[16] By 1956 Rosenblatt was able to train a perceptron to classify certain types of patterns as similar and to separate these from other patterns that were dissimilar. By 1959 he too was jubilant and felt his approach had been vindicated:

It seems clear that the . . . perceptron introduces a new kind of information processing automaton: For the first time, we have a machine which is capable of having original ideas. As an analogue of the biological brain, the perceptron, more precisely, the theory of statistical separability, seems to come closer to meeting the requirements of a functional explanation of the nervous system than any system previously proposed. . . . As concept, it would seem that the perceptron has established, beyond doubt, the feasibility and principle of non-human systems which may embody human cognitive functions. . . . The future of information processing devices which operate on statistical, rather than logical, principles seems to be clearly indicated.[17]

In the early sixties both approaches looked equally promising, and both made themselves equally vulnerable by making exaggerated claims. Yet the results of the internal war between the two research programs were surprisingly asymmetrical. By 1970 the brain simulation research, which had its paradigm in the perceptron, was reduced to a few lonely, underfunded efforts, while those who proposed using digital computers as symbol manipulators had undisputed control of the resources, graduate programs, journals, and symposia that constitute a flourishing research program.

Reconstructing how this change came about is complicated by the myth of manifest destiny that any ongoing research program generates. Thus, it looks to the victors as if symbolic information processing won out because it was on the right track, while the neural network or connectionist approach lost because it simply didn't work. But this account of the history of the field is a retrospective illusion. Both research programs had ideas worth exploring, and both had deep, unrecognized problems.

Each position had its detractors, and what they said was essentially the same: each approach had shown that it could solve certain easy problems but that there was no reason to think either group could extrapolate its methods to real-world complexity. Indeed, there was evidence that as problems got more complex, the computation required by both approaches would grow exponentially and so would soon become intractable. In 1969 Marvin Minsky and Seymour Papert said of Rosenblatt's perceptron:

> Rosenblatt's schemes quickly took root, and soon there were perhaps as many as a hundred groups, large and small, experimenting with the model. . . .
>
> The results of these hundreds of projects and experiments were generally disappointing, and the explanations inconclusive. The machines usually work quite well on very simple problems but deteriorate very rapidly as the tasks assigned to them get harder.[18]

Three years later, Sir James Lighthill, after reviewing work using heuristic programs such as Simon's and Minsky's, reached a strikingly similar negative conclusion:

> Most workers in AI research and in related fields confess to a pronounced feeling of disappointment in what has been achieved in the past 25 years. Workers entered the field around 1950, and even around 1960, with high hopes that are very far from having been realized in 1972. In no part of the field have the discoveries made so far produced the major impact that was then promised. . . .
>
> [O]ne rather general cause for the disappointments that have been experienced: failure to recognize the implications of the 'combinatorial explosion'. This is a general obstacle to the construction of a . . . system on a large knowledge base which results from the explosive growth of any combinatorial expression, representing numbers of possible ways of grouping elements of the knowledge base according to particular rules, as the base's size increases.[19]

As David Rumelhart and David Zipser have succinctly summed it up, "Combinatorial explosion catches you sooner or later, although sometimes in different ways in parallel than in serial."[20] Both sides had, as Jerry Fodor once put it, walked into a game of three-dimensional chess, thinking it was tick-tack-toe. Why then, so early in the game, with so little known and so much to learn, did one team of researchers triumph at the total expense of the other? Why, at this crucial branchpoint, did the symbolic representation project become the only game in town?

Everyone who knows the history of the field will be able to point to the proximal cause. About 1965, Minsky and Papert, who were running a laboratory at MIT dedicated to the symbol-manipulation approach and therefore competing for support with the perceptron projects, began circulating drafts of a book attacking the idea of the perceptron. In the book they made clear their scientific position:

> Perceptrons have been widely publicized as "pattern recognition" or "learning" machines and as such have been discussed in a large number of books, journal articles, and voluminous "reports." Most of this writing . . . is without scientific value.[21]

But their attack was also a philosophical crusade. They rightly saw that traditional reliance on reduction to logical primitives was being challenged by a new holism:

Both of the present authors (first independently and later together) became involved with a somewhat therapeutic compulsion: to dispel what we feared to be the first shadows of a "holistic" or "Gestalt" misconception that would threaten to haunt the fields of engineering and artificial intelligence as it had earlier haunted biology and psychology.[22]

They were quite right. Artificial neural nets may, but need not, allow an interpretation of their hidden nodes* in terms of features a human being could recognize and use to solve the problem. While neural network modeling itself is committed to neither view, it can be demonstrated that association does not *require* that the hidden nodes be interpretable. Holists like Rosenblatt happily assumed that individual nodes or patterns of nodes were not picking out fixed features of the domain.

Minsky and Papert were so intent on eliminating all competition, and so secure in the atomistic tradition that runs from Descartes to early Wittgenstein, that their book suggests much more than it actually demonstrates. They set out to analyze the capacity of a one-layer perceptron,† while completely ignoring in the mathematical portion of their book Rosenblatt's chapters on multilayer machines and his proof of the convergence of a probabilistic learning algorithm based on back propagation‡ of errors.[23] According to Rumelhart and McClelland,

Minsky and Papert set out to show which functions can and cannot be computed by [one-layer] machines. They demonstrated, in particular, that such perceptrons are unable to calculate such mathematical functions as parity (whether an odd or even number of points are on in the retina) or the topological function of connectedness (whether all points that are on are connected to all other points that are on either directly or via other points that are also on) without making use of absurdly large numbers of predicates. The analysis is extremely elegant and demonstrates the importance of a mathematical approach to analyzing computational systems.[24]

---

* Hidden nodes are nodes that neither directly detect the input to the net nor constitute its output. They are, however, either directly or indirectly linked by connections with adjustable strengths to the nodes detecting the input and those constituting the output.

† A one-layer network has no hidden nodes, while multilayer networks do contain hidden nodes.

‡ Back propagation of errors requires recursively computing, starting with the output nodes, the effects of changing the strengths of connections on the difference between the desired output and the output produced by an input. The weights are then adjusted during learning to reduce the difference.

But the implications of the analysis are quite limited. Rumelhart and McClelland continue:

> Essentially . . . although Minsky and Papert were exactly correct in their analysis of the *one-layer perceptron*, the theorems don't apply to systems which are even a little more complex. In particular, it doesn't apply to multilayer systems nor to systems that allow feedback loops.[25]

Yet in the conclusion to *Perceptrons,* when Minsky and Papert ask themselves the question, Have you considered perceptrons with many layers? they give the impression, while rhetorically leaving the question open, of having settled it:

> Well, we have considered Gamba machines, which could be described as "two layers of perceptron." We have not found (by thinking or by studying the literature) any other really interesting class of multilayered machine, at least none whose principles seem to have a significant relation to those of the perceptron. . . . [W]e consider it to be an important research problem to elucidate (or reject) our intuitive judgment that the extension is sterile.[26]

Their attack on gestalt thinking in AI succeeded beyond their wildest dreams. Only an unappreciated few, among them Stephen Grossberg, James A. Anderson, and Teuvo Kohonen, took up the "important research problem." Indeed, almost everyone in AI assumed that neural nets had been laid to rest forever. Rumelhart and McClelland note:

> Minsky and Papert's analysis of the limitations of the one-layer perceptron, coupled with some of the early successes of the symbolic processing approach in artificial intelligence, was enough to suggest to a large number of workers in the field that there was no future in perceptron-like computational devices for artificial intelligence and cognitive psychology.[27]

But why was it enough? Both approaches had produced some promising work and some unfounded promises.[28] It was too early to close accounts on either approach. Yet something in Minsky and Papert's book struck a responsive chord. It seemed AI workers shared the quasi-religious philosophical prejudice against holism that motivated the attack. One can see the power of the tradition, for example, in Newell and Simon's article on physical symbol systems. The article begins with the scientific hypothesis that the mind and the computer are intelligent by virtue of manipulating discrete symbols, but it ends with a revelation: "The study of logic and computers has revealed to us that intelligence resides in physical-symbol systems."[29]

Holism could not compete with such intense philosophical convictions. Rosenblatt was discredited along with the hundreds of less responsible network research groups that his work had encouraged. His research money dried up, and he had trouble getting his work published. By 1970, as far as AI was concerned, neural nets were dead. In his history of AI, Newell says the issue of symbols versus numbers "is certainly not alive now and has not been for a long time."[30] Rosenblatt is not even mentioned in John Haugeland's or Margaret Boden's histories of the AI field.[31]

But blaming the rout of the connectionists on an antiholistic prejudice is too simple. There was a deeper way philosophical assumptions influenced intuition and led to an overestimation of the importance of the early symbol-processing results. The way it looked at the time was that the perceptron people had to do an immense amount of mathematical analysis and calculating to solve even the most simple problems of pattern recognition, such as discriminating horizontal from vertical lines in various parts of the receptive field, while the symbol-manipulating approach had relatively effortlessly solved hard problems in cognition, such as proving theorems in logic and solving combinatorial puzzles. Even more important, it seemed that given the computing power available at the time, the neural net researchers could do only speculative neuroscience and psychology, while the simple programs of symbolic representationists were on their way to being useful. Behind this way of sizing up the situation was the assumption that thinking and pattern recognition are two distinct domains and that thinking is the more important of the two. As we shall see later in our discussion of the commonsense knowledge problem, to look at things this way is to ignore both the preeminent role of pattern discrimination in human expertise and also the background of commonsense understanding that is presupposed in everyday real-world thinking. Taking account of this background may well require pattern recognition.

This thought brings us back to the philosophical tradition. It was not just Descartes and his descendants who stood behind symbolic information processing, but all of Western philosophy. According to Heidegger, traditional philosophy is defined from the start by its focusing on facts in the world while "passing over" the world as such.[32] This means that philosophy has from the start systematically ignored or distorted the everyday context of human activity.[33] The branch of the philosophical tradition that descends from Socrates through Plato, Descartes, Leibniz, and Kant to conventional AI takes it for granted, in addition, that understanding a domain consists in having a *theory* of that domain. A theory formulates the relationships among objective, *context-free* elements (simples, primitives, features, attributes, factors, data points, cues, etc.) in terms of abstract principles (covering laws, rules, programs, etc.).

Plato held that in theoretical domains such as mathematics and perhaps ethics, thinkers apply explicit, context-free rules or theories they have learned in another life, outside the everyday world. Once learned, such theories function in this world by controlling the thinker's mind, whether he or she is conscious of them or not. Plato's account did not apply to everyday skills but only to domains in which there is a priori knowledge. The success of theory in the natural sciences, however, reinforced the idea that in any orderly domain there must be some set of context-free elements and some abstract relations among those elements that account for the order of that domain and for man's ability to act intelligently in it. Thus, Leibniz boldly generalized the rationalist account to all forms of intelligent activity, even everyday practice:

> [T]he most important observations and turns of skill in all sorts of trades and professions are as yet unwritten. This fact is proved by experience when passing from theory to practice we desire to accomplish something. *Of course, we can also write up this practice, since it is at bottom just another theory more complex and particular....* [italics added][34]

The symbolic information-processing approach gains its assurance from this transfer to all domains of methods that have been developed by philosophers and that are successful in the natural sciences. Since, in this view, any domain must be formalizable, the way to do AI in any area is obviously to find the context-free elements and principles and to base a formal, symbolic representation on this theoretical analysis. In this vein Terry Winograd describes his AI work in terms borrowed from physical science:

> We are concerned with developing a formalism, or "representation," with which to describe ... knowledge. We seek the "atoms" and "particles" of which it is built, and the "forces" that act on it.[35]

No doubt theories about the universe are often built up gradually by modeling relatively simple and isolated systems and then making the model gradually more complex and integrating it with models of other domains. This is possible because all the phenomena are presumably the result of the lawlike relations between what Papert and Minsky call "structural primitives." Since no one *argues* for atomistic reduction in AI, it seems that AI workers just implicitly *assume* that the abstraction of elements from their everyday context, which defines philosophy and works in natural science, must also work in AI. This assumption may well account for the way the physical symbol system hypothesis so quickly turned into a revelation and for the ease with which Papert and Minsky's book triumphed over the holism of the perceptron.

Teaching philosophy at MIT in the mid-sixties, one of us—Hubert—was soon drawn into the debate over the possibility of AI. It was obvious that researchers such as Newell, Simon, and Minsky were the heirs to the philosophical tradition. But given the conclusions of the later Wittgenstein and the early Heidegger, that did not seem to be a good omen for the reductionist research program. Both these thinkers had called into question the very tradition on which symbolic information processing was based. Both were holists, both were struck by the importance of everyday practices, and both held that one could not have a theory of the everyday world.

It is one of the ironies of intellectual history that Wittgenstein's devastating attack on his own *Tractatus*, his *Philosophical Investigations*,[36] was published in 1953, just as AI took over the abstract, atomistic tradition he was attacking. After writing the *Tractatus*, Wittgenstein spent years doing what he called phenomenology[37]—looking in vain for the atomic facts and basic objects his theory required. He ended by abandoning his *Tractatus* and all rationalistic philosophy. He argued that the analysis of everyday situations into facts and rules (which is where most traditional philosophers and AI researchers think theory must begin) is itself only meaningful in some context and for some purpose. Thus, the elements chosen already reflect the goals and purposes for which they are carved out. When we try to find the ultimate context-free, purpose-free elements, as we must if we are going to find the primitive symbols to feed a computer, we are in effect trying to free aspects of our experience of just that pragmatic organization which makes it possible to use them intelligently in coping with everyday problems.

In the *Philosophical Investigations* Wittgenstein directly criticized the logical atomism of the *Tractatus:*

> "What lies behind the idea that names really signify simples"?—Socrates says in the *Theaetetus:* "If I make no mistake, I have heard some people say this: there is no definition of the primary elements—so to speak—out of which we and everything else are composed. . . . But just as what consists of these primary elements is itself complex, so the names of the elements become descriptive language by being compounded together." Both Russell's 'individuals' and my 'objects' *(Tractatus Logico-Philosophicus)* were such primary elements. But what are the simple constituent parts of which reality is composed? . . . It makes no sense at all to speak absolutely of the 'simple parts of a chair.'[38]

Already, in the 1920s, Martin Heidegger had reacted in a similar way against his mentor, Edmund Husserl, who regarded himself as the culmination of the Cartesian tradition and was therefore the grandfather of AI.[39] Husserl argued that an act of consciousness, or noesis, does not on its own grasp an object; rather, the act has intentionality (directedness) only by virtue of an "abstract form," or meaning, in the noema correlated with the act.[40]

This meaning, or symbolic representation, as conceived by Husserl, is a complex entity that has a difficult job to perform. In *Ideas Pertaining to a Pure Phenomenology,*[41] Husserl bravely tried to explain how the noema gets the job done. Reference is provided by "predicate-senses," which, like Fregean *Sinne,* just have the remarkable property of picking out objects' atomic properties. These predicates are combined into complex "descriptions" of complex objects, as in Russell's theory of descriptions. For Husserl, who was close to Kant on this point, the noema contains a hierarchy of strict rules. Since Husserl thought of intelligence as a context-determined, goal-directed activity, the mental representation of any type of object had to provide a context, or a "horizon" of expectations or "predelineations" for structuring the incoming data: "a rule governing *possible* other consciousness of [the object] as identical—possible, as exemplifying essentially predelineated types."[42] The noema must contain a rule describing all the features that can be expected with certainty in exploring a certain *type* of object—features that remain "inviolably the same: as long as the objectivity remains intended as *this* one and of this kind."[43] The rule must also prescribe predelineations of properties that are possible, but not necessary, features of this type of object: "Instead of a completely determined sense, there is always, therefore, a *frame of empty sense*. . . . "[44]

In 1973 Marvin Minsky proposed a new data structure, remarkably similar to Husserl's, for representing everyday knowledge:

> A *frame* is a data-structure for representing a stereotyped situation, like being in a certain kind of living room, or going to a child's birthday party. . . .
>
> We can think of a frame as a network of nodes and relations. The top levels of a frame are fixed, and represent things that are always true about the supposed situation. The lower levels have many *terminals*—slots that must be filled by specific instances or data. Each terminal can specify conditions its assignments must meet. . . .
>
> Much of the phenomenological power of the theory hinges on the inclusion of expectations and other kinds of presumptions. *A frame's terminals are normally already filled with "default" assignments.*[45]

In Minsky's model of a frame, the "top level" is a developed version of what, in Husserl's terminology, remains "inviolably the same" in the representation, and Husserl's predelineations have become "default assignments"—additional features that can normally be expected. The result is a step forward in AI techniques from a passive model of information processing to one that tries to take account of the interactions between a knower and the world. The task of AI thus converges with the task of transcendental phenomenology. Both must try in everyday domains to find frames constructed from a set of primitive predicates and their formal relations.

Heidegger, before Wittgenstein, carried out, in response to Husserl, a phenomenological description of the everyday world and everyday objects like chairs and hammers. Like Wittgenstein, he found that the everyday world could not be represented by a set of context-free elements. It was Heidegger who forced Husserl to face precisely this problem by pointing out that there are other ways of "encountering" things than relating to them as objects defined by a set of predicates. When we use a piece of equipment like a hammer, Heidegger said, we actualize a skill (which need not be represented in the mind) in the context of a socially organized nexus of equipment, purposes, and human roles (which need not be represented as a set of facts). This context, or world, and our everyday ways of skillful coping in it, which Heidegger called "circumspection," are not something we *think* but part of our socialization, which forms the way we *are*. Heidegger concluded:

> The context . . . can be taken formally in the sense of a system of relations. But . . . [t]he phenomenal content of these 'relations' and 'relata' . . . is such that they resist any sort of mathematical functionalization; nor are they merely something thought, first posited in an 'act of thinking'. They are rather relationships in which concernful circumspection as such already dwells.[46]

This defines the splitting of the ways between Husserl and AI on the one hand and Heidegger and the later Wittgenstein on the other. The crucial question becomes, Can there be a theory of the everyday world as rationalist philosophers have always held? Or is the commonsense background rather a combination of skills, practices, discriminations, and so on, which are not intentional states and so, *a fortiori*, do not have any representational content to be explicated in terms of elements and rules?

By making a move that was soon to become familiar in AI circles, Husserl tried to avoid the problem Heidegger posed. Husserl claimed that the world, the background of significance, the everyday context, was merely a very complex system of facts correlated with a complex system of beliefs, which, since they have truth conditions, he called validities. One could, in principle, he held, suspend one's dwelling in the world and achieve a detached description of the human belief system. One could thus complete the task that had been implicit in philosophy since Socrates: one could make explicit the beliefs and principles underlying all intelligent behavior. As Husserl put it,

> [E]ven the background . . . of which we are always concurrently conscious but which is momentarily irrelevant and remains completely unnoticed, still functions according to its implicit validities.[47]

Since he firmly believed that the shared background could be made explicit as a belief system, Husserl was ahead of his time in raising the question of the possibility of AI. After discussing the possibility that a formal axiomatic system might describe experience and pointing out that such a system of axioms and primitives—at least as we know it in geometry—could not describe everyday shapes such as "scalloped" and "lens-shaped," Husserl left open the question whether these everyday concepts could nonetheless be formalized. (This was like raising and leaving open the AI question whether one can axiomatize commonsense physics.) Taking up Leibniz's dream of a mathesis of all experience, Husserl added:

> The pressing question is . . . whether there could not be . . . an idealizing procedure that substitutes pure and strict ideals for intuited data and that would . . . serve . . . as the basic medium for a mathesis of experience.[48]

But, as Heidegger predicted, the task of writing out a complete theoretical account of everyday life turned out to be much harder than initially expected. Husserl's project ran into serious trouble, and there are signs that Minsky's has too. During twenty-five years of trying to spell out the components of the subject's representation of everyday objects, Husserl found that he had to include more and more of the subject's commonsense understanding of the everyday world:

> To be sure, even the tasks that present themselves when we take single types of objects as restricted clues prove to be extremely complicated and always lead to extensive disciplines when we penetrate more deeply. That is the case, for example, with . . . spatial objects (to say nothing of a Nature) as such, of psycho-physical being and humanity as such, culture as such.[49]

He spoke of the noema's "huge concreteness"[50] and of its "tremendous complication,"[51] and he sadly concluded at the age of seventy-five that he was a perpetual beginner and that phenomenology was an "infinite task."[52]

There are hints in his paper "A Framework for Representing Knowledge" that Minsky has embarked on the same "infinite task" that eventually overwhelmed Husserl:

> Just constructing a knowledge base is a major intellectual research problem. . . . We still know far too little about the contents and structure of common-sense knowledge. A "minimal" common-sense system must "know" something about cause-effect, time, purpose, locality, process, and types of knowledge. . . . We need a serious epistemological research effort in this area.[53]

To a student of contemporary philosophy, Minsky's naiveté and faith are astonishing. Husserl's phenomenology *was* just such a research effort. Indeed, philosophers from Socrates through Leibniz to early Wittgenstein carried on serious epistemological research in this area for two thousand years without notable success.

In the light of Wittgenstein's reversal and Heidegger's devastating critique of Husserl, one of us—Hubert—predicted trouble for symbolic information processing. As Newell notes in his history of AI, this warning was ignored:

> Dreyfus's central intellectual objection . . . is that the analysis of the context of human action into discrete elements is doomed to failure. This objection is grounded in phenomenological philosophy. Unfortunately, this appears to be a nonissue as far as AI is concerned. The answers, refutations, and analyses that have been forthcoming to Dreyfus's writings have simply not engaged this issue—which indeed would be a novel issue if it were to come to the fore.[54]

The trouble was, indeed, not long in coming to the fore, as the everyday world took its revenge on AI as it had on traditional philosophy. As we see it, the research program launched by Newell and Simon has gone through three ten-year stages. From 1955 to 1965 two research themes, representation and search, dominated the field then called "cognitive simulation." Newell and Simon showed, for example, how a computer could solve a class of problems with the general heuristic search principle known as means-end analysis—namely, to use any available operation that reduces the distance between the description of the current situation and the description of the goal. They then abstracted this heuristic technique and incorporated it into their General Problem Solver (GPS).

The second stage (1965–75), led by Marvin Minsky and Seymour Papert at MIT, was concerned with what facts and rules to represent. The idea was to develop methods for dealing systematically with knowledge in isolated domains called "microworlds." Famous programs written around 1970 at MIT include Terry Winograd's SHRDLU, which could obey commands given in a subset of natural language about a simplified "blocks-world," Thomas Evan's analogy problem program, David Waltz's scene analysis program, and Patrick Winston's program, which could learn concepts from examples.

The hope was that the restricted and isolated microworlds could be gradually made more realistic and combined so as to approach real-world understanding. But researchers confused two domains, which, following Heidegger, we shall distinguish as "universe" and "world." A set of interrelated facts may constitute a *universe,* like the physical universe, but it does not constitute a *world.* The latter, like the world of business, the world of theater, or the world of the physicist, is an organized body of objects, purposes, skills, and practices on the basis of which human activities have meaning or make sense. To see the difference, one can contrast the *meaningless* physical universe with the *meaningful* world of the discipline of physics. The world of physics, the business world, and the theater world make sense only against a background of common human concerns. They are local elaborations of the one commonsense world we all share. That is, subworlds are not related like isolable physical systems to the larger systems they *compose* but rather are local elaborations of a whole that they *presuppose.* Microworlds are not worlds but isolated meaningless domains, and it has gradually become clear that there is no way they could be combined and extended to arrive at the world of everyday life.

In its third stage, roughly from 1975 to the present, AI has been wrestling with what has come to be called the commonsense knowledge problem. The representation of knowledge was always a central problem for work in AI, but the two earlier periods—cognitive simulation and microworlds—were characterized by an attempt to avoid the problem of commonsense knowledge by seeing how much could be done with as little knowledge as possible. By the middle 1970s, however, the issue had to be faced. Various data structures, such as Minsky's frames and Roger Schank's scripts, have been tried without success. The commonsense knowledge problem has kept AI from even beginning to fulfill Simon's prediction of twenty years ago that "within twenty years machines will be capable of doing any work a man can do."[55]

Indeed, the commonsense knowledge problem has blocked all progress in theoretical AI for the past decade. Winograd was one of the first to see the limitations of SHRDLU and all script and frame attempts to extend the microworlds approach. Having "lost faith" in AI, he now teaches Heidegger in his computer science course at Stanford and points out "the difficulty of formalizing the commonsense background that determines which scripts, goals and strategies are relevant and how they interact."[56]

What sustains AI in this impasse is the conviction that the commonsense knowledge problem must be solvable, since human beings have obviously solved it. But human beings may not normally use commonsense *knowledge* at all. As Heidegger and Wittgenstein pointed out, what commonsense *understanding* amounts to might well be *everyday know-how*. By "know-how" we do not mean procedural rules but knowing what to do in a vast number of special cases.[57] For example, commonsense physics has turned out to be extremely hard to spell out in a set of facts and rules. When one tries, one either requires more common sense to understand the facts and rules one finds or else one produces formulas of such complexity that it seems highly unlikely they are in a child's mind.

Doing theoretical physics also requires background skills that may not be formalizable, but the domain itself can be described by abstract laws that make no reference to these background skills. AI researchers mistakenly conclude that commonsense physics too must be expressible as a set of abstract principles. But it just may be that the problem of finding a *theory* of commonsense physics is insoluble because the domain has no theoretical structure. By playing with all sorts of liquids and solids every day for several years, a child may simply learn to discriminate prototypical cases of solids, liquids, and so on and learn typical skilled responses to their typical behavior in typical circumstances. The same might well be the case for the social world. If background understanding is indeed a skill and if skills are based on whole patterns and not on rules, we would expect symbolic representations to fail to capture our commonsense understanding.

In the light of this impasse, classical, symbol-based AI appears more and more to be a perfect example of what Imre Lakatos has called a degenerating research program.[58] As we have seen, AI began auspiciously with Newell and Simon's work at Rand and by the late 1960s turned into a flourishing research program. Minsky predicted that "within a generation the problem of creating 'artificial intelligence' will be substantially solved."[59] Then, rather suddenly, the field ran into unexpected difficulties. It turned out to be much harder than one expected to formulate a theory of common sense. It was not, as Minsky had hoped, just a question of cataloguing a few hundred thousand facts. The commonsense knowledge problem became the center of concern. Minsky's mood changed completely in five years.

He told a reporter that "the AI problem is one of the hardest science has ever undertaken."[60]

The rationalist tradition had finally been put to an empirical test, and it had failed. The idea of producing a formal, atomistic theory of the everyday commonsense world and of representing that theory in a symbol manipulator had run into just the difficulties Heidegger and Wittgenstein had discovered. Frank Rosenblatt's intuition that it would be hopelessly difficult to formalize the world and thus to give a formal specification of intelligent behavior had been vindicated. His repressed research program (using the computer to instantiate a holistic model of an idealized brain), which had never really been refuted, became again a live option.

In journalistic accounts of the history of AI, Rosenblatt is vilified by anonymous detractors as a snake-oil salesman:

> Present-day researchers remember that Rosenblatt was given to steady and extravagant statements about the performance of his machine. "He was a press agent's dream," one scientist says, "a real medicine man. To hear him tell it, the Perceptron was capable of fantastic things. And maybe it was. But you couldn't prove it by the work Frank did."[61]

In fact, he was much clearer about the capacities and limitations of the various types of perceptrons than Simon and Minsky were about their symbolic programs.[62] Now he is being rehabilitated. David Rumelhart, Geoffrey Hinton, and James McClelland reflect this new appreciation of his pioneering work:

> Rosenblatt's work was very controversial at the time, and the specific models he proposed were not up to all the hopes he had for them. But his vision of the human information processing system as a dynamic, interactive, self-organizing system lies at the core of the PDP approach.[63]
>
> The studies of perceptrons . . . clearly anticipated many of the results in use today. The critique of perceptrons by Minsky and Papert was widely misinterpreted as destroying their credibility, whereas the work simply showed limitations on the power of the most limited class of perceptron-like mechanisms, and said nothing about more powerful, multiple layer models.[64]

Frustrated AI researchers, tired of clinging to a research program that Jerry Lettvin characterized in the early 1980s as "the only straw afloat," flocked to the new paradigm. Rumelhart and McClelland's book *Parallel Distributed Processing* sold six thousand copies the day it went onto the market, and thirty thousand are now in print. As Paul Smolensky put it,

> In the past half-decade the connectionist approach to cognitive modeling has grown from an obscure cult claiming a few true believers to a movement so vigorous that recent meetings of the Cognitive Science Society have begun to look like connectionist pep rallies.[65]

If multilayered networks succeed in fulfilling their promise, researchers will have to give up the conviction of Descartes, Husserl, and early Wittgenstein that the only way to produce intelligent behavior is to mirror the world with a formal theory in the mind. Worse, one may have to give up the more basic intuition at the source of philosophy that there must be a theory of every aspect of reality—that is, there must be elements and principles in terms of which one can account for the intelligibility of any domain. Neural networks may show that Heidegger, later Wittgenstein, and Rosenblatt were right in thinking that we behave intelligently in the world without having a theory of that world. If a theory is not *necessary* to explain intelligent behavior, we have to be prepared to raise the question whether in everyday domains such a theoretical explanation is even *possible.*

Neural net modelers, influenced by symbol-manipulating AI, are expending considerable effort, once their nets have been trained to perform a task, in trying to find the features represented by individual nodes and sets of nodes. Results thus far are equivocal. Consider Hinton's network for learning concepts by means of distributed representations.[66] The network can be trained to encode relationships in a domain that human beings conceptualize in terms of features, without the network being given the features that human beings use. Hinton produces examples of cases in which some nodes in the trained network can be interpreted as corresponding to the features that human beings pick out, although these nodes only roughly correspond to those features. Most nodes, however, cannot be interpreted semantically at all. A feature used in a symbolic representation is either present or not. In the net, however, although certain nodes are more active when a certain feature is present in the domain, the amount of activity not only varies with the presence or absence of this feature but is affected by the presence or absence of other features as well.

Hinton has picked a domain—family relationships—that is constructed by human beings precisely in terms of the features that human beings normally notice, such as generation and nationality. Hinton then analyzes those cases in which, starting with certain random initial-connection strengths, some nodes can, after learning, be interpreted as representing those features. Calculations using Hinton's model show, however, that even his net seems to learn its associations for some random initial-connection strengths without any obvious use of these everyday features.

In one very limited sense, any successfully trained multilayer net can be interpreted in terms of features—not everyday features but what we shall call highly abstract features. Consider the simple case of layers of binary units activated by feed-forward, but not lateral or feedback, connections. To construct such an account from a network that has learned certain associations, each node one level above the input nodes could, on the basis of the connections to it, be interpreted as detecting when one of a certain set of input patterns is present. (Some of the patterns will be the ones used in training, and some will never have been used.) If the set of input patterns that a particular node detects is given an invented name (it almost certainly won't have a name in our vocabulary), the node could be interpreted as detecting the highly abstract feature so named. Hence, every node one level above the input level could be characterized as a feature detector. Similarly, every node a level above those nodes could be interpreted as detecting a higher-order feature, defined as the presence of one of a specified set of patterns among the first level of feature detectors. And so on up the hierarchy.

The fact that intelligence, defined as the knowledge of a certain set of associations appropriate to a domain, can always be accounted for in terms of relations among a number of highly abstract features of a skill domain does not, however, preserve the rationalist intuition that these explanatory features must capture the essential structure of the domain so that one could base a theory on them. If the net were taught one more association of an input-output pair (where the input prior to training produced an output different from the one to be learned), the interpretation of at least some of the nodes would have to be changed. So the features that some of the nodes picked out before the last instance of training would turn out not to have been invariant structural features of the domain.

Once one has abandoned the philosophical approach of classical AI and accepted the atheoretical claim of neural net modeling, one question remains: How much of everyday intelligence can such a network be expected to capture? Classical AI researchers are quick to point out—as Rosenblatt already noted—that neural net modelers have so far had difficulty dealing with stepwise problem solving. Connectionists respond that they are confident that they will solve that problem in time. This response, however, reminds one too much of the way that the symbol manipulators in the sixties responded to the criticism that their programs were poor at the perception of patterns. The old struggle continues between intellectualists, who think that because they can do context-free logic they have a handle on everyday cognition but are poor at understanding perception, and gestaltists, who have the rudiments of an account of perception but no account of everyday cognition.[67] One might think, using the metaphor of the right and the left brain, that perhaps the brain or the mind uses each strategy when appropriate. The problem would then be how to combine the strategies. One cannot just switch back and forth, for as Heidegger and the gestaltists saw, the pragmatic background plays a crucial role in determining relevance, even in everyday logic and problem solving, and experts in any field, even logic, grasp operations in terms of their functional similarities.

It is even premature to consider combining the two approaches, since so far neither has accomplished enough to be on solid ground. Neural network modeling may simply be getting a deserved chance to fail, as did the symbolic approach.

Still, there is an important difference to bear in mind as each research program struggles on. The physical symbol system approach seems to be failing because it is simply false to assume that there must be a theory of every domain. Neural network modeling, however, is not committed to this or any other philosophical assumption. Nevertheless, building an interactive net sufficiently similar to the one our brain has evolved may be just too hard. Indeed, the commonsense knowledge problem, which has blocked the progress of symbolic representation techniques for fifteen years, may be looming on the neural net horizon, although researchers may not yet recognize it. All neural net modelers agree that for a net to be intelligent it must be able to generalize; that is, given sufficient examples of inputs associated with one particular output, it should associate further inputs of the same type with that same output. The question arises, however: What counts as the same type? The designer of the net has in mind a specific definition of the type required for a reasonable generalization and counts it a success if the net generalizes to other instances of this type. But when the net produces an unexpected association, can one say it has failed to generalize? One could equally well say that the net has all along been acting on a different definition of the type in question and that that difference has just been revealed. (All the "continue this sequence" questions found on intelligence tests really have more than one possible answer, but most human beings share a sense of what is simple and reasonable and therefore acceptable.)

Neural network modelers attempt to avoid this ambiguity and make the net produce "reasonable" generalizations by considering only a prespecified allowable family of generalizations—that is, allowable transformations that will count as acceptable generalizations (the hypothesis space). These modelers then attempt to design the architecture of their nets so that they transform inputs into outputs only in ways that are in the hypothesis space. Generalization will then be possible only on the designer's terms. While a few examples will be insufficient to identify uniquely the appropriate member of the hypothesis space, after enough examples only one hypothesis will account for all the examples. The net will then have learned the appropriate generalization principle. That is, all further input will produce what, from the designer's point of view, is the appropriate output.

The problem here is that the designer has determined, by means of the architecture of the net, that certain possible generalizations will never be found. All this is well and good for toy problems in which there is no question of what constitutes a reasonable generalization, but in real-world situations a large part of human intelligence consists in generalizing in ways that are appropriate to a context. If the designer restricts the net to a predefined class of appropriate responses, the net will be exhibiting the intelligence built into it by the designer for that context but will not have the common sense that would enable it to adapt to other contexts, as a truly human intelligence would.

Perhaps a net must share size, architecture, and initial-connection configuration with the human brain if it is to share our sense of appropriate generalization. If it is to learn from its own "experiences" to make associations that are humanlike rather than be taught to make associations that have been specified by its trainer, a net must also share our sense of appropriateness of output, and this means it must share our needs, desires, and emotions and have a humanlike body with appropriate physical movements, abilities, and vulnerability to injury.

If Heidegger and Wittgenstein are right, human beings are much more holistic than neural nets. Intelligence has to be motivated by purposes in the organism and goals picked up by the organism from an ongoing culture. If the minimum unit of analysis is that of a whole organism geared into a whole cultural world, neural nets as well as symbolically programmed computers still have a very long way to go.

ENDNOTES

[1]Ludwig Wittgenstein, *Last Writings on the Philosophy of Psychology* (Chicago: Chicago University Press, 1982), vol. 1, 504 (66e). (Translation corrected.)

[2]David E. Rumelhart and Donald A. Norman, "A Comparison of Models," *Parallel Models of Associative Memory,* ed. Geoffrey Hinton and James Anderson (Hillsdale, N.J.: Lawrence Erlbaum Associates, 1981), 3.

[3]Allen Newell, "Intellectual Issues in the History of Artificial Intelligence," in *The Study of Information: Interdisciplinary Messages,* ed. F. Machlup and U. Mansfield (New York: Wiley, 1983), 196.

[4]Allen Newell and Herbert Simon, "Computer Science as Empirical Inquiry: Symbols and Search," reprinted in *Mind Design,* ed. John Haugeland (Cambridge: MIT Press, 1981), 41.

[5]Ibid., 42.

[6]Thomas Hobbes, *Leviathan* (New York: Library of Liberal Arts, 1958), 45.

[7]Leibniz, *Selections,* ed. Philip Wiener (New York: Scribner, 1951), 18.

[8]Ibid., 20.

[9]Ibid., 10.

[10]Ludwig Wittgenstein, *Tractatus Logico-Philosophicus* (London: Routledge and Kegan Paul, 1960).

[11]D. O. Hebb, *The Organization of Behavior* (New York: Wiley, 1949).

[12]Frank Rosenblatt, "Strategic Approaches to the Study of Brain Models," *Principles of Self-Organization,* ed. H. von Foerster (Elmsford, N.Y.: Pergamon Press, 1962), 386.

[13]Ibid., 387.

[14]Herbert Simon and Allen Newell, "Heuristic Problem Solving: The Next Advance in Operations Research," *Operations Research* 6 (January–February 1958):6.

[15]Ibid. Heuristic rules are rules that when used by human beings are said to be based on experience or judgment. Such rules frequently lead to plausible solutions to problems or increase the efficiency of a problem-solving procedure. Whereas algorithms guarantee a correct solution (if there is one) in a finite time, heuristics only increase the likelihood of finding a plausible solution.

[16]David E. Rumelhart, James L. McClelland, and the PDP Research Group in their recent collection of papers, *Parallel Distributed Processing: Explorations in the Microstructure of Cognition,* vol. 1 (Cambridge: MIT Press, 1986), describe the perceptron as follows:

> Such machines consist of what is generally called a *retina,* an array of binary inputs sometimes taken to be arranged in a two-dimensional spatial layout; a set of *predicates,* a set of binary threshold units with fixed connections to a subset of units in the retina such that each predicate computes some local function over the subset of units to which it is connected; and one or more decision units, with modifiable connections to the predicates. (p. 111)

They contrast the way a parallel distributed processing (PDP) model like the perceptron stores information with the way information is stored by symbolic representation:

> In most models, knowledge is stored as a static copy of a pattern. Retrieval amounts to finding the pattern in long-term memory and copying it into a buffer or working memory. There is no real difference between the stored representation in long-term memory and the active representation in working memory. In PDP models, though, this is not the case. In these models, the patterns themselves are not stored. Rather, what is stored is the *connection strengths* between units that allow these patterns to be re-created. (p. 31)
>
> [K]nowledge about any individual pattern is not stored in the connections of a special unit reserved for that pattern, but is distributed over the connections among a large number of processing units. (p. 33)

This new notion of representation led directly to Rosenblatt's idea that such machines should be able to acquire their ability through learning rather than by being programmed with features and rules:

> [I]f the knowledge is [in] the strengths of the connections, learning must be a matter of finding the right connection strengths so that the right patterns of activation will be produced under the right circumstances. This is an extremely important property of this class of models, for it opens up the possibility that an information processing mechanism could learn, as a result of tuning its connections, to capture the interdependencies between activations that it is exposed to in the course of processing. (p. 32)

[17]Frank Rosenblatt, *Mechanisation of Thought Processes: Proceedings of a Symposium held at the National Physical Laboratory* (London: Her Majesty's Stationery Office, 1958), vol. 1, 449.

[18]Marvin Minsky and Seymour Papert, *Perceptrons: An Introduction to Computational Geometry* (Cambridge: MIT Press, 1969), 19.

[19]Sir James Lighthill, "Artificial Intelligence: A General Survey" in *Artificial Intelligence: A Paper Symposium* (London: Science Research Council, 1973).

[20]Rumelhart and McClelland, *Parallel Distributed Processing,* 158.

[21]Minsky and Papert, *Perceptrons,* 4.

[22]Ibid., 19.

[23]Frank Rosenblatt, *Principles of Neurodynamics, Perceptrons and the Theory of Brain Mechanisms* (Washington, D.C.: Spartan Books, 1962), 292. See also:

> The addition of a fourth layer of signal transmission units, or cross-coupling the A-units of a three-layer perceptron, permits the solution of generalization problems, over arbitrary transformation groups. (p. 576)
>
> In back-coupled perceptrons, selective attention to familiar objects in a complex field can occur. It is also possible for such a perceptron to attend selectively to objects which move differentially relative to their background. (p. 576)

[24]Rumelhart and McClelland, *Parallel Distributed Processing,* 111.

[25]Ibid., 112.

[26]Minsky and Papert, *Perceptrons,* 231–32.

[27]Rumelhart and McClelland, *Parallel Distributed Processing,* 112.

[28]For an evaluation of the symbolic representation approach's actual successes up to 1978, see Hubert Dreyfus, *What Computers Can't Do,* 2d ed. (New York: Harper and Row, 1979).

[29]Newell and Simon, "Computer Science and Empirical Inquiry," 197.

[30]Newell, "Intellectual Issues," 10.

[31]John Haugeland, *Artificial Intelligence: The Very Idea* (Cambridge: MIT Press, 1985); and Margaret Boden, *Artificial Intelligence and Natural Man* (New York: Basic Books, 1977). Work on neural nets was continued in a marginal way in psychology and neuroscience. James A. Anderson at Brown University continued to defend a net model in psychology, although he had to live off other researchers' grants, and Stephen Grossberg worked out an elegant mathematical implementation of elementary cognitive capacities. For Anderson's position see "Neural Models with Cognitive Implications" in *Basic Processing in Reading,* ed. D. LaBerse and S. J. Samuels (Hillsdale, N.J.: Lawrence Erlbaum Associates, 1978). For examples of Grossberg's work during the dark ages, see his book *Studies of Mind and Brain: Neural Principles of Learning, Perception, Development, Cognition and Motor Control* (Boston: Reidel Press, 1982). Kohonen's early work is reported in *Associative Memory—A System-Theoretical Approach* (Berlin: Springer-Verlag, 1977).

At MIT Minsky continued to lecture on neural nets and to assign theses investigating their logical properties. But according to Papert, Minsky did so only because nets had interesting mathematical properties, whereas nothing interesting could be proved concerning the properties of symbol systems. Moreover, many AI researchers assumed that since Turing machines were symbol manipulators and Turing had proved that Turing machines could compute anything, he had proved that all intelligibility could be captured by logic. On this view a holistic (and in those days statistical) approach needed justification, while the symbolic AI approach did not. This confidence, however, was based on confusing the uninterpreted symbols of a Turing machine (zeros and ones) with the semantically interpreted symbols of AI.

[32]Martin Heidegger, *Being and Time* (New York: Harper and Row, 1962), sec. 14–21; Hubert Dreyfus, *Being-in-the-World: A Commentary on Division I of Being and Time* (Cambridge: MIT Press, forthcoming, 1988).

[33]According to Heidegger, Aristotle came closer than any other philosopher to understanding the importance of everyday activity, but even he succumbed to the distortion of the phenomenon of the everyday world implicit in common sense.

[34]Leibniz, *Selections,* 48.

[35]Terry Winograd, "Artificial Intelligence and Language Comprehension," in *Artificial Intelligence and Language Comprehension* (Washington, D.C.: National Institute of Education, 1976), 9.

[36]Ludwig Wittgenstein, *Philosophical Investigations* (Oxford: Basil Blackwell, 1953).

[37]Ludwig Wittgenstein, *Philosophical Remarks* (Chicago: University of Chicago Press, 1975).

[38]Wittgenstein, *Philosophical Investigations,* 21.

[39]See *Husserl, Intentionality and Cognitive Science,* ed. Hubert Dreyfus (Cambridge: MIT Press, 1982).

[40]"Der Sinn . . . so wie wir ihn bestimmt haben, ist nicht ein konkretes Wesen im Gesamtbestande des Noema, sondern eine Art ihm einwohnender abstrackter Form." See Edmund Husserl, *Ideen Zu Einer Reinen Phänomenologie und Phänomenologischen Philosophie* (The Hague: Nijhoff, 1950). For evidence that Husserl held that the noema accounts for the intentionality of mental activity, see Hubert Dreyfus, "Husserl's Perceptual Noema," in *Husserl, Intentionality and Cognitive Science.*

[41]Edmund Husserl, *Ideas Pertaining to a Pure Phenomenology and to a Phenomenological Philosophy,* trans. F. Kersten (The Hague: Nijhoff, 1982).

[42]Edmund Husserl, *Cartesian Meditations,* trans. D. Cairns (The Hague: Nijhoff, 1960), 45.

[43]Ibid., 53.

[44]Ibid., 51.

[45]Marvin Minsky, "A Framework for Representing Knowledge," in *Mind Design,* ed. John Haugeland (Cambridge: MIT Press, 1981), 96.

[46]Heidegger, 121–22.

[47]Edmund Husserl, *Crisis of European Sciences and Transcendental Phenomenology,* trans. D. Carr (Evanston: Northwestern University Press, 1970), 149.

[48]Edmund Husserl, *Ideen zu einer reinen Phänomenologie und phenomenologischen Philosophie,* bk. 3 in vol. 5, *Husserliana* (The Hague: Nijoff, 1952), 134.

[49]Husserl, *Cartesian Meditations,* 54–55.

[50]Husserl, *Formal and Transcendental Logic,* trans. D. Cairns (The Hague: Nijhoff, 1969), 244.

[51]Ibid., 246.

[52]Husserl, *Crisis,* 291.

[53]Minsky, "A Framework," 124.

[54]Newell, "Intellectual Issues," 222–23.

[55]Herbert Simon, *The Shape of Automation for Men and Management* (New York: Harper and Row, 1965), 96.

[56]Terry Winograd, "Computer Software for Working with Language," *Scientific American* (September 1984):142.

[57]This account of skill is spelled out and defended in Hubert Dreyfus and Stuart Dreyfus, *Mind Over Machine* (New York: Macmillan, 1986).

[58]Imre Lakatos, *Philosophical Papers,* ed. J. Worrall (Cambridge: Cambridge University Press, 1978).

[59]Marvin Minsky, *Computation: Finite and Infinite Machines* (New York: Prentice-Hall, 1977), 2.

[60]Gina Kolata, "How Can Computers Get Common Sense?" *Science* 217 (24 September 1982):1237.

[61]Pamela McCorduck, *Machines Who Think* (San Francisco: W. H. Freeman, 1979), 87.

[62]Some typical quotations from Rosenblatt's *Principles of Neurodynamics:*

> In a learning experiment, a perceptron is typically exposed to a sequence of patterns containing representatives of each type or class which is to be distinguished, and the appropriate choice of a response is "reinforced" according to some rule for memory modification. The perceptron is then presented with a test stimulus, and the probability of giving the appropriate response for the class of the stimulus is ascertained. . . . If the test stimulus activates a set of sensory elements which are entirely distinct from those which

were activated in previous exposures to stimuli of the same class, the experiment is a test of "pure generalization." The simplest of perceptrons ... have no capability for pure generalization, but can be shown to perform quite respectably in discrimination experiments particularly if the test stimulus is nearly identical to one of the patterns previously experienced. (p. 68)

Perceptrons considered to date show little resemblance to human subjects in their figure-detection capabilities, and gestalt-organizing tendencies. (p. 71)

The recognition of sequences in rudimentary form is well within the capability of suitably organized perceptrons, but the problem of figural organization and segmentation presents problems which are just as serious here as in the case of static pattern perception. (p. 72)

In a simple perceptron, patterns are recognized before "relations"; indeed, abstract relations, such as "A is above B" or "the triangle is inside the circle" are never abstracted as such, but can only be acquired by means of a sort of exhaustive rote-learning procedure, in which every case in which the relation holds is taught to the perceptron individually. (p. 73)

A network consisting of less than three layers of signal transmission units, or a network consisting exclusively of linear elements connected in series, is incapable of learning to discriminate classes of patterns in an isotropic environment (where any pattern can occur in all possible retinal locations, without boundary effects). (p. 575)

A number of speculative models which are likely to be capable of learning sequential programs, analysis of speech into phonemes, and learning substantive "meanings" for nouns and verbs with simple sensory referents have been presented in the preceding chapters. Such systems represent the upper limits of abstract behavior in perceptrons considered to date. They are handicapped by a lack of a satisfactory "temporary memory," by an inability to perceive abstract topological relations in a simple fashion, and by an inability to isolate meaningful figural entities, or objects, except under special conditions. (p. 577)

The applications most likely to be realizable with the kinds of perceptrons described in this volume include character recognition and "reading machines," speech recognition (for distinct, clearly separated words), and extremely limited capabilities for pictorial recognition, or the recognition of objects against simple backgrounds. "Perception" in a broader sense may be potentially within the grasp of the descendants of our present models, but a great deal of fundamental knowledge must be obtained before a sufficiently sophisticated design can be prescribed to permit a perceptron to compete with a man under normal environmental conditions. (p. 583)

[63]Rumelhart and McClelland, *Parallel Distributed Processing,* vol. 1, 45.

[64]Ibid., vol. 2, 535.

[65]Paul Smolensky, "On the Proper Treatment of Connectionism," *Behavioral and Brain Sciences,* forthcoming.

[66]Geoffrey Hinton, "Learning Distributed Representations of Concepts," in *Proceedings of the Eighth Annual Conference of the Cognitive Science Society* (Amherst, Mass.: Cognitive Science Society, August 1986).

[67]For a recent influential account of perception that denies the need for mental representation, see James J. Gibson, *The Ecological Approach to Visual Perception* (Boston: Houghton Mifflin, 1979). Gibson and Rosenblatt collaborated on a research paper for the U.S. Air Force in 1955; see J. J. Gibson, P. Olum, and F. Rosenblatt, "Parallax and Perspective During Aircraft Landing," *American Journal of Psychology* 68 (1955):372–85.

What Is Information?

David Israel and John Perry

Introduction

In this paper we provide an account of information and informational content, show how it accords with certain intuitive principles of information, and use it to resolve an apparent tension among those principles.[1]

Our aim is not to provide a semantics for talk about information, but to provide an account of information itself. Still, it will be helpful to begin with some observations about the structure and logical properties of *information reports*.

(1) The x-ray indicates that Jackie has a broken leg.
(2) The acoustic waves from the speaker carry the information that the announcer said, "Nancy Reagan is irritated."
(3) The fact that the x-ray has such and such a pattern indicates that Jackie has a broken leg.

(1) and (2) have a structure similar to reports of propositional attitudes. We call an information verb or verb phrase ('shows,' 'indicates,' 'carries the information'), together with the preceding noun phrase, an *informational context*. We shall call the proposition designated by the 'that'-clause the *informational content*. The object designated by the initial noun phrase of a report like (1) or (2) we shall call the *carrier* of the information; the fact designated by the initial noun phrase of a report like (3) we shall call the *indicating fact*.

Both styles of information reports are *factive*. That is, if the report is true, the informational content is true too. If the x-ray indicates that Jackie has a broken leg, then she does. In particular, if the fact that the x-ray has such and such a pattern indicates that her left hind leg is broken, then it is. In this way information reports differ from reports of some cognitive attitudes and linguistic acts, but are similar to others. What is believed or conjectured or asserted or denied need not be true, although what is seen or known must be. And in this way information reports differ from reports of what is possible, and are similar to reports of what is necessary.

Information contexts, like modal contexts and propositional attitude contexts, are clearly not truth-functional. Reports of cognitive attitudes and linguistic acts differ from modal statements, in that substitution of necessarily equivalent statements in the latter preserve truth value, while this is not so with the former. On this issue, information reports are like reports of cognitive attitudes and linguistic acts. For example, it does not follow from (1) that the x-ray shows that Jackie has a broken leg and $7 + 5 = 12$.

Like 'believes,' and 'is necessary,' 'indicates' distributes across *and* but not across *or*.

> If x indicates that P and Q, then x indicates that P and x indicates that Q.
> x may indicate that P *or* Q, even though x neither indicates that P nor indicates that Q.

Reports of linguistic acts and cognitive attitudes are notoriously opaque — substitution of codesignative terms in the content sentences does not always preserve the truth value of the whole report. As we might expect given the emphasis in recent philosophy of language on the different semantic properties of names and definite descriptions, it is important to distinguish two kinds of opacity. Opacity with respect to definite descriptions is relatively noncontroversial, common, and well understood. Modal, cognitive, linguistic, and informational reports all exhibit such opacity, when read in a certain way. Even though Jackie is Jonny's dog, we cannot infer from (1) that the x-ray indicates that Jonny's dog has a broken leg, *if* we take this to mean that Jonny's ownership of the dog is part of what is indicated.

Opacity with respect to proper names is less common, more controversial, and less well understood. It seems that if Tully was necessarily human, so was Cicero; that if Cicero was possibly the best philosopher of his age, so was Tully. But it seems that someone might well say or believe that Cicero was the best Roman philosopher, while not believing or even explicitly denying that Tully was. Should we say that such a person said or believed that Tully was the best Roman philosopher, simply because he said or believed that Cicero was? This would be misleading. Would it be false? Philosophers differ over whether the opacity is real and semantic or apparent and pragmatic. If the former, then it seems that on this score, information reports are closer to modal statements than to reports of cognitive attitudes and linguistic acts. If the entrails of some animal showed that Tully had a broken leg, then they showed that Cicero did.

Information contexts, then, are factive and not truth-functional; substitution of necessarily equivalent content statements does not preserve truth; they distribute across *and* but not across *or*; they may support opaque readings with definite descriptions in the content sentences, but not with proper names.

With our intuitions thus sharpened, let us turn from information reports to information itself.

THE PRINCIPLES

We now turn to stating some intuitive principles of information. We use such terms as 'fact' and 'situation' in their ordinary senses; in the next section we give explications of them within situation theory.

We take the second sort of information report, exemplified by (3), as canonical. Where *X* is a noun phrase designating the carrier of the information, '*X* indicates that such and such' is elliptical for '*X*'s being so and so indicates that such and such.' For example, we bring Jackie, who has been limping badly, to the vet, who takes an x-ray of Jackie's left hind leg, the one she's been favouring. The x-ray is developed. At this point the vet might say something fully explicit like (3).

So our first principles are as follows:

(A) Facts carry information.[2]
(B) The informational content of a fact is a true proposition.

What underlies the phenomenon of information is the fact that reality is lawlike; that what is going in one part of reality is related to what is going on in some other part of reality, by laws, nomic regularities, or as we shall say, *constraints*. Our point of view may be taken as a generalization of Hume's. He took constant conjunctions to be contingent matters of fact, that one type of event was *constantly conjoined* with another. We take constraints to be contingent matters of fact, that one type of situation *involves* another. Involving implies constant conjunction: if one type of situation involves another, then if there is a situation of the first type, there is one of the second type. But we leave open the question of whether constant conjunction implies involvement.

In a world knitted together by constraints — whether these be constant conjunctions or some more metaphysically potent connections — situations carry information. The fact that there is a situation of one type carries the information that there are situations of the types that one involves. If it is a constraint that objects left unsupported near the surface of the earth fall, then the fact that a certain apple near the surface of the earth is left unsupported carries the information that it will fall.

This conception licenses the notion of the information carried by a fact relative to a constraint. It is this relative notion of informational content that we think is implicit in our actual thinking about information and important for theoretical purposes. From it one *might* derive an absolute notion of the information carried by a situation, as that information carried by the situation relative to some constraint or other. We do not think this is a useful notion.

(C) The information a fact carries is relative to a constraint.

Hume saw constant conjunction as supplying the world with enough structure so that events contained information, which experience enabled us to recognize. But this structure did not require that there be any intrinsic connections between events; no event contained information in virtue of its intrinsic properties. If the event were embedded in a different sort of world, where different constraints held sway, it would carry quite different information than it actually does.

(D) The information a fact carries is not an intrinsic property of it.

The informational content of a fact can involve objects quite remote from those involved in the fact. Jackie is not a part or aspect of the x-ray mentioned in (3), nor is she a constituent of the fact that the x-ray has such and such a pattern, but something remote from it. The x-ray is not broken, and does not have bones. Information typically involves a fact indicating something about the way things are elsewhere and elsewhen, and this is what makes information useful and interesting.

(E) The informational content of a fact can concern remote things and situations.

This conception of information can explain how an x-ray could carry the information that some dog had been x-rayed and had a broken leg. But it is not clear how it can account for the specific information the x-ray carries about Jackie that is reported in (3). As we noted above, Jackie is not a part of the x-ray, and it does not seem that her having a broken leg could be constantly conjoined with x-rays exhibiting the pattern that the vet recognizes. So how can the informational content of the x-ray have her as a constituent?

We shall call the sort of information reported, e.g., in (3), *incremen-*

tal information. The conception is most easily grasped if we think of what the x-ray indicates *to* the vet. If she does not know which dog the x-ray is of, it simply indicates that some dog has been x-rayed that has a broken leg. We call this *pure* information. But if she knows that Jackie was x-rayed, then the pattern on the x-ray indicates to her the additional or incremental information that Jackie has a broken leg. This is the incremental information carried by the x-ray, given the fact that the x-ray is of Jackie. The fact that is given *connects* the indicating situation and the specific objects the information is about, so we shall call it the *connecting fact*. We must be careful that this example does not mislead as to our intentions, however. Incremental information is important in understanding the use humans make of information, but humans and mental states need not be brought into its analysis. Incremental information about specific objects is an objective feature of the world that is there for us to use.

(F) Informational content can be specific; the propositions that are informational contents can be about objects that are not part of the indicating fact.

(G) Indicating facts contain such information only relative to connecting facts; the information is incremental, given those facts.

If we put the x-ray in a drawer for a day or a month, it will still indicate that Jackie had a broken leg. After a month, of course, it will not indicate that Jackie has a broken leg *then*, for the leg might have mended. It will still indicate that Jackie had a broken leg at the time the x-ray was taken. This illustrates two important points about information.

First, different facts can carry the same information. Suppose that t is the time the x-ray was taken, and t' is a month later. The fact that the x-ray exhibits a certain pattern at t and the fact that it exhibits that pattern at t' are different, yet they carry the same information. And of course many facts, exhibiting more radical differences from the original state of the x-ray, could carry the same information about Jackie's leg — the way she limped, the vet's remarks after feeling the leg, and the notations in Jackie's file years later.

In the case of the stored x-ray, though, the later fact contains the information that Jackie had a broken leg *because* the earlier one did. And this is the second point illustrated by the example. For this is a (very) simple case of the storage of information. Note that what goes on in this case is that the carrier of the information is itself stored, in the drawer say, whence it and the information it carries can be retrieved. This storage system works so long as the manner in which the indicating object is stored preserves the indicating property. The world is to be arranged in such a way that the carrier has the indicating property over a usefully long stretch of time. No storage system works forever.

Now imagine that a xerox is made of the x-ray and the copy sent to a vet in another city. It, too, will indicate that Jackie has a broken leg. That is, it's having such and such a pattern will indicate that Jackie has a broken leg. This is a simple case of the *flow of information*. Notice here that it's crucial that the copy be a copy, that is, that it be related in a certain way to the original carrier and its indicating property. But things can be otherwise. In some cases storage and transmission of information involves varying both the carrier and the indicating properties. Thus, the x-ray's indicating pattern could be digitized and sound waves produced by scanning the binary array. (This process could even be reversible, up to the stipulated quantization.)

Later we look closely at a more complex case of the flow of information due to Dretske.[3] An announcer speaks into a microphone, the microphone is connected through a transmitter to a transmitting antenna. The modulation of the electromagnetic signal transmitted by the antenna contains information about what the announcer says because it contains information about the way the microphone diaphragm vibrates, and that contains information about the voice.

(H) Many different facts, involving variations in objects, properties, relations and spatiotemporal locations, can indicate one and the same informational content — relative to the same or different constraints.

(I) Information can be stored and transmitted in a variety of forms.

The x-ray's being such and such at *t* carries the information that Jackie's left hind leg is broken; but what good does this do the x-ray? None. What good does it do Jackie? Perhaps a lot. If, that is, the vet has the information that Jackie has a broken leg, the chances of her doing Jackie some good increase dramatically. It has often been noted that books contain a lot of information, too, yet that fact seems not to be of any use to books. There is a distinction between carrying or containing information and *having* information. We shall suggest that an agent or device has the information that P just in case it is in a state that both carries the information that P, and controls the behaviour of the device in a way appropriate to the truth of P.

(J) Having information is good; creatures whose behaviour is guided or controlled by information (by their information carrying states) are more likely to succeed than those which are not so guided.

There is a certain tension between (J) and the rest of our principles. They all emphasize that the information carried by an agent or device being in a certain state is a contingent, extrinsic fact about that agent or device. Given different constraints or specific facts, the information carried by the agent or device being in the state would be quite different. Yet the effect that being in the state has on the device cannot depend on these remote contingencies. How then can such states control behaviour in ways that are appropriate to this information? We shall see, however, that when we think through our principles in a careful way, this tension is only apparent.

THE FRAMEWORK

We have noted that indication is a relation between facts and propositions. We have also said that what underlies information are laws or constraints involving types of situations. So what are all these things? And what precisely are we saying about them?

Situations

A basic idea of situation theory is that there is a concrete reality, which has concrete parts but not concrete alternatives. This reality can be thought about, perceived, studied, and analysed in a variety of different ways, from a variety of different perspectives, for a variety of different purposes. But ultimately everything that exists, everything that happens, everything that is true, has its status because of the nature of this reality. The parts of reality are what we call *situations*. Situation theory is committed to there being situations, but not to there being a largest total situation of which the rest are parts.

Relations, argument roles, locations, individuals, issues, positive and negative states of affairs

When we think or talk about reality, we need some way of analysing it. This we call a *system of classification and individuation*. Such a system consists of domains of situations, relations, locations, and individuals. The commonplace that different schemes can be used to study the same reality is one to which situation theory subscribes. But this fact should not be thought of as showing that situations are structureless, with their properties projected onto them by language or thought. Rather, situations are rich in structure, and support a variety of schemes, suited (or unsuited) to various needs.

Each relation R comes with a set of argument roles. For example, the relation of *eating* comes with the roles of *eater, eaten,* and *location of eating*. Objects of appropriate sorts play these roles. The eater must be some sort or organism. The eaten must be a physical object or quantity of stuff. The location of eating must be a spatio-temporal location.

A relation, together with appropriate objects assigned to its roles, gives rise to an *issue,* namely, the issue of whether or not the objects stand in the relation. There are two possibilities, and each of these we call a *state of affairs*.

Example. If *eating* is the relation, Reagan is the eater, a certain quantity of succotash is the eaten and the White House at a certain time is the location (call it *l*), then there are the following two states of affairs:

$\ll$ *Eats, Loc*: *l*, *Eater*: *Reagan*, *Eaten*: *the succotash*;1 $\gg$
$\ll$ *Eats, Loc*: *l*, *Eater*: *Reagan*, *Eaten*: *the succotash*;0 $\gg$

The first state of affairs resolves the issue positively, the second, negatively. We say the first has a positive and the second a negative polarity.

The relation of *eating* is the major constituent of these states of affairs; Reagan, the location *l* and the quantity of succotash are the minor constituents. The polarities should not be thought of as constituents at all.

Officially, we don't assume that the argument roles of a relation have a natural order — that is, an order independent of the order in which they are expressed in a given language or in a given construction in a language. But in this paper we shall often use the order suggested by English to identify argument roles, without explicitly mentioning them.[4] For the first state of affairs above we write:

$\ll$ *Eats, l, Reagan, the succotash*; 1 $\gg$

Facts and other states of affairs; makes-factual; the partiality of situations

Situations determine whether a given state of affairs or its dual (the one with the same relation, and same assignment of constituents to roles but the other polarity) is a fact. This primitive relation we call *making factual* or *supporting*.

$s \models \sigma$ means that *s makes σ factual*.

We will also make use of the property of *being factual*. A state of affairs is factual iff some real situation supports it.

$\models \sigma$ means that *σ is factual*.

The following are uncontroversial theses about the $\models$ relation:

Given a state of affairs and its dual,

- some situation will make one of them factual;
- no situation will make the other one factual;
- some situations will leave the issue unresolved, i.e., will make neither of them factual.

The following is a controversial thesis about this important relation:

- some situation resolves all issues.

This, of course, is the thesis that there is a largest total situation.

The third thesis tells us that situations are partial. They do not resolve all the issues (except, perhaps, for the total situation called for in the fouth thesis). Because of the partiality of situations, we must distinguish between two ways a situation *s* can fail to make a given state of affairs σ factual:

— *s* may make the dual of σ factual
— *s* may fail to resolve the σ issue one way or the other.

Parameters and anchors

For theoretical purposes, it is useful, though not strictly necessary, to have a domain of *parameters* corresponding to individuals and locations.[5] Where $\ll \ldots, a, \ldots \gg$, is a state of affairs with *a* as a minor constituent, and **a** is a parameter, $\ll \ldots, \mathbf{a}, \ldots \gg$ is a *parametric state of affairs* or *infon*.[6]

The step from states of affairs to infons is a sort of abstraction.[7] To get from the infons back to states of affairs, we need *anchors*. An anchor is a partial function from the domain of parameters to appropriate objects. Where *f* is an anchor, $> \ll \ldots, \mathbf{a}, \ldots \gg [f] = \ll \ldots, f[\mathbf{a}], \ldots \gg . <$

An anchor *f satisfies* an infon *i* relative to a situation *s* iff $s \models i[f]$. An anchor *f* satisfies an infon *i simpliciter* iff $\models i[f]$, i.e., if there is a situation *s* such that $s \models i[f]$.

Compound infons

We need to characterize two sorts of compound infon, the *meet* of a set of infons, $\wedge I$, and the *existentialization* of an infon with respect to parameter x, $\exists x(i)$. We characterize the conditions under which an anchor satisfies each:

- f satisfies $\wedge I$ iff $i[f]$ is factual for each $i \in I$.[8]
- f satisfies $\exists x(i)$ iff for some object a, $i[f_{x}/a]$ is factual.

Types, constraints, and involvement

Now we need to define the notions which are at the heart of our account of information.

Where σ is a state of affairs, $[s \mid s \models \sigma]$ is the *type of situation* that supports σ. Where i is an infon (i.e., a parametric state of affairs), $[s \mid s \models i]$ is a *parametric type*, and i is the *conditioning infon* of T (*cond*(T)). A situation s is *of* parametric type T relative to f if $s \models i[f]$, where i is the conditioning infon of T and f is defined on all of the parameters of i.

Since infons and parametric types are the entities most used from now on, we shall mean parametric types when we say "types"; non-parametric types may be thought of as the special case.

We take constraints to be states of affairs with types of situations as constituents. *Simple involvement* is a binary relation. If T involves T', then for every situation of type T, there is one of type T'.[9] We write:

$$\ll Involves, T, T', 1 \gg$$

Relative involvement is a ternary relation. If T involves T' relative to T'', then, for any pair of situations of the first and third types, there is a situation of the second type. We write:

$$\ll Involves_{R}, T, T', T'' 1 \gg$$

Propositions

We take propositions to be nonlinguistic abstract objects that have absolute truth values. From the perspective of situation theory, this means that a proposition requires not only a type — that which corresponds or doesn't correspond to the way things are — but also a situation for the type to correspond to. Two basic kinds of propositions are recognized in situation theory. An *Austinian proposition* is determined by a situation and a type and is true if the situation is of the type. A *Russellian proposition* is determined by a type alone, and is true if some situation or other is of that type. If we adopted the fourth thesis, that there is a total situation, Russellian propositions could be taken as Austinian propositions determined by this total situation.[10]

Propositions are not infons. Infons characterize situations; propositions are truth bearers. We shall assume that for each type of situation and each situation there is an Austinian proposition that is true just in case that situation is of that type. With respect to Russellian propositions, we shall assume that for each type, there is a proposition that is true just in case some situation is of that type. This last is a strong assumption, that can lead to paradox. We shall not concern ourselves with such issues in the present paper; instead we urge all interested parties to consult the treatment in Barwise and Etchemendy's *The Liar*.[11]

Infons may have individuals and locations as constituents. When an infon with an individual or location as a constituent is the conditioning infon of a type, then we also say that the type has that individual or location as a constituent, as does the proposition determined by that type. A proposition whose type contains no such constituents, because each argument role has been quantified over, is *general*, in Kaplan's terminology; others are *singular*. We shall say that a singular proposition is *about* its constituents.

INFORMATION

We now turn to constructing our theory of information within the version of situation theory just sketched.

Let C be some constraint. The fact *σ carries the pure information that P relative to C* iff

(1) $C = \ll Involves, T, T'; 1 \gg$.[12]

(2) For any anchor f such that $\sigma = cond(T)[f]$, $P =$ the proposition that $\exists s'(s' \models \exists a_1, \ldots a_n(cond(T')[f]))$.

Informally, we would have the following in the case of the x-ray:

> The x-ray's being Φ-ish indicates that there is a dog, of whom this is an x-ray, and that dog has a broken leg.[13]

We are often interested in more specific information. For instance, to guide her action appropriately, the vet has to know which dog. It is not enough for her to be acquainted with the indicating fact and aware of the constraint. She must know that the x-ray was of Jackie's left hind leg; she must know that the information it carries is *about* Jackie — what we have called *incremental* information. To capture the notion of incremental information, we need a more complex constraint, one of relative involvement, the third type being the *connecting type*, the type of the *connecting situation*. We also call such constraints, *relative constraints*.

Let C be some relative constraint, then the fact *σ carries the incremental information that P relative to C and the fact σ'* iff

(1) $C = \ll Involves_R, T, T', T''; 1 \gg$.

(2) For any anchor f such that $\sigma = cond(T)[f] \wedge \sigma' = cond(T'')[f]$, $P =$ the proposition that $\exists s' (s' \models \exists a_1, \ldots a_n(cond(T')[f]))$.

Again, informally, in our case, the connecting fact is that the x-ray in question is of Jackie's left hind leg, and it is in virtue of Jackie's being a constituent of this fact that she is a constituent of the indicated proposition, the proposition that Jackie's left hind leg is broken.[14]

An application of the theory

Let's now apply the theory more formally and fully to our example involving Jackie's leg and the x-ray. We can consider this as a case of *pure information* or of *incremental information*.

In both cases, the indicating fact σ is the x-ray's being of a certain type at t. When we consider the pure information, we have in mind the following simple constraint: whenever there is a state of affairs consisting of some x-ray's having such and such a pattern at some time t, then there is a state of affairs involving a dog's leg having been the object of that x-ray and that leg's being broken at t.[15] So the indicated proposition is that there is a dog of which this is the x-ray, and it has a broken leg. The pure information is about the x-ray, but not about Jackie, or her leg.

Using the resources of situation theory, we represent the simple constraint as follows:

$$T = [s \mid s \models \ll \textit{X-ray}, \mathbf{x}, \mathbf{t}; 1 \gg \wedge \ll \textit{Has-pattern-}\Phi, \mathbf{x}, \mathbf{t}; 1 \gg]$$
$$T' = [s \mid s \models \ll \textit{Is-x-ray-of}, \mathbf{x}, \mathbf{y}, \mathbf{t}; 1 \gg \wedge \ll \textit{Has Broken Leg}, \mathbf{y}, \mathbf{t}; 1 \gg]$$
$$C = \ll \textit{Involves}, T, T'; 1 \gg$$

The indicating situation, σ, is

$$\ll \textit{X-ray}, a, t'; 1 \gg \wedge \ll \textit{Has-pattern-}\Phi, a, t'; 1 \gg$$

where a is the x-ray and t' the time. We assume that σ is factual, that is that $\exists s(s \models \sigma)$. Now let f be any anchor defined on **x** and **t** (at least) such that

$$\sigma = cond(T)[f] = \ll \textit{X-ray}, \mathbf{x}, \mathbf{t}; 1 \gg \wedge \ll \textit{Has-pattern-}\Phi, \mathbf{x}, \mathbf{t}, 1 \gg [f]$$

(Thus, $f(\mathbf{x}) = a$ and $f(\mathbf{t}) = t'$.) Then P = the proposition that

$$\exists s'(s' \models \exists y(\ll \textit{Is-x-ray-of}, x, y, \mathbf{t}; 1 \gg \wedge \ll \textit{Has Broken Leg}, y, \mathbf{t}; 1 \gg)[f])$$

Thus P is the proposition that the state of affairs which consists of some dog being the object of a, the x-ray in question (at t', the time in question) and that dog's having a broken leg (at the time in question) is factual. Or, more simply, it is the proposition that there is some dog whose leg is depicted by a at t' and whose leg is broken at t'.

When we consider this as a case of incremental information, we have in mind the relative constraint that if an x-ray is of this type, and it is the x-ray of a dog, then that dog had a broken leg at the time the x-ray was taken. The fact that the x-ray was of Jackie is the connecting fact, and the incremental informational content is the proposition that Jackie has a broken leg. This proposition is about Jackie, but not about the x-ray.

The relevant relative constraint is:

$$C' = \ll \mathit{Involves}_R, T, T', T''; 1 \gg$$

where T, the indicating type is as before. T', the indicated type is

$$[s \mid s \models \ll \mathit{Has\ Broken\ Leg}, \mathbf{y}, \mathbf{t}; 1 \gg]$$

and T'', the connecting type is:

$$[s \mid s \models \ll \mathit{Is\text{-}x\text{-}ray\text{-}of}, \mathbf{x}, \mathbf{y}, \mathbf{t}; 1 \gg].$$

As before, σ is:

$$\ll X-ray, a, t'; 1 \gg \wedge \ll Has-pattern-\Phi, a, t'; 1 \gg.$$

Again, we assume that σ is factual. Further, we assume that the connecting state of affairs, σ' is factual. Where b is Jackie, $\sigma'/\mathbf{y}$-*is*

$$\ll Is-x\text{-}ray-of, a, b, t'; 1 \gg.$$

Any anchor f, such that $\sigma = cond(T)[f]$ and $\sigma' = cond(T')$, must be defined on the parameter $\mathbf{y}$ of the connecting type, in particular, it must anchor $\mathbf{y}$ to Jackie. Thus, for any such anchor f, the proposition carried incrementally by σ relative to C and σ' is the proposition that

$$\exists s''(s'' \models \ll \mathit{Has\ Broken\ Leg}, b, t'; 1 \gg).$$

This is a singular proposition about Jackie, and not at all about the x-ray. And it is, after all, Jackie that we're concerned about.

The flow of information

Now consider a case in which it is natural to speak of "information flow." The manner in which the diaphragm of a certain microphone is vibrating carries information about what a certain announcer is saying. The modulation of the electromagnetic signal arriving at a certain antenna carries information about the way in which that microphone diaphragm is vibrating. And finally, the modulation of the elecro-magnetic signal arriving at the antenna carries information about what the announcer is saying, for instance, "Nancy Reagan is irritated."

How does the modulation of the electromagnetic signal at the antenna carry information about the words the announcer spoke? Let's look at the constraints and connecting facts that are involved.

The first constraint we call $C_{voice\text{-}info}$: If the diaphragm of a microphone vibrates in a certain way (T_{mike}), then the announcer's voice produced certain sounds (T_{voice}), given that the announcer was speaking into the mike ($T_{mike\text{-}voice}$).

$$C_{voice\text{-}info} = \ll Involves_R, T_{mike}, T_{voice}, T_{mike\text{-}voice}; 1 \gg$$

The connecting fact, that the announcer was speaking into the microphone we call $\sigma_{\text{mike-voice}}$.

The second constraint we call $C_{mike\text{-}info}$: if the electromagnetic signal reaching the antenna is of a certain type ($T_{antenna}$), then the diaphragm of the microphone vibrates in a certain way (T_{mike}), given that the antenna and the microphone are connected in a certain way ($T_{antenna\text{-}mike}$).

$$(C_{mike\text{-}info}), = \ll Involves_R, T_{antenna}, T_{mike}, T_{antenna\text{-}mike}; 1 \gg$$

The connecting fact, that the antenna and the mike are connected in this way, we call $\sigma_{\text{antenna-mike}}$.

The third constraint we call $C_{info\text{-}flow}$: if the electromagnetic signal reaching the antenna is of a certain type ($T_{antenna}$), then the announcer's voice produced certain sounds (T_{voice}), given that the announcer was speaking into the mike and the antenna and the microphone are connected in a certain way ($T_{antenna\text{-}mike} \wedge T_{mike\text{-}voice}$).[16]

$$C_{info\text{-}flow}) = \ll Involves_R, T_{antenna}, T_{voice}, (T_{antenna\text{-}mike} \wedge (T_{mike\text{-}voice}); 1 \gg$$

The connecting fact, that the antenna, mike and voice are connected in this way, we call ($\sigma_{\text{antenna-mike}} \wedge \sigma_{\text{mike-voice}}$).

Let P be the proposition that the announcer said "Nancy Reagan is irritated." Let Q be the proposition that the diaphragm of the mike in question is vibrating in such and such a way — the way that is the major constituent of type T_{mike}. Then

- σ_{antenna} carries the information that Q relative to $C_{mike\text{-}info}$, given the connecting fact $\sigma_{\text{antenna-mike}}$.

Moreover, we say that

- σ_{antenna} carries the information that P relative to $C_{info\text{-}flow}$, given ($\sigma_{\text{antenna-mike}} \wedge \sigma_{\text{mike-voice}}$).

In such a case, we also say information of type T_{voice} flows along channels of type ($T_{antenna\text{-}mike} \wedge T_{mike\text{-}voice}$). We can derive something more like the normal use of the term if we move to the individual objects, the carriers, that are constitutents of the connecting types.[17]

We might as well generalize, and state the following principle of information:

(K) There are laws of information flow.

Laws of information flow involve compound infons and relations among the parameters of those infons. In plain(er) English: laws of information flow involve relations among states of various components of information systems, states of various objects remote from those systems and connections between these. These laws are useful or exploitable to the extent that these relations and connections are controllable or at least knowable.[18]

The Helpfulness of Information

Now we must face the question of how information, as we conceive it, can be helpful. Clearly, for information to be of use to some agent, or to enable some device to do what it is supposed to, it is not enough that the states of the agent or device *carry* the information. The agent or device must in some sense *have* the information.

We want to develop an account of having information as being in a state that plays two roles. First, the agent's being in the state carries certain information relative to a constraint. Second, an agent's being in that state has an effect (relative to some other constraint) that is appropriate given the information. In that case, we want to say that the agent not only carries but has the information.

But there seems to be a large problem standing in the way of developing such an account on the basis of an approach to information of the sort we have been putting forward. On our account, the information that an object carries in virtue of being in a certain state is not *intrinsically* connected to the object's being in that state. The x-ray's being in state Φ carries the information that Jackie's leg is broken *only* relative to a constraint and a fact. Relative to other constraints and facts, that very same state will carry different information.

But the effect of that state on other parts of the system of which it is a part will not depend on these constraints and facts. How then can the resulting response be appropriate to the information? Our strategy for analysing the having of information, given our account of information, seems to require something like action at a distance.

These problems, however, are merely apparent.

Let's consider a simple example. You stick a pencil in an electric pencil sharpener; a lever is depressed; a circuit is closed; the motor turns on, the blade spins; the pencil is sharpened. In this case, the insertion of the pencil caused the pencil sharpener to be in a certain state, having a lever depressed, that carried information. Under normal usage, this state only occurs when a pencil is inserted, and so carries the information that this is so. This state causes things to happen inside the pencil sharpener: the circuit closes, the motor starts, the blade spins. So, the state of having the lever depressed plays two roles. It carries information, relative to constraints, about the wider circumstances in which the system finds itself — that a pencil has been inserted. And it causes things to happen in the system.

Note that we say that the electric pencil sharpener worked, or did what it was supposed to do, or responded appropriately because we have in mind the goal of sharpening pencils. Relative to another goal, say frustrating people who want their pencils sharpened, it did not work. One might convert a device that works, relative to the first goal, to one that works, relative to the second, by putting in a different kind of blade — say one that leaves the end of the inserted pencil blunt. Whenever we talk about success or failure, or the appropriateness of an action, we have in the background some goal or measure of success.

Let us suppose:

(1) G is a goal, say of sharpening pencils.
(2) *Lever-depressed*, *circuit-closed*, and *blades-spinning*, etc. are states of systems of a certain kind K.
(3) There is a constraint $C_{pure\text{-}info}$: if a system a of kind K is in *lever-depressed* at location l, then there is a pencil inserted in a at l.
(4) There is a constraint C_K that governs the internal workings of the system: if a is in state *lever-depressed* at l, a will go into state *circuit-closed*, then state *blades-spinning*.
(5) There is a constraint $C_{pure\text{-}result}$: if a is in state *blades-spinning* then if there is a pencil in contact with the blades of a, that pencil will be sharpened.

The pencil sharpener of kind K has been designed so that the state that carries the information that a pencil has been inserted sets in motion a chain of events that promotes the goal for which it was designed, sharpening pencils. The design will be successful only in an environment in which the depressing of the lever will carry the information that a pencil has been inserted, and the motion of a blade against a pencil will leave it sharpened. We say that the system is *attuned* to these constraints, relative to the goal of sharpening pencils.

Thus there is no particular problem about how an agent or device may be caused, by the state that carries remote information, to respond in ways appropriate to that information, and so be said not merely to carry but to have that information. The problem may still seem to apply to the case of incremental information, however. What can be the point of saying that the state of a device or an agent has the information that ...*b*...? In such a case, the state of the agent or device will *carry* the information that ...*b*... relative to some fact that connects the agent or device with *b*. It could have been connected with some other object, *c*, in which case it would carry the information that ...*c*.... But it could be in exactly the same state *S* in the two cases. In this case the effects would be the same, so in what sense can the presence of *b* rather than *c* be relevant?

This argument is fallacious, however, for the effects need not be the same. The immediate effects of being in state *S* will be the same, no matter what the remote cause of being in state *S* might be. But the remote effects of being in state *S* may depend on facts that vary with the remote causes. These remote effects may be the ones that are relevant to the success or failure of the system's response, relative to a given goal.

In our example, the insertion of a pencil *p* into our sharpener depresses a lever, which closes a circuit, causing a motor to impel the blades. The lever would have been depressed in the same way, had another pencil *p′* been inserted rather than *p*. But given that *p* is inserted, *p* gets sharpened; had *p′* been inserted, *p′* would have been sharpened. The remote effects of inserting the different pencils differ, even though the local effects are the same.

The following factors are involved:

(1) *G* is a goal.
(2) *lever-depressed, circuit-closed, blades-spinning,* etc. are states of systems of a certain kind *K*.
(3) There is a relative constraint $C_{inc\text{-}info}$: *if a system a* kind *K* is in *lever-depressed* at location *l*, then pencil *c* is inserted in *a*, given that *c* is depressing the lever of *a*.
(4) There is a constraint C_K that governs the internal workings of the system: if *a* is in state *lever-depressed* at *l*, *a* will go into state *circuit-closed*, then into state *blades-spinning*.
(5) There is a relative constraint $C_{inc\text{-}result}$: if *a* is in state *blades-spinning*, pencil *c* will be sharpened, given that *c* is in contact with *a*'s blade.
(6) There is a constraint, $C_{how\text{-}things\text{-}are}$: if a pencil *c* is depressing the lever of a device of kind *K*, it will be in contact with the blades of that device.

Note the last constraint, that connects the fact of a pencil depressing the lever of the sharpener and the pencil being in contact with the blades of the sharpener. These facts are rather intimately connected, given the construction of an electric pencil sharpener.[19] In cases involving information flowing to an agent from more remote events, which then performs actions whose appropriateness moreover depends on remote effects, the analogous connection between facts that accounts for the agent's success, may be quite a bit more complex and fragile. When such contingencies relate the objects an agent has information about with the objects its actions need to affect to promote its goals, mere *attunement* may not suffice. In such cases, having information may require a system of representation to keep track of these contingencies.[20]

NOTES

1 The work presented here was supported by the System Development Foundation under a grant to the Center for the Study of Language and Information, Stanford University, and SRI International. Many of the ideas reported here reflect the work of the STASS (Situation Theory and Situation Semantics) group at CSLI; we are particularly indebted to Jon Barwise.

2 As we shall see, this is really shorthand for the following. Situations carry information in virtue of making certain states of affairs factual.

3 *Knowledge and the Flow of Information* (Cambridge, MA: MIT Press 1981), 58.

4 The argument role for spatiotemporal locations will always be displayed last.

5 In our paper *What Are Parameters?* (in preparation), we address the issue of what parameters are, and whether they are a necessary part of situation theory.

6 The term 'infon' is to suggest that parametric states of affairs are theoretical entities that are the basic units of information. It is due to Keith Devlin. 'Infon' and 'state of affairs' are close in meaning: an infon is a parametric state of affairs; a state of affairs is a nonparametric infon.

7 This is a bit misleading; see *What Are Parameters?*.

8 This characterization partially reflects the postulation of a complete lattice of infons. For the meet of two infons σ, σ', we use the notation $(\sigma \wedge \sigma')$.

9 Note that the definition does not require that when s is of type T that *it* also be of type T'.

10 See Jon Barwise and John Perry, *Situations and Attitudes* 139–40. The distinction is further clarified and the present terminology introduced in Jon Barwise and John Etchemendy, *The Liar* (Oxford: Oxford University Press 1987) where it plays a key role in the treatment of semantic paradox. See also the postscript to the 2nd edition, forthcoming.

11 In what follows, we will avail ourselves of propositions in which the situation parameter is existentially quantified. The reader should not take this as the expression of a substantive commitment on our part.

12 We simplify by treating the *involves* relation, as well as the relation of *relative involvement* as not having an argument role for locations. We should also note that relative constraints are not to be confused with what in *Situations and Attitudes* were called conditional constraints.

13 In what follows, we shall simply assume that the x-ray's being Φ-ish indicates that it is of a dog's leg.

14 As we shall see, this reflects the fact that the anchor for the connecting type, that is for T'', must assign Jackie to the role of being the object whose leg is x-rayed and thus the indicated type, T' — and the indicated proposition — will be about her.

15 For the sake of simplicity, we shall assume that the x-ray is developed essentially instantaneously.

16 The complete lattice of infons induces a complete lattice of types. A situation *s* is of $(T_1 \wedge T_2)$ iff *s* is of T_1 and *s* is of T_2.

17 Strictly speaking, such objects figure as the values of anchors for the parameters of the conditioning infons.

18 The reader should compare the above with what Dretske, *Knowledge and the Flow of Information*, calls the *Xerox Principle*.

19 Given, that is, *how-things-are*.

20 For more on these issues, the reader may consult Israel's *The Role of Propositional Objects of Belief in Action*, CSLI Report No. 72 and Perry's *Circumstantial Attitudes and Benevolent Cognition*, CSLI Report NO. 53, reprinted from J. Butterfield, ed., *Language, Mind and Logic* (Cambridge, Eng.: Cambridge University Press 1986), 123–33. We hope to address these issues further in a series of papers.

When Is Information Explicitly Represented?

David Kirsh*

INTRODUCTION

Computation is a process of making *explicit*, information that was *implicit*. In computing 5 as the solution to $\sqrt[3]{125}$, for example, we move from a description that is not explicitly about 5 to one that is. We are drawing out numerical consequences of the description $\sqrt[3]{125}$. We are extracting information implicit in the problem statement. Can we precisely state the difference between information that is implicit in a state, structure or process and information that is explicit?

Most discussions of implicit/explicit belief, knowledge, and representation confidently assume that we know what it is for information to be explicitly encoded; the problematic notion — if any notion is problematic at all — is implicit information.[1] What inspires this confidence is a particular vision of computation.

Let us suppose that to understand a computation it is necessary to track the trajectory of informational states the computing system follows as it winds its way to an explicit answer. If a computer is seen as a mechanism which applies rules to syntactically structured representations, it is natural to view explicit information as an encoding of information in syntactic structures that are interpretable according to a well-behaved theory of content, such as a truth theory. We can then point to a syntactic structure in the system and say 'that form encodes this content.' This, I believe, is our underlying idea behind our intuitions about explicit encodings.

As different kinds of computational mechanisms are discovered and explored — PDP systems, massive cellular automata, analogue relaxation systems — it is becoming increasingly difficult, however, to track the trajectory of informational states these mechanisms generate. There is no doubt that we must find some method of tracking them; otherwise there is no reason to think of them as more than complex causal systems.[2] But it is at present an open question whether the model of rules operating on explicit representations is a perspicuous model of their style of computation.

Once the lid has been raised on new styles of computation we are forced to re-examine our uncritical intuitions about basic notions. We already know that there are many ways information can be implicit in a state, structure or process, and that we are largely ignorant of the full variety of ways that information can be built into architecture, internal dynamics, and environment-system interaction. It seems to follow that one reason it is hard for us to track informational trajectories is that we don't yet know how to determine what information is in a system.

The same problem arises for computational systems that are familiar: we do not know how to determine unambiguously exactly what information is encoded in a system, even explicitly.

For instance, what information is contained in a system that has lost its pointers to one of its data sets? The data is still recorded in the system, in the sense that if the system could regain its obliterated pointers, the full data set could be retrieved. But *ex hypothesis* those pointers are unrecoverable. The states are unusable. Does the system still explicitly encode the data even though they are absolutely inaccessible?

Suppose the pointers are not simple address locations, themselves stored in a look-up table, but rather are calculated by solving a complex function. Or suppose the data is not found in a single location but spills over to many cell locations connected by pointers of the most complex sort. Is the data explicitly encoded?

Again, suppose a set of axioms is represented in a language as expressive as first order predicate calculus. Is the whole deductive closure of the set implicit? Even if that set is infinite, or would require exponential computation to derive its members? What about the $2^{100^{100}}$ digit of π? Is that implicit in the state of an arithmetical engine?

Or suppose that a system has highly ambiguous encodings and must deliberate in order to choose the right interpretation for a given word. What information is encoded explicitly? Is any? Must explicit encodings be non-ambiguous?

That such questions arise is proof that we have unsettled intuitions about the meaning of explicit and implicit information even in familiar programmable symbol manipulating systems. Computer and cognitive scientists talk as if they have a precise idea of these concepts. But they do not.

My intent in what follows is to articulate a particular conception of explicit information that at least may serve as a stable basis for subsequent inquiries into the meaning of implicit information. When I began this inquiry I too assumed that our notion of explicit was unproblematic. No longer. The paper is divided into three sections.

In the first, I show, in greater detail, why the notions of explicit and implicit need elucidation. Our intuitions are not consistent; nor is there any settled view how to resolve them. Yet the concepts are important for both computer and cognitive scientists.

In the second section, I explore efforts to identify explicit information with syntactically and semantically well-defined representations. It is hard to imagine any more natural image of explicit encodings of information than sentences in a natural language. But as we shall see it is not enough that information be present in an encoding; it must be usably present, it must be 'instantly' accessible. This condition of use places a heavy constraint on what sorts of representations can encode information explicitly.

In a brief third section, I mention some of the implications of my view. My approach throughout will be informal.

OUR INTUITIONS ABOUT EXPLICITNESS ARE INCONSISTENT

Perhaps the simplest and most persistent intuition we have about what explicit means is that information is explicit if it is there, for all to see, much like an unambiguous word in a book. This image of words in a text has four properties which it is tempting to ascribe to explicit representations generally:

(1) locality: they are visible structures with a definite location;
(2) movability: no matter where in a book a word is to be found, or where in a library the book is stored, that word retains its meaning and retains its explicitness;
(3) meaning: words have a definite informational content;
(4) availability: the informational content of a word is directly available to the system reading it; no elaborate translation or interpretation process is necessary to extract the information it represents.

On the surface, these four properties seem to explain some obvious facts. For instance, we believe that the number 3 is explicitly represented as being *in* the set A: {1,5,3,7,4,4} because the information that 3 is a member of the set is *on the surface* of the data structure. The meaning of the numeral '3' is readily understood by any numerically literate agent, so its informational content is directly available. It is not so context sensitive that the agent must read the entire data structure or the entire contents of current memory to determine that meaning. And it has a specific location in the data structure. We can point to what in the data structure explicitly carries meaning.

By contrast, if we say that an element is a member of a set iff it satisfies a given list of properties, say $\{x \mid x \text{ is an even integer and } 0 \leq x \leq 9\}$ we designate a unique set but in a manner which requires computation on the part of the user. The elements cannot be just read off. It is true that we are stating the property list explicitly as opposed to using the elliptical ... notation to denote the elements, as in $\{0,2,4,\ldots\}$, which specifies the properties of the elements implicitly. But both specifications fail to present the elements in a manner that can be directly read off. They do not explicitly encode the elements of the set.

The same difference holds between a table of trigonometric functions where there is a separate entry for each value of sin $n°$, and Euler's equation $e^{ix} = cosx + i \sin x$ for generating trigonometric values. Euler's equation is a *compact* way of describing a trigonometric table. But it does not explicitly represent the table. Taken to a first approximation, and restricted within certain bounds, Euler's equation offers the same information as the table. Yet it is in a different form. The informational content of the table is not directly available in the equation; an elaborate reasoning process is necessary to extract the information explicitly contained in the table.

Another way a representation can carry information inexplicitly is by display. For instance, the number of elements in A: $\{1,5,3,7,4,4\}$ – A's cardinality — is not explicitly represented by A, even though each digit in A is explicit and ready to be counted. *A displays* its cardinality; it does not explicitly represent or encode it.

Let us say that information is displayed if there is a process in a system which can, in short order, *extract* that information, while it is explicitly represented if there is a process in the system which can *immediately grasp* the information. Information that is displayed lies just beneath the surface. Information that is explicitly represented lies on the surface.

The trouble with using immediate graspability, or better *immediate readability* as the mark of explicitness is that we run into problems as soon as we ask whether to count accessing time as part of the reading process. Are the elements in large sets immediately readable? Suppose we have a matrix 10,000 by 10,000 and we want to know the identity of the element in position (6754,9629). Even if each position in the matrix is marked by two numbers representing row and column, we shall have to expend some computational energy in locating the right position and identifying the symbol found there. The task of finding a position seems no different in principle from determining cardinality, both involve counting, or some other numerical operation. Both require computation. But then if we deny that cardinality is explicitly encoded because it can be determined only through computation, shall we not also have to deny that the value at location (i,j) is explicit?

The point at issue here is whether symbols which are *on the surface* in a structural sense may be below the surface in a process sense. I believe they can, and that this difference between structural immediacy and process immediacy lies at the heart of confusions about explicitness.

From a process perspective information is explicit only when it is *ready to be used*. No computation is necessary to bring the content into a usable form. From a structural perspective information is explicit when it has a definite location and a definite meaning. The confusion arises when a representation that seems to be in a usable form when viewed structurally turns out to be in a non-immediately usable form procedurally.

For instance, imagine a reader who wishes to use the suggestions in a book to help him solve a particular engineering problem. The suggestions are there, in a phrase or a line somewhere, but if the book has no index or no obvious ordering, the reader will have to scan an arbitrary amount of the book to find the information he needs. Should we say that the sought-after information is explicit for that reader? Relative to his goal of problem-solving, an indexless book is an inefficient representation of the information he needs. It fails to record the information in an easy to use form.

It will no doubt be objected that there is an important difference between finding information and using it once found. Most everyone will agree that if information is encrypted in a baroque code requiring lengthy decryption before being comprehensible then that information is not explicit. Encrypted information requires preprocessing. The information is present, in some sense, but not present in a usable enough form to be deemed explicit.

But in the case of our imagined engineer, there is no question that once the representation is actually retrieved it is easy to read. The question is whether the accessing process should be viewed as part of the representation's readableness. Is there a relevant difference between spending time and effort to locate information, and spending time and effort to decrypt? Both retrieval and decryption are algorithmic processes; both involve some form of pattern matching or network following.

My own view is that there is not a relevant difference. Explicitness is tied to usability. And usability implies a match up between the procedures available to the agent and the forms the content is encoded in. Granted, these are matters over which we have no fixed intuitions. But we have biases. Are words that are hidden in a tangle of other words any different than encryptions? A standard method of passing secret information is to send a book to one's ally with the unwritten understanding that message words are found in certain spots. Was the secret message encrypted? The question is open to dispute. Suppose the reader must *deliberate* to determine which passages in the book are the relevant ones. Does the book explicitly encode the information he needs?

From a purely computational standpoint there is no fundamental difference between spending time and cycles in finding a datum in space (memory) and spending a similar measure of time and cycles computing that datum in time. It may seem that there is a principled difference here, just as it seems that there is a principled difference between space and time. But we have learned otherwise. Accordingly, just taking computational effort as the measure of explicitness, there is no way of choosing whether to represent a given block of information by a powerful procedure plus limited data or by a weak procedure plus exhaustive data. Either form may be able to provide the information we want when we want it and in the form we want it. Accordingly, out structural notion of explicitness may run at odds with our procedural notion. Despite out intuitions about what is on the surface we cannot decide what is explicit without knowing in detail how a system works.

OUR INTUITIONS ABOUT IMPLICITNESS ARE INCONSISTENT

Our intuitions are even more unsettled concerning *implicit* information. It is natural to suppose that information is implicit if it is *mediately* readable; the information is structurally hidden and/or procedurally distant but nonetheless *recoverable* by additional processing. It can be made explicit. Thus, it is often thought that the hallmark of implicit information is that it is not explicit but could be made explicit.

To take the canonical example, in formal logic it is generally assumed that formulas which are not part of a given axiom set are implicit if they lie anywhere in the set's deductive closure. Structurally they are absent but procedurally they are recoverable. Given enough processing they can be brought to the surface and represented explicitly.

This definition, however, runs into problems as soon as we try to say what 'in principle, recoverable' means. Returning to deduction, shall we say that certain formulas are implicit regardless of how much effort is required to recover those formulas? Our intuitions are not decisive here. For any set of premisses, there are going to be certain theorems that are easy to prove — nearby in lemma space — and certain others that are computationally distant.[3] Are all these theorems equally implicit? Perhaps implicitness is a matter of degree? But in that case what shall we say about theorems that are infinitely distant, or infinitely hard to reach? And what shall we say about as yet unproven theorems? Is Fermat's last theorem implicit in Peano's axioms? We know that most interesting representational systems are incomplete. It is possible, then, that Fermat's last theorem is neither provably true nor provably false. Assuming that it is true but not provable is it implicit? On one account it is not, for it does not lie in the deductive closure of the axioms. Yet if the theorem is true (and constructivists are right), then there must exist some non-deductive processes that can extract that information from the axiom set. Shall we say that a given datum of information is implicit in a representation only relative to a set of operations?

To press the point, consider a system able to discover generalizations. For such a system Euler's equation might be discovered by reasoning about a trigonometric table. Euler's equation is potentially implicit in a trigonometric table for that system. Yet whether we think the equation is actually implicit depends on how much other knowledge we believe is necessary to make the discovery. A system which can draw generalizations has a *chance* at discovering Euler's equation. But such a discovery would be remarkable. For one thing, the equation contains more information than the table itself — it applies to any real value of x — so it represents a powerful abstraction. The generalization is more than a simple interpolation of the data. It generalizes to new entities. No one knows what is required for such abstractions. Often they are inspired guesses. This is particularly true where the generalization refers to a fundamental concept, such as e, which is not in the descriptive language of the data. e is like a theoretical entity: supported by observations but not reducible to them. How these new concepts are discovered depends on so many factors that it is impossible, in general, to determine whether a given agent will ever stumble on the correct generalization. But then should we allow that generalizations are implicit in data?

Given these difficulties it is hard to make precise a notion of recoverability which can serve to demarcate the realm of the implicit accurately. I still think it is hard to imagine a more natural criterion of implicitnes that has any chance of working than *that which is not explicit but which could be made so*. But not everyone would agree.

For example, it has become popular in some circles[4] to call information implicit if it is latent in a system even if it is unrecoverable. It is well known that a computation can often be made more efficient by exploiting regularities rather than by explicitly representing them. These regularities are really assumptions about the environment, or about the interaction of the agent with the environment. For instance, a vision module designed to extract a 3-D shape from two stereoscopic images works rapidly if it is equipped with an algorithm which differentiates. Such an algorithm will work if the assumption about the world — in this case, that objects change in shape smoothly and continuously — is true.

Smoothness is a condition of the world that justifies differentiation. It is a *success condition* determining whether the algorithm will work. If the condition is false the algorithm will fail to compute a correct answer. A designer who wishes to determine the algorithm's reliability will need to know how often the assumption is correct. For the truth of the assumption is the theoretical justification of the algorithm. But shall we say that the algorithm implicitly represents the assumption? Or that information about the visual world is implicitly encoded in certain of the states, structures or processes of the visual system? Clearly, this assumption is not recoverable by the system itself because the vocabulary of early vision does not include terms such as smoothness. We find expressions of values for wavelength, physical intensity, zero-crossings, surface contours, depth measures, and so on. But nowhere in this vocabularly does a term for smoothness appear. Nonetheless, it has become fashionable to speak of the system as having an implicit theory of the world. Some would argue that the information is causally effective. Is this just sloppy language?

To take another case, some robots currently under research navigate without maps. Such systems are equipped with a compass, with knowledge of their orientation with respect to an origin, and suitable instructions to find their way from any point in a maze to any other. These robots explicitly represent information of the form *if at position A then to get to B orient* 90° *go 10 steps, turn* 120° *then go 15 steps*. It is easy to prove that the total information contained in such instruction sets is sufficient to define a structural map giving the position of all points and identifying all open corridors. A structural map is, in principle, *recoverable* from the instruction set, though not recoverable by the system itself unless it has certain analytic skills.

Should we say that information about structural relations is implicit in the instruction set? By our condition of explicit recovery we must not. According to the condition of recoverability, a system does not encode information implicitly unless it can recover that information and explicitly encode it. Because the robot lacks the ability to translate from its instructions to structural representations of its environment we are obliged to say the instructions do not contain structural information implicitly. Yet what shall we make of the intuition that it is because the instructions *do* contain structural information implicitly that when they are interpreted correctly they generate the right behaviour? If the instruction set did not conform to the structure of the world what could explain its success? *Prima facie*, the instructions succeed because they implicitly encode information about the structure of their environment. They contain structural information.

What these examples show, I believe, is that we have not yet any settled view about our intuitions about explicit and implicit information. On the one hand, it is reasonable to require that information be *actually* recoverable to be implicit. Yet, on the other, it is reasonable to grant that information can be embedded in a system so that it is causally efficacious despite being unrecoverable. Recoverability is contingent on a host of other arguably incidental processes. This, at any rate, is a position some would like to defend.

Why It Matters Whether Our Intuitions Are Unsettled

Such inconsistencies would be unproblematic if terms like explicit and implicit never appear in psychological and philosophical theories. But they do.

Fodor,[5] for instance, maintains that mental states are functional relations to explicit representations. To know or believe a certain fact is to be in a certain computational relation to a representation which explicitly encodes information about that fact. Explicitness is important to Fodor. Yet he never states what explicitness amounts to short of saying it must satisfy some ill-defined formality condition. This leaves us groping for a workable criterion of formal. We do not know, for example, whether cardinality when displayed rather than represented directly is a formal property. The same applies to the relation of having a location in a matrix, or to the relation of being connected to, or being beside. Some of these properties are usually represented, others are displayed. Are they formal properties? How we answer these questions has deep consequences. For, according to Fodor, it determines what shall count as an episode in our mental life.

Gibson and his followers, too, make strong claims about implicit information. They maintain that information about shape and distance, for example, is implicit in the ambient flux of light energy striking our retinas. The visual system, we are told, does not explicitly represent edges etc., then construct further representations of shape. It picks up the invariants implicit in visual energy fields and puts that information to use in controlling behaviour "directly," without ever representing it. Because such information is put directly to use, the visual system has no facility for explicitly naming invariants; it never represents them explicitly. Visual invariants in Gibson's sense, fail to be implicit by our condition of recoverability. For by that condition a system can implicitly encode information only if it can, in principle, explicitly encode it as well, since to recover information it must be possible to represent that information explicitly. How shall we interpret Gibson's remarks? Can information about visual invariants be implicit in light energy?

More recently, Perry, Smith, and Rosenschein[6] have contended that information can be implicit in a system because that system is embedded in a particular environment. A system well-adapted to its environment contains information about that environment and its momentary relations to that environment, even though that information is built into the design of the system and so is in principle inaccessible. On their account, information need not be amenable to eventual explicit representation to be implicit. The information we decide is present in a sytem is not identical to the sum of information that is explicit plus the information that is recoverable. Once again information can be implicit but unrecoverable. Yet again what are we to make of these claims?

The upshot, it seems to me, is that we know somewhat less about information processing than we suppose. Information processing has always been understood as a process of transforming representations — transforming explicit representations. But owing to the variety of physical mechanisms that are often interpreted to be computing functions, this view is no longer universally held. This does not mean that information processing is *not* explicit representation processing. But until we have an adequate theory of the relation of implicit to explicit information we cannot decide the issue.

TOWARDS A THEORY OF EXPLICITNESS

Because implicit is defined largely negatively as information that is present but not explicitly encoded, any inquiry into implicit information must presuppose a theory of explicit information. If I am right, however, our structural and procedural intuitions about explicitness are so confused that there is no easy theory to offer. We may offer a stipulative theory but it will never satisfy all our intuitions.

I shall argue that the source of confusion lies in the bewitching image of a word printed on a page. Words on a printed page have four properties that make them an attractive model of explicitness: locality, movability, meaningfulness, and immediate readability. When we look closely at each attribute we find each is, in some manner, misleading.

In the remainder of this paper, I will discuss each attribute in an effort to separate truth from fantasy. My own positive account emerges along the way.

Four Conditions on Explicitness

Locality. It is a fact of English and all other natural languages that words are represented by written tokens that are spatially compact and readily separable from their spatial neighbours. It is tempting to suppose that all explicit encodings of information share this property. Explicit information, after all, is encoded in codings. These codings must present the information in a modular, readily surveyable manner; otherwise they could not present the information in a ready to use form.

If locality were true, however, it would eliminate, in one stroke, the possibility of distributed connectionist systems ever having explicit representations. This seems to me a good reason to deny it. The kernal of truth in the locality condition is that a word, however it be represented, must be a *determinate* something. It must have identity conditions. It is pointless talking of a state, structure or process encoding information explicitly unless we can be precise about which state, structure or process does the encoding. But it certainly does not follow that these identity conditions mandate spatial isolation. They don't. They require, of course, that the system using the representation must have operators which can recognize those representations. Humans find spatial boundaries especially easy to use for individuation. But there is no *a priori* reason why symbols must be spatially separate. To demand spatial separation places an unmotivated restriction on the range of recognition devices that non-humans might use in reading and communicating.

For example, we can readily imagine a system which encodes information in the wavelengths of the visible spectrum. Since many wavelengths and intensities can be superposed on the same spatial region but later filtered out, one colour, such as a shade of white or pink, can actually explicitly encode many different pieces of information. A system appropriately endowed with colour filters can read off the information immediately. It "sees" separate colour tokens and reads them directly. To anyone without the filters, however, the information is invisible.

The same principle applies to information encoded in scatter diagrams. We can imagine a fax machine, for instance, which distributes information like buckshot sprayed over a page. Several such pages could be superposed. To a system appropriately set up, each page is separable without loss. But again, only to a system with the appropriate operators to read the buckshot distribution. Humans would find such distributions unreadable because they lack edges and simple spatial forms. The problem would be compounded by superposition. Yet what humans are able to see is irrelevant. There are many codes we cannot read unaided.

The only constraint on explicitness that locality imposes, then, has little to do with spatial forms, spatial cohesiveness or spatial size. It is about identity conditions: a representation that explicitly encodes information must be made up of tokens that are readily separable from their surroundings. This separation process may vary arbitrarily from system to system. To be sure, there are limits. A system must be able to identify tokens quickly without engaging in substantial computation. Later I will state more precisely what this means. But for now the point is that locality does not mean spatial isolation. It means separability by the host system.

This then is the first condition on explicit encoding of information:

> **Condition (1)**: The states, structures, or processes — henceforth symbols — which explicitly encode information must be easily separable from each other.

Movability. The ideal of *operational* identity conditions also lies at the bottom of the movability condition. In its simplest form the movability condition states that a word can occur in more than one location and still carry its meaning. That is, the identity of a word is largely independent of context.

There is a profound justification for this idea. If we grant that there is no fundamental difference between transmitting information across space, and transmitting it across time, then transmission across time is storage, while transmission across space is spatial communication. Words serve as compact vehicles for meaning. They are the carriers of information. It is natural, then, to assume that we can use them both to store and to send information.

This view leads quite naturally to the idea that a word retains its meaning whether on page 1 or page 601. In principle, it could be sent from one page to the other. Either in token or in type. One consequence of this view, however, is that context is largely irrelevant to word content. This follows because if the information content of a word changed once it was transmitted we would have no way of reliably sending information. The very idea of a word is of a physical vehicle that holds its meaning across situations. But then the identity of a word must be largely independent of where and when the word appears in a system.

Now symbols which are totally mobile and which retain their identity whatever their context lie at one extreme of a continuum of symbol systems. Such symbols can never by polysemous; they can never have indexical elements; and they can never be read differently by different operators. In short, an information processing system using totally mobile symbols must be uniform throughout: there can be no regions where the symbol is interpreted differently, and no states which the system can enter into which cause exactly similar symbols to be read differently.

To see just how restrictive this constraint is I shall briefly examine several representational languages. We can then test the reasonableness of movability as a condition on explicit encoding. For if we believe that we *can* encode information explicitly in a language that violates the movability condition we have grounds for rejecting movability as just construed as a condition on explicit encoding.

Which languages satisfy movability? By a language I mean any set of individuatable states, structures or processes which can be paired with meanings. In the simplest cases, the theory which specifies a language consists of two components: a notational component and a meaning component.

The notational component tells us what to accept as allowable variation in the structure of a token. It is the theory of symbol separation. So, for example, although my writing changes from page to page as I change my posture, a good notational component would specify enough variability in tokens to cluster my written words into correct equivalence classes. It gives the identity conditions of atomic symbols.

The meaning component tells us what information is carried by each symbol. So, for example, a meaning theory for the symbols on a map will tell us that '•' means *cities with populations in excess of 50,000*.

Now just how restrictive is a language that allows no ambiguity whatsoever? Restrictive, very restrictive. Such systems can have no syntax, even a simple syntax. For instance, simple languages such as Arabic notation for numbers will have too complex a structure. Perfect notational mobility implies that the '5' in 105 and the '5' in 501 must carry the same information. It implies that identical notational elements encode identical information whatever their context. But of course the meaning of '5' changes with position. In 105, '5' means units, in 501, '5' means 500.

In order to capture this variability of meaning with position, we need to introduce a syntax. The point of syntax is to allow us to determine how to adapt the information content of a symbol to its position. For languages with syntax, the meaning component must factor in the contribution to meaning which the word's syntactic role makes. Since most languages do have syntax, a theory of language will usually contain, in addition to its notational and meaning components, a third component — a syntactic component — which describes the syntactic role symbols play when combined into compound structures.

In the case of Arabic notation the contribution to meaning made by position is trivial. Defining position as location in a string read from right to left, we then interpret '5' as follows:

'5' in position i means $5 \times 10^{i-1}$

The language for counting based on Arabic numerals has a very simple syntax. Yet even this syntax, we have seen, violates the movability condition. I think that few of us would deny that Arabic numerals represent numbers explicitly. So movability in its extreme form is too restrictive. But there are many other natural languages in which position is not all that can affect meaning. The symbols which come before or after may matter. Can these encode information explicitly?

For instance, a standard trick for extending an instruction set beyond the limits set by the individual keys on a keyboard is to use some characters as *switches*. A control character, for example, allows any character that follows it to be interpreted as a command rather than as a typed letter. *A* in the context of *Control-a* does not have its normal meaning. The control character switches *a*.

To accomodate switches we need to increase the complexity of the syntax of languages discussed so far. Up until now a syntactically primitive symbol has had no apparent structure. Our notational theory told us exactly what symbols were syntactically atomic. Now, however, we must treat certain *strings* of characters as syntactically simple. They are to be accorded the same syntactic role as atomic symbols despite their apparent molecular structure. This will have no real effect on our meaning theory. For once a language has syntax, its meaning rules are defined over syntactic elements. Thus, in our meaning theory we will find axioms such as:

'Control-a' means *move cursor to line's beginning*
'Control-e' means *move cursor to line's end*

These revisions extend the representational power of a language by adding more primitive symbols to its list of meaningful expressions. Because these syntactically primitive symbols are not notationally primitive, however, the host system has a slightly more complex recognition task, for it must first recognize the notation for 'control' and the notation for 'a' before it can recognize the presence of 'control-a' as a syntactic primitive.

Is the presence of a set of switches in a language sufficient to prevent it from encoding information explicitly? That depends on how local is the connection between a switch and the notational element it changes. For instance, if a switch may be set at an arbitrarily early point in a sentence, then the user of the language must keep track of which switches have been set. This never gets complicated in a computational sense because the user need only keep a stack of active switches and compare each current element against the stack. In fact, even if a switch once turned on may be switched off by a later switch, the job of tracking which switches are on is still simple. For again, the user need only check the current element against the stack. If that element is a switch, the user removes a member from the stack. If it is a non-switch, the user either changes its meaning (and removes a switch), or the user interprets the element with its standard meaning. Accordingly, the only taxing feature of this language is that one must remember which switches have been set. If there are few switches, and each switch is a distinct notational element such as Meta or Control which cannot itself be switched in meaning, this task should be trivial. If humans do not, in fact, find reading this language trivial, that they may tell us something about how long, and how large is the stack which humans can manage with ease.

Switches are a simple method for expanding the vocabulary of a language while keeping notation concise. But they do not allow us to compact our meaning theory: for every switched symbol there must be a meaning axiom.

In most economical languages, however, the same switch can effect different symbols in similar ways. For instance, the manual describing the commands available for my editor tells me that 'a' and 'e' when following 'Control' and 'Meta' mean *beginning* and *end* respectively, while 'Control' and 'Meta', when preceding 'a' and 'e,' indicate *line* and *sentence* respectively. Thus *'Control-a'* means *move cursor to line's beginning*, while *'Meta-a'* means *move cursor to sentence's beginning*.[7]

Such systematic variation in meaning allows us to compact our meaning theory. We can save memory. But it does not save computation. Once again, a stack will be needed to mark the switches that are on, and once again each notational element will be compared against it. Memory is saved because we can get by with fewer meaning axioms. But now instead of determining the meaning of *Control a* by looking up that entry in a memory intensive meaning theory, we must compute its meaning by looking up *Control* and *a* separately, and combining those meanings according to a general rule of combination. Computation increases.

Should we say such languages explicitly encode information? Again, it seems an open question. As codes go, such languages are no more compact than ordinary switched languages. They do get by with a more memory-compact decoder; but that decoder may take slightly longer to apply than one which just looks up the answer. Everything turns on how much time it takes to determine meaning. If the set of switches is small, or the host's decoder is highly parallel, then meaning may be determined almost instantly.

Let us grant that there is room for doubt whether languages with dedicated switches can be counted on always to encode information explicitly. There can be no doubt, however, that if we allow that *any* symbol may serve as a switch for any other, then information will sometimes be hidden. For now every symbol may, in principle, be ambiguous.

The net effect of unconstrained ambiguity is that syntactic rules may be arbitrarily complex because the disambiguations they must help to perform may be arbitrarily complex. The set of syntactic rules necessary, for example, for deciding which type of 'a' we find in a given expression, may enjoin us to examine many letters, or combinations of letters, before and after *a*. Because each of these letters in turn might be ambiguous we might eventually require a set of syntactic rules that computes a function of staggering complexity. For instance, to decide what *a* means in a certain context we might have to compute a function such as $a = f(b,c,f_1(d), f_2(f_3(f_4(e))), \ldots)$ to determine the particular *a* we are dealing with, and then look up its meaning.

To take an example from English, the sentence *Police police police police police*[8] is in principle grammatical. Read as: Police who are policed by policemen, are themselves policers of policemen, we see that each occurrence of 'police' has a unique syntactic and semantic identity. In some contexts 'Police' means *policeman,* in others it means *to enforce*. Complexity enters because there are so many combinations of meanings to consider. The amount of computation needed just to determine what a single expression means rises exponentially with the length of the sentence. Should we say that each occurrence of 'police' is explicit when it is so hard to identify the symbol?

If there remains any doubt here it is because we have not completely resolved whether to base our judgment of explicitness on the computational cost of recognizing and using a symbol or on the fact that the notational and syntactic elements are well-defined. On the other hand, it is tempting to go with our eyes and say that if we can see there in front of us a well defined symbol we know to be meaningful, it must be explicit. We can see the term *police,* so its meaning must be explicitly encoded. Its identity is well defined, though hard to determine. On the other hand, if efficiency is important then it is not enough that there exists *some* mechanism, however complex, for recognizing the symbol. For by that token, structure hidden arbitrarily deeply in a represention could also be called explicit. Thus, an edge might be said to be explicitly encoded on a retinal intensity matrix because there is an effective procedure for extracting it. This is absurd. Surely there is a substantive difference between information that is explicitly encoded and information that must recovered? But then efficiency does matter; it is the driving condition.

Accordingly, each step away from total movability — total context independence — is a step which increases the complexity of the processes which recognize a symbol and its meaning. At some point these recognition costs become too high and a language becomes unable to encode information explicitly. Such languages are too complex to be read and understood immediately. The truth in the movability condition then is this:

> **Condition (2)**: An ambiguous language may explicitly encode information only if it is trivial to identify the syntactic and semantic identity of the symbol.

Immediately readable. I have been arguing that for an expression in a language to encode information explicitly it must be trivial for a user of that language to recognize the notational components of the expression; trivial for that user to recognize the syntactic role of those components, and trivial as well for it to recognize the meaning of both the components and the expression as a whole. In short, I have been arguing that the expression must be immediately readable.

But what does it really mean for a recognitional process to be trivial? Can we say in more precise computational terms what immediately readable amounts to?

The definition I propose is that we call a recognitional process *trivial* if there is a mechanical process that identifies the relevant property in *constant time*. Constant time is a measure of the absolute computational complexity of a process. It means that the number of computational operations needed to solve a problem is a constant independently of the size of the problem instance. For example, the time needed to recognize whether a binary number is even is constant regardless of size because the test for evenness is local, it involves checking the last digit. Similarly, to decide if an encoding is all 1's, all we need to do is add 1 and check to see if the new number overflows, i.e., has a longer encoding length. This too can be done in constant time.

Constant time is the smallest complexity order known. Few computations fall within it. Accordingly, in saying that an expression explicitly encodes information only if it can be parsed and interpreted in constant time, we are placing a strong and precise condition on explicitness. Instead of vague intuitions about structures being *immediately usable* or permitting their information to be *directly read off*, we now have a precise principle for interpreting immediacy.

The criterion of constant time, like all complexity orders, is meaningful only if we know what can be done in a single step. For example, on some machines a piece of information can be retrieved in a few steps regardless of how big the memory storage unit is. On such machines, retrieval is a constant time operation. On other machines, as memory size increases the number of steps needed to find information rises logarithmically. On these machines, memory retrieval is a log time operation.

The one weakness in using constant time as a mark of immediacy is that sometimes we may recognize small inputs immediately, even though the recognitional process for arbitrary inputs takes non-constant time. Strictly speaking, complexity is not meaningful for finite inputs; for in principle the answers to any finite problem can be stored in a giant look-up table, where the minimal amount of computation required to find an answer would be approximately the same across all problems.

Yet sometimes this is exactly what we believe is the case: patterns are recognized immediately because they are matched in memory.

To accommodate this intuition let us think of operators as having a certain spatial *attention span*. We may think of the attention span of an operator as its input window, the number of basic notational elements that may be in focus at any time. In a sense, it is the measure of parallelism inherent in the operator.

For example, to determine whether a given encoding is symmetric — as in *0110*, where one half is a mirror image of the other — a system with an attention span of 1 will iteratively compare numerals at each end. In our own case, however, if the number of digits is small, we can tell at a glance, without aid of iteration, if the two are mirror images. We gestalt this *global* property of the numeral. And so we can decide symmetry in constant time for any numeral up to some length n. Once n is reached there are too many digits to fit inside our attentional field. At that point, we too must iteratively scan. And so the property is no longer explicit. We no longer just 'see' it.

Attention span sets an upper bound on what can be immediately gestalted. That means that the net affect of attention span for larger problems is, at best, to reduce by a constant factor the absolute number of steps required.[9] This has the effect that complexity orders are unchanged by attention span. If a problem was order log it remains order log, except for problem instances that fall within the attention span. The upshot is recognition processes that are normally non-constant time, such as recognizing switched symbols, remain so, unless the symbols are, for instance, close together in time or space.

Accordingly:

Condition (3): symbols explicitly encode information if they are either:

- readable in constant time; or
- sufficiently small to fall in the attention span of an operator.

Meaning. The final condition of explicitness is that every expression that contains explicit information must have a definite information content. It is tautological that a symbol can explicitly encode information only if there is some information that it encodes. Although I have been arguing that the question of explicitness really concerns how quickly information can be made available in an encoding, I have yet to explain what I mean by *information*.

Just what it is for a state, structure, or process to express meaning remains the premiere issue of twentieth-century philosophy. My objective here, though, is not to clarify what information means, but to show that whatever theory of meaning one holds, the same concept of immediate apprehension can apply. Accordingly, let us consider some contenders.

The first theory of meaning is the most widely held:

A system immediately recognizes the meaning of a symbol if it grasps the contribution which the symbol makes to the meaning of the larger expression of which it is a part.

For instance, recognizing the meaning of 'cat' in *the cat in the hat*, on this view, consists in entering a state which contributes to the larger state of knowing the truth conditions of the whole sentence. To discharge the question-begging term 'knowing' we might reformulate the claim in more verificationist terms. Thus, recognizing the meaning of 'cat' in *the cat in the hat* consists in turning on a subset of the abilities involved in recognizing when a cat is in a hat. Associated with 'cat,' then, would be a set of abilities, or dispositional states, some of which are perceptual and motor, which are triggered (in constant time) by the appearance of the symbol 'cat' and which can combine with other abilities triggered by other symbols. The substance of the theory lies in first identifying the relevant abilities, and second explaining how they come to be triggered in just the right way and just the right order to produce appropriate composite abilities.

When understood in its referential version, this theory requires that the agent be able to 'know the referent' of an expression in constant time. If we identify this condition with the agent's being in a certain state, then we can say that a symbol explicitly encodes a certain datum of information for a system *S* only if *S* can enter a state of knowing the truth conditions of the expression in constant time. It is an empirical and conceptual problem to determine what this state is for any given system.

The second theory of meaning also attempts to explain in process terms what understanding consists in. Unlike the first, this theory places most emphasis on reasoning skills.

> A system immediately recognizes the meaning of a symbol if it directly enters a state that rationally constrains the system's future inferences and judgements.

For instance, recognizing the meaning of 'cat' in *the cat in the hat* may consist in entering a state which constrains the class of deductions and inductions that the system might make about cats, hats, being inside, and so on. These possible inferences and judgements are somehow *rationally regimented* by the semantic import of 'cat.' The substance of the theory lies in explaining first, the norms of reasoning and judgment, and second, how a given proposition fares in the cognitive economy of a rational agent. If we accept the second theory of meaning, then, we will say that a symbol explicitly encodes a certain datum of information for S only if S can, in constant time, enter a state which appropriately constrains S's possible trajectories of reasoning and judgment. It is an empirical and conceptual problem to determine what these constraints are for any given system.

The third theory of meaning I shall mention, unlike the other two, does not attempt to provide a full blooded account of meaning that grounds understanding in a set of abilities to recognize truth conditions or to reason rationally. This theory offers no explanation of the abilities an agent must have to understand a concept. It does, however, tie understanding to the activation of symbols. These symbols in turn might activate abilities.

> A system immediately recognizes the meaning of a symbol if it accesses (in constant time) any relevant associated symbols.[10]

For instance, recognizing the meaning of 'cat' in *the cat in the hat* may consist in retrieving certain other symbols. Eventually this process must ground out in basic abilities to act, perceive, and reason. Because these grounding abilities might be slow to activation they cannot be part of the explicit content of a symbol. They may be part of the symbol's total meaning. But they are not explicitly encoded.

Thus to take an example from English once again, the symbol "him" in the sentence 'Then John read *him* his rights.' explicitly encodes only that information that can be directly read from it. The referent is not part of this information, for a parser may have to look arbitrarily back among other sentences to locate it. Sometimes this process of locating the referent of a pronoun can be done by syntactic means. There are binding rules and in certain cases these will suffice to determine reference. In short sentences, though, the referent may be within the attention span of the agent. Hence explicitly encoded. For example, *John shot himself*. In other cases, the parser may have to rely on extra-syntactic knowledge which no agent could have within its attention span. For instance, to determine the referent of 'it' in 'Christine put the candle onto the wooden table, lit a match, and lit *it*,' the interpreter must exploit knowledge about tables and candles. Tables are rarely lit, and especially not simply by applying matches to them. The knowledge that is employed to decide that *it* refers to the candle, is located somewhere in the system, but there is no predetermined place it must be. It could be encoded in the state of the interpreter, in rules for meta-level control, or in a lexical data base. Determining where this state is could take arbitrarily long. Accordingly, its content is not explicitly present.

Sketchy as these accounts of meaning are they provide us with a hint at the fourth condition, for they share a common feature: namely that whatever meaning is, the states, structures, or processes that instantiate apprehension of that meaning must be able to be turned on in constant time. Thus:

> **Condition (4)**: The information which a symbol explicitly encodes is given by the set of associated states, structures, or processes it activates in constant time.

IMPLICATIONS

I have claimed throughout this paper that our intuitions about explicit information are confused. Explicitness really concerns how quickly information can be accessed, retrieved, or in some other manner put to use. It has more to do with what is present in a process sense, than with what is present in a structural sense. Three notable consequences follow.

The first consequence is that not everything which we can assign a meaning to is explicitly encoded. If a sentence takes longer than constant time to interpret, then its meaning is not on the surface. Again this holds whether the sentence is a declarative, such as *Buffalo buffalo buffalo buffalo buffalo*[11] or a procedure. For instance, the sentence (add(square 2) (5th-root 3125)) in one sense means (add 4 5). But not explicitly. On the surface, it means to add the square of 4 to the 5th root of 3125.

On the other hand, if (add 4 5) were a constant time procedure we would be obliged to say that its evaluation *was* explicitly represented. This has the consequence that information may be explicit even if it is not represented by its canonical symbol. Returning to our adding example, (add 1 1) explicitly encodes 2 for any system that can add in constant time or which has memorized the answer and can trivially retrieve it. Normally, we would expect that the difference between 2 and (add 1 1) is precisely that the first explicitly encodes 2 while the second explicitly encodes information about a procedure. Yet, while it is true that (1 + 1) does explicitly encode information about adding, it also explicitly contains information about the evaluation of the procedure. This ambiguity rarely occurs, however, because usually, procedures do not evaluate in constant time. So the information they contain is not explicit. It is only when the procedure is a constant time procedure, or when the performance of the procedure is in the attention span of the host, that the symbols become ambiguous. In such cases, there is no reason not to regard the procedure call as both a call to a certain procedure with certain values, and a special name for its evaluation.

If this seems unreasonable, consider a related case. In binary notation the last digit which ordinarily encodes explicitly the number of units, also encodes whether a number is even or odd. Should we say information about evenness is explicitly present? I think we must. We would not likely find an entry in a Tarski meaning theory stating that '. . . 0 means even number.' But if the host system has an understanding of what even or odd is, and it tests for evenness by checking the last digit, then what grounds have we for denying that the last digit carries two meanings explicitly? It is reasonable to suppose that '1' in the units location just is how we represent oddness. To be sure, a system may not always make use of information that is explicit. Being explicit is not the same as being *occurrent*. Occurrent states are occurrent because control has passed to a procedure which interprets the symbol. The control makes occurrent an interpretation. But what a symbol explicitly represents is independent of what is happening in the control structure. The only connection is that if we do not *know* all the constant time procedures that might act on the representation we cannot know all the bits of information the representation might encode explicitly.

The upshot is that an ordinary meaning theory for a language will not specify all the meanings of a symbol unless that theory was constructed with foreknowledge of the constant time procedures present in the system, and foreknowledge of what can be the contents of a span of attention.

This need for foreknowledge is one reason procedural semantics is hard. But by restricting the focus of procedural semantics to the constant time effects a representation can have rather than to arbitrarily long term effects, the project of procedural semantics may become more tractable. This, I take it, is one substantial virtue of the proposed theory of explicitness.

A second consequence of tying explicitness to rate of access is that there is no principled distinction between declarative and procedural representations. It is irrelevant whether 'place 10' means a location in some vector, or it means some compiled procedure which when invoked starts a set of processes for placing object 10 somewhere. Either meaning may be explicitly encoded. What counts is that the link to the vector location or to the compiled procedure be negotiable in constant time.

This focus on process is significant because it encourages us to think about information processing in terms of informational movement. Representations are inert unless coupled with processes which interpret them. This trivial point is often ignored in correlational theories of meaning. Thus we find correlationists looking for static structures to interpret as representations even in essentially dynamic systems such as relaxation networks. The truth, however, is that for such dynamical systems, information content is to be found in the coupling of structure with process. It is the union of structure and process which can explicitly encode information.

The final and most philosophically significant point is that the

Language of Thought as usually conceived is capable of generating representations that are not actually explicit in the proprietary sense I have been discussing. This has the consequence that, at a minimum, one of the following is *false*:

- the language of thought is the best level of analysis to represent perspicuously the episodes in our *mental life;*
- the events in our mental life are identical with operations on explicit representations;
- the language of thought perspicuously describes human information processing.

The primary motive for postulating a language of thought, it will be recalled, is that there are important regularities in thought, belief and action that would otherwise be missed were we to look for explanations at the neural level alone or at the competence level alone. Competence theories are above all structural theories: they tell us what is computed, what knowledge a system must have to be able to perform those computations, and, in the best competence theories, they tell us something about the decompositional structure of the computational process. But the details of the actual computational trajectories they leave undescribed. The opposite is true at the neural level: so many details are available about particular computational trajectories individual people follow that it is hard to find a level of characterization which perspicuously captures the important informational transitions that generalize well. The language of thought is meant to be the right level of abstraction to describe these informational transitions.

Does the language of thought successfully describe this middle level? In most discussions, the language of thought is assumed to be as complex as first order predicate calculus. Yet we know that parsing and assigning a semantic interpretation to first order predicate calculus is a non-constant time process. Something must give. We cannot believe the language of thought to be simultaneously a complete description of human information processing and a complete description of human mental life. If we opt for the language of thought as a complete description of the mental, then we must forsake identifying mental activity with computation on explicit representations.

If any of these three conclusions seems counterintuitive it is because we tend to think of explicitness as a local property of a data structure: something which can be ascertained without studying the system in which it is embedded. But that is a mistake.

Acknowledgement

My thanks to Eric Saund, Greg Smith, and Bob Stalnaker for many helpful hours of discussion.

Notes

* Support for this work has been provided in part by DARPA under Office of Naval Research contracts N00014-85-K0124, and by the Army Institute for Research in Management, Information and Communication Systems contract number DAKF11-88-C-0045.

1 See, for instance, Dennett, Three Kinds of Intentional Psychology, reprinted in *The Intentional Stance,* Cambridge, MA: Bradford/MIT Press 1987), 55–6; Hector Levesque, and Ron Brachman, "A Fundamental Tradeoff in Knowledge Representation and Reasoning," reprinted in *Readings of Knowledge Representation,* eds. Brachman and Levesque (1985), 41–70; Rob Cummins, "Inexplicit Information," in *The Representation of Knowledge and Belief,* eds. M. Brand and R.M. Harnish. (Tuscon: University of Arizona Press 1986).

2 Even if we choose to see them as computers merely because we can interpret them at an input output level as implementing functions, we certainly can never know that they are computing those functions correctly unless we can interpret intermediate states.

3 The issue here is not whether we can decide *after* a successful proof has been found just how many inferential steps are required to reach a given theorem. The issue is that there is no means of determining during the course of searching for a proof how far away that particular theorem remains. We cannot tell whether we are getting closer or moving farther away from the theorem.

4 Cf. Noam Chomsky, *Rules and Representations* (Oxford: Blackwell 1980); Stan Rosenschein, "Formal Theories of Knowledge and AI and Robotics." (*SRI* 1985; Hubert Dreyfus, *What Computers Can't Do,* (New York: Harper and Row 1979); and Terry Winograd and Fernando Flores, in *Understanding Computers and Cognition* (New York: Addison-Wesley 1987).

5 For instance, in *Psychosemantics: The Problem of Meaning in the Philosophy of Mind* (Cambridge, MA: MIT Press 1987), 25, Fodor states: "According to the Representational Theory of Mind, programs — corresponding to the 'laws of thought' — *may* be explicitly represented; but 'data structures' — corresponding to the contents of thoughts — *have to be*" (Fodor's emphasis).

6 Brian Smith, "On the Threshold of Belief," to appear in *Foundations of Artificial Intelligence,* special edition of *Artificial Intelligence,* ed. D. Kirsh; Rosenschein, "Formal Theories of Knowledge in AI and Robotics."

7 It is clear that the designers of this editor chose command names they thought reflected some systematicity, in order to make the commands easier to remember. The commands themselves, however, they implemented by a look-up table, thereby treating names as fusions. This design choice was a typical store versus compute choice. It is clearly more efficient to store all the combinations of letter sequences as molecular primitives, if the number of combinations is small, rather than parse each sequence each occasion of use. But as a vocabulary increases it pays to parse. For bigger applications it may be wiser to use compositional axioms, instead of a look-up table.

8 This example, and the proof that unbounded ambiguity leads to exponential computation is drawn from *Computational Complexity and Natural Language* by Barton, Berwick, and Ristad (Cambridge, MA: MIT Press 1987).

9 Of course, if attention span could be flexibly expanded, then the complexity

profile could be altered. A machine that is able to dedicate the ever-increasing hardware and memory required to enlarge its input window can potentially "see" the answer to ever larger problems. But the overhead in terms of the number of wires and connections needed to sustain an enlarged window of attention will grow at the same rate as the number of steps grows for systems with fixed attention span. So there will always be relatively narrow attention spans.

10 Cf. Allen Newell, "Physical Symbol Systems," *Cognitive Science* 4 (1980): 135–83; and Allen Newell, "The Knowledge Level," *Artificial Intelligence* 18: 1 (1982): 18–127.

11 Meaning: Buffalo from Buffalo outwit buffalo from Buffalo.

MACHINES AND THE MENTAL[1]*

Fred Dretske
University of Wisconsin/Madison

Computers are machines and there are a lot of things machines can't do. But there are a lot of things *I* can't do: speak Turkish, understand James Joyce, or recognize a nasturtium when I see one. Yet, numerous as are my disabilities, they do not materially affect my status as a thinking being. I lack specialized skills, knowledge and understanding, but nothing that is essential to membership in the society of rational agents. With machines, though, and this includes the most sophisticated modern computers, it is different. They *do* lack something that is essential.

Or so some say. And so say I. In saying it, though, one should, as a philosopher, be prepared to say what *is* essential, what are the conditions for membership in this exclusive club. If an ability to understand James Joyce isn't required, what, then, *must* one be able to understand? If one doesn't have to know what nasturtiums look like, is there something else one must be able to identify? What might this be? If one is told that there is no specific thing one has to understand, identify or know but, nonetheless, something *or other* towards which one must have a degree of competence, it is hard to see how to deny computers admission to the club. For even the simple robots designed for home amusement talk, see, remember and learn. Or so I keep reading in the promotional catalogs. Isn't this enough? Why not?

I happen to be one of those philosophers who, though happy to admit that minds computer, and in this sense *are* computers, have great difficulty seeing how computers could be minded. I'm not (not *now* at least) going to complain about the impoverished inner life of the computer--how they don't feel pain, fear, love or anger. Nor am I going to talk about the mysterious inner light of consciousness. For I'm not at all sure one needs feelings or self consciousness to solve problems, play games, recognize patterns and understand stories. Why can't pure thought, the sort of thing computers purportedly have, stand to ordinary thought, the sort of thing we have, the way a solitary stroll stands to a hectic walk down a crowded street? The same thing--walking--is going on in both cases. It just *seems* different because, in the latter case, so much else is going on at the same time. A mathematician's calculations are no less brilliant, certainly no less deserving of classification as mental, because he or she is blind, deaf and emotionally stunted--because, in other words,

----

*Presidential Address delivered before the Eighty-third Annual Meeting of the Western Division of the American Philosophical Association, Chicago, Illinois, April 26, 1985.

the calculations occur within a comparatively anemic sensory and emotional environment. Why can't we think of our machines as occupying a position on the far right of this mental continuum? Just a bit to the right of Star Trek's Doctor Spock? We don't, after all, deny someone the capacity for love because they can't do differential calculus. Why deny the computer the ability to solve problems or understand stories because it doesn't feel love, experience nausea, or suffer indigestion?

Nor am I going to talk about how bad computers are at doing what most children can do--e.g., speak and understand their native language, make up a story or appreciate a joke. For such comparisons make it sound like a competition, a competition in which humans, with their enormous head start, and barring dramatic breakthroughs in AI, will remain unchallenged for the foreseeable future. I don't think the comparison should be put in these terms because I don't think there is a genuine competition in this area at all. It isn't that the best machines are still at the level of two-year-olds, requiring only greater storage capacity and fancier programming to grow up. Nor should we think of them as idiot savants, exhibiting a spectacular ability in a few isolated areas, but having an overall IQ too low for fraternal association. For machines, even the best of them, don't have an IQ. They don't *do* what we do--at least none of the things that, when we do them, exhibit intelligence. And it's not just that they don't do them the way we do them or as well as we do them. They don't do them at all. They don't solve problems, play games, prove theorems, recognize patterns, let alone think, see and remember. They don't even add and subtract.

To convince you of this, it is useful to look at our relationship to various instruments and tools. The preliminary examination will not take us far, but it will set the stage for a clearer statement of what I take to be the fundamental difference between minds and machines.

In our descriptions of instruments and tools we tend to assign them the capacities and powers of the agents who use them. We often think, or at least talk, of artifacts--tools, instruments and machines--as telling us things, recognizing, sensing, remembering and, in general, doing things that, in our more serious, literal, moments, we acknowledge to be the province of rational agents. In most cases this figurative use of language does no harm. No one is really confused. Though we open doors, and keys open (locked) doors, no one seems to worry about whether keys open doors better than we do, whether we are still ahead in this competition. No one is trying to build a fifth generation key that will surpass us in this enterprise. Why not? Since both keys and people open doors, why doesn't it make sense to ask who does it better? Because, of course, we all understand that doors are opened *with* keys. *We* are the agents. The key is the instrument. That we sometimes speak of the instrument in terms appropriate to the agent, speak of the key as doing what the agent does with the key, should not tempt us into supposing that, therefore, there are some things we do that keys can also do. We catch fish *with* worms; *we*, not the worms, catch the fish.

Before concluding, however, that computers are, like keys, merely fancy instruments in our cognitive tool box--and, thus, taken by themselves, unable to do what we can do with them--consider another case. Who really picks up the dust, the maid or the vacuum cleaner? Is the vacuum cleaner merely an instrument that the maid uses to pick up dust? Well yes, but not *quite* the way one uses a key to open a door or a hammer to pound a nail. One pushes the vacuum cleaner around but *it* picks up the dust. In this case (unlike the key case) the question: "Who picks up dust better: people or vacuum cleaners?" *does* make good sense, and the answer, obviously, is the vacuum cleaner. We may never have had any real competition from keys for opening doors, but we seem to have lost the race for picking up dust to vacuum cleaners.

What such examples reveal is that the agent-instrument distinction is no certain guide to who or what is to be given credit for a performance. We do things. Machines do things. Sometimes we do things with machines. Who gets the credit depends on what is done and how it is done. To ask whether a simple pocket calculator can really multiply or whether it is *we* who multiply *with* the calculator is to ask, whether, relative to this task, the agent-instrument relation is more like our use of a key in opening a door or more like our use of a vacuum cleaner in picking up dust.

Well, then, are computers our computational keys? Or are they more like vacuum cleaners? Do they literally do the computational tasks that we sometimes do without them but do it better, faster, and more reliably? This may sound like a rather simple-minded way to approach the issue of minds and machines, but unless one gets clear about the relatively simple question of *who* does the job, the person or the pocket calculator, in adding up a column of figures, one is unlikely to make such progress in penetrating the more baffling question of whether more sophisticated machines exhibit (or will some day) some of the genuine qualities of intelligence. For I assume that if machines can really play chess, prove theorems, understand a text, diagnose an illness, and recognize an object--all achievements that are routinely credited to modern machines by sober members of the artificial intelligence community--if these descriptions are *literally* true, then to that degree they participate in the intellectual enterprise. To that degree they are minded. To that extent they belong in the club however much we, with our prejudice in favor of biological look-alikes, may continue to deny them full admission.

So let me begin with a naive question: Can computers add? We may not feel very threatened if this is *all* they can do. Nevertheless, if they do even this much, then the barriers separating mind and machine have been breached and there is no reason to think they won't eventually be removed.

The following argument is an attempt to show that whatever it is that computers are doing when we use them to answer our arithmetical questions, it isn't addition. Addition is an operation on numbers. We add 7 and 5 to get 12, and 7, 5 and 12 are numbers. The operations computers perform, however, are not operations on numbers. At best, they are operations on certain physical tokens that *stand for*, or are interpreted as standing for, the numbers. Therefore, computers don't add.

In thinking about this argument (longer than I care to admit) I decided that there was something right about it. *And* something wrong. What is right about it is the perfectly valid (and relevant) distinction it invokes between a representation and what it represents, between a sign and what it signifies, between a symbol and its meaning or reference. We have various ways of representing or designating the numbers. The written numeral "2" stands for the number 2. So does "two." Unless equipped with special pattern recognition capabilities, machines are not prepared to handle these particular symbols (the symbols appear on the keyboard for *our* convenience). But they have their own system of representation: open and closed switches, the orientation of magnetic fields, the distribution of holes on a card. But whatever the form of representation, the machine is obviously restricted to operations on the symbols or representations themselves. It has no access, so to speak, to the *meaning* of these symbols, to the things the representations represent, to the numbers. When instructed to add two numbers stored in memory, the machine manipulates representations in some electromechanical way until it arrives at another representation--something that (if things go right) stands for the sum of what the first two representations stood for. At no point in the proceedings do numbers, in contrast to numerals, get involved. And if, in order to add two numbers, one has to perform some operation on the numbers themselves, then what the computer is doing is not addition at all.

This argument, as I am sure everyone is aware, shows *too* much. It shows that *we* don't add either. For whatever operations may be performed in or by our central nervous system when we add two numbers, it quite clearly isn't an operation on the numbers themselves. Brains have their own coding systems, their own way of representing the objects (including the numbers) about which its (or our) thoughts and calculations are directed. In this respect a person is no different than a computer. Biological systems may have different ways of representing the objects of thought, but they, like the computer, are necessarily limited to manipulating these representations. This is merely to acknowledge the nature of thought itself. It is a *vicarious* business, a *symbolic* activity. Adding two numbers is a way of thinking *about* two numbers, and thinking *about* X and Y is not a way of pushing X and Y around. It is a way of pushing around their symbolic representatives.

What is wrong with the argument, then, is the assumption that in order to add two numbers, a system must literally perform some operation on the numbers themselves. What the argument shows, if it shows anything, is that in order to carry out arithmetical operations, a system must have a way of representing the numbers and the capacity for manipulating these representations in accordance with arithmetic principles. But isn't this precisely what computers have?

I have discussed this argument at some length only to make the point that all cognitive operations (whether by artifacts or natural biological systems) will necessarily be realized in some electrical, chemical or mechanical operation over physical structures. (Or, if materialism isn't true, they will be realized in or by transformations of mind-stuff.) This fact alone doesn't tell us anything about the cognitive nature of the operations being performed--whether, for instance, it is an inference, a thought or the taking of a square root. For what makes these operations into thoughts, inferences, or arithmetical calculations is, among other things, the meaning or, if you prefer, the semantics of those structures over which they are performed. To think about the number 7 or your cousin George, you needn't do anything with the number 7 or your cousin George, but you do need the internal resources for representing 7 and George and the capacity for manipulating these representations in ways that stand for activities and conditions of the things being represented.

This should be obvious enough. Opening and closing relays doesn't count as addition, or as moves in a chess game, unless the relays, or their various states, stand for numbers and chess moves. But what may not be so obvious is that these physical activities cannot acquire the relevant kind of meaning merely by *assigning* them an interpretation, by letting them mean something *to* or *for us*. Unless the symbols being manipulated mean something *to the system manipulating them*, their meaning, whatever it is, is irrelevant to evaluating what the system is doing when it manipulates them.[2] I cannot make you, someone's parrot, or a machine think about my cousin George, or the number 7, just by assigning meanings in accordance with which this is what your (the parrot's, the machine's) activities stand for. If things were this easy, I could make a tape recorder think about my cousin George. Everything depends on whether this is the meaning these events have to you, the parrot, or the machine.

Despite some people's tendency to think that the manipulation of symbols is *itself* a wondrous feat, worthy of such inflated descriptions as "adding numbers," "drawing conclusions," or "figuring out its next move" the process is, in fact, absolutely devoid of cognitive significance.[3] I once watched a gerbil manipulate a symbol, a symbol that, according to conventional standards--standards that I, but not the gerbil--understood, stood for my bank balance. I didn't have the slightest temptation to see in this symbol manipulation (actually *consumption*) process anything of special significance. Even if I trained a fleet of gerbils to arrange symbols in some computationally satisfying way (e.g., to balance my checkbook), I don't think *they* should be credited with balancing my checkbook. *I* would merely be using the gerbils to balance my checkbook in the way I use worms to catch fish.

To understand *what* a system is doing when it manipulates symbols, it is necessary to know, not just what these symbols mean, what interpretation they have been, or can be, *assigned*, but what they mean to the system performing the operations. John Searle and Ned Block have dramatized this point.[4] Searle, for instance, asks one to imagine someone who understands no Chinese manipulating Chinese symbols in accordance with rules expressed in a language he does understand. Imagine the rules cleverly enough designed so that this person can carry on a correspondence in Chinese--responding to (written) Chinese questions with (written) Chinese answers in a way that is indistinguishable from the performance of a native speaker of Chinese. Clearly, though a correspondent might not be able to discover this fact, the symbol manipulator himself doesn't understand Chinese. Nor does the system of which he is a part. Understanding Chinese is not just a matter of manipulating meaningful symbols in some appropriate way. These symbols must mean something *to* the system performing the operations.

This should not be taken to imply that machines cannot serve as useful models for cognitive processes. On the contrary. Their prevalent use in cognitive psychology indicates otherwise. What it does imply is that the machines do not literally *do* what we do when we engage in those activities for which they provide an effective model. Computer simulations of a hurricane do not blow trees down. Why should anyone suppose that computer simulations of problem solving must themselves solve problems?

But how does one build a system that is capable not only of performing operations on (or with) symbols, but one *to which* these symbols mean something, a machine that, in this sense, understands the meaning of the symbols it manipulates? Only when we can do this will we have machines that not only produce meaningful output, but machines whose activities in producing that output bear the mark of the mental. Only then will we have machines that we can not only *use* to balance our checkbook, but machines that will do it for us, machines that will not only print out answers to our questions, but machines that will *answer* our questions.

One thing seems reasonably clear: if the meaning of the symbols on which a machine performs its operations is a meaning wholly derived from us, its users--if it is a meaning that *we* assign the various states of the machine and, therefore, a meaning that we can change at will without altering the *way* these symbols are processed by the machine itself--then there is no way the machine can acquire understanding, no way these symbols can have a meaning to *the machine itself.* Unless these symbols have what we might call an intrinsic meaning, a meaning they possess which is independent of our communicative intentions and purposes, then this meaning *must* be irrelevant to assessing what the machine is doing when it manipulates them. The machine is processing meaningful (to us) symbols, to be sure, but the *way* it processes them is quite independent of *what they mean*--hence, nothing *the machine* does is explicable in terms of the meaning of the symbols it manipulates or, indeed, of their even having a meaning. Given the right programming and data base, we can contrive to make the sentences a machine produces answers to our questions. But the machine itself is no more answering our questions than is an automatic teller (now so prevalent in the banking industry) embezzling money when it keeps our deposit without crediting our account.

In order, therefore, to approximate something of genuine cognitive significance, in order to give a machine something that bears *a* mark, if not *all* the marks, of the mental, the symbols a machine manipulates must be given a meaning of their own, a meaning that is independent of their user's purposes and intentions. Only by doing this will it become possible to make the meaning of these symbols relevant to what the machine does with them, possible, in other words, to make the machine do something *because* of what its symbols mean, possible, therefore, to make these symbols mean something to the machine itself.

And how might this be done? In the same way, I submit, that nature arranged it in our case. We must put the computer into the head of a robot, into a larger system that has the kind of sensory capabilities, the perceptual resources, that enable what goes on inside the computer to mean something, in Paul Grice's natural sense of meaning[5], about what goes on outside the computer. The elements over which the computer performs its operations will then have a meaning that is independent of the conventions of its users. They will then mean something in the same way the swing of a galvanometer needle means something regarding the electrical activity in the circuit to which it is connected, the way expanding mercury means something about the surrounding temperature, the way a voltage spike in our visual cortex means something about the distribution of light impinging on the retina. This kind of meaning is sometimes called information.[6] It is the kind of meaning we associate with reliable signs and trustworthy indicators, the kind of meaning possessed by dark clouds, shadows, prints, leaf patterns, smoke, acoustic vibrations, and the electrical activity in the sensory pathways. The difference between a robot and the disembodied computer found in our office buildings and laboratories is that the former, unlike the latter, have symbol systems that are also *sign* systems: signs being symbols having a meaning quite independent of what *we* might say or think they mean. The only intrinsic meaning in most computers is the meaning derived from the array of pressure sensitive transducers on its keyboard. The activities in the computer may mean a move to KB-3 *to us*, but all they mean *to the computer* is that key 37 has been depressed.

This is only to say that information, *real* information, the kind of meaning associated with natural signs, is irrelevant to the operation of high speed digital computers in a way it is not irrelevant to the operation of living systems. If a sea snail doesn't get information about the turbulence in the water, if there isn't some state *in* the snail that functions as a natural sign of turbulent water, it risks being dashed to pieces when it swims to the surface to obtain the micro-organisms on which it feeds. If (certain) bacteria did not have something inside that meant that *that* was the direction of magnetic north, they could not orient themselves so as to avoid toxic surface water. They would perish. If, in other words, an animal's internal sensory states were not rich in information, intrinsic natural meaning, about the presence of prey, predators, cliffs, obstacles, water and heat, it could not survive. It isn't enough to have the internal states of these creatures mean something *to us*, for it to have *symbols* it can manipulate. If these symbols don't somehow register the conditions in their possessor's surroundings, the creature's symbol manipulation capacity is completely worthless. Of what possible significance is it to be able to handle symbols for food, danger and sexual mates if the occurrence of these symbols is wholly unrelated to the actual presence of food, danger and sexual mates?

In a sense, then, work on machine perception, pattern recognition, and robotics has greater relevance to the cognitive capacities of machines than the most sophisticated programming in such purely intellectual tasks as language translation, theorem proving, or game playing. For a pattern recognition device is at least a device whose internal states, like those of the bacterium, snail and human being, mean something about what is happening, or the conditions that exist, around it. There is actually something *in* these machines that means something regarding what is happening outside them and, moreover, something that means this whether or not we, the users of the machine (or, indeed, the machine itself), recognize it. We are not free to assign or withhold this meaning--anymore than we are free to say what the screech of a smoke alarm means. We can *say* that the alarm means there are leopards nearby, and for certain purposes (e.g., in a children's game of make-believe) we may even want to give it that meaning. But that isn't actually what the sound means. That isn't what it is a sign of, not the information it carries. And for the same reason, the meaning of the internal states of a pattern recognition device, or a robot equipped with sensory capacities, is a meaning these states have which, if it isn't actually a meaning *for* the machine itself, is the only meaning that shows any promise of being promoted into something that is relevant to assessing what these machines are doing when they mobilize these meaningful elements to produce an output.

But have we come any closer to understanding genuine mentation, the capacity to add, subtract, plan, play games, understand stories, and think about one's cousin George? What we have so far required of any aspiring symbol-manipulator is, in effect, that *some* of its symbols be actual signs of the conditions they signify, that there *be* some system-to-world correlations that confer on these symbols an intrinsic meaning, a meaning they do not derive wholly from the purposes and intentions of their users. This puts the symbol-manipulator *in the world* in a way it would not otherwise be. But have we come any closer to understanding how an element, symbol *or* sign, could have meaning *to* the symbol manipulator itself, how this meaning, and not just the sign having this meaning, could be relevant to *what* the system is doing when it manipulates these signs?

Think about a dog that has been trained to detect marijuana. Custom's agents can use these dogs to find concealed marijuana. When the dog barks, wags its tail, or does whatever it was trained to do when it smells marijuana, this alerts the agent to its presence. As a result of the dog's behavior, the official comes to believe that there is marijuana in the suitcase. But what does *the dog* believe? Surely not what the agent believes--*viz*., that there is marijuana in the suitcase. Why not? There is obviously something in the dog that is sensitive to the presence of marijuana, some neural condition whose occurrence is a sign, and in this sense means, that there is marijuana nearby. Furthermore, this something is (as a result of training) getting the dog to wag its tail or bark. Why isn't this enough to justify attributing a belief to the dog, a belief with the content: there is marijuana nearby? If we had a Stanford robot that could perform half as well with blocks on a table, we would doubtless be hearing about its extraordinary recognitional capacities. But nobody seems terribly impressed with the dog. The dog, one can hear them saying, has a wonderfully discriminating sense of smell. It has *sensory* powers that exceed those of its trainers, but its *conceptual* or *cognitive* capacities are modest indeed. It can smell marijuana, sure enough. It can even be trained to respond in some distinctive way to this smell. But it doesn't have the conceptual resources for believing *of* what it smells *that* it is marijuana.

If we are going to treat the dog in this deflationary way, we should be prepared to do the same with machines--including fancy robots. In industrial applications of machine vision, for example, it is said that machines can recognize short circuits on the printed circuit boards they examine. Not so. The machine merely searches for breaks or discontinuities in the metallic deposit. It is concerned with *spatial* discontinuities. We, its users, are worried about electrical discontinuities. Under the right circumstances, we can use something that detects the first as an instrument, a means, for identifying the second, but, just like the dog, the instrument should not be credited with the *conceptual* talents of its users, what *we* are able to discover by using it. The machine is no more able to have electricity thoughts than the dog is able to have marijuana thoughts.

Some people think that what machines lack is conscious awareness. Perhaps they do. But our marijuana sniffing dog should teach us that this isn't the missing ingredient, not what we need to manufacture a thinker of thoughts out of a sign manipulator. For the dog *is,* whereas the custom's agent is not, *aware of* the concealed marijuana. The dog smells it and the agent does not. To give a system the kind of meaning we now seek, to give it genuine understanding, it is not enough to give it conscious awareness *of* the stuff it is supposed to cognize. It isn't even enough to make the creature's conscious awareness of the stuff *cause* it to behave in some appropriate way *toward* the stuff. For, as our trained dog illustrates, all this can be true without the system, animal or machine, having the slightest conception of what it all means. And what we are after, of course, is something that wags its tail, activates its printer, or starts its motors, not just because it is aware of, say, marijuana, but because it thinks, judges, or believes that it is marijuana. What we are after is *con*ception, not *per*ception.

The difference between machines (or dogs) and the agents who use them is that although machines (and dogs) can pick up, process and transmit the information we need in our investigative efforts (this is what makes them useful tools), although they can respond (either by training or programming) to meaningful signs, it isn't the meaning of the signs that figures in the explanation of why they do what they do. Some internal sign of marijuana, some neurological condition that, in this sense, means that marijuana is present, can cause the dog's tail to move, but it isn't the fact that it means this that explains the tail movement. This, I submit, is the difference between the dog and its master, between the machine and its users, between the robot and the people it replaces. When I smell marijuana, my finger wagging is produced, not simply (as in the case of the dog) by a neurological condition that means that marijuana is present, but by the *meaning* of this neurological condition, by the fact that it means this and not something else. In *my* case the motor activity is produced by the meaning of an occurrent sign; in the dog's case by the occurrence of a sign having that meaning. To say that the smell of marijuana means something to me that it doesn't mean to the dog is merely to say that its meaning what it does makes a difference to what I do but not to what the dog does. That is why it is true of me, but not the dog, that I wag my finger because I think marijuana is present, because I am in an internal state having this content. The dog is in a state with the same content, to be sure, but it isn't this content that wags the tail. The difference between a thinker of marijuana thoughts (me) and the mere detector of marijuana (dog or machine) is not, then, merely a difference in what our internal signs mean, but a difference in whether, and if so, how, these meanings are implicated in the management of the signs themselves.

I seem to have painted myself into a corner. At least I expect to be told as much by those philosophers who are deeply suspicious of meaning. I expect to be told that meaning is an abstraction, not something that *could* play a role in the activities of a symbol manipulating system. From the control point of view, meaning is an epiphenomenon. It is causally inert. Even if one agrees that there are signs in the head, it is the signs themselves, not their meaning, that turn the cranks, pull the levers, and depress the accelerator. It is the grey stuff inside, not what it means, that activates the motor neurons. Just ask the neurobiologists. If, in order to promote a processor of meaningful signs into a system with genuine understanding, into a real thinker of thoughts, we must give the meaning of these signs a role to play in the *way* these signs are processed, in the way the motor control system operates with them, then the prospects for effecting such a promotion, not just for machines, but for human beings as well, look bleak indeed.

Such pessimism, though widespread these days, is unwarranted. Meanings, of the kind now in question, *are* what philosophers like to call abstract entities, but they are *no more* abstract, and certainly no less capable of exercising a causal influence, than are, say, differences in weight, brightness and orientation. Just as the difference in weight between a basketball and a bowling ball may be responsible, causally responsible, for the behavior of a beam balance, the correlations constituting the meaning of a sign can, and regularly *do*, affect the way a system processes that sign. The correlation between a ringing bell and someone's presence at one's door, the kind of correlation that confers on the ringing bell the meaning that someone is at the door, *changes* the way a (suitably exposed) nervous system processes the internal sign of a ringing bell. Exposure (either directly or indirectly) to this correlation produces a difference in whether, and if so, which, motor neurons are activated by the internal sensory sign of a ringing bell. This, it seems to me, is a case where the meaning of a sign, and not just the sign that has that meaning, makes a difference in *how* a system processes that sign--hence, a case where the sign's meaning, and not the sign itself, helps to explain the behavior of the system in which that sign occurs.

My doorbell example is a homely example of the causal role of meaning. Some may think it ignores all the interesting questions. For it involves an agent already possessed of the conceptual resources for interpreting signs, understanding meanings, and modifying his or her behavior in the light of experienced correlations. This is true, but irrelevant. For the very same phenomenon can be illustrated at almost every biological level, every level at which *learning* occurs. It is, in fact, merely an instance of what learning theorists describe as the contingencies modifying the way a system processes, and hence responds to, the internal signs for stimulus conditions. Even the lowly snail mentioned earlier changes the way it processes signs by exposing it to the correlations constituting the meaning of these signs. And it is, surely, the fact that our internal states are correlated with certain kinds of external conditions that helps to determine the ultimate outcome of the motor activities produced by these internal states. It is the correlations, therefore, that help to determine what kind of feedback we received from such activities and, hence, the likelihood of our repeating them in the same circumstances. It is, therefore, the correlations, not merely the internal correlates, that shape--hence, *explain*--learned behavior. Learning, in fact, *is* a process in which the meaning of internal signs (i.e., their correlation with external conditions), not (merely) the signs themselves, helps to determine how these signs are exploited for purposes of motor control. For such systems the internal signs not only have meaning, this meaning affects the way the system manages these signs; and it is in this sense that the signs mean something *to* the system in which they occur.

This, it seems to me, is a fundamental difference between the sign processing capabilities of various systems. It is a difference that helps explain why it seems so natural to say of some of them (human beings and some animals) but not others (machines and simple organisms) that the symbols they manipulate mean something to the symbol manipulator. It is a difference, I submit, that underlies our conviction that we, but not the machines and a variety of simple organisms, are genuine thinkers of thoughts. What *gives* us the capacities underlying this difference is a long and complicated story. It involves, I think, issues in learning theory, our multiple sensory access to the things we require to satisfy our needs, and the kind of feedback mechanisms we possess that allow us to modify *how* we manipulate internal signs by the kind of results our previous manipulations have produced. But this, clearly, is a story that we expect to hear from neurobiologists, not from philosophers. All I have been trying to tell is a simpler story, a story about the entrance requirements for admission to the club. I leave it to others to worry about how different systems manage, each in their own way, to satisfy these requirements.

Footnotes

1. My thanks to Denny Stampe for careful criticism and many useful suggestions. I also want to acknowledge the help given me by Fred Adams and the other sceptics in the audience at Augustana College where I read an early draft of this paper. They convinced me that the draft I read them was *earlier* than I ever suspected.
2. This is what Haugeland calls "original intentionality," something that, according to Haugeland, computers don't have: "To put it bluntly: computers themselves don't mean anything by their tokens (any more than books do)--they only mean what we say they do. Genuine understanding, on the other hand, is intentional

in its own right" and not derivatively from something else. *Mind Design*, John Haugeland (ed.), Bradford Books; Montgomery, Vt., 1981, pp. 32-33. A number of authors have made essentially this point in their own way; e.g., Jerry Fodor, "Tom Swift and His Procedural Grandmother," *Cognition*, 6 (1978), reprinted in *Representations*, MIT/Bradford, 1981; Hilary Putnam, "Brains in a Vat," *Reason, Truth and History*, Cambridge University Press, 1981, pp. 10-11; Rob Cummins, *The Nature of Psychological Explanation*, MIT/Bradford, 1983, p. 94; Tyler Burge, "Belief *De Re*," *The Journal of Philosophy*, LXXILV, 6 (1977); John Searle, "Minds, Brains and Programs," *The Behavioral and Brain Sciences* 3:3 (1980).

3. In explaining why he thinks computers *can* (or will someday), Marvin Minsky (in "Why People Think Computers Can't," *AI Magazine*, Fall 1982), seems most impressed, for instance, with the fact that "computers can manipulate *symbols*."
4. John Searle, "Minds, Brains and Programs," *The Behavioral and Brain Sciences*, 3:3 (1980); Ned Block, "Troubles with Functionalism," in Wade Savage (ed.), *Perception and Cognition: Issues in the Foundations of Psychology*, Minnesota Studies in the Philosophy of Science, Vol. 9, Minneapolis, Minn.; 1978.
5. Paul Grice, "Meaning," *Philosophical Review*, vol. 66 (1957), pp. 377-388.
6. See my *Knowledge and the Flow of Information*, MIT/Bradford: Cambridge, Mass., 1981.

Ways of Establishing Harmony

Daniel C. Dennett

Folklore has many tales in which the hero goes in search of some precious thing – a holy grail, a magic talisman – and eventually, thanks to his many virtues, acquires the sought-for treasure *but only after rejecting it, unrecognized, several times*. In the final dénouement, he is shown that what he wanted so badly he had already had within reach.

One can see in Fred Dretske's career just such a quest – with just such a happy result. I am pleased to be the bearer of glad tidings, especially since, in Dretske's particular saga, he has often mistaken me for one of the villains (or better: worthy opponents), rather than the protector, all along, of the magic key. What Dretske has sought, with increasing clarity of purpose over the years, is the key to *how meaning makes a difference to us*, and now that he has described his quest so vividly, the rest of us can see better what we were trying to say and do as well.

In a recent paper (1985, p. 31), Dretske gives a particularly clear and telling example of the difference that he is trying to capture: the marijuana-detecting dog whose tail wags because an event occurs in its brain "meaning" (carrying the information) that marijuana is present, but which doesn't wag *because* the event means what it means. Unlike the dog's tell-tale tail-wag, Dretske insists, *our* bodily actions often happen *because of* what the states that cause them mean: "it is the structure's having this meaning (its semantics), not just the structure that has this meaning (the syntax), which is relevant to explaining behavior" (personal correspondence, quoted in Dennett, 1987, p. 307).

In a more recent paper (Dretske, SOFIA conference, 1988), on which this will focus,[1] he puts it even better: he has been "increasingly preoccupied with the question, not of what meaning (or content) *is*, but what meaning (or content) *does*." He wants to give meaning "some explanatory bite," (p. 5 of Dretske's conference paper, hereafter MS) and ideally, this would involve showing "the way meaning ... *can* figure in the explanation of why" an event causes what it does.

What difficulty lies in the way of this goal? The arguments, from myself and others, to the effect that the meaning of a particular event always must be, in Dretske's terms, *epiphenomenal* with regard to that event's actual causal powers. In *Content and Consciousness* (1969) I argued that the intentional interpretation of neural events is always at best a "heuristic overlay", and in "Intentional Systems" (1971) I tried to show how physical-stance predictions of the effects of structures always had hegemony over predictions based on the powers attributable to those structures (in idealization) in virtue of their meaning – as discerned from the intentional stance. More recently (1981, 1983, 1987), I have spoken, as Dretske notes, of the *impotence* of meaning; the brain is first and foremost a syntactic engine, which can be fruitfully viewed as reliably mimicking a semantic engine, but in which meanings themselves never overrule, overpower, or so much as influence the brute mechanistic or syntactic flow of local causation in the nervous system. (A semantic engine, I claim, is a mechanistic impossibility – like a perpetual motion machine, but a useful idealization in *setting the specs* for actual mechanisms.) Others have made similar claims: Fodor has long insisted on the inescapability of what he calls the Formality Constraint, and Dretske attributes to Schiffer (1987) the view that meaning is an "excrescence" which can do nothing and explain nothing.

Dretske's response to these claims is ambivalent. On the one hand he makes it entirely clear that he would truly love to defend a doctrine of brains as real semantic engines, with real meanings locally throwing their weight around and making the most direct imaginable difference – but he knows better. He is convinced by the arguments that show, in LePore and Loewer's terms, that the historical facts on which the meaning of a structure supervenes are *screened off* from the explanation of the structure's causal powers and behavior. (In a similar vein, I have spoken of "inert historical facts.") In fact, his own presentation of the argument, drawing the analogy to the difference between value and perceived value, is the clearest yet. He has reached the First Camp, and he finds it a hateful place but one he must endure now that he has cleaned it up.

What he will not endure, however, is any of the paths to the Second Camp. The well-known responses to the Lesson of the First Camp all involve finding some more indirect way in which there can be a regular, reliable correspondence between the meaning of a (neural) structure and its effects on behavior. For instance, Fodor's *language of thought* hypothesis is essentially an attempt to describe a system that satisfies what Haugeland has called the Formalists' Motto:

> If you take care of the syntax, the semantics will take care of itself. (1985, p. 106.)

This motto lies at the heart of what Haugeland calls GOFAI (Good Old Fashioned AI) and I call "High Church Computationalism" (Dennett, 1986). There are other, more noncommittal, ways in which materialists who have reached the First Camp can postulate a reliable correspondence between semantics and mechanism, but Dretske finds them all intolerable. I think it is wonderful that he chose to illuminate this "corner materialists have painted themselves into" by some old-fashioned labels: "epiphenomenalism" and "pre-established harmony." These dreaded relics of prescientific philosophy of mind, these desperate and doomed escape routes from Cartesian dualism, are sure to strike terror in the heart of complacent materialists, and Fred tells us exactly why he cannot abide them: any view of meaning according to which there is merely a pre-established harmony between the causal facts and the facts of meaning may permit us to *predict* an agent's behavior, and *control* an agent's behavior, but will not permit us to *explain* an agent's behavior – "and that," he says quite reasonably, "is what it takes to vindicate belief-desire psychology or our ordinary view about the causal efficacy of thought – that we stopped, for example, *because* we thought the light was red."[2]

But since Dretske has reluctantly accepted the conclusion of the First Camp, he realizes that a straightforward vindication of this intuition is not in the cards. What he offers us instead is an attempt to salvage, if not *locally potent meanings*, then the next best thing: "the fact that *A* means *M*, though it fails to explain why *B* occurred, may help explain a closely related fact, the fact that events of type *A*, when they occur, cause events of type *B* . . . And this fact, especially when we are trying to explain the behavior of a system, is a fact eminently worth explaining" (p. 11 of Dretske's conference paper).

What we need, in short, is not just a brute pre-established harmony, but an *explanation* of why and how the harmony is pre-established. Moreover (if Dretske has his druthers) this explanation will make an ineliminable appeal to the meanings of the elements thus linked. Now apparently he thinks that we pre-established harmony guys have failed to offer such an explanation, for he is forthright in his opposition: "I don't think this works. Or, if it does work, it does so at a cost that I'm not prepared (unless forced) to pay" (p. 9 of Dretske's conference paper). But this is where he makes his mistake, for in the end, he does not offer us an alternative to pre-established harmony, but a version of it, a truncated version, in fact, of the very version I have offered. (We have reached the turning point in the saga. Reach out, Fred, and *take the key!*)

There are exactly five ways in which such a correspondence – a "pre-established harmony" between the meanings of structures and their causal powers – could (in principle) come into existence. Fred encounters them all, but fails to recognize them for what they are.

First, there are the Three Cousins:

1. the correspondence is designed by natural selection;
2. the correspondence is designed by a learning process of some sort in the individual brain;
3. the correspondence is designed by an engineer creating an artifact, such as a robot or computer.

Then there is the Philosopher's Fantasy:

4. the correspondence is the result of a Cosmic Coincidence.

Finally, there is the Theologian's Hope:

5. the correspondence is created and maintained by God.

Desperate though he is to wed meaning and causation together, Fred rightly dismisses this fifth possibility with only a passing allusion, for the obvious reason that it would be, quite literally, a *deus ex machina*. It is interesting to me that philosophers who would be embarrassed to spend more than a passing moment dismissing this fifth alternative are nevertheless irresistibly drawn to extended discussions of the implications of the fourth, Cosmic Coincidence, which is actually a more fantastic and negligible "possibility in principle."

Notice that there really cannot be a sixth route to pre-established harmony. If such a harmony is not just a single, large ("Cosmic") coincidence (4), or a miracle (5), it must be the product, *somehow*, of lots of tiny, well-exploited coincidences, for the moral of the First Camp is that meanings cannot *directly* cause things to happen – and hence they cannot *directly* cause themselves to correspond to any causal regularities in the world. So it will have to be via an indirect process of fortuitous coincidences that are duly "appreciated" or "recognized" or "valued" or "selected" by something – either something blind and mechanical, such as natural selection or operant conditioning or "neural Darwinism" (Edelman, 1988) (1 and 2), or something foresightful and intelligent, such as an engineer (3). Any such process is a design process, and must consist, at bottom, of such generate-and-test cycles, where the generation of diversity to be tested is somewhat random or coincidental (see "Why the Law of Effect Will Not Go Away", Dennett, 1974, 1978).

Let me preview Dretske's encounters with the Ways, before setting out the details: he *endorses* the first two Cousins, natural selection and conditioning, while *rejecting* the third Cousin, engineering, never recognizing that *by his own principles* they are inseparable kin who stand or fall together. He then uses his allies, the first two Cousins, to defeat the fourth Way, Cosmic Coincidence, which really doesn't pose a threat in the first place. What clouds our hero's vision? As we shall see, it is his overzealous vow of allegiance to the intuitions of folk-psychology.

Now the details. Dretske begins his attempt to give meaning explanatory bite by nicely distinguishing between explaining B's happening (A caused it) and explaining A's causing B. He then tells a story about how a neural assembly can come to have a meaning, either via species evolution or via phenotypic learning – a kind of intra-cerebral evolutionary process of conditioning. The upshot is that such a story can explain why it is that As, meaning what they do, cause Bs. So far as I can see, this account follows precisely the path I laid out in *Content and Consciousness*, in my discussion of "the evolution of appropriate structures" (pp. 47–63).

Dretske describes an organism with a need to develop an avoidance mechanism against the highly toxic condition F, while I described different strains of organism which were different wired up to avoid, approach, or ignore a particular stimulus condition that happens to be "more often than not" – an important proviso – injurious (p. 49). The result of both thought experiments is the same: the lucky ones who happen to be wired up to avoid the toxic, *ceteris paribus*, are the ones who survive to reproduce, their coincidentally happy correspondence being selected for by natural selection. Dretske goes on to suggest that the same result could also be achieved by redesign during an individual organism's lifetime via a conditioning process, or as I put it, via a process of "intra-cerebral evolution" which can, in principle, yield all and only the new designs which the much slower process of species evolution could produce (pp. 56–63).

Note, however, that while Dretske now agrees with me about this, his doing so requires that he abandon, or at least soften, the hard line he has previously taken on these issues, in *Knowledge and the Flow of Information* (1981), and more recently in "Machines and the Mental" (1985) and "Misrepresentation" (1986). In his book, he attempted to erect meaning on a foundation of information. That is, he developed an account of semantic information (the sort of meaning needed for psychology – a *functional* notion that applies only to *designed* channels) from a base of nonfunctional, nonsemantic information channels, through which traveled items with "natural meaning" – items that informed (by definition) with *perfect reliability*; where natural meanings are concerned, no misrepresntation is possible. The task then was to turn the corner, somehow, from natural meaning to semantic or "natural functional meaning" (in which misrepresentation *is* possible), without, as he has more recently put it, "artificially *inflating*" the attributions of meaning to a structure one is so interpreting. Dretske has tried to hold the line against inflation by insisting on what he now calls the "indicator relation." But, although the current paper is not forthright about it, the indicator relations he now endorses (thanks to his endorsement of natural selection as a Way) can only approximately carry information about the distal conditions one is tempted to say they are designed to inform the organism about.

The indicator relation, which he heralds as "a plausible, at least a *possible*, partial basis for meaning" need only be a rough-and-ready guide to the meaning of the chosen structure. At least Dretske *ought* to recognize this, for that is how evolution, at the species or neural level, works. Mother Nature is a stingy, opportunistic engineer who takes advantage of rough correspondences whenever they are good enough for the organism's purposes, given its budget. Fred correctly wants to boast that his account *does* find an explanatory role for meanings: it is *because of what a structure happens to indicate* that it is "selected for" or "reinforced in" a further causal role in the economy of control of the organism, but it will be selected for, or reinforced in, this role *whenever* it is "close enough for government work" as the engineers say.

The most Dretske can get out of Cousins (1) and (2), then, is an explanatory account that makes ineliminable appeal to *quasi-indicator relations* or *approximate meanings*. Mother Nature never holds out for high-priced indicator relations.

As my frequent allusions to engineering suggest, and as I have argued in *The Intentional Stance* (chapter 8), the design processes one encounters in (1) and (2) are not only fundamentally the same, but fundamentally the same as the *artificial* design process encountered in (3). It is striking that Dretske resists this conclusion, most emphatically in "Machines and the Mental" but still strongly in evidence, with somewhat difference emphasis, in the current paper. If it is an engineer or computer scientist – rather than natural selection or a learning history – who does the selecting (who esteems a structure for its quasi-indicator relations and harnesses it in a particular functional role in a robot's control structure), this somehow gives the structure an illegitimate ancestry, in Dretske's eyes. But why?

Why should selection by an engineer disqualify a structure for one of Dretske's why-explanations, while "natural" selection does not? One might even suppose that engineer-selection had an advantage over its "blind," inefficient competition. One might say: whereas one must use scare-quotes when talking of natural selection's "appreciation" of the potential meaning of a structure, engineers sometimes really and truly respond to these potential meanings in the course of their conscious, deliberate, designing. But Dretske does not find this line of thought palatable, in spite of the fact that in the present paper his illustration of the wiring of the light switch explicitly appeals to just such different appreciations or intentions on the part of circuit designers. Is it just because he has a bad case of *orqanophilia* (otherwise known as *silicophobia*)? I think not. I suspect that he is distracted by an illusion: the illusion that somehow in ways (1) – and (2) – but in (3) not – the organism itself (or even: its mind or soul) does the understanding – responds directly to the meaning. After all, one might naturally but confusedly say, if some engineer is responsible for appreciating the meaning of a neural or computer structure, and is responsible for designing its further role in the light of that meaning, there is nothing left for the organism or robot to do – no *task of understanding* left over. But of course if *that* were so, the very same consideration would disqualify natural selection, for if it is the process of natural selection that has set up an innate correspondence between meaning and causation, there would likewise be no supervisory role for the organism (or its central, understanding homunculus) to play. (For more on this see my commentary on Ewert's "Prey-Catching in Toads," in *Behavioral and Brain Sciences*, (1988) "Eliminate the Middletoad!")

Now the reason I suspect that Dretske is beguiled by this line of thought is that in earlier work, he endorsed only (2), a learning history, and resisted endorsing (1), natural selection, as a legitimate Way to Harmony.[3] Both in his book, and more recently in his articles (and in personal correspondence, quoted in *The Intentional Stance*, p. 306), he held the line against innate, unlearned meanings. "Beliefs and desires, *reasons* in general (the sort of thing covered by the intentional stance), are (or so I would like to argue) invoked to explain patterns of behavior that are acquired during the life history of the organism exhibiting the behavior (i.e., learned)."

Why then has Dretske been tempted to favor individual learning histories exclusively? Because, apparently, they seemed to give the organism itself a proper role in the acquisition and appreciation of the meanings in question. But once again, of course, if "mere conditioning" is responsible for the redesign of the individual organism's brain, this too looks like taking responsibility away from the inner understander that Dretske is so loath to lose.

"But where does the *understanding* happen?" One might ask this, having been treated to an account of the way in which an organism was caused, thanks to its design, to respond appropriately (first internally, and eventually externally) to events impinging on it. It is as if one held out the hope of *locating* a moment of understanding by using a more powerful microscope, but in fact the understanding is, must be, located more diffusely, in the happy interactions of all those well-designed mechanisms.

This is, I think, the primary source of Dretske's earlier (and continuing!) opposition to natural selection and his continuing opposition to engineering design as sources of Harmony. In fact, in recent correspondence with me, he made it quite clear that he put so much stock in learning history, that he was prepared to grant real meaning even to the structures in an artifact, *so long as they were produced, in part, by individual learning* by the artifact: "I think we could (logically) create an artifact that *acquired* original intentionality, but not one that (at the moment of creation as it were) *had* it " (personal correspondence, quoted in *The Intentional Stance*, p. 305).

Now here we must distinguish two claims, one plausible and important, and the other – Dretske's – obscurely motivated and, I think, strictly negligible. The plausible and important claim is that it is astronomically unfeasible to create, by the usual engineer's methods, the sorts of structures that are naturally and efficiently created by learning histories of the sort he champions. This suspicion strikes at the heart of a particular fantastic hope of some in AI, who would *hand-craft* the myriads of beliefs that would constitute the "world knowledge" of an adroit robot. Not only have some thought this was possible in principle; there is a multi-million dollar project in AI with that as its explicit goal: Douglas Lenat's CYC project, an effort which Lenat himself supposes will take *person-centuries* of programming to accomplish. (See my discussion in *Daedalus* (1988a).) The majority opinion in AI, however, is that this is a hopeless approach, for reasons well-canvassed by David Waltz (1988).

Dretske's point, in contrast, is philosophical, not practical. It is that even if the engineers could hand-craft all those structures, they wouldn't have any meaning until they had been somehow annealed in the fire of experience. He puts the astronomically unfeasible product of engineering design in the same category with the even more astronomically unlikely case of Cosmic Coincidence, in spite of the fact that in the former case, there would be explanations of the provenance of structures that made appeal to meanings. He imagines that a physical duplicate of himself might "materialize – miraculously or randomly – out of some stray collection of molecules" (ms p. 19), and goes to some length to insist that this biological twin's motions would not be *actions*, with *meanings* behind them.

> I move my arm in this way *in order* to frighten away a pesky fly. With such a purpose I am, let us say, *shooing away a fly*. That is my *action*. My biological twin, though he moves his arm in the same way (with the same result) does not shoo away a fly, He doesn't have wants or beliefs, the kind of purposes I have in moving my arm. He isn't therefore, performing the same action. (ms, p. 19)

Your intuitions may agree with his, or recoil, but in either case, they concern something negligible, for as he goes on to acknowledge, there is a loophole: this metaphysically shocking state of affairs is apt to be short-lived, since it will persist only "until the twin accumulates enough experience – until, that is, his internal processes acquire the requisite extrinsic relations – to give his control processes, the processes governing the movement of his hand, the same kind of explanation as mine" (ms, p. 20).

How long, one wonders, should "acquiring the requisite extrinsic relations" take? I should think it would be instantaneous.[4] Signals from the bio-double's peripheral vision (or perhaps a faint blip from cutaneous sensors on the shoulder) happen to put the bio-double into what would be a bogus fly-out-there-sensing state – except that this time it is caused by a real fly. Moreover, the real fly's trajectory intimately determines the hand – eye coordination series that promptly leads to the (bogus or real?) "shooing" motions. How many flies must buzz around the head of a bio-double before he can start shooing them? If that isn't an angels-dancing-on-the-head-of-a-pin question, what would be?

This curious question, of how much traffic with the world is enough, somehow, to ensure that genuine meaning has been established, is simply the enlargement (via a *Cosmic* Coincidence) of the curious question that has bedeviled some evolutionary theorists: how much selection is required to endorse a tiny coincidence (a random mutation) as a genuine *adaptation*? (See my discussion in *The Intentional Stance*, pp. 320–1 and footnotes on those pages, and in my response to commentary in *BBS*). But if nothing but arbitrary answers (e.g., 42 generations of selection) could "settle" the question for natural selection, only arbitrary answers (e.g., 42 flies must buzz) could settle the question for a learning history, for the processes have the same structure – they must begin with a fortuitious or coincidental coupling, thereupon favored – and they have the same power to design structures in indirect response to meaning.

One might hold out some hope of a less arbitrary answer in the special case of design by conscious, deliberater engineers, for one could require that a structure could acquire only those meanings that were "explicitly recognized" by the designers, but such a reliance on the Word would be of dubious value since, as I argued in *The Intentional Stance* (pp. 284–6), and as Dretske has also shown in his current arguments in support of *screened off history*, the results of the three different processes can be indistinguishable: there is no surefire way of telling, for instance, that some correspondence in your own brain is *not* the result of ancient tampering by visiting extraterrestrial bio-engineers.

There remains a marginal sense in which (1) and (2) are more "natural" ways of establishing meanings, but this is a sense of no theoretical importance. In just the same sense, a weasel's short legs are natural, while a dachshund's, as a product of *artificial* selection, are not. It is an interesting historical fact, but it makes no difference to the integrity of any explanation that appeals to the function, or meaning, or implications, of those features.

This should leave us, and Dretske, with three equally legitimate Ways to Harmony, and indeed he comes within a hair's breadth of granting this. Consider the fundamental claim that underlies his paper: his analysis of why the meaning of a structure cannot figure in causal explanations of its effects:

> If meaning supervenes, at least in part, on the *extrinsic* properties of an event – historical and relational facts that *need not* be mirrored in the event's current (= the time at which it has its effects) physical constitution or structure – then if *A* causes *B*, then the fact, if it is a fact, that *A* means *M* will not – indeed, cannot – figure in a causal explanation of *B*. It cannot because, in *similar circumstances* [my italics] an event lacking this meaning, but otherwise the same, will have exactly the same effects. So it isn't *A*'s having meaning *M* that explains why *B* occurred. (Ms p. 10)

This would be a significant worry if "similar circumstances" were apt to be forthcoming with non-zero probability in cases where *A* did not mean *M*, but we can rest assured that we will never encounter such an anomaly. That is to say, it is no accident that events with the meanings they have get to play the causal roles they play (and Fred gives a good account of this), but the other side of that coin is that the odds are astronomical against the occurrence of an event or structure that *lacked* the relevant meaning somehow arising to cause a bogus *B*-type event. We don't need any special history of experience to ensure that any harmonies we encounter are robust, and Dretske's own arguments show that a learning history, "acquisition of *extrinsic* relations," *could not* impart any *intrinsic* power to those harmonies.

Let me review Dretske's view, and compare it with the view he *says* he will not accept, unless forced to. On Dretske's view, an account of the historical process of "acquiring the requisite extrinsic relations" explains *why* structure types (As) cause their associated Bs. This is fine, even if he slights some perfectly good varieties of historical process. But, to quote Dretske's earlier remark: "Meaning, on this view of things, has to do with the etiology of a structure type, with how (and perhaps why) it was developed to service an organism's needs." (ms, p. 7). Dretske ends up showing how, even if meaning cannot be locally potent, it can be put into reliable pre-established harmony with locally potent structures.

So I think Dretske and I end up, if not yet in perfect harmony, at least in possession of all the same themes with which to explain how – and to what extent – meanings can be cited in the explanation of events.

Postscript

So matters seemed to me until Dretske's Postscript arrived, recanting his endorsement of natural selection (or more fairly, denying that he had ever meant to endorse natural selection as a Way to Harmony). He gives this account of the difference between a learning history and a selection history:

> Natural selection gives us something quite different: reflex, instinct, tropisms, fixed-action-patterns, and other forms of involuntary behavior – behavior that is (typically) *not* explained in terms of the actor's beliefs and desires (if any). These genetically determined patterns of behavior often involve (as triggers for response) internal indicators (information-carrying elements), but, unlike, belief, it isn't *their* content that explains the way they affect output. That is determined by the genes.

What exactly is the contrast?

> In order to get meaning itself (and not just the structures that have meaning) to play an important role in the explanation of an *individual's* behavior (as beliefs and desires do) one has to look at the meaning that was instrumental in shaping the behavior that is being explained. This occurs only during individual learning. Only then is the meaning of the structure type (the fact that it indicates so-and-so about the animal's surroundings) responsible for its recruitment as a control element in the production of appropriate action.

The only difference I can discern, however, is that the "structure type" in the case of natural selection is a type that is identified in the genotype, while the structure type in the case of intra-cerebral evolution is a type that is identified only in the phenotype. In both cases "meaning was instrumental in shaping the behavior" – that is, in shaping the behavior-*type*, and in neither case was meaning instrumental in shaping any particular, individual token of a behavioral type.

Let us compare the particular case Dretske describes – his shooing of the fly – with a near neighbor produced, presumably, by an evolutionary history rather than a learning history – the shooing of a fly by a horse swishing its tail. Whatever the actual facts about such cases, let us stipulate that Dretske's arm-swing is a genuine *action*, for the reasons he gives, and that the horse's superficially similar tail-swing is a mere reflex, genetically programmed.

The horse's tail-swing belongs to a type which is designed to be provoked or caused by various other internal types, normally produced by flies buzzing around its rump; if these mediating types hadn't meant what they have meant over evolutionary history, the horse wouldn't be wired up to caused by them now to issue one of the tail-swing type behaviors. But of course, right now, given the way nature has set up the horse's wiring, a particular event of one of these mediating types *however it in particular is caused, and regardless of what, if anything, it in particular means*, will cause a tail-swing. That's the way it is with reflexes: no locally potent meaning.

Is there a contrast, however, in the case of Dretske's shooing action? In virtue of his individual learning history, he has come to acquire various beliefs and desires, among them the belief that when he sees or feels something roughly *like that*, it is apt to be a fly or bug or something in need of shooing, and a desire to shoo whatever needs shooing. Such belief–desire pairs, when provoked by particular circumstances, are designed to cause the formation of shooing intentions which forthwith get executed. (The particulars of this rough-and-ready account of beliefs, desires and intentions is not meant to bear any weight; I assume that Dretske has some such scheme in mind, and I mean to address what must be true of any such scheme.)

Now let us look at a particular case: at time t the fly buzzes and at $t + \delta$ Dretske shoos. What has happened during δ? The fly causes a mediating perceptual event p, which causes the mediating belief-state b, which, along with desire-state d, causes the intention i, which causes Dretske's arm to move – something like that. In short, a lot of internal events happen, and all together they amount to his coming to think a fly is buzzing and then deciding to take some action, viz., shooing. And in fact, given his learning history, all these mediating events and states mean what they ought to mean and cause what they ought to cause, but *had any particular component been "wild"* the sequence would have occurred just the same; that's the way it is with actions: no locally potent meanings. Now Dretske says, in the postscript quoted above, that "one has to look at the meaning that was instrumental in shaping the behavior that is being explained," but no meaning was "instrumental" in shaping *this particular action*; it would have happened just as it happened, no matter what each element occurring during δ meant or failed to mean. We do have room to advert to meanings if what we want to explain is how it comes to be that events of these (structural) types cause a behavior of this (structural) type at time $t + \delta$. But that is also what we do when we account for the etiological ancestry of reflexes. It is not that there is no difference at all between a reflex and an action. Of course there is. But it does not lie in the domain that Drestske explores.

Notes

1 This paper is an elaboration of my reply to Dretske at the SOFIA conference on information-based semantics at Tepoztlan, Mexico, August, 1988. The proceedings of that conference are published by Basil Blackwell in *Information, Semantics and Epistemology* (1990) edited by Eurique Villanueva. Dretske composed a postscript to his paper, published in that volume, responding to the objections I had raised in Tepoztlan, and the present paper responds in turn to that postscript.

2 It is interesting that here Dretske announces his allegiance to the same goal that motivates Fodor – the vindication of folk psychology taken neat – while dismissing Fodor's own solution as insufficiently responding to the folk-psychological intuition that (the Formality Condition be damned) *meanings make it happen.*

3 As Dretske's postscript makes clear, he did not intend to endorse natural selection in the paper under discussion. See the discussion of this postscript below.

4 See, for instance, my discussion (in "Mechanism and Responsibility," in *Essays on Freedom of Action* (London: Routledge and Kegan Paul, 1973), ed. T. Honderich, of the parallel case of the bogus belief (that he has an older brother living in Cleveland) surgically inserted into Tom (in *Brainstorms*, pp. 251–3); the discussion of the Panamanian debut of the two-bitser (how long does it take for the new functions to be "real"?); and my reply to Goldman, forthcoming in *Behavioral and Brain Sciences*.

References

Dennett, D. 1969: *Content and Consciousness*. London: Routledge and Kegan Paul.

—— 1971: Intentional Systems. *Journal of philosophy*, 8 (1971), pp. 8–106.

—— 1975: Why the Law of Effect Will Not Go Away. *Journal of the Theory of Social Behavior*, 5, pp. 169–87.

—— 1978: *Brainstorms*. Cambridge, Mass: MIT Press/Bradford Books.

—— 1981: The Kinds of Intentional Psychology. In *Reduction, Time and Reality*, ed. R. Healey, Cambridge, Cambridge University Press.

—— 1983: Intentional System in Cognitive Ethology: the Panglossian Paradigm Defended. *Behavioral and Brain Sciences*, 6, pp. 34–90.

—— 1986. The Logical Geography of Computational Approaches: A View from the East Pole. In *Representation of Knowledge and Belief*, ed. M. Harnish M. Brand, University of Arizona Press.

—— 1987: *The Intentional Stance*. Cambridge: MIT Press/ Bradford Book.

—— 1988a: When Philosophers Encounter Artificial Intelligence. *Daedalus*, winter (issue on Artificial Intelligence), pp. 283–95.

—— 1988b: Précis of *The Intentional Stance*. *Behavioral and Brain Sciences*, 11, pp. 493–544.

Dretske, F. 1981: *Knowledge and the Flow of Information*. Cambridge, Mass.: MIT Press/Bradford Book

—— 1985: Machines and the Mental. *Proceedings and Addreses of the American Philosophical Association*, 59 (1985), pp. 23–33.

—— 1986: Misrepresentation. In *Belief*, ed. R. Bogdan Oxford, Oxford, University Press.

Edelman, G. 1988 *Neural Darwinism*. New York: Basic Books.

Haugeland, J. 1985 *Artificial Intelligence: The Very Idea*. Cambridge, Mass.: MIT Press/Bradford Books.

Schiffer, S. 1987: *Remnants of Meaning*. Cambridge, Mass MIT Press/ Bradford Books.

Waltz, D. 1988: The Prospects for Building Truly Intelligent Machines *Deadalus* winter (issue on artificial intelligence), pp. 191–212.

Acknowledgments

Turing, A.M. "Computing Machinery and Intelligence." *Mind* 59 (1950): 433–60. Reprinted with the permission of the Oxford University Press.

Haugeland, John. "Semantic Engines: An Introduction to Mind Design." In *Mind Design: Philosophy, Psychology, Artificial Intelligenge,* (Cambridge: MIT Press, 1981): 1–34. Reprinted with the permission of MIT Press.

Searle, John R. "Mind, Brains, and Programs." In *Mind Design: Philosophy, Psychology, Artificial Intelligence,* (Cambridge: MIT Press, 1981): 282–306. Reprinted with the permission of MIT Press.

Harnad, Stevan. "The Symbol Grounding Problem." *Physica* 42 (1990): 335–46. Reprinted with the permission of North-Holland.

Churchland, Paul M. and Patricia Smith Churchland. "Could a Machine Think?" *Scientific American* 262 (January 1990): 32–37. Reprinted with the permission of Scientific American, Inc.

Chalmers, David J. "On Implementing a Computation." *Minds and Machines* 4 (1994): 391–402. Reprinted with the permission of Kluwer Academic Publishers.

Newell, Allen. "You Can't Play 20 Questions with Nature and Win: Projective Comments on the Papers of this Symposium." In *Visual Information Processing,* edited by William G. Chase (New York: Academic Press, 1973): 283–308. Reprinted with the permission of Academic Press.

Marr, D. "Artificial Intelligence: A Personal View." *Artificial Intelligence* 9 (1977): 37–48. Reprinted with the permission of North Holland.

Reeke, George N., Jr. and Gerald M. Edelman. "Real Brains and Artificial Intelligence." *Daedalus* 117 (Winter 1988): 143–73. Reprinted by permission of *Daedalus,* Journal of the American Academy of Arts and Sciences.

Dreyfus, Hubert L. and Stuart E. Dreyfus. "Making a Mind Versus Modeling the Brain: Artificial Intelligence Back at a Branchpoint." *Daedalus* 117 (Winter 1988): 15–43. Reprinted by permission of *Daedalus,* Journal of the American Academy of Arts and Sciences.

Israel, David and John Perry. "What Is Information?" In *Information, Language, and Cognition,* edited by Philip P. Hanson (Vancouver: University of British Columbia Press, 1990): 1–19. Reprinted with the permission of University of British Columbia Press.

Kirsh, David. "When Is Information Explicitly Represented?" In *Information, Language, and Cognition,* edited by Philip P. Hanson (Vancouver: University of British Columbia Press, 1990): 340–65. Reprinted with the permission of University of British Columbia Press.

Dretske, Fred. "Machines and the Mental." *Proceedings and Addresses of the American Philosophical Association* 590 (1985): 23–33. Reprinted with the permission of the American Philosophical Association.

Dennett, Daniel C. "Ways of Establishing Harmony." In *Dretske and His Critics,* edited by Brian P. McLaughlin (Oxford: Blackwell, 1991): 118–30. Reprinted with the permission of Blackwell Publishers.